Health Plants of the World

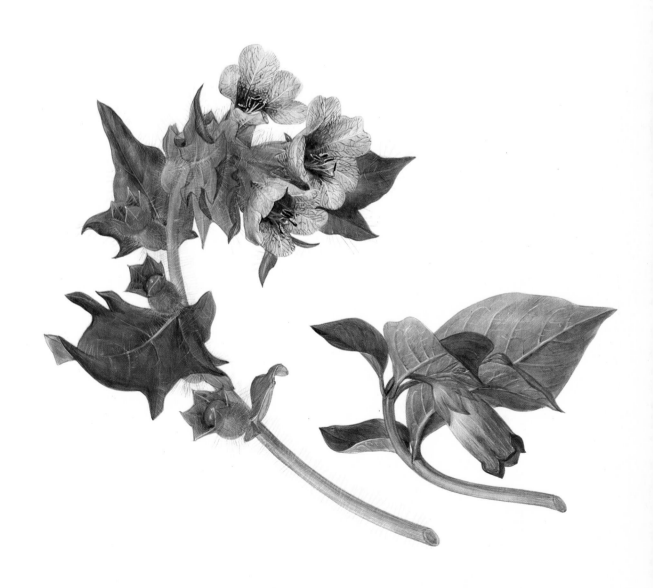

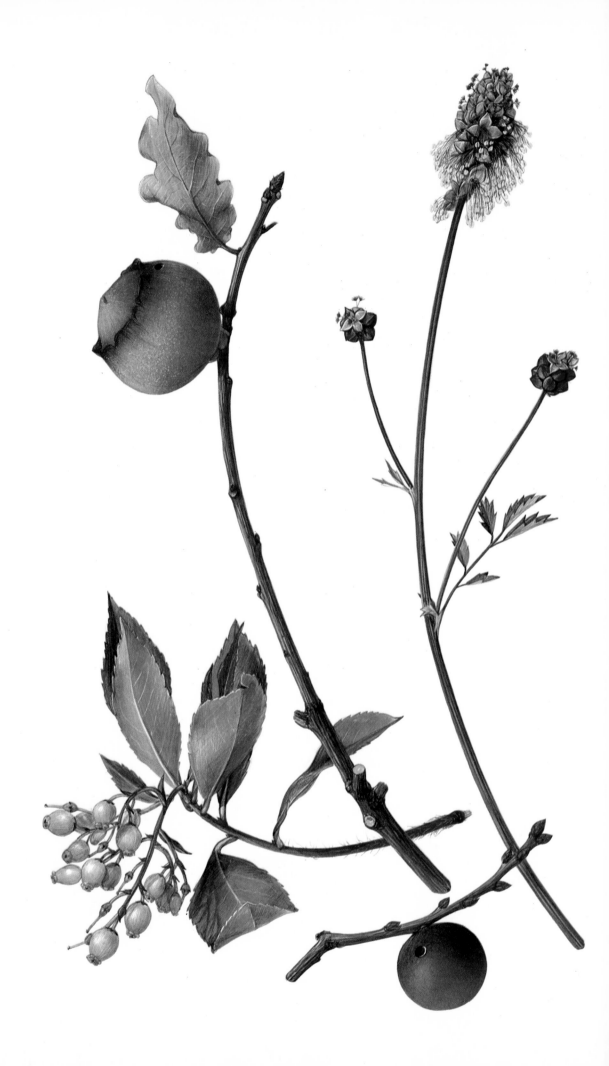

Francesco Bianchini
Francesco Corbetta

HEALTH PLANTS
of the
WORLD
Atlas of Medicinal Plants

Illustrations by Marilena Pistoia
English adaptation by M. A. DEJEY

Newsweek Books, New York

CASSELL & COMPANY LTD
an imprint of
Cassell & Collier Macmillan Publishers Ltd
35 Red Lion Square, London WC1R 4SG
and at Sydney, Auckland, Toronto, Johannesburg
*and an affiliate of The Macmillan Publishing Company
Inc, New York*

Originally published in Italian as
LE PIANTE DELLA SALUTE
Copyright © 1975 by Arnoldo Mondadori
CEAM Milan
English translation copyright © 1977 by
Cassell & Company Ltd
ISBN 0 304 29790 9

1977 First American Edition

© 1975 Arnoldo Mondadori Editore, Milano
All rights reserved under International and
Pan-American Copyright Conventions.
Published in the United States by Newsweek, Inc., New York.
Published simultaneously in Great Britain under the title
The Kindly Fruits by Cassell & Company, Ltd.

Library of Congress Cataloging in Publication Data
        F. Bianchini and F. Corbetta
        Health Plants of the World
    Index, Glossary and Bibliography
1. Plants—Worldwide.   2. Authors, Italian—Atlas.
3. Medicinal History of Plants.
Library of Congress Card Number 76-46692
ISBN 0-88225-250-X

Printed and Bound in Italy

Contents

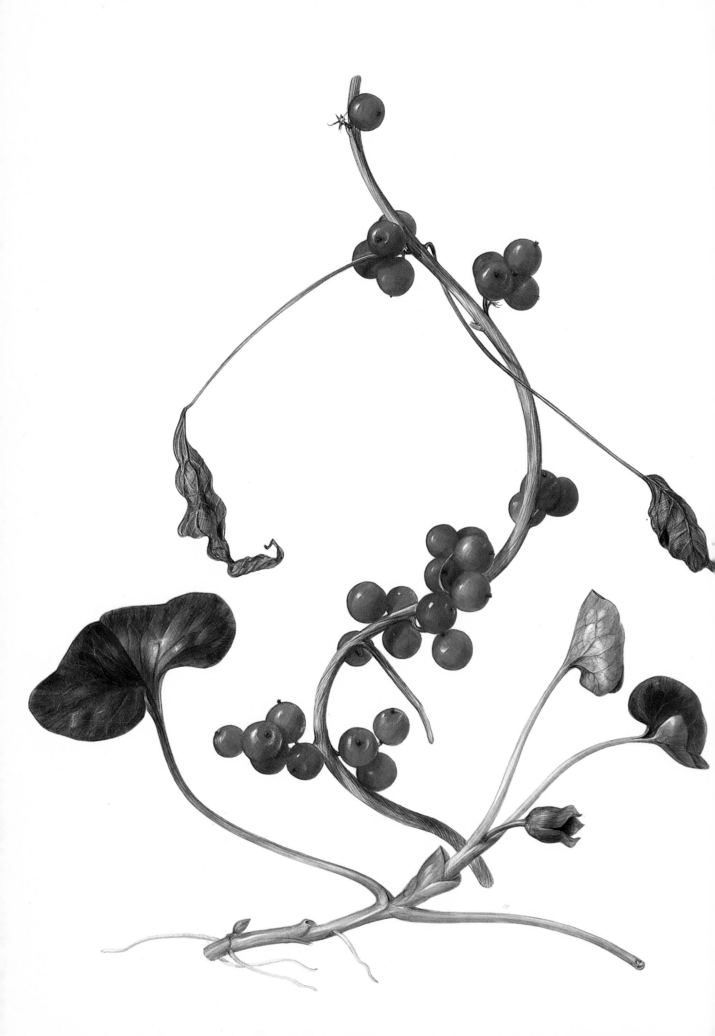

Introduction

The celebrated English divine William Cole (d. 1600), wrote the following on the history of herbs: 'It is a subject as ancient as the Creation, yea, more ancient than the sun or moon or stars, they being created on the fourth day, whereas plants were the third.' With the present revival of interest in ecology and the increasing use of such words as 'nature' and 'herbs' it is appropriate that man, constructing a new relationship with his surroundings, should seek a less artificial way of life, choosing more natural foods and rediscovering herbs, not only to add to his cooking but to cure his ailments. An anthology dedicated to these 'simples' some of which were in use thousands of years ago, is a hopeful sign of the new direction in which increasingly more people are turning.

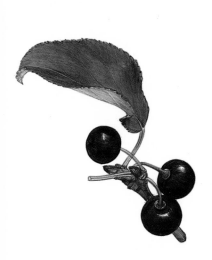

For far too long herbal medicine has been neglected in favour of synthetic drugs, many of them good, but some of them seeming too good to be true, and because of misuse or abuse, losing their efficacy, and in some cases producing side effects which have become a social evil.

In central Europe and some northern countries, natural medicine has never been completely abandoned, and the old methods of healing are now being revived. However, simply to read books on herbs is not to know all about them, and certainly not to be able to doctor oneself. If this book provokes the hoped-for reaction the reader will try to broaden his basic knowledge:

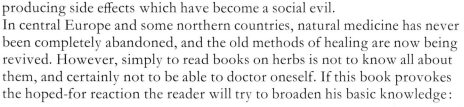

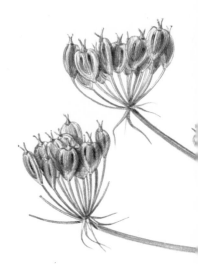

to study the herbs found in the countryside, and to seek out the herbalists'
shops where they continue to work amidst the fragrant scents that recall
other days when Charlemagne was ordaining which medicinal herbs should
be grown in monastery 'physicke' gardens, and great herbalists like
Dodoens, Gerard and Culpeper were writing their *Herballs* for future
generations in the centuries to come.

It must be accepted that the doctor has to be consulted in cases of illness;
the reader cannot heal himself, nor can the herbalist, nor the chemist.
Caution must be used with most herbs, and there are a few that must
definitely be avoided, except when prescribed by a physician, and then
taken preferably in homoeopathic doses. This does not, of course, apply to
a cup of chamomile tea nor to a tisane of lime blossoms, which, even if not
the specific remedy, can do no harm to anyone. This book is not intended
as a substitute for the medical advice of physicians. The reader should
regularly consult a doctor in all matters relating to his or her health, and
particularly in respect of any symptoms which may require diagnosis or
medical attention.

These plants have been grouped in separate sections according to their
principal areas of operation; though these areas overlap in many cases. The
chemical action of each herb is given and also the ills for which it may be
beneficial. Most of the scientific information is found in the appendix. The
text has been written not for the scholar, nor even for those who wish to be
instructed, but for people who love plants; who find delight in looking at
beautiful illustrations of fruits and flowers, and reading the old names:
heart's-ease, herb of grace, sweet sedge, meadowsweet, which recall the
times when market gardens flourished in the centre of great cities, and the
earth chestnut could be found 'in the next field to the conduit heads of
Maribone, near the way that leads to Paddington by London' and mallow
grew 'hard by the place of execution, Tyburn'.

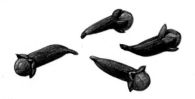

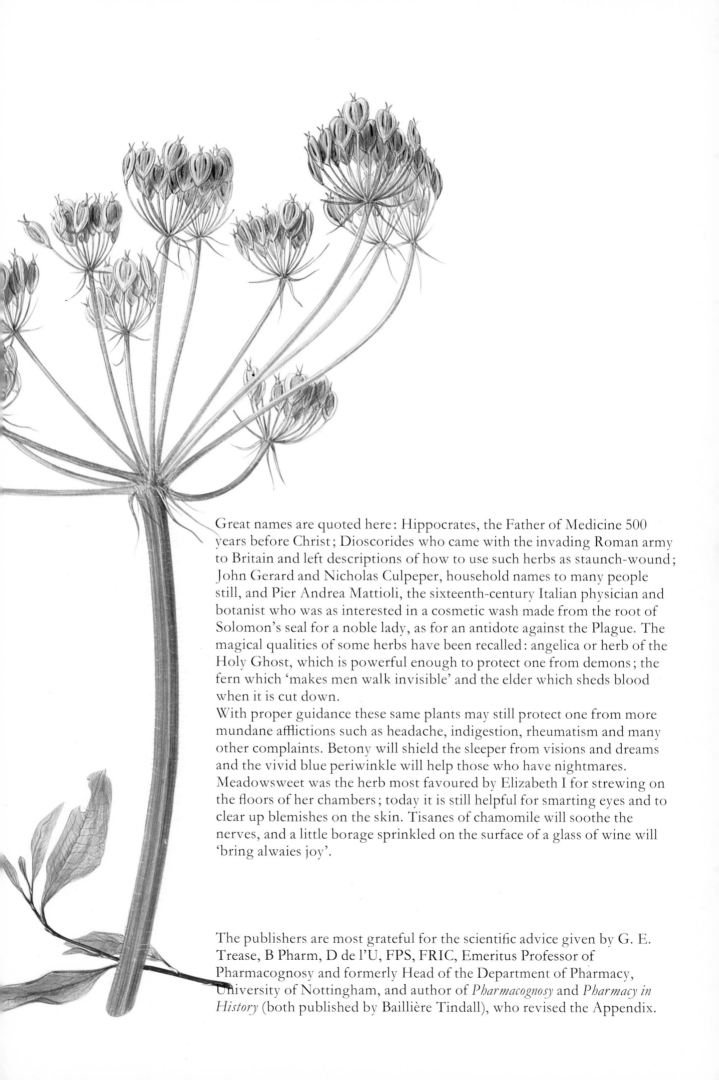

Great names are quoted here: Hippocrates, the Father of Medicine 500 years before Christ; Dioscorides who came with the invading Roman army to Britain and left descriptions of how to use such herbs as staunch-wound; John Gerard and Nicholas Culpeper, household names to many people still, and Pier Andrea Mattioli, the sixteenth-century Italian physician and botanist who was as interested in a cosmetic wash made from the root of Solomon's seal for a noble lady, as for an antidote against the Plague. The magical qualities of some herbs have been recalled: angelica or herb of the Holy Ghost, which is powerful enough to protect one from demons; the fern which 'makes men walk invisible' and the elder which sheds blood when it is cut down.

With proper guidance these same plants may still protect one from more mundane afflictions such as headache, indigestion, rheumatism and many other complaints. Betony will shield the sleeper from visions and dreams and the vivid blue periwinkle will help those who have nightmares. Meadowsweet was the herb most favoured by Elizabeth I for strewing on the floors of her chambers; today it is still helpful for smarting eyes and to clear up blemishes on the skin. Tisanes of chamomile will soothe the nerves, and a little borage sprinkled on the surface of a glass of wine will 'bring alwaies joy'.

The publishers are most grateful for the scientific advice given by G. E. Trease, B Pharm, D de l'U, FPS, FRIC, Emeritus Professor of Pharmacognosy and formerly Head of the Department of Pharmacy, University of Nottingham, and author of *Pharmacognosy* and *Pharmacy in History* (both published by Baillière Tindall), who revised the Appendix.

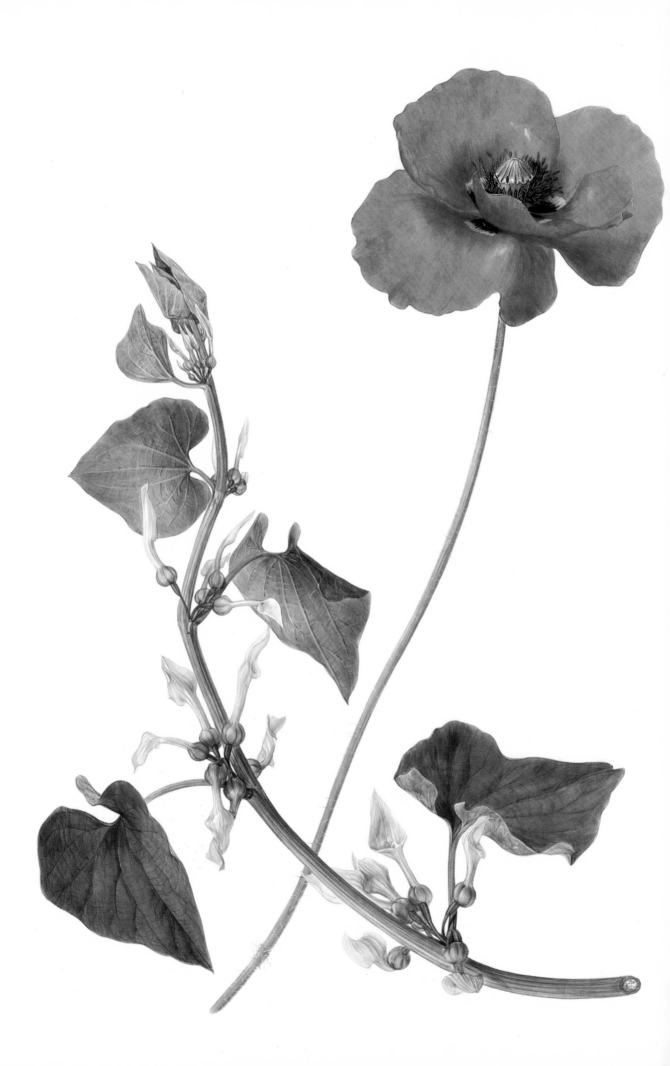

Health Plants of the World

Holy thistle
Star thistle
Holly

The blessed or **Holy thistle** (*Cnicus benedictus*) is of the Compositae (daisy or thistle family). Originally found only around the Mediterranean, it has been naturalized in North America and South Africa. The drug is derived from the flowering plant and the flowering tops and leaves detached from the stalk. Holy thistle provides a bitter tonic which stimulates the appetite acting in a manner similar to that of quassia (*v.* p. 178). The diuretic, diaphoretic, febrifuge and cholagogic properties of this herb are also important pharmaceutically. Today it is principally used as a eupeptic for certain forms of dyspepsia. Holy thistle is mentioned in the writings of the Venerable Bede (*c.* 672–735), but its connections with sanctity came from the ancient belief that it was a cure-all and had supernatural powers.

According to the great Greek physician Dioscorides, who is thought to have been an army doctor with the occupying Roman troops in Britain in the first century AD, parts of the holy thistle 'are a remedy for those that have their bodies drawne backwards.'

Many species of the genus *Centaurea* are known for their therapeutic virtues in folk medicine. Of particular importance is the **Star thistle** (*C. calcitrapa*), also called knapweed, of the Compositae. This plant may be used as a substitute for holy thistle. It grows in sand and gravelly places and flowers between July and September. The flowering heads contain a bitter glucoside giving the herb a bitter-tonic characteristic. The leaves and flowers have active principles with a febrifuge action; the roots and fruits have diuretic properties. In the Middle Ages the powdered root was used against the Plague.

'Holly he hath berries as red as any rose' are the words of a fifteenth-century carol, and they evoke the beautiful vivid fruits of the 'Holy tree' as it became known after the Christian Church had adopted it as part of its Christmas festivities. Superficially the leaves of the **Holly** (*Ilex aquifolium*) resemble those of certain forms of evergreen oak or ilex (*Quercus ilex*), as is emphasized by the generic part of its botanical name. Holly, as a bush or small tree, is widespread in Europe, western Asia and North Africa. The pharmacological action derives from the leaves which are bitter-tonic, febrifuge and sedative. According to some authorities they may be collected throughout the year; other herbalists believe that the best time is just before flowering. The leaves have a bitter taste due to the presence of a glucoside, ilicin. Holly also contains rutin, and active principles with similar action to the leaves have been found in the bark; they are used in the treatment of hepatic disturbances. Before the advent of patent medicines holly was made into infusions or decoctions for colic, digestive difficulties and malarial fevers, and for a long time was one of the chief remedies for smallpox. Extracts of the berries have a purgative and emetic activity, and have occasionally caused cases of serious poisoning in children, characterized by vomiting, diarrhoea and eventual collapse. In parts of Corsica a drink similar to coffee is made from roasted and powdered holly berries.

Culpeper, the seventeenth-century English herbalist, recommended the bark or leaves 'used in fomentations, for broken bones and such members as are out of joint.' Pliny, in his *Natural History* (77 AD), said that the flowers would repel poison and had the power to turn water into ice. An old country superstition claims that a house will never be struck by lightning if a holly bush is planted near it.

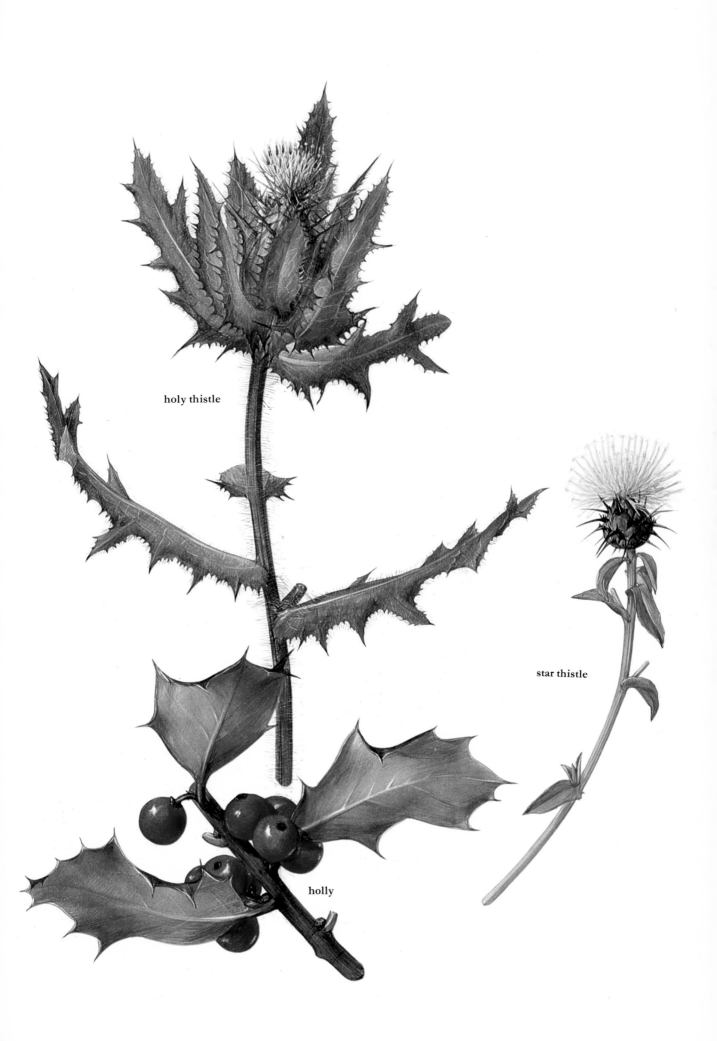

holy thistle

star thistle

holly

Wall germander
Common centaury
Balm

The **Wall germander** (*Teucrium chamaedrys*) of the Labiatae or mint family owes its specific name, the ancient Greek word for 'ground oak', to the resemblance of its leaves to those of the oak tree; its English name is a corruption of the same word. It is found growing on walls and ruins in southern Europe, western Asia and North Africa. In ancient times it was known chiefly as a vulnerary, and is still prescribed today for healing sores and ulcers. In mediaeval times it was also known as a cure for dropsy, jaundice and gout. It has now been brought into general use as a remedy for digestive and liver troubles, anaemia and bronchitis, because of its astringent, stimulant, diuretic and antiseptic qualities. Taken as a tisane this herb reduces inflammation anywhere in the body.

The **Common centaury** (*Centaurium erythraea*), a plant of the Gentianaceae or gentian family, grows throughout Europe, western Asia and North Africa. It was renowned in the time of Dioscorides for its emmenagogic and anti-bilious properties, and even more for the healing of wounds. Its generic name derives from the legend of the Centaur Cheiron who, it is said, was cured of a wound in the foot by an application of the fresh leaves and flowers of the plant. In the fifteenth century ladies used an infusion of the herb to bleach their hair, though with small success. At about this time the true therapeutic qualities of centaury were recognized, and are still valued today. The whole plant, including the flower itself, from which the drug is made, is used as a stomachic, digestive, cholagogic, febrifuge and astringent tonic. Applied externally to sores, ulcers and eczema it is found to have valuable healing properties. Its active ingredients consist of a bitter glycoside; centaurin, erythrocentaurin and oleanolic acid, and some alkaloids, including erycitrin. Gum, resin and sugar are also present. Common centaury is often prescribed for stimulating the digestive juices in cases of acidity or indigestion.

An extract of the herbs forms the basis of tinctures, draughts, syrups and an aperitive. It is a popular ingredient of many alcoholic drinks because of its remarkable bitter quality. Nicholas Culpeper said of it ''Tis very wholesome, but not very toothsome.' It is also used to allay fever and is believed to be the most effective substitute for quinine.

Balm, or lemon balm (*Melissa officinalis*), of the Labiatae, is one of the herbs beloved by healers since time immemorial. In the original Greek, *melissa* denotes not only the plant but also the bee, an insect which, according to Pliny, was 'delighted with this herb above others' and accounts for balm's less well known name of *apiastrum*. In ancient Greece sprigs of balm were put into bee hives to attract swarms. Balm was held in high esteem in early medicine, and was much used by the Arabs in Spain. Avicenna, the great Arab physician and philosopher of the eleventh century, believed that 'it causeth the mind and heart to become merry.' It was also known in early cookery, especially as an ingredient of the aromatic liqueurs distilled in Italian monasteries. Today, too, it is used as a flavouring for certain cheeses in parts of Switzerland, and is widely used in domestic cookery in salads, omelettes and summer drinks, such as 'May Wine' (*v.* p. 128). The drug is prepared from the flowering plant or from the leaves picked before flowering. The active ingredients, including an essential oil, gives it stomachic, sudorific and, more importantly, antispasmodic and sedative properties. It is prescribed in the form of an infusion, as a palliative for stomach cramps of a nervous type, vomiting and insomnia. Culpeper in his seventeenth-century herbal recommends a syrup made of balm and sugar to 'be kept in every gentlewoman's house to relieve the weak stomachs and sick bodies of their poor and sickly neighbours.'

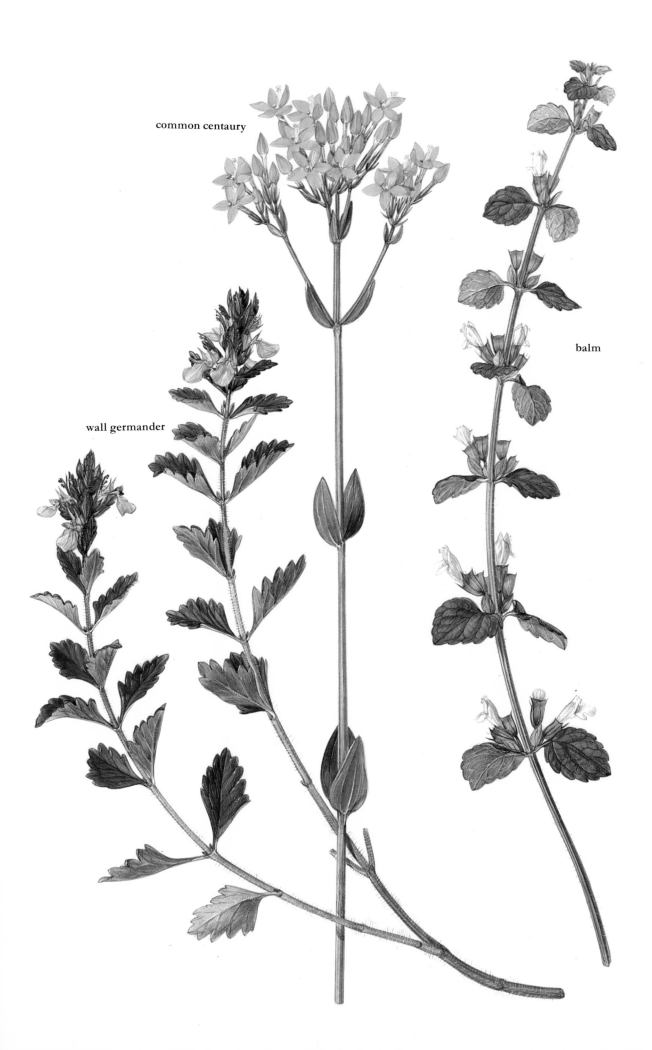

common centaury

balm

wall germander

Pepper
Saffron
Ginger
Cinnamon

Pepper (*Piper nigrum*), a member of the Piperaceae, originated in India and is cultivated in other tropical countries. The drug is derived from the fruits, which are small drupes. Three forms of pepper are available commercially, black, white and green. The first comes from fruits gathered while still immature, and dried. White pepper is obtained from the mature fruits, which are red. These are fermented in heaps or macerated in water for several days. The fruits are rubbed to detach the skin and fleshy part leaving the white pepper, which is less pungent than black pepper. Green pepper is also gathered when immature and stored in boxes. In small doses pepper has tonic and appetite-stimulating properties, but its principal use is in cooking. It is one of the earliest known spices in Europe, and came from Arabia via the Red Sea which was the old spice route used before the destruction of Rome. Hippocrates (*c.* 460–*c.* 377 BC), the Father of Medicine, made great use of pepper in his prescriptions.

Saffron (*Crocus sativus*) originated in Asia Minor and was introduced into Spain by the Arabs, before spreading to France and the western Mediterranean as a result of the Crusades. It was probably derived by cultivation of related wild forms. Today it is widely grown in Europe, Persia, Afghanistan, India and China. It flowers in autumn. Unlike most plants, the drug is obtained from the dried stamens. If they are mixed with the styles the spice is called 'female saffron' and is of less value commercially. Saffron was known as a medicinal plant in ancient Egypt and is mentioned by Hippocrates, Theophrastus in his treatises, and later, Galen (*c.* 130–*c.* 200) who attributed various medicinal and culinary properties to it. Apart from its domestic uses, particularly in *bouillabaisse* and *risotto*, saffron aids the digestion and is used as a sedative. It was also believed to help dimness of sight. The Romans used it as a dye plant.

Ginger (*Zingiber officinalis*) is a perennial herbaceous plant unknown in the wild state. It belongs to the Zingiberaceae, and originated in Malabar and Bengal. The drug comes from the rhizome and is available commercially in two forms: *grey* which is not decorticated and comes in tubercles, and *white*, which is scraped to remove the corky outer skin, powdered with chalk and sold in smaller pieces. Ginger is the *gengiovo* of Boccaccio. Mattioli (1500–1577), wrote that 'it has the capacity to warm and digest . . . move the body gently . . . is useful to the stomach, valuable in all impediments and should be found in all antidotes . . .' He also mentions the popularity of candied ginger in India and China. Ginger can be used as a digestive and carminative, as well as in cooking, baking and liqueur-making. Candied ginger grated, and mixed into vanilla ice cream with the syrup used as a sauce, is a delicious dessert. Applied externally ginger has a revulsive action and is counted among the correctives. Taken internally it relieves cramp in the hands and feet, and is excellent for warding off colds.

Cinnamon (*Cinnamomum zeylanicum*) is a tree of medium height, of the Lauraceae. It originated in Sri Lanka (Ceylon) and is now cultivated in Java, Brazil, Jamaica and Martinique. It is especially used in treating diarrhoea because of the presence of tannic acid which has an astringent effect. In strong doses it produces an increase in heart rate and respiration, increased salivation, lachrymation, and a slight rise in temperature, but taken in the correct dosage can improve the circulation. It also has antiseptic properties. Pharmaceutically many different preparations based on cinnamon are used as digestive and general stimulants. The only medicinal cinnamon is the *Ceylon cinnamon* which is sold in small sticks of rolled bark. *Chinese cinnamon*, which is cheaper, is inferior in quality with a less pleasant taste, though its uses in cooking and liqueur-making are many. One of the earliest mentions of cinnamon is in a thirteenth-century encyclopaedia compiled by Bartholomaeus Anglicus, an English monk. Even at that time all spices, which were rare and extremely costly, were supposed to come from the Garden of Eden, by way of the Euphrates, 'a river which floweth from Paradise.'

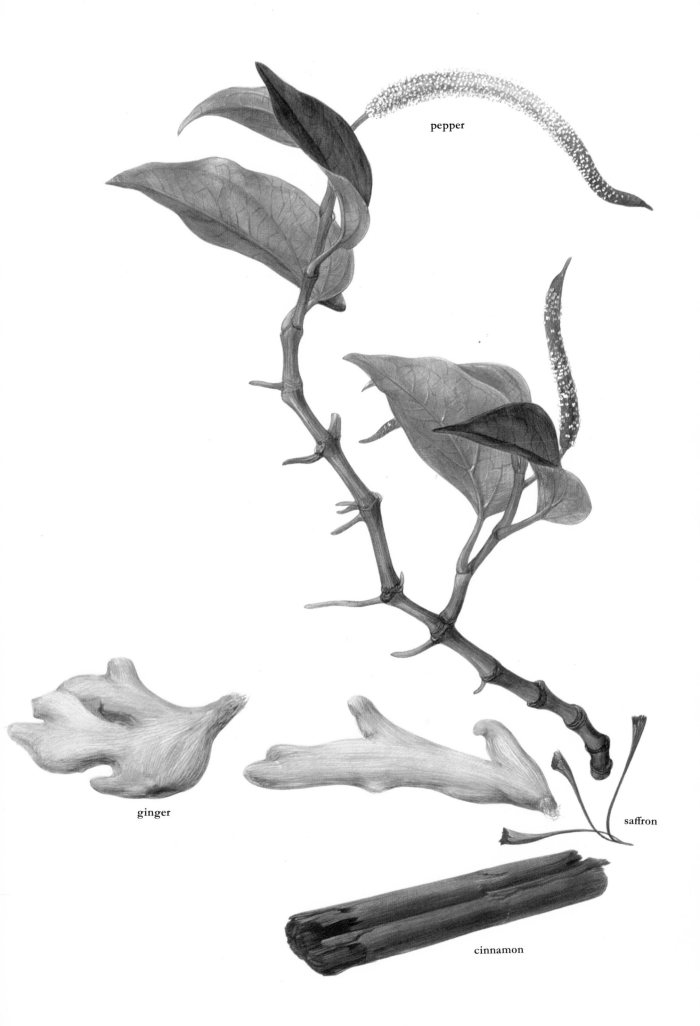

pepper

ginger

saffron

cinnamon

Garden thyme
Horseradish
White mustard

The etymology of **Garden thyme** (*Thymus vulgaris*) is said to derive from the Greek verb *thyo*, 'I sacrifice', alluding to the smell of incense. The plant, a small shrub with grey-green leaves, of the Labiatae, has a strong, aromatic scent and a pungent flavour. As a medicinal herb it has been used since ancient times and is mentioned by Pliny, Dioscorides and Theophrastus. It lost favour in the Middle Ages and did not reappear until the sixteenth century as an important plant in herbals. John Gerard, the renowned Elizabethan herbalist (b. 1545), wrote of thyme, 'It helpeth against the bitings of any venomous beast, either taken in drinke, or outwardly applied.'

The whole plant, especially the lateral branches which are gathered at the flowering stage, constitutes a versatile drug with a tonic effect. It is used in cases of anaemia, bronchial and intestinal disturbances, and as an antiseptic against tooth decay. It gives relief from catarrh and coughs, and also provides an essence which is used in the liqueur and perfume industries. It is one of the most popular herbs in cooking.

'The bees alluring thyme' of Spenser is the wild thyme (*T. serpyllum*, *v.* p. 104) a cultivated variety with similar though less pronounced characteristics. It is famous as a bee plant, and is often grown with lavender, the two plants being very sympathetic to each other. Pliny wrote 'For the sake of honey we have brought thyme out of Attica, but there is great difficulty in raising it from seed . . .' It grows all over western Europe, and will flourish equally well in a small plant-pot on a kitchen windowsill, as in a herb garden.

The original etymology of the name *Nasturtium armoracia* of the Cruciferae, known familiarly as **Horseradish**, derives from a fusion of the Latin words, *nasus* and *tortus*, meaning a sharp smell which makes the nose wrinkle up. *Armoracia* is also Latin in origin, referring to Brittany, the ancient Armorica, a region where this plant was once cultivated. Medicinal properties are found in the root, which, when sliced, gives off a faint smell which becomes very pungent when the root is crushed or grated. The basic active principles are an essential oil, asparagine; glutamine, glucides such as sucrose, fructose, and glucose, and vitamins B_1 and C.

The drug is used in bronchial-pulmonary infections, and for infections of the urinary passages; as an anti-scorbutic; and in particular as a digestive stimulant. It should also be remembered that the root, when crushed and used externally, acts as a counter-irritant. Horseradish is used in small doses, and with the addition of vinegar may be used as a kitchen condiment in the preparation of a spicy sauce. If commercially prepared horseradish is mixed with double the amount of whipped cream and then frozen, it can be served with cold salmon or other fish, in place of mayonnaise.

The seeds of **White mustard** (*Sinapis alba* of the Cruciferae) and the powder that is obtained from them, are among the herbs that activate the gastric juices. The seeds are gathered at the height of summer when the plant is turning yellow. There are many varieties of mustard differing from one country to another. In Britain it is sold as a powder and mixed with a little water before being served. France produces more sophisticated varieties; Dijon mustard mixed with verjuice, or Bordeaux mustard mixed with unfermented wine. Both are sold ready for use, in heavy jars. In Italy a syrupy variety called Cremona mustard contains different kinds of crystallized fruit and is usually served with cold meats.

Mustard was a popular condiment of the ancient Romans who introduced it into Gaul where its use became widespread. It acts directly on the gastric mucous membrane, stimulating secretion. Occasionally mustard seeds are recommended as a laxative, though the practice is now much less common. Their strength is well illustrated in the Gospel of St. Matthew (xvii;20): 'If ye have faith as a grain of mustard seed, ye shall say unto this mountain; Remove hence to yonder place; and it shall remove.'

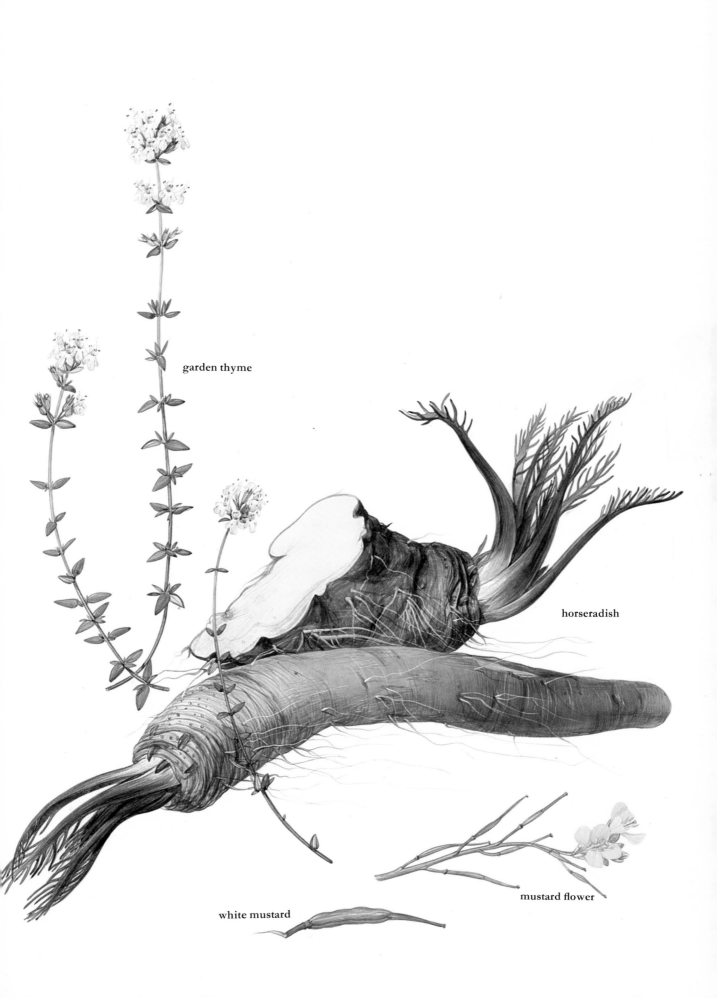

garden thyme

horseradish

mustard flower

white mustard

Gentians

The etymological derivation of the generic name of the **Gentian** plant is from the discovery by the Illyrian King, Genthius, of the yellow gentian (*Gentiana lutea*), the most important of the Major gentians. Of the numerous species of the genus *Gentiana* of the Gentianaceae, those of particular pharmacological and botanical interest belong to the Greater or Major gentians, including *G. lutea*, *G. purpurea* and *G. pannonica*. The term Lesser or Minor gentians, comprises such species as *G. asclepiadea* and *G. cruciata*, while the well-known species *G. acaulis* with its brilliant blue flowers, is known by the Italian name gentianella. The beautiful yellow gentian grows in alpine meadows on calcareous soil in central and southern Europe. It may also be found in valleys in the Alps, places in the Apennines, the Black Forest and the Sardinian Gennargentu. The drug is derived from the dried fermented rhizome and roots (*Gentianae radix*) of *G. lutea* which should be collected in autumn or spring. These contain numerous bitter glycosides, enzymes, sugars such as sucrose, and starch, galactan, inulin and a yellow colouring substance called gentisic acid. The gentians have a typically bitter-tonic and eupeptic action, and have been widely used for many centuries as aids to digestion. Their great value as a tonic is that they do not cause constipation. They are also employed in the manufacture of various aperitives and medicaments to help loss of appetite and dyspepsia. In combination with iron compounds and other restoratives they are used in the treatment of anaemia, and for convalescents and cases of physical exhaustion. They are widely employed in the manufacture of confectionary and liqueurs, especially in *Gentiane*, a digestive liqueur made in Switzerland and parts of France. Those who wish to prepare gentian bitters domestically, should not confuse it with the poisonous *Veratrum* or hellebore. Another less known but ancient use of the gentian in folk medicine, is as an antimalarial, due to the bitter glucoside, gentiopicrin, which has effective anti-febrile and anti-malarial properties. In small doses gentian exhibits a stimulant activity on the central nervous system, but large doses are depressant and finally paralysing.

One of the easiest gentians to cultivate is the willow gentian (*G. asclepiadea*) which flowers in July and August. In the United States in midsummer, parts of the prairies are covered with a rose-coloured gentian (*Sabbiata campestris*). The amarella gentian with little lavender flowers also grows well in America. The old country names for the gentian plants are baldmoney, bitterwort and fillwort.

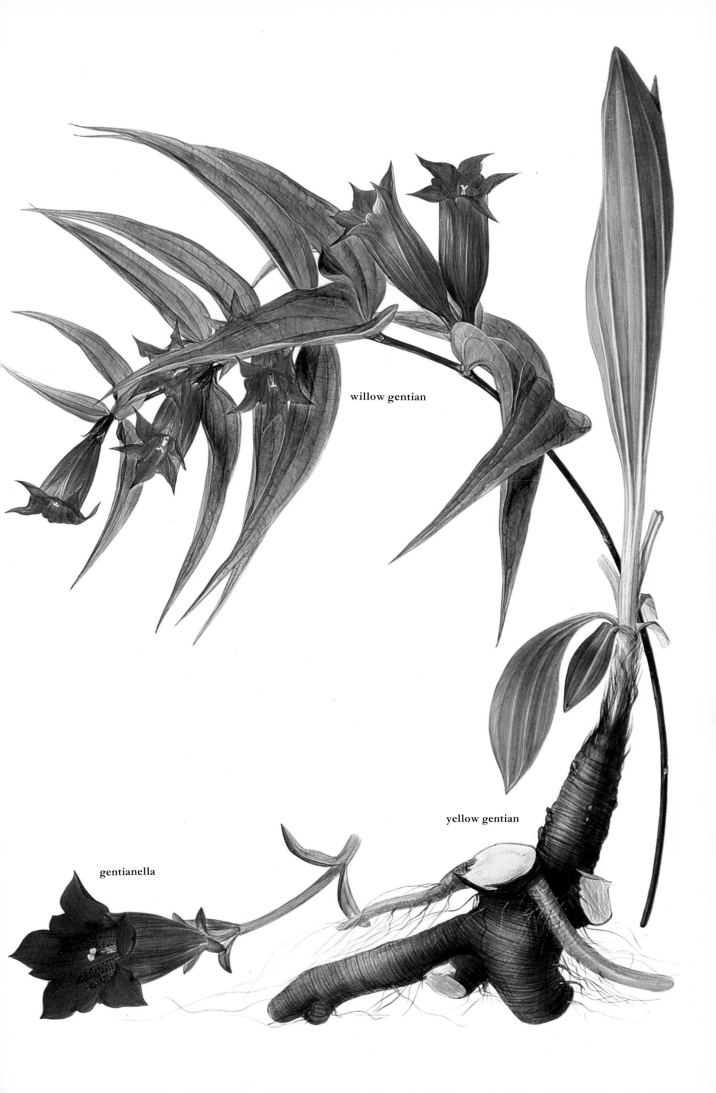

willow gentian

gentianella

yellow gentian

Rhubarb
Bay laurel

Rhubarb is a large, herbaceous, perennial plant originating in Tibet and north-west China, belonging to the Polygonaceae. It is now cultivated in Europe both commercially, and in small kitchen gardens.

There is some terminological confusion surrounding the various types of rhubarb; the old names of Chinese, Persian, Russian and Turkish rhubarb, in fact simply indicated the countries of origin of commercially sold rhubarb.

Rhubarb has been known for centuries and is mentioned in the Chinese herbal *Pen-king*, which is thought to date from 2700 BC. It may have been brought to Europe by the army of Charles V and was subsequently grown by monks as a medicinal plant because of its mild astringent and purgative qualities.

The typical form known today has been cultivated from roots brought from the East by two explorers; Nicholai Prjevalsky (or Przewalsky), who, in 1872, introduced a species with less deeply incised leaves than the typical plant, and Julius Tafel, who brought back a form in 1906, with more deeply incised leaves, *Rheum tanguticum*. Rhapontic rhubarb is botanically *R. rhaponticum*, which is cultivated widely in Europe and Britain. The stems are used in pies, fruit compotes or jam. In the United States it is also served as a side-dish. Plenty of sweetening is needed, and the plant is never eaten raw. The leaves are highly poisonous, and may cause severe abdominal pain, vomiting, cramp, and eventually convulsion, coma and death.

R. palmatum, the Turkish or Chinese rhubarb, is used pharmaceutically. The drug is obtained from the rhizome, which, after being deprived of its bark, is either sun dried or kiln dried. It contains gallic acid, tannin, resins, organic acids, water-soluble glycosides, essential oil and potassium oxalate. Because of the last constituent rhubarb must never be cooked in a copper saucepan. In small doses the drug promotes digestion, cleanses the blood and stimulates the appetite. In medium doses it acts as a laxative and in larger quantities is used as a purgative. It is a very good cure for dysentery, and does not harm weak stomachs and intestines. Commercially it is widely used in the manufacture of aperitifs and liqueurs. There is some prejudice against rhubarb because it can cause rheumatism. This however, is due to its action in stirring up whatever poisons are in the blood before eliminating them, and if the fruit is regularly eaten the rheumatic symptoms will finally disappear with the poisons.

The **Bay laurel**, or sweet bay (*Laurus nobilis* of the Lauraceae) is an evergreen shrub, or more rarely, a tree, which can grow as high as 15 to 20 metres (50 to 60 feet). It grows spontaneously in scrubland and woods in Europe and around the Mediterranean and in California. Some of the largest species are to be found in Italy in the woods of Policoro in Lucania. It is also popular as an ornamental in gardens.

L. nobilis, which is well named for its wholesome properties, has been used since the earliest times to flavour food. The drug is provided by the leaves and fruits which contain a volatile oil used in the treatment of rheumatic complaints. Also present are bitter principles and tannic acid. As well as being a culinary herb, bay is used medicinally in infusions or decoctions as a general stimulant, as a stimulant of gastric secretion, and as a diaphoretic and carminative. The fruits are drupes, rich in essential oil, fats and tannin. Their particular use is in the manufacture of laurel oil or butter which is a vital ingredient of laurin ointment. This is a popular remedy for rheumatism, gout, and in the treatment of the spleen. It is also used in veterinary medicine.

Laurel has aroused various feelings in poets throughout the centuries. Milton wrote of its 'berries harsh and crude' (*Lycidas*), but Théodore de Banville, over a century later, did not consider the woods worth visiting after the laurels had been cut down: 'Nous n'irons plus aux bois, les lauriers sont coupés.'

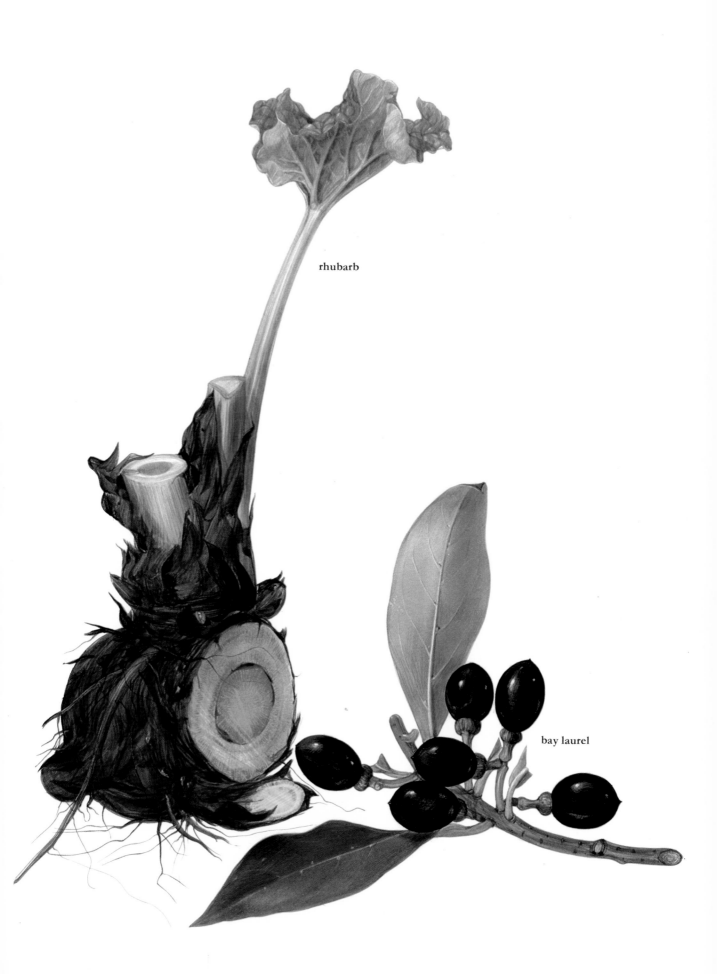

rhubarb

bay laurel

Aloe
Lemon
Capsicum

Pharmacologically the term **Aloe** covers a variety of products obtained from the fleshy leaves of the plant; a xerophyte of the Liliaceae. The most interesting species commercially are the *Aloe vera* which, with *A. chinensis*, a West Indian species, provides Barbados aloes. *A. ferox* from South Africa yields Cape aloes; *A. perryi*, a species from the island of Socotra is the source of one of the oldest medicines, Socotrine aloes. *A. vera* or *A. vulgaris* is indigenous to Africa but is cultivated widely in the West Indies and on the northern shores of the Mediterranean.

A gum resin is extracted from the leaves. Its slow purgative action is due to the glycoside aloin, which after absorption slowly hydrolyses and produces emodin. In Annam certain species yield an edible starch. In small doses the aloe has a bitter-tonic, eupeptic and cholagogic effect; in larger doses it is a laxative, but in certain cases it has been proved to be habit-forming. It should not be taken as a laxative during pregnancy. Externally it is sometimes used in the treatment of ulcers and dermatitis, because of its antibacterial properties. The wood of the tree is believed to have the power to keep away evil spirits, and is still burnt as incense in temples in parts of India and China.

'Kennst du das Land wo die Zitronen blühn?' asked Goethe, and the land where the lemon-trees flowered was India and possibly also China. The **Lemon** (*Citrus medica* var. *limon* or *C. limonia* of the Rutaceae) is a small evergreen tree widely cultivated along the Mediterranean coastline, in California, and in Argentina. The drug comes from the coloured part of the rind which contains pectin and a volatile oil, used as a flavouring agent as is the dried or fresh peel.

The lemon, in addition to its general anti-scorbutic and anti-infectious properties which are due to the quantity of vitamin C in the juice, also acts as a depressant of the central nervous system; as an anti-bacterial and disinfectant agent both in the operating theatre and in dermatology; as a counter-irritant, a corrective and as a tonic and eupeptic. The fruit is used in distilling.

The **Capsicum** or red pepper (*Capsicum minimum*) is a small shrub of the Solanaceae or potato family. It is perennial in suitable climatic conditions, but is more often cultivated as an annual, and originates in tropical regions. Commercially three varieties of *C. minimum* occur, known as African chillies. The drug, which is provided by the fruit, contains a pungent principle called capsaicin; a fixed oil; a liquid alkaloid; and a red colouring substance. The drug is used internally as a carminative against flatulence and dyspesia, and externally in the form of ointment or medicated wool as a counter-irritant against chilblains, neuralgia, certain forms of rheumatism and bad circulation.

Another variety, *C. annuum*, provides larger and less pungent fruits from which the seasoning paprika is obtained. Being milder than *C. minimum* it is eaten raw as a salad vegetable or cooked in various ways, usually stuffed with meat and rice, or in a *ratatouille*. The capsicum has taken its name from a Greek word meaning 'to bite'. Under this name it was first mentioned in the eleventh century by the Greek writer Actuarius.

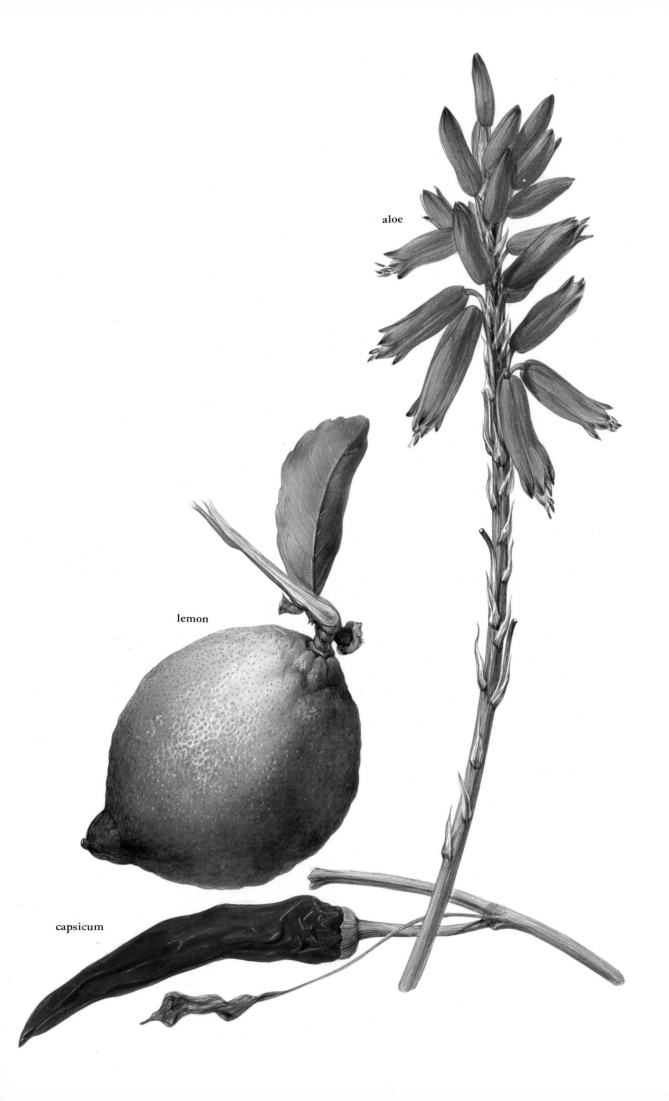

aloe

lemon

capsicum

Rosemary
Boldo
Artichoke

The etymology of the term *Rosmarinus* is derived from *ros maris*, dew of the sea, a poetic expression to describe the humidity that condenses during the night along coastlines, or alternatively, minute drops of spray. Coastal regions are particularly suitable for **Rosemary** (*Rosmarinus officinalis*), a Labiate with a typically Mediterranean distribution, but which is also found under cultivation in areas far from its natural surroundings. This plant was known in ancient times, and was woven into heroes' crowns with myrtle and laurel as well as being employed medicinally. It was also used in orgies and banquets because of its aromatic perfume.

Various medicinal properties were attributed to it and it was widely used by Arab physicians in the early centuries AD. It is mentioned in Charlemagne's Capitularies and by many early herbalists including Gerard, who records that 'there is such plenty thereof in Languedocke, that the inhabitants burne scarce any other fuell.' He adds that 'The distilled water of the floures of Rosemary being drunke at morning and evening first and last, taketh away the stench of the mouth and breath, and maketh it very sweet . . .' Today the herb is known for its tonic, eupeptic, carminative and emmenagogic properties and is also thought to be beneficial in modifying bronchial secretions. It is used to treat dyspepsia and stomach pains. The drug comes from the leaves, which should be gathered during the flowering stage, preferably in spring, with or without the twigs. Rosemary has many culinary uses; the leaves and young branches are particularly full of flavour; and it is also used in the cosmetic industry.

Pharmacological studies of **Boldo** (*Peumus boldus* of the Monimiaceae) only began in the nineteenth century. Boldo contains a volatile oil, the alkaloid boldine, and a glucoside called boldoglucin. The dried leaves of the plant are used as a diuretic and stimulant of the liver, bladder and urethra, and for hepatic illnesses and kidney stones. It is also manufactured pharmaceutically as a tonic-digestive. An oil rather like that of chenopodium is found in glands on the leaves' surface. The fruit is edible.

The plant is indigenous to South America, especially Chile and Peru. From these countries it was introduced into Europe and has now become acclimatized to the dry zones of the Mediterranean. Its importance in medicine is so great that it is imported into almost every country in the world.

The **Artichoke** was popular in Roman times, both for its therapeutic properties, and as a food. The botanical name for artichoke, *Cynara scolymus*, is derived partly from the custom of fertilizing the plant with ashes, and partly from the Greek *skolymos*, meaning 'thistle', from the spines which are found on the involucral bracts (they are not leaves) which enclose the flowering heads and form the edible part. The bitter-tasting cauline leaves contain the active principles used pharmacologically. The artichoke possesses cholagogic, liver-protective, nutritive, tonic, stomachic, astringent, diuretic and hypoglycaemicizing properties. Preparations of the drug, in the form of fluid extracts and tinctures are used for the excretion of bile and anti-toxic functions of the liver, and as a diuretic for malfunctions of the urinary system, and in arteriosclerosis. The artichoke is also used in dermatology, to reduce forms of infantile pruritis, urticaria and eczema.

Artichokes can be eaten hot or cold, but must first be boiled fast for 30 to 35 minutes. During this time the lid must be left off the saucepan as otherwise the vegetable will taste very bitter. After boiling, they should be turned upside down to drain thoroughly.

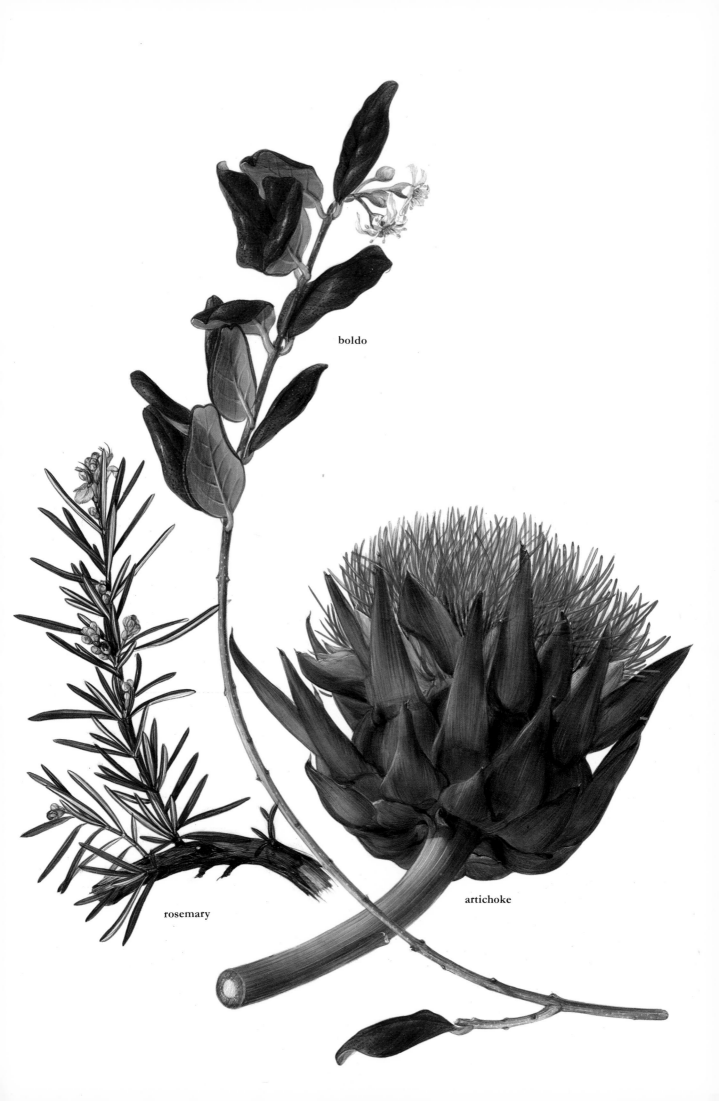

boldo

rosemary

artichoke

Garlic
Sage
Clary

Allium sativum, the scientific name of **Garlic**, is said by Sweet to come from the Celtic word *all*, which means burning or smarting and refers to its taste. Its place of origin is controversial; Linnaeus suggested Sicily; Kunth Egypt; de Candolle maintained that in the wild it was found only in the Kirghiz desert, and Wallich claimed to have found it in India. It is certain that garlic has been used since antiquity as both a culinary and a medicinal herb. The ancient Egyptians, Chinese, Greeks and Romans cultivated it for its therapeutic virtues. Dioscorides used it as a cure for worms and both he and Pliny praised its tonic, diuretic and anti-asthmatic properties, while in the Middle Ages it was held in high esteem as a cure for deafness and leprosy, and carried in the pocket as a talisman against witchcraft and vampires. Garlic also helped animals. The seventeenth-century farrier Gervase Markham made balls of garlic, aniseed and liquorice for horses that had nightmares. Its ancient reputation has been largely confirmed by modern pharmacology and clinical experiment. The medicinal content is in the bulb, or more correctly the cloves or segments into which it is sub-divided. Two thirds is composed of water, nitrates, some lipids and mineral ash, while almost all the rest consists of glycosides. The active ingredients are derived from an essential oil and sulphur compounds. In addition to its stimulant, antifebrile, eupeptic and anthelminthic properties, garlic eases bronchial secretion and acts as a vaso-dilator; it is found in preparations for the treatment of bronchial asthma and arteriosclerosis. Applied externally as a liniment or poultice, it makes an effective counter-irritant. In parts of the Far East it is used as an antidote to snake bites.

Sage (*Salvia officinalis*), one of the Labiatae, owes its generic name to the Latin word *salvere*, to heal, evidence of the high regard in which it was held in ancient times. Its popularity continued throughout the Middle Ages. In his Capitularies Charlemagne advised its cultivation, and contributed to the herb's diffusion across northern and central Europe. The medicinal virtues of the plant are contained in the leaves, which are picked in late spring just before the flowers completely open. There are about 500 different species all with a pleasant scent and a slightly bitter, aromatic flavour. Commercially, the most prized varieties are all French: the *grande sauge* or great sage with slightly thicker and hairy leaves; the very small Catalogne sage; and the *petite sauge de Provence*, which is not quite as small as the Catalogne, but which has a much stronger scent. They are all used to flavour vinegar. As well as being a culinary herb which helps the digestion, sage has a stimulant effect in dyspepsia, and gastro-intestinal atonia. It also possesses a hypoglycaemic, haemagogic, diuretic, cholagogic and vulnerary action, being both astringent and antiseptic. The last quality makes it a useful antidote for mouth infections and bleeding gums. It is used in the cosmetic industry in place of certain animal products. An old English saying advises, 'Eat sage in May and you'll live for aye.' It was reputed to flourish only where there was a domineering wife.

Clary (*Salvia sclarea*) is another Labiate of southern Europe and southwest Asia, and is very similar to *S. officinalis*. The drug is made from the flower head, which yields an essence employed in perfumery and distilling. *S. sclarea*, as well as being used in cooking and to flavour liqueurs and wines, is valued for its stomachic, anti-perspirant and haemagogic properties.

Culpeper had much to say on how clary should not be used. After recommending it for men and women with weak backs 'to helpeth the reins' he continues: '. . . many men when they have got the running of the reins, or women the whites, run to the bush of clary, exclaiming – Maid, bring hither the frying-pan, and fetch me some butter quickly. Then they will eat fried clary just as hogs eat acorns, and this they think will cure their disease, forsooth! Whereas, when they have devoured as much clary as will grow upon an acre of ground, their backs are as much better as though they had never touched it. We will grant that clary strengthens the back; but this we do deny, that the cause of the running of the reins . . . lies in the back . . . and therefore for medicine is as proper as for me, when my toe is sore, to lay a plaster on my nose.'

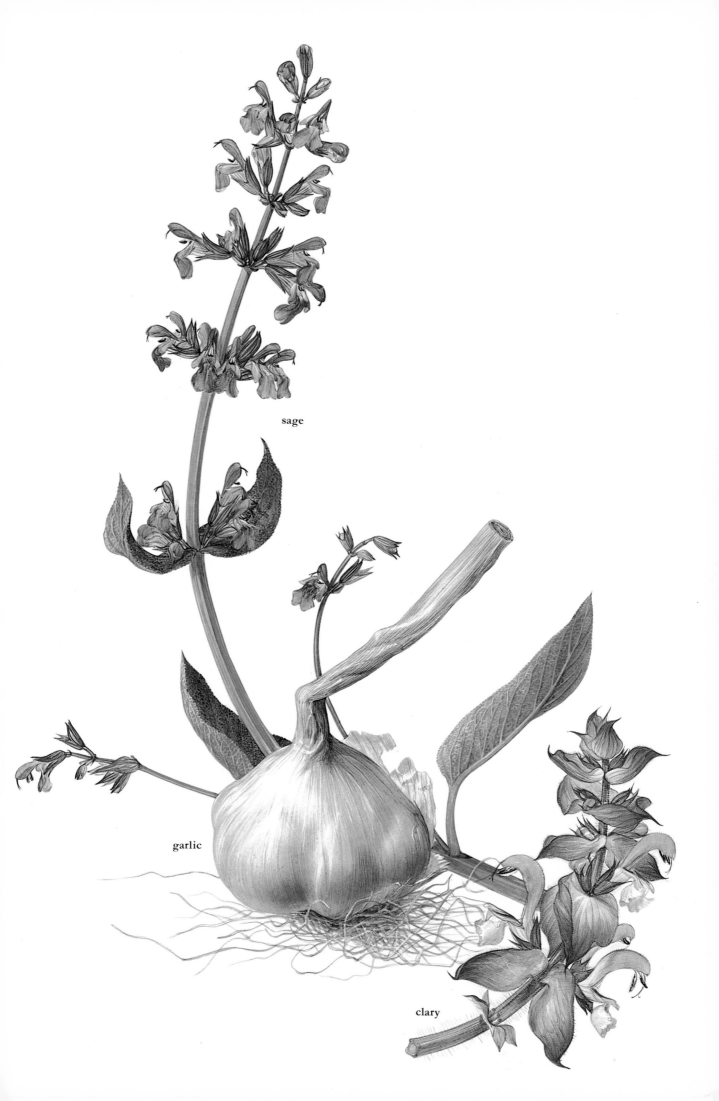

sage

garlic

clary

Meadow sage
Hemp agrimony
Sweet fern

Meadow sage (*Salvia pratensis*) possesses similar properties to those of *S. officinalis*. The active principles have been used in the treatment of excessive sweating especially during puberty and the menopause. The bitter-tonic qualities of this plant are well known, and are particularly valuable in treating those suffering from atonia nervosa and periodic depression. Meadow sage is indigenous to the British Isles, but is more rare than *S. officinalis*. In mediaeval times it was believed that this herb would flourish when the master of the house was doing well, but if ill fortune overtook him it would wither and die. King Mithridates Eupator seems to have been the inspiration of those eighteenth-century botanists who gave **Hemp agrimony** its Latin name: *Eupatorium cannabinum*. Avicenna, the eleventh-century Arab doctor, knew it as *eupatoria*. It is widely spread throughout the Old World and Australia. Medicinally it is not much in demand. In the past, however, it was used by the Greeks and Romans, and was still employed in mediaeval times to aid digestion and constipation, as well as to remove stray earwigs from the ears. The entire plant was used to provide the drug. It should be collected at the moment of flowering, the major heads removed and used either fresh, or within a short time, as otherwise its activity is considerably reduced. The roots of hemp agrimony possess cholalogic and laxative qualities, and the leaves have bitter-tonic, diuretic and sudorific properties. The drug acts particularly on the bile, increasing its secretion and is therefore effective in cases of constipation due to glandular insufficiency, and in congestion or disease of the liver or spleen.

The **Sweet fern**, also called wood liquorice or common polypody (*Polypodium vulgare*) is an attractive fern commonly found in the temperate regions of Eurasia and Africa. *Polypodium* is a term derived from the Greek, meaning 'many feet', an allusion to the numerous stipes of this plant. These represent the remains of the old leaves left on the trunk of the plant. The 'sweet' part of the plant's name refers to the sweet taste of the rhizome which resembles liquorice, and constitutes the pharmacologically active part of *Polypodium*. It should be collected during autumn and the lowermost scales, pale brown in colour, which conceal the stipes or 'stumps', removed. By the time it has been well cleaned and prepared for commercial use, the flavour is considerably less sweet and a nauseatingly bitter taste is released if it is briefly chewed. The active principles in the drug have a purgative and cholagogic action, and so, in the form of tisanes, fluid extracts or other preparations, can be administered to patients with jaundice, or those suffering from chronic constipation aggravated by an insufficiency of bile. It has been denied that *Polypodium* has any drastic effects or any direct action on the intestines.

Because the fern bore no flowers and the seeds were hidden on the backs of the fronds, an ancient belief in its power to make people invisible endured for many centuries. It was generally worn in the shoes or carried in the pockets. Ben Jonson refers to this: 'I had no medicine, sir, to walk invisible, no fern seed in my pocket.'

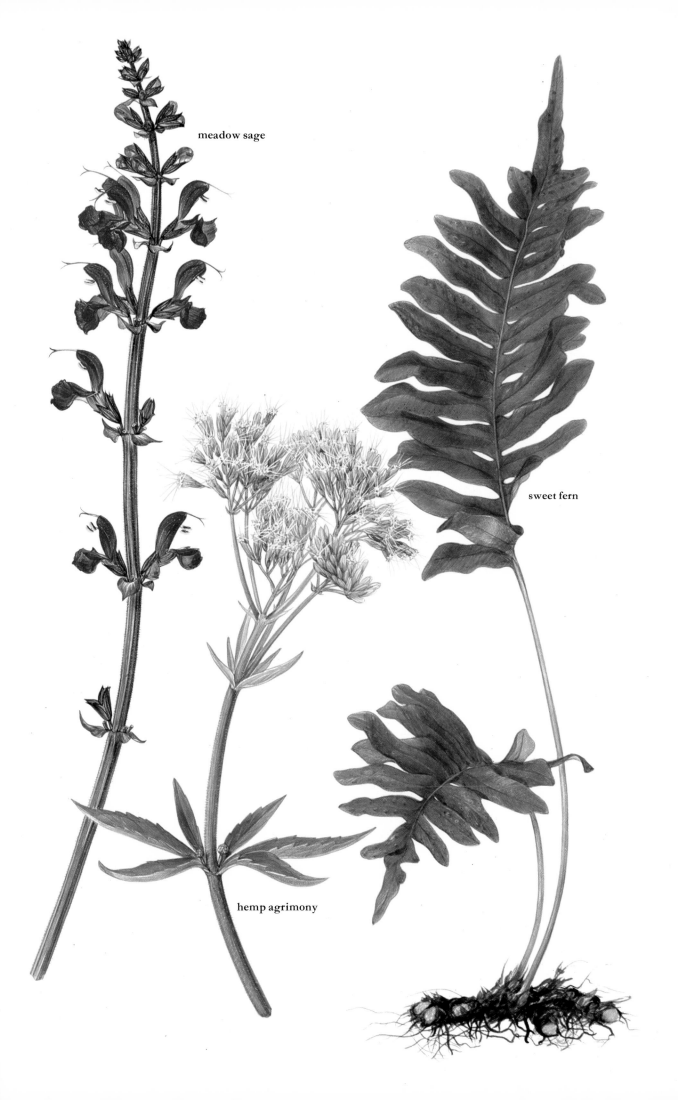

meadow sage

hemp agrimony

sweet fern

Dandelion
Succory

Although the **Dandelion** (*Taraxacum officinale*) is usually considered as an edible plant, it has many well-tried therapeutic virtues, and has been used by herbalists for many centuries. Its familiar use has inspired a number of popular names: fairy clock in its seeding stage (Gerard's 'round downy blowbal') and piss-a-beds, referring to its diuretic property. This member of the Compositae is now naturalized in all the cool and temperate zones of the world, although its distribution was originally confined to Europe, north and central Asia, North Africa and North America. The dandelion's food value is limited, since it is poor in protein and glucosides and contains no fats. On the Continent, but only rarely in the British Isles, the central leaves of the rosette are often eaten in salads, or cooked in the same way as spinach. In France the roots are made into soup, and in Germany they are added to salads. As a medicinal herb the dandelion has a certain importance due to its anti-bilious, diuretic and bitter tonic properties; it is also good for the liver in general and is sometimes used as a mild laxative. As long ago as the eleventh century Avicenna, the great Arab physician, was using it as an alterative and emmenagogue. The drug, which is called taraxacum, is made from the dried roots which should be gathered in autumn, washed, dried at a temperature of about 30°C, and preserved. For commercial use they are supplied either whole, or cut into very fine slices, longitudinally or across. The active ingredients contained in the root consist of inulin, tannin, sugars, waxy and resinous substances, mucilage, and a milky juice, latex, the constituents of which include taraxacin. This last chemical is also found in the leaves. As a remedial drug, the dandelion is often prescribed for liver troubles, gastritis, kidney disease, inflammation of the gall bladder and dyspepsia. It can also be used as an astringent. Externally it is sometimes used to treat eczema and ulcers. Health-food manufacturers make a form of coffee from the root, which can be drunk even by those with weak digestions.

Succory (*Cichorium intybus*), one of the Compositae of Eurasia and North Africa but naturalized all over western Europe, was already known at the time of Pliny, who recognized its value as a food plant and also its remarkable effectiveness in purifying the blood.

Today, through the accumulated experience of physicians and herbalists and through modern pharmaceutical research, further qualities have been revealed: astringent, stomachic, aperient and anti-bilious properties, and hypoglycaemic action. The medicinal content comes from the leaves, which should be picked at the start of flowering, and the root harvested in late autumn. The leaves contain inulin, fructose and other constituents, while the root produces terpene with the resins derived from it, gum and fats. The herb is used where there is lack of gastric tone, bile deficiency and chronic skin troubles. Its leaves, applied externally, are thought to be good for boils and abscesses. Even in the seventeenth century Culpeper was advising the juice of the bruised leaves used with a little vinegar 'to wash pestiferous sores.'

Commercially the root, when dried, roasted and ground, is used to adulterate coffee, or as a coffee-substitute, but it has a very bitter taste.

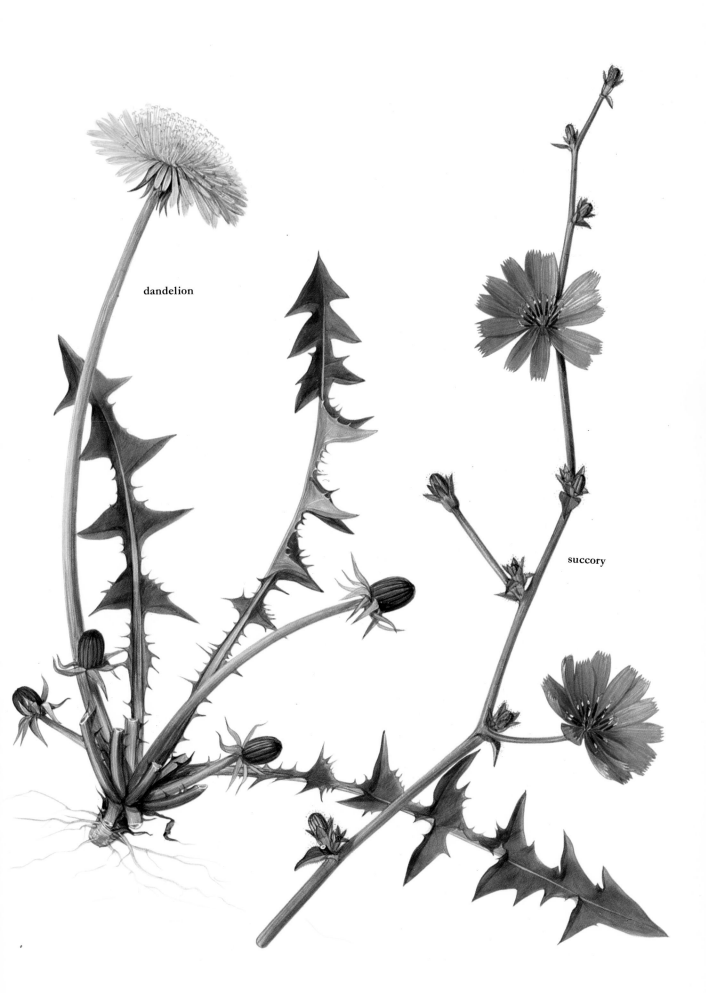

dandelion

succory

Aubergine
Buckbean
Vanilla

The **Aubergine**, known in the United States as eggplant, is the *Solanum melongena* of the Solanaceae (potato family). It originated in India and has been recognized there for its culinary and pharmacological properties since ancient times. It did not arrive in Europe however until around the beginning of the fourteenth century, possibly via Africa. It is mentioned in thirteenth-century Arab prescriptions. Today it is widely cultivated wherever the climatic conditions are suitably warm. It is particularly associated with the cookery of Provence, being one of the main ingredients of many classic dishes of that region.

Pharmaceutically the drug is derived from the fruits which are large berries varying in colour from purple to white, and in shape from oblong to round. They contain various caffeic substances, an alkaloidal glycoside called solanine, anthocyanins and some vitamins. Some authorities believe that the unripe fruits may be haemolytically toxic due to the amount of solanine present, but it is claimed that the solanine is eliminated during cooking, and certainly the young, unripe fruits are more tender and better-tasting than the ripe ones.

The aubergine actively aids the excretion of bile by the liver so that there is a greater excretion of biliary constituents. It also promotes the flow of bile into the duodenum from the gall bladder; reduces the level of cholesterol and acts as a diuretic.

The **Buckbean** (*Menyanthes trifoliata*), also called marsh trefoil or bug bean, is of the Gentianaceae. With its frothy pinkish-white flowers it is one of the most beautiful marsh plants in Europe, but although quite common it is difficult to find owing to the inaccessible bogs and marshy places where it grows. Since ancient times its healing qualities have been recognized and it is still used in country districts, especially in northern Britain, as an infusion for feverish colds.

In early times it was a popular remedy for dropsy, catarrh, scabies and 'hot rotten agues'. Its tonic properties led it to be used in the treatment of scurvy. The drug, which has stomachic and tonic properties, is provided by the leaves which are collected during the flowering stage. They contain various organic acids, fats and a glycoside called menyanthine. Modern herbalists prescribe it for rheumatic complaints, skin diseases and for reducing fevers. It is recognized as an aid to digestion and a stimulant to the appetite.

Vanilla (*Vanilla planifolia*) is a herbaceous epiphyte of the Orchidaceae. It originated in Mexico and is now extensively cultivated in many tropical regions. The drug is obtained from the fullgrown, cured but unripe fruits. These are long thin capsules, black in colour, called sticks or pods. To develop the vanilla's distinctive aroma the pods are plunged into boiling water, and before drying out completely, are shut into airtight tins. The aromatic constituent of vanilla is called vanillin.

Vanilla was introduced into Spain after the discovery of America, and spread from there to France, England, and other European countries. It is well known in the confectionery, distilling and cosmetic industries. The Bourbon pod is said to be the best for domestic use: added to ices, chocolate and creams, it imparts an appetizing fragrance and delicate flavour. Pharmaceutically it is used for its stimulant properties to fight loss of appetite, and lack of tone in the gastrointestinal system.

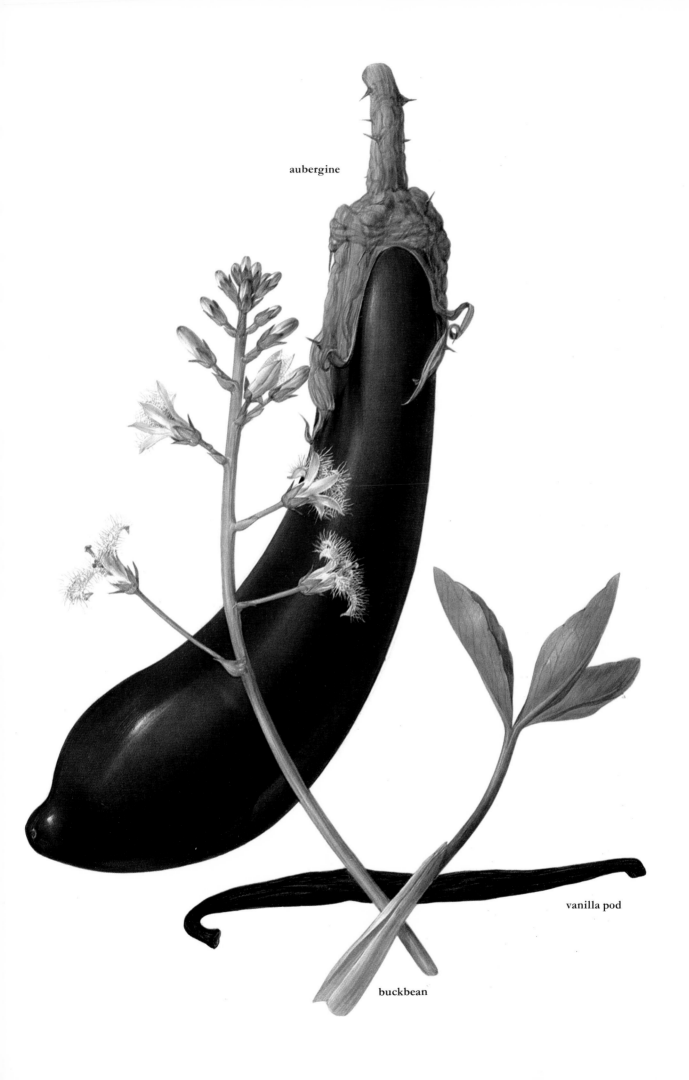

aubergine

buckbean

vanilla pod

Seville orange
Angelica
Wild cherry
Rasberry

The **Seville** or **bitter orange** (*Citrus aurantium* var. *amara*) is an evergreen of the Rutaceae, native to India, and known since ancient times for its medicinal properties. The Crusaders introduced it into Italy, and the Arabs brought it to Spain, the south of France and East Africa. Its Sanscrit name was *Nagrunga*.

The longest-living bitter orange tree was planted in 1422 by Eleanora of Castille, wife of Charles III of Navarra. It eventually found its way to the gardens of Fontainebleau and then to Versailles, where it died in 1858.

As a food the bitter orange is used only in English marmalade (the continental *confiture d'oranges*) but pharmaceutically it is used for its carminative properties. The peel is used as a flavouring in medicine, and the flowers provide Neroli oil, much used in perfumery. Orange-flower water is also made from the blossoms and is used both in perfumery and confectionery. The bitter orange is valued for its bitter tonic, stomachic and digestive properties, and has been found beneficial in cases of dyspepsia and loss of appetite.

Angelica, called more poetically angelic herb, after its botanical name *Angelica archangelica*, is a large biennial herb of the Umbelliferae. It is indigenous to northern Russia, Lithuania, Bohemia and Germany, but will thrive in gardens everywhere.

Culpeper berates the 'heathens and papists' for their blasphemy in calling angelica 'an herb of the Holy Ghost', but its Latin denomination possibly derives from the old belief that it flowered on the feast of St Michael the Archangel. In medieval times it was widely supposed to possess angelic powers against witchcraft and evil spells.

Medicinally angelica has always been recognized for its carminative, stomachic, sudorific, stimulant and antispasmodic properties. It is mainly cultivated for the roots and stalks and is chiefly used in bronchial ailments, coughs, colds, and digestive troubles. Angelica is highly prized in the liqueur industry where it is used in chartreuse, strega, vespetro (which was drunk by Louis XV of France to restore his failing health), English bitters, gin and melissa cordial.

The **Wild cherry** (*Prunus cerasus*) originated in Persia and northern Anatolia. It was prized for its medicinal properties by the ancient Egyptians, Greeks and Romans. The Roman general Lucullus was responsible for bringing the tree into Italy from Pontus. Later herbalists also appreciated its virtues; Culpeper loved the cherry for many reasons: 'The gum of the cherry tree dissolved in wine is good for colds, coughs and hoarseness of the throat; mends the colour of the face, sharpens the eye sight and provokes appetite, and dissolved, the water thereof is of much use to break the stone and to expel gravel and wind.' The American wild black cherry (*P. serotina*) has mild sedative properties and is used in preparations for bronchial complaints and coughs. This plant is very beautiful, and may have been A. E. Houseman's inspiration when he wrote 'Loveliest of trees, the cherry now/Is hung with bloom along the bough.' (*A Shropshire Lad*)

The **Raspberry** (*Rubus idaeus*), a shrub of the Rosaceae or rose family, was known to man many centuries before Christ, as is shown by fossil remains in prehistoric Swiss lake-dwellings. It grows both spontaneously and by cultivation. Early herbalists valued it for many reasons. Gerard (b. 1545), who called it the 'Raspis', claimed that 'they heale the eies that hang out', and that the leaves 'make a most excellent lotion' that 'fastneth the teeth.' It was also widely believed that the boiled leaves helped women during labour, and it has now been proved that they do contain a water-soluble principle called fragarine which acts on the mother's pelvic muscles and relieves uterine pains. The raspberry is used pharmaceutically to improve the flavour of various medicines, and is believed to have a mildly laxative and diruetic effect.

Gastronomically it makes an excellent liqueur brandy, and is used in jams and jellies.

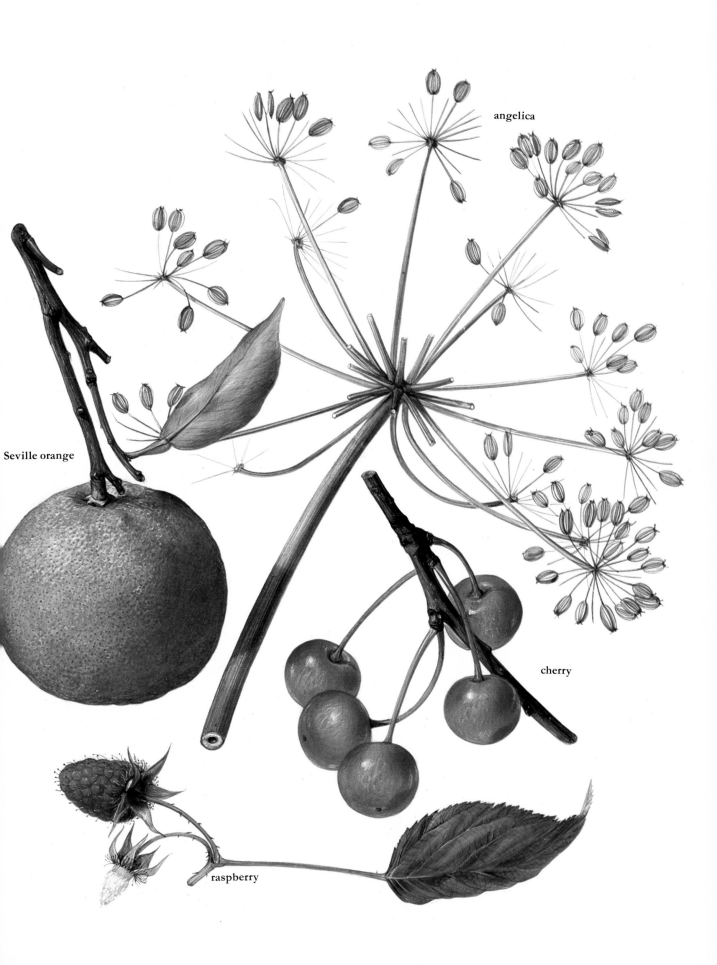

Seville orange

angelica

cherry

raspberry

Peppermint
Hyssop
Aniseed
Cardomom

Peppermint (*Mentha piperita*) is one of the many species to be found in the Labiatae family. There are two varieties, black and white. They are both used in dispensary, although the white peppermint is superior in quality and fetches a higher price than does the black mint.

M. piperita has been cultivated for its medicinal properties since ancient times. It has been found in Egyptian tombs dating back to 1000 BC, and earlier, and the Japanese have been growing it to obtain menthol for at least two thousand years. It is one of the therapeutic herbs that Charlemagne, in his Capitularies, ordered to be specially cultivated. In the early seventeenth century Culpeper was prescribing it as a 'great strengthener of the stomach.' *M. piperita* as it is known today, is probably a hybrid of *M. aquatica* and *M. viridis*. It requires damp, rich soil, but should not be planted where it is too shady, as a shrubby plant is required to provide the leaves from which the drug derives. This is a volatile oil distilled from the fresh plants from which menthol or crystals of camphor mint can be extracted. It is used to flavour unpleasantly tasting medicines, in prescriptions for digestive troubles, in toothpaste and also as a herbal tea, which throughout several centuries has retained its popularity as a soothing drink. The Japanese peppermint, *M. arvensis* var. *piperascens*, provides an oil containing as much as 90% menthol, but it is inferior in flavour to *M. piperita*. The latter species is also known as English mint as its largest cultivation is found in that country, although it also flourishes in Europe, the United States and Japan. Pliny remarked that 'it stirred up the mind and taste to a greedy desire of meat' which may account for the fact that domestically its most common usage is as a sauce to flavour roasts of lamb.

Hyssop has been so favoured throughout the centuries by all herbalists and physicians that Gerard wrote of it 'Dioscorides that gave so many rules for the knowledge of simples, hath left Hyssope altogether without description, as being a plant so well knowne that it needed none:' and he recommended that 'A decoction of Hyssope made with figges, water, honey, and rue, and drunken, helpeth the old cough.' Culpeper prescribed it for such varied complaints as dropsy and singing in the ears. The Persians used distilled hyssop water as a body lotion to give a fine colour to their skin.

Hyssop grows profusely around the Mediterranean and in various other parts of Europe including the British Isles, where it was probably introduced by the Romans. It is found as far afield as Siberia and the Himalayas. Today this little plant with its aromatic smell is used as a carminative and to treat coughs.

It is also used in the distilling industry to flavour many liqueurs.

Hyssopus officinalis of the Labiatae was called 'a holy herb' in ancient times and is mentioned in the Psalms (51:7) 'Purge me with hyssop, and I shall be clean:'.

Aniseed, or anise as it is often called in recipe books, is one of the valued oil-bearing seed plants of the Umbelliferae or parsley family. It is cultivated for the presence of a volatile oil consisting largely of anethole. It is used in dispensary for its carminative and expectorant properties, and in the distilling and confectionery industries as a flavouring. Sometimes parsley seed, after the pubescence is removed, is sold dishonestly as aniseed. It has long been recognized for its therapeutic and commercial properties, and is mentioned in the New Testament: 'for ye pay tithes of mint and anise and cumin.'

Cardamom (*Elettaria cardamomum*) which belongs to the Zingiberaceae, possesses properties similar to those of anise and hyssop. It is grown in Ceylon and southern parts of India. Only the seeds are used, and contain a volatile oil with carminative properties. It is used as a flavouring agent both for medicines and in liqueurs, and as a spice, particularly in curries. In parts of South America two or three cardamom seeds are sometimes added to coffee while it is brewing. The whole fruits are distilled to produce Oil of Cardamom.

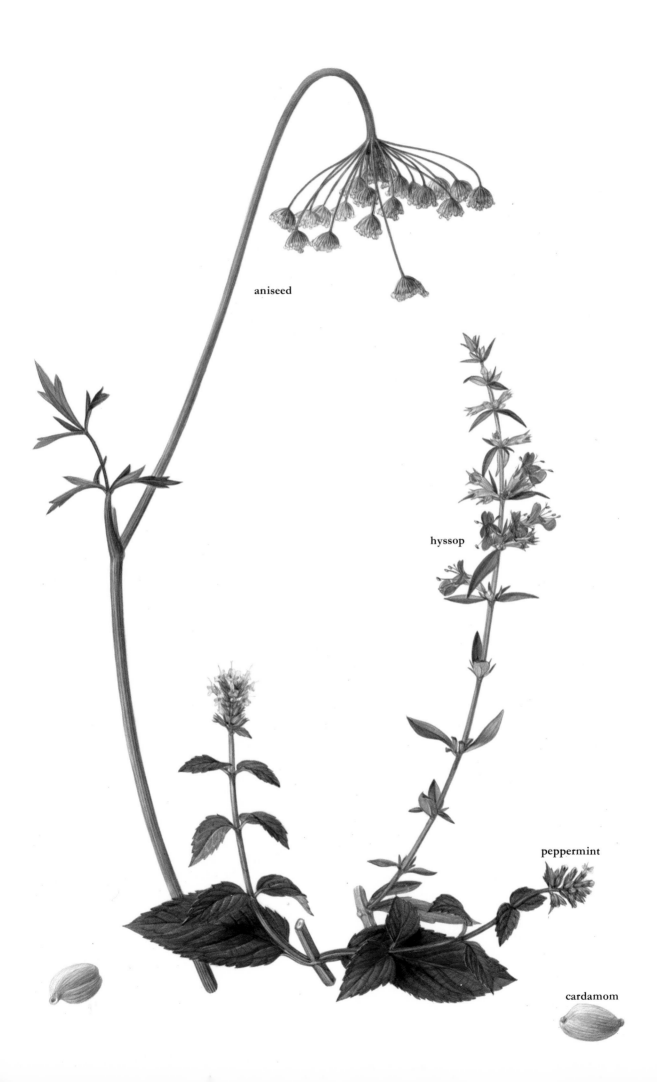

aniseed

hyssop

peppermint

cardamom

Iris
Sweet sedge

The beautiful **Iris**, despite its botanical name, *Iris florentina*, is actually derived from *I. pallida*. It belongs to the Iridaceae and is a perennial cultivated for commercial and decorative purposes. It grows well in gardens under cultivation, and flourishes in the wild state in arid, rocky places in continental Europe, around the Mediterranean and in Mexico, from where most of the root was originally imported. It is cultivated on a large scale in France for the perfume industry. The dried root provides Orris powder which is used in cosmetics. It has a fragrance similar to that of violets.

Another variety *I. germanica*, which has darker coloured flowers, is used in medicine. The part of the plant used is the decorticated rhizome. It is employed as a diuretic and expectorant, and in the liqueur industry.

The iris is Gerard's Floure de-luce, which, 'in two daies at the most take away the blacknesse or blewnesse of any bruise.'

Sweet sedge (*Acorus calamus* of the Araceae) or sweet flag is aptly named as all parts of the plant have a fragrant scent. Several centuries ago it was strewn about as a floor covering, and one of the criticisms levelled at Cardinal Wolsey was his extravagance in having large quantities of sweet sedge brought from Norfolk to use in his London house.

It grows on river banks and at the edges of ponds and streams. It has a blunt, thick spike or inflorescence composed of many brownish-yellow flowers. The drug is provided by the root-stock or rhizomes, which are collected in late autumn or early spring. After being cleaned they are cut into 4 inch-long pieces and dried until brittle. Sweet sedge is used as a bitter tonic, a corrective and in the liqueur industry. It was probably brought to England from the Middle East in the sixteenth century. The *Calamus* which is mentioned so often in the Bible is thought to be sweet sedge, which also has its place in poetry : 'The sedge is withered from the lake,/And no birds sing.' (*La Belle Dame Sans Merci*, Keats.)

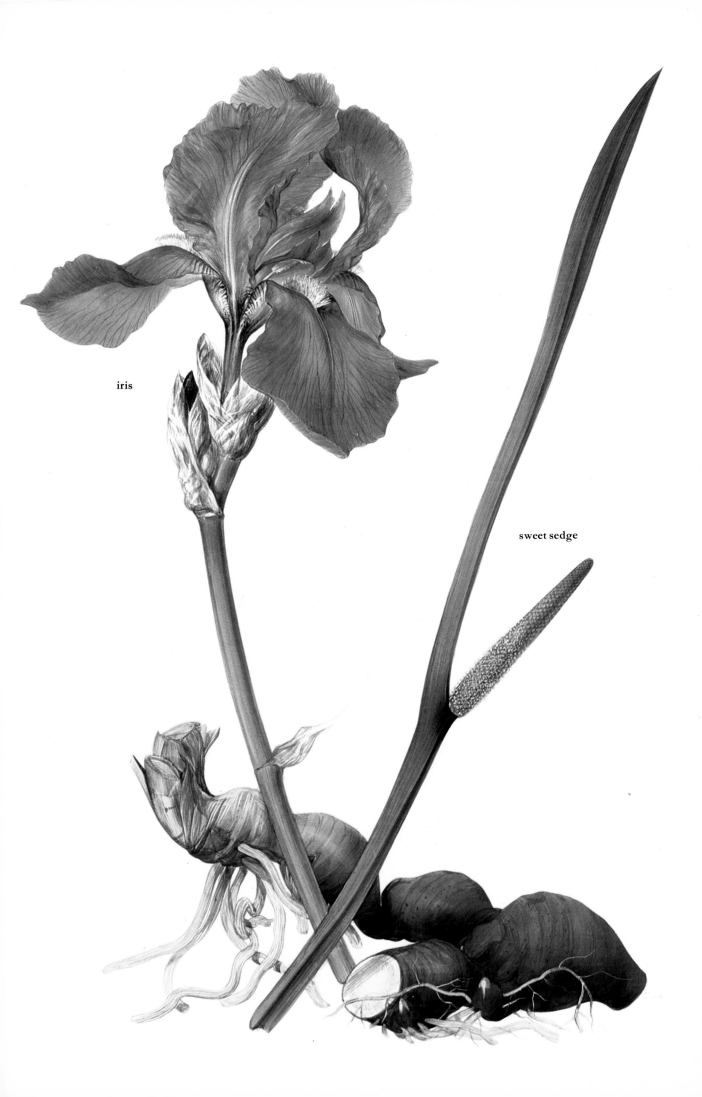

iris

sweet sedge

Wild orchid

Possibly only those who have visited the Near East, Greece or Russia will have heard of salep, and might even have tasted it, either in the form of a refreshing jelly or a spicey soup. This substance that provides the basis of these foods is also endowed with definite medicinal properties. Pharmaceutically salep is a food or drug made from the dried tubers of various species of **Wild orchid**; the early purple orchid (*Orchis mascula*), and two other species, *O. latifolia* and *O. maculata*. They are collected when the plant is in flower, and the tubers are swollen with nutritious substances. They are then washed in boiling water to prevent germination, and dried, threaded together in small bunches until needed, when they are reduced to a powdery consistency. Nearly half of this is composed of a floury substance and gelatine, about a third is starch, and the remainder is made up of protein, sugar and traces of cumarin, from which it derives a delicate aroma.

The use of salep as a foodstuff can be traced back to before the time of Theophrastus and Dioscorides. It was popular with the Persians and the Turks, and has remained so to this day. Salep was unknown in Europe until around the fifteenth century, and then its diffusion as a food was very limited because of its strangeness to western palates, although it does in fact slightly resemble sago. However, its medicinal virtues soon began to be appreciated. Its high mucilage content makes it very suitable as a demulcent administered either orally or rectally to allay irritation and to protect the mucous membranes. It is also an easily digested food for those suffering from gastric disturbances. At one time salep was prescribed for serious cases of infantile diarrhoea because of its supposed sedative and nutritive qualities, but it has been superseded by other, more modern remedies.

Commercial consumption of salep was mostly confined to the Near East and neighbouring countries, and is still not exported on a large scale to Europe due to the manufacture of many predigested foods.

In some parts of Britain the *Orchis morio* or green-winged orchid, the *O. militaris* or soldier orchid, and the *O. purpurea* or lady orchid, and others belonging to the Orchidaceae, are to be found in the wild state. These indigenous orchids can also be dried in the sun when it is strong enough, and prepared to make a comparable salep to that of the East. With the addition of vegetable stock and a little soya sauce and tarragon it makes a tasty soup, especially good for invalids and convalescents. If pineapple syrup or an equivalent is added with a little cinnamon, it can be made into a jelly. Dr Leclerc used to tell the story of some famous French gastronomes who had been served salep as Birds' Nest soup, and had been completely taken in.

Culpeper, who knew the wild orchid well, called it 'one of the most valuable plants growing . . . the salep contains the greatest quantity of nourishment in the smallest bulk, and will support the system in privation and during famine.' But half a century earlier Gerard had written 'It is not used in physicke, that I can finde in any authorite either of the antient or later writers . . .' The early herbalists also knew the different species of wild orchid as goat-stones, dog-stones and fool-stones.

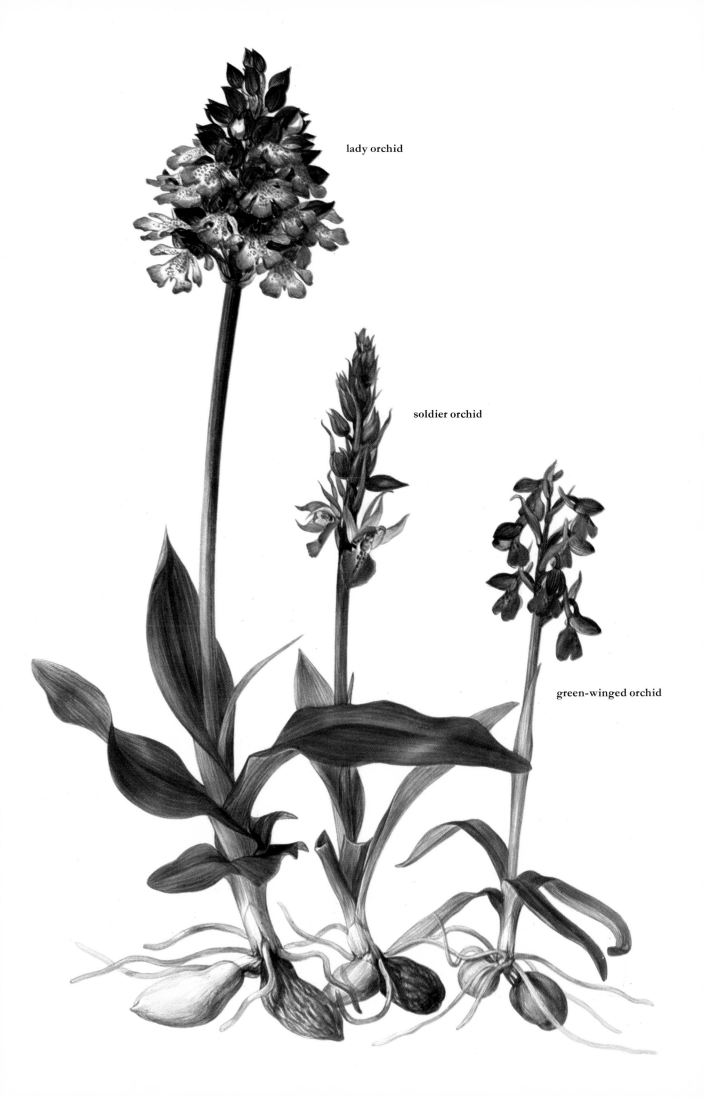

lady orchid

soldier orchid

green-winged orchid

Dog rose
Sea buckthorn
Blackcurrant

Although their medicinal properties differ greatly, both the **Dog rose** and the **Sea buckthorn** bear fruit containing a high percentage of ascorbic acid, more commonly known as vitamin C. The history of vitamins is comparatively recent, going back to the early years of the twentieth century, although for some hundreds of years the presence of these elements in foodstuff has been suspected. It was the Polish chemist Kazimierz Funk who, in 1911, gave the name vitamins to certain complex substances which, although they exist only in minute proportions in both the animal and vegetable kingdoms, are indispensable in the regulation of vital functions in the animal and human organisms. Animal organisms, however, cannot synthesize vitamins for themselves, and can receive them only through plant foods, either directly or in the form of provitamins that are subsequently converted into vitamins. The score or so of vitamins that have so far been identified can be divided into two principal groups: those that are water-soluble and those that are liposoluble, that is, fat-soluble. Their importance in the human and animal body is proved by the onset of various deficiency diseases as soon as there is an insufficient supply in the diet. For this reason vitamins are often described by the functions they govern; vitamin A is known as the anti-xerophthalmic and anti-infection vitamin; B is anti-neuritic, anti-dermatitis and pellagra-preventing; D is anti-rachitic; K anti-haemorrhagic; C is anti-scorbutic and E is anti-sterility. Fruits, especially citrus fruits, salads and green vegetables are the chief sources of vitamin C. Unfortunately a great deal of the vitamin content is lost in cooking, so that the best way to obtain the necessary amount of vitamin C is by eating fresh fruits and vegetables whenever possible.

Two other fruits which are not eaten fresh, but are just as rich in vitamin C, are the fruit receptacles or hips of the dog rose (*Rosa canina* of the Rosaceae) and the berry of sea buckthorn (*Hippophae rhamnoides*), a plant of the Elaeagnaceae. The wild or dog rose is the more common of the two, and the more beautiful. Its delicate pink flowers bloom between May to July in most country hedgerows. Its familiar name is derived from the Anglo-Saxon word *dagge*, which means 'dagger' and not 'dog'. It could refer either to the sharp thorns or to the hard wood which used to be made into handles for daggers. In the Middle Ages many desserts were made with rose hips because of the scarcity of cultivated fruit. Gerard praises the wild rose, writing '. . . the fruit maketh the most pleasant meates and banketting dishes or tartes.' The dog rose is mentioned in an eleventh-century Anglo-Saxon herbal, but much earlier Hippocrates was including it in his prescriptions. The ancient Romans used rose petals lavishly, strewing their banqueting tables with them and filling their baths to scent the water.

In Britain rose hips, which also contain some vitamin A and vitamin P, are mainly used in a syrup for children and invalids. As well as helping the general growth of healthy bones, teeth and tissue, rose hip syrup combats anaemia by assisting in the production of the red cells in the blood. Many rheumatic sufferers believe that this syrup is beneficial to them. In other parts of the world, chiefly Bulgaria, France, Germany, Russia and the Scandinavian countries, the dog rose is used commercially and domestically in jams, jellies and various sweetmeats.

Sea buckthorn, which is harder to find in Britain than the dog rose, proliferates along coastlines and riverbanks in most of Europe and western Asia. Although not as decorative as the wild rose it is nonetheless valuable in pharmacy for possessing similar qualities.

The **Blackcurrant** (*Ribes nigrum*) has long ago outlived its old reputation for breeding worms in the stomach. The leaves and fruit contain active ingredients which are believed to be therapeutic in the treatment of gout, arthritis, rheumatism and many other complaints. They possess tonic, cordial and blood-purifying properties. In France it is highly valued commercially in the distillation of a liqueur called *Cassis* and in the manufacture of jams and jellies.

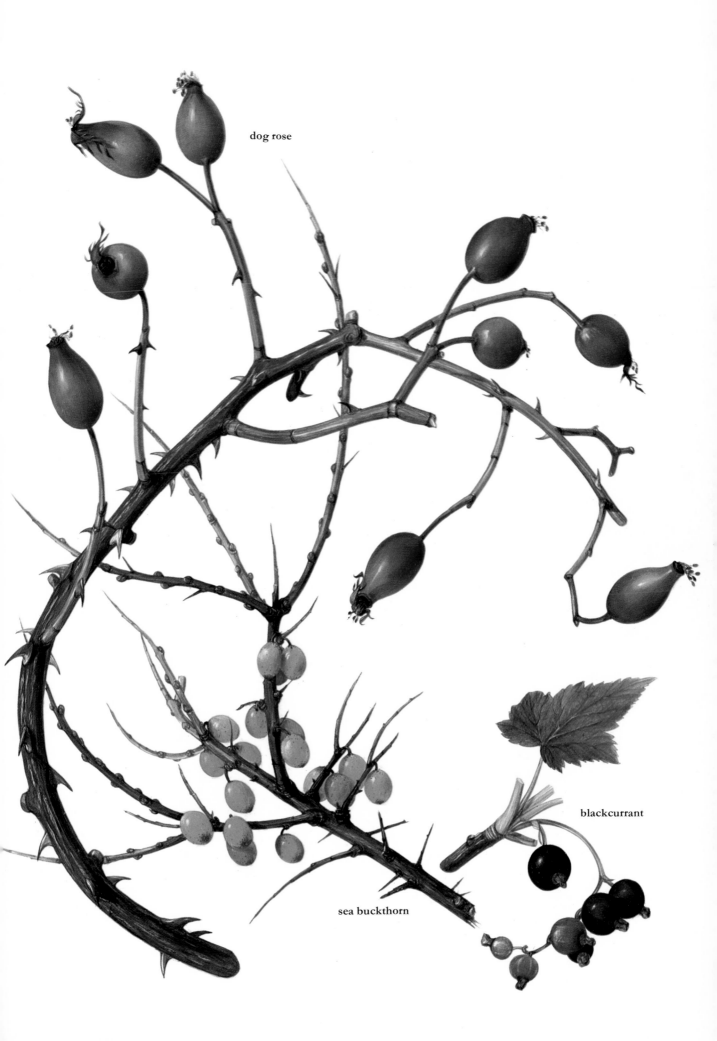

dog rose

blackcurrant

sea buckthorn

Black bryony
Asarabacca

Tamus communis or **Black bryony**, of the Dioscoreaceae, has over the centuries acquired many familiar names such as wild vine, Madonna's needle and Virgin's root. This plant is distributed around the Mediterranean and throughout Europe. The active principles contained in the fleshy tuberous root are used in pharmacology. The root contains a glycoside called saponin which has a strong emetic and purgative action. Black bryony has lost its popularity in herbal medicine although it is still used in remote country districts as a vulnerary. It is said to be good for healing bruises with remarkable speed, and for this reason is called by the women of the French countryside *herbe-aux-femmes-battues*. In the seventeenth century Culpeper used the dried root for cleaning 'gangrene and tetters', to help lepers and to remove freckles.

Asarum europaeum, of the Aristolochiaceae, is commonly called **Asarabacca**, and in some country districts is known more simply as wild nard. It is found in central and southern Europe and western Asia. Its botanical name is derived from the Greek *asarum*, meaning hazelwort, and Pliny writes of it as being one of the plants not permitted to be used in garlands and laudatory crowns: '*Asaron invenio vocitari, quoniam in coronis non addatur.*' The active principles of the plant are contained in the dried rhizome and roots which are gathered either in spring, or, preferably, during autumn. The leaves which are also used in pharmacology, are collected between April and August.

For various reasons asarabacca has not retained its popularity as a medical herb. Once the plant is picked its active principles soon lose their therapeutic power. The asarone in the roots, being volatile, largely disappears when they are dried. Also, it has been discovered that, as an emetic and expectorant, the drug's effect could be too powerful, causing excessive vomiting and damaging the organs involved; the kidneys and the lungs especially. The essential oil in asarabacca is toxic, and in large doses can cause nephritis, metritis, hyperaemia of the internal organs, and, in extreme cases, death. The dried roots are known to have a local irritant action. However, in small quantities asarabacca is used as an antiseptic and stimulant, and is said to bring relief as an expectorant in cases of chronic bronchitis and similar illnesses. Even Culpeper, so long ago, advised discretion in its use, declaring that he fancied 'purging and vomiting medicines as little as any man breathing doth, for they weaken nature . . .'

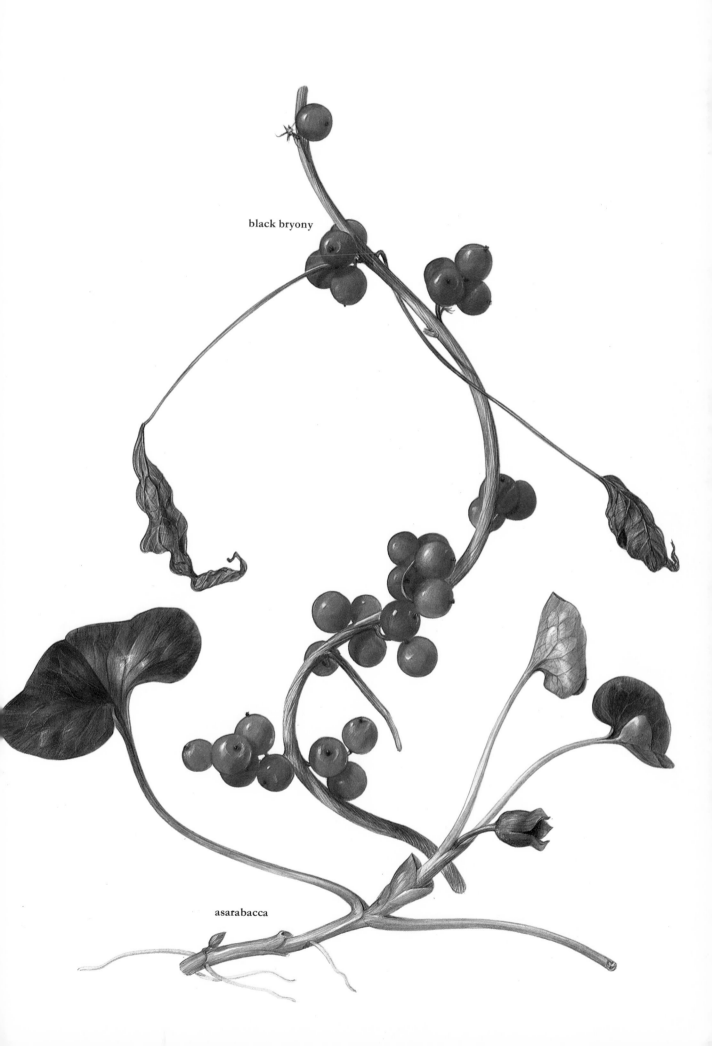

black bryony

asarabacca

Black hellebore
Green hellebore
Winter aconite

The **Black hellebore** or Christmas rose (*Helleborus niger*) is a herbaceous perennial with a creeping rhizome, and sparse shiny and leathery leaves. It blooms between December and February, with the flowers being most profuse at Christmas, for which reason it has earned its common name. In mediaeval times it was called Christ's herb because of the time of its flowering. The stems carry one to two large white flowers, slightly veined with rose on the exterior. They have no scent. Black hellebore grows in mountainous woods in central-southern Europe, and is also found in the Alps and along the ridges of the Appenines. It is a member of the Ranunculaceae. The drug is provided by the rhizome and contains lipids, traces of essential oil, resin, a bitter principle, the saponin called helleborein, and the glucoside helleborin. This plant is toxic and should be used very carefully. It possesses various properties; the powdered rhizome has a sternutatory activity; helleborein is a cardiotonic; helleborin has a strong narcotic action, and also acts as an emetic and emmenagogue.

In the sixteenth century Gerard prescribed 'purgations of Hellebor . . . for mad and furious men' and for those that were 'molested with melanccholy.'

The **Green hellebore** (*H. viridis*) is another herbaceous perennial growing in woods and thickets in western and central Europe. Many varieties are recognized. It produces abundant greenish flowers carried on a stem which is much longer than that of *H. niger*. Flowering lasts from December to early April. Green hellebore has similar properties to those of black hellebore and contains certain alkaloids. Today, because of its toxicity it is no longer in much demand, but it is still sometimes used as a cardiotonic, an emetic, a purgative and an anthelminthic. Both *H. niger* and *H. viridis* are used in veterinary medicine. Similar purgative and anthelminthic properties are found in stinking hellebore (*H. foetidus*), whose distribution is like that of *H. viridis*. It has persistent stems readily visible, and leaves which are coriaceous and finely incised. Stinking hellebore is so named because of the terrible smell which is emitted by the green tissues.

Winter aconite (*Eranthis hyemalis*) is a characteristic small herbaceous plant having a tuberous rhizome which is remarkable for the fact that during the major part of its life it exists in a latent state. Within the course of two months or less, the plant develops, flowers and fruits. In the depths of winter it produces small golden-yellow flowers. It is diffused across Europe and has been naturalized in North America. Its habitat is along the edges of ditches and small streams, and in fields.

The drug is derived from the rhizome, and has the same action as hellebore. It is inadvisable to use this plant in home medicine because of its toxic nature.

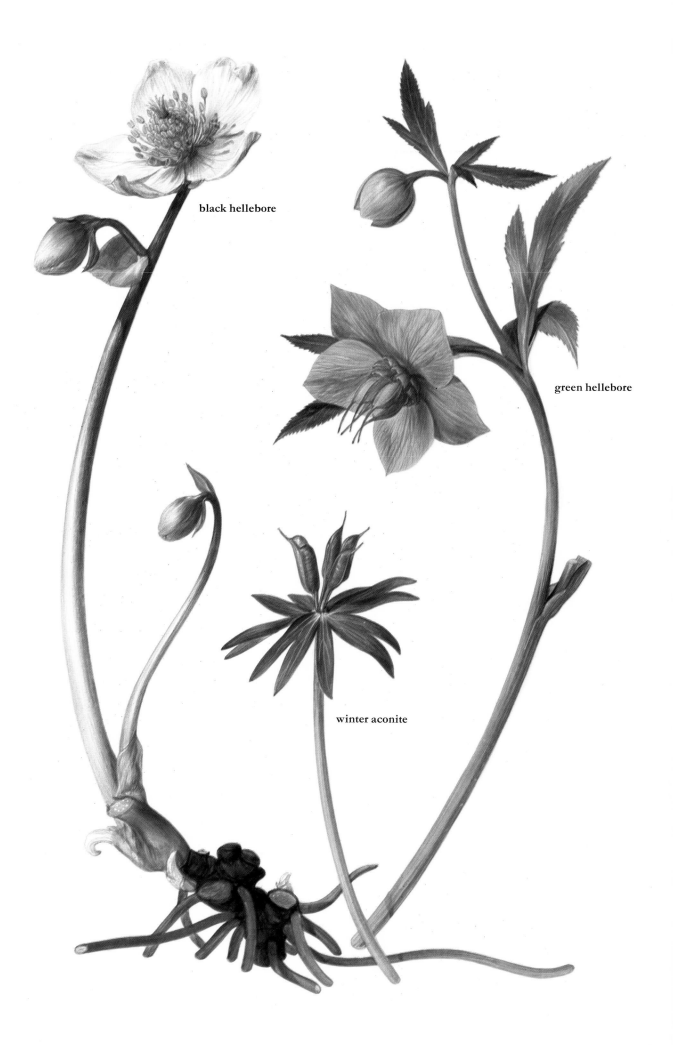

black hellebore

green hellebore

winter aconite

Wormwood
Pomegranate
Coralline
American wormseed

Long renowned for its medicinal virtues, *Artemisia absinthium*, commonly called
Wormwood, of the Compositae, is diffused throughout Europe, parts of Asia and North
Africa, and is naturalized elsewhere. The active ingredients of this strongly aromatic herb
are obtained from the leaves and flowerhead: an essential oil, absinthol, and a crystallin
compound called absinthiin, as well as vitamins B and C. Wormwood is known as a bitter
tonic, digestive, febrifuge, and mild anthelminthic. It is also a cerebral stimulant, and is
dangerous in large doses, for which reason its use in drinks is now prohibited in most
countries. In the nineteenth century the widespread consumption of absinthe caused
madness and premature death in many people. Another species of the same genus, musk
milfoil, is used in the manufacture of a Swiss liqueur, *Irabitter*. Alpine yarrow, another
species, is employed in the preparation of herb teas.
Wormwood is believed to be the herb which Shakespeare had in mind when Oberon
lifted the spell from Titania with the juice of 'Dian's bud'. Botanically the herb is called
after the goddess Artemis, whose Roman name is Diana. 'Dian's bud' was probably
invented by Shakespeare as it is unknown elsewhere. Thomas Tusser (b. *circa* 1523),
author of a great work on husbandry and huswifery, advises as one of the tasks for July,
'While wormwood hath seed, get a handful or twain/To save against March, to make flea
to refrain:/Where chamber is sweeped, and wormwood is strown,/No flea, for his life,
dare abide to be known.' Together with rue, wormwood was held in high repute in
mediaeval times, against all forms of infection.
The **Pomegranate** (*Punica granatum*), of the Punicaceae, is distinguished for its beautiful
fruit and flowers, although it has little actual food value. Its uses as a medical plant
however, have been celebrated since antiquity. A native of Persia, this shrub or small tree
was also associated with the religious rites of the ancient Egyptians, Greeks and Romans.
Its anthelminthic properties were recorded by Dioscorides, Pliny and Celsus and, much
later, in the thirteenth century by the English monk Bartholomaeus Anglicus. After this the
pomegranate's popularity declined, until in the eighteenth century, it came into use again,
mostly as a vermifuge, and more details of its efficacy as an astringent remedy for
dysentery and diarrhoea were received from as far away as China.
The drug contains various alkaloids, one of which, pelletierine, acts as a vermifuge.
Infusions of this are believed to totally paralyse tapeworms, after which they can be
eliminated by a good purgative. Commercially, the pomegranate is used in the
manufacture of grenadine syrup, and in jams and jellies. In literature it also has a place;
Shakespeare has chosen it for his nightingale when 'Nightly she sings on yon pomegranate
tree' (*Romeo and Juliet*, III. v.2).
Corallina officinalis or **Coralline**, a delicate pink or purplish seaweed with calcareous coral-
like incrustations, common along both the Atlantic and Mediterranean coasts, also has
anthelminthic properties. It is said to be particularly good against *ascaris* which infects the
small intestine, and *oxyuris*, the human threadworm. Its use declined towards the end of
the eighteenth century when it was superseded by the grey coralline or Corsican moss,
which proved to be equally effective, and was more common and therefore easier to find.
The remedy is made from the whole thallus of the seaweed, after it has been carefully
cleaned of all impurities such as grains of sand and rock fragments. The active ingredient
comes from the gelatine that makes up 60 per cent of the thallus.
The flowerheads of **American wormseed** (*Chenopodium ambrosioides*) are also credited with
mild vermifugal qualities, especially the variety *anthelminthicum*. The plant is a member of
the Chenopodiaceae, and is commonly found in the eastern states of America.
Chenopodium oil is now almost the only form of the drug which is used. It is obtained
from the fresh flowering and fruiting plants and consists mostly of ascaridole. It cures
roundworms and hookworms, and was also thought to be a cure for scurvy.

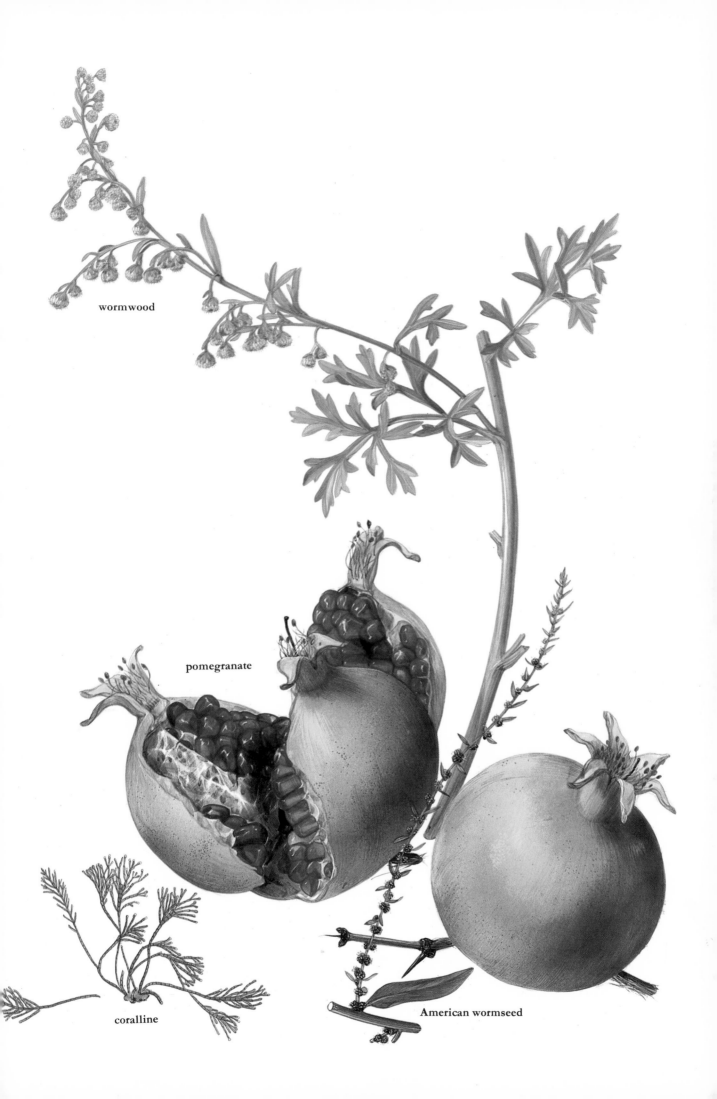

wormwood

pomegranate

coralline

American wormseed

Male fern
Santolina
Feverfew

The **Male fern** (*Dryopteris filix-mas*) of the Aspidiaceae, has been recognized since very ancient times as a most useful taenifuge. Theophratus, Dioscorides and Pliny all described its anthelminthic properties. They advised mixing the dried rhizome with honey to combat tapeworms, and to cure other types of smaller worms they prescribed the plant's use with wine and barley meal. During the Middle Ages the male fern was yet another plant that fell into disuse, and it was not until the eighteenth century that it, also, was again mentioned in pharmacopoeias. Both Louis XV of France and Frederick II of Prussia are said to have paid vast sums of money for remedies containing this drug. The male fern finally came into its own at the start of the nineteenth century, in Geneva, where two brothers, both pharmacists, recommended the use of an ether extract of fresh rhizomes instead of using it in dried and powdered form. The efficacy of the drug when used in this way was soon proved, and it began to be widely used.

The rhizome should be gathered in summer when the active medical principles are most highly concentrated. It is considered to be an excellent anthelminthic, particularly against tapeworms, but it must be used with discretion, especially as an ether extract, and it should not be given to children. It is advisable to be taken under medical supervision as excessive doses could be poisonous.

Another plant with anthelminthic properties is **Santolina** (*Santolina chamaecyparissus*), known in country districts by the prettier names of lavender cotton or holy flax. Because of its active principles this member of the Compositae is used as a stimulant, stomachic, emmenagogue, antiseptic and vulnerary. The parts used in pharmacy are the flowerheads and the seeds. Pliny recommended it to be drunk in wine to cure snake-bites, and Gerard thought it 'to be equall with the usuall worme-seed.' The vermifuge powder that was once made from the seeds has now given way to mass-produced products.

Culpeper, as well as confirming the importance of santolina as a cure for worms 'not only in children but also in people of riper years . . .' added that 'the body bathed with a decoction of it, helps scabs and the itch.'

Similar therapeutic properties to those of santolina are found in **Feverfew** (*Chrysanthemum parthenium*). The flowerheads contain active principles which are emmenagogic and vulnerary, and may also be used as a substitute for chamomile to ease menstrual pain. It has even been known on the Continent to have been sold fraudently as chamomile.

In mediaeval times feverfew was frequently mixed with wine and honey as a cure for 'them that are giddie in the head' and 'such as be melancholike'. There is little doubt that wine and honey could do a lot for depression, if only temporarily, but as a cure for vertigo the efficacy of either, and of feverfew, has not been proved.

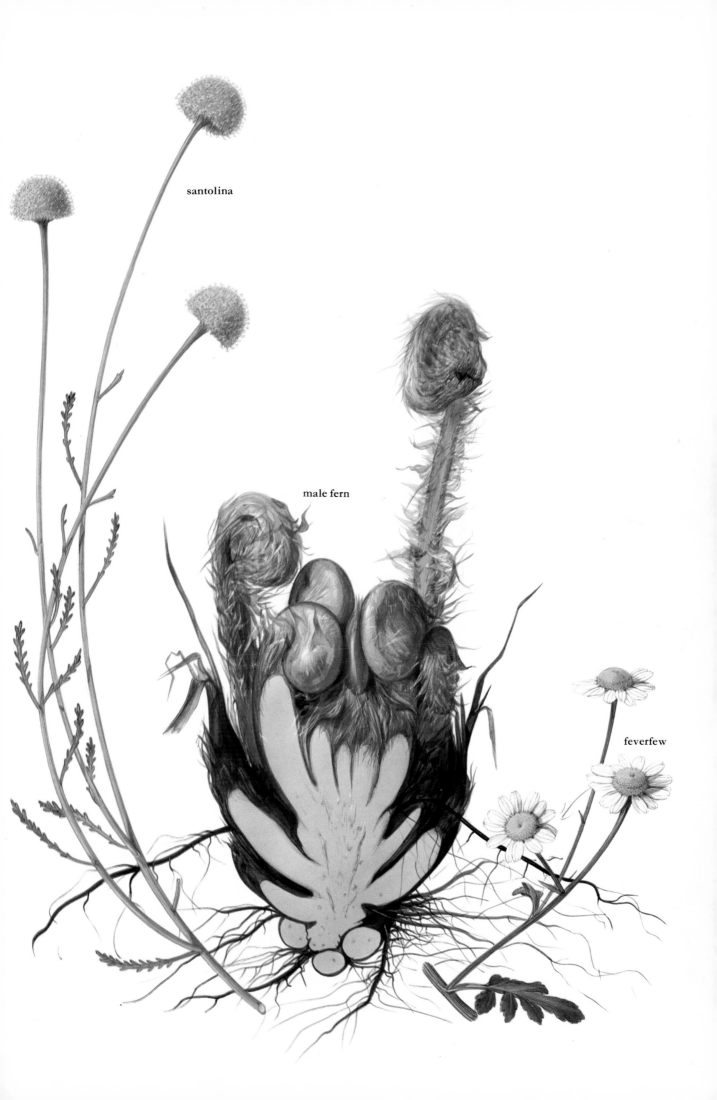

santolina

male fern

feverfew

Carob
Black mulberry
Manna ash

The **Carob** (*Ceratonia siliqua*), of the Leguminosae, is a tree of moderate height bearing leathery, persistent leaves. Indigenous to the Orient, possibly Levant, it is widely cultivated in western Europe, where it is also sometimes found growing spontaneously. The trees in Sicily are especially noted for their fleshy fruit with abundant sugar content. The carob's common name is derived from the Persian *haruba*, and its generic name, *Ceratonia*, from its horn-shaped fruits. In ancient times carob seeds were used as units of weight for gold, the carat; and the term is still in use today.

The drug is provided by the fruits. These produce a mucilage when boiled in water, and contain large quantities of saccharose which is extracted industrially for consumption by both humans and animals. The seeds show the presence of mannan, galactan, pentosans, protein and cellulose. The endosperms from the seeds of the carob, or locust beans, produce carob gum. The carob's activities are contrasting: a decoction of the flowers can be taken as a mild laxative, while the meal or flour made from the seeds, is a good antidiarrhetic, and is sometimes used in the diet of unweaned babies to help against persistent vomiting and regurgitation. A cough linctus is manufactured from the carob, and it is sold in health food stores as a substitute for chocolate. It is believed to have been the locusts eaten by John the Baptist in the desert.

The **Black mulberry** (*Morus nigra*) belongs to the Moraceae. It is a tree of medium height which originated either in the southern part of the Caucasus or in the mountains of Nepal. Today it is largely grown in Turkestan and Iraq where varieties with very large, seedless fruits have been obtained. Like the white mulberry, *Morus nigra* was once widely cultivated to feed silkworms, and was certainly known to the ancient Greeks and Romans who prized it highly for its fruit. The berries contain almost 9 per cent sugar with malic and citric acid. They are usually cooked, rather than being eaten raw. The juice is used to give colour to wines. It has slightly laxative and expectorant properties, and can also be used in a soothing drink for febrile patients. The fruit is made into jams, jellies and a slightly tart syrup. George Peele (*c*. 1558–1597) saw the mulberry in a less prosaic light when he wrote *David and Bethsabe*, 'God in the whizzing of a pleasant wind/Shall march upon the tops of mulberry trees.'

The **Manna ash** (*Fraxinus ornus*) grows either as a tree of modest size, or, more frequently, as a large bush. It belongs to the Oleaceae, and is commonly found in dry, sunny woods on hillsides and mountains. It is cultivated in southern Europe, particularly in Sicily, for the sweetish juice called *manna*, which contains about 50 per cent of mannitol and has a gentle laxative action. In summer the bark of the tree is incised with a sort of bill-hook or sickle which causes the *manna* to exude. It takes on the appearance of amorphous sugar when it has set. The laxative obtained from *manna* may be safely given to children. In association with other drugs, such as senna, a stronger purgative can be prepared.

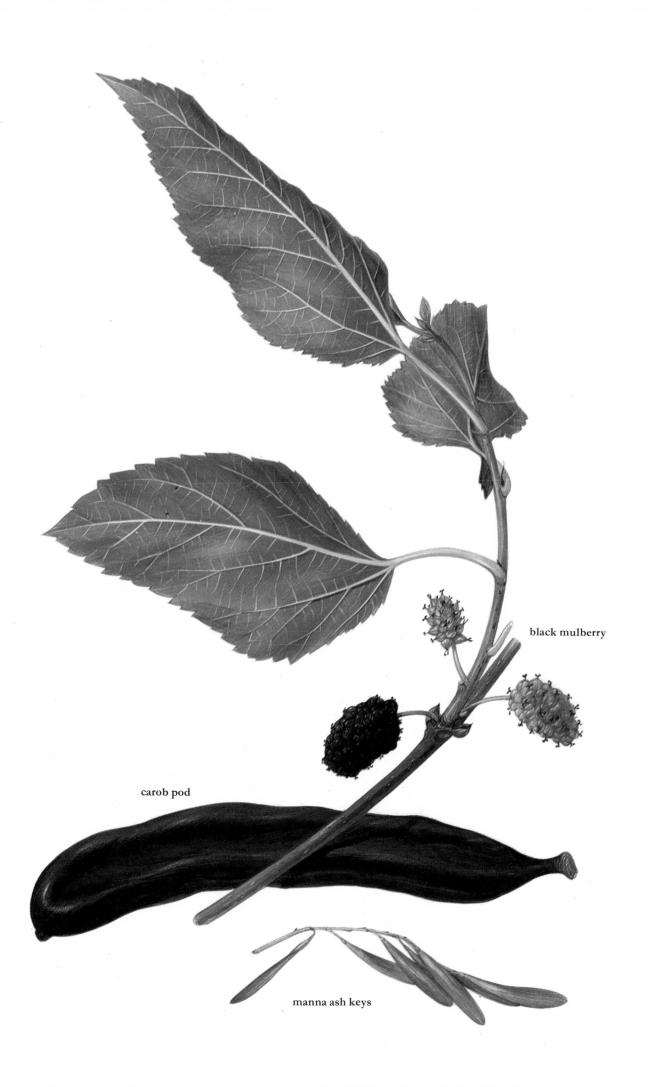

black mulberry

carob pod

manna ash keys

Mullein
Flax
Tamarind

Mullein (*Verbascum thapsus*), of the Scrophulariaceae, has always been known by many names, and there are, besides, several species. The tall, straight stems of the plant with their long spikes of golden-yellow flowers have earned it the names of candleflower and candlewick, and it was known to early herbalists as higtaper, torches or longwort. Gerard wrote that country people, 'especially the husbandmen of Kent, do give their cattel the leaves to drink against the cough of the lungs, being an excellent approved medicine for the same, whereupon they call it Bullocks Lungwort.' Mullein has been used by man since ancient times. Pliny recorded that 'figs do not putrifie at all that are wrapped in the leaves of mullein.' In the Middle Ages, possibly because of the ghostly appearance of the whitish-grey leaves, the plant was believed to be a protection against demons, and monks grew mullein in large quantities in their herb gardens for many medicinal purposes. Culpeper employed black mullein (*V. nigrum*) for colic, coughs, all chest ailments and haemorrhoids, and used white mullein (*V. lychnitis*) as a cure for such diverse afflictions as gout and warts. For many years it was official in the *British Pharmacopoeia*.

The drug is derived from the leaves and flowers which are gathered in July and August. They contain a saponin, saccharose, essential oil and mucilaginous substances. The leaves also have bitter principles, waxes and resins. Mullein is used as the basis of soothing emollients, and in liquid form for bronchial troubles. In certain country districts Culpeper's influence is still felt, for the flowers are made into an infusion to bring relief to sufferers from gout, and into poultices for neuralgia.

Flax (*Linum usitatissimum*), of the Linaceae, is a herbaceous annual which originated in southern Europe, but is now extensively cultivated for textile fibre and for the seeds, which, when ripened and dried, yield linseed oil. The oval, characteristically shiny seeds are also used in pharmacy. They contain principally oil and mucilaginous substances which help to alleviate constipation and refresh the intestinal mucosa. They can also be made into poultices for the chest or abdomen, and are said to be good against certain skin diseases. Commercially, the oil is used in the manufacture of varnish. The fibrous part of the plant is spun into linen cloth.

The **Tamarind** (*Tamarindus indica*) is a large tree, attaining a height of about 20 metres (80 feet), belonging to the Caesalpinioideae. It originated in tropical Africa; despite its name it is doubtful whether it is a spontaneous species of India, where it is more probably a fugitive from cultivation. In mediaeval times the Arabs brought it from India to Europe, where it is now grown extensively. Arab physicians were the first to recognize the emollient and laxative properties of the tamarind, and Pier Andrea Mattioli, although he was misled by the Arabic name *Tamr hindi*, meaning 'Indian date', into believing that the tree was a sort of date palm, also appreciated its medicinal value and wrote that it 'makes the body to move.'

The drug comes from the acid pulp of the berries, and contains a high concentration of malic, citric, tartaric and oxalic acids, as well as glucose, fructose, sucrose, potash and pectin. Today the tamarind is used to make a refreshing type of *limonade* and a vinegar substitute, and in pharmacy is manufactured into a mild laxative. The tree is also used for its timber, and even for the leaves, which provide a red or yellow dye.

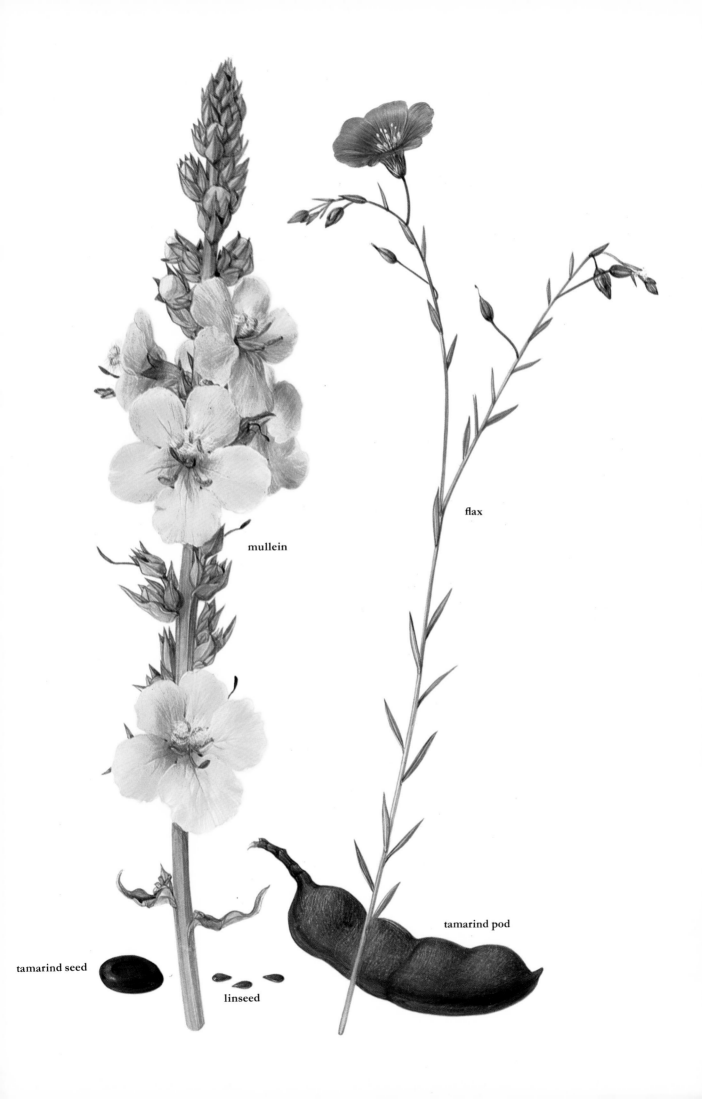

mullein

flax

tamarind seed

linseed

tamarind pod

Tormentil
Cornelian cherry
Sanicle

For several centuries most of the *Potentillas* were believed to have special astringent properties. In the seventeenth century Culpeper included both the *P. erecta* or common **Tormentil**, and the *P. reptans* or creeping cinquefoil, in his herbal, and used them to heal so many afflictions: toothache; wounds; jaundice; dysentery and bleeding noses among them, that it seems surprising that he should have needed to employ any other herbs. Gerard attributed virtues similar to those of cloves to tormentil: 'The decoction of the roots held in the mouth doth mitigate the paine of the teeth.'

Tormentil is of the Rosaceae and grows abundantly on moors and mountains. It flowers between June and September. The drug is provided by the rhizome which contains large quantities of tannin as well as a red colouring agent. It should be gathered in the spring or autumn and dried in the sun. Tormentil is used as an astringent and tonic against diarrhoea. Other active principles, although present in smaller proportions, have useful stomachic, tonic and febrifuge action.

Cornelian cherry or cornel (*Cornus mas*) produces acidulous fruits of moderate sweetness. They are about the size of cherries, and are preserved in sugar, or sometimes, honey. They are also made into jellies, or pickled as a relish. The fruits contain malic and citric acids, glucose, and tannic and gallic acids, and have a mildly astringent action. The same fruits, when eaten fresh, are a good gastro-intestinal astringent. The bark of the tree also contains several active principles, including the bitter substance, cornin, and tannin. Apart from its astringent properties, cornel bark can be used as a tonic and febrifuge. *Cornus mas* is a member of the Cornaceae, and grows throughout western Asia and south-central Europe, although today its cultivation is limited.

Sanicle (*Sanicula europaea*), often called by its country name of strawberry herb, is found in damp shaded woods in Europe, Asia and Africa. Of the Umbelliferae, sanicle is the only one of its genus, and although fairly common, it is not easy to recognize, being only about 12 inches high and not having any particular morphological characteristics. It is a pretty herb, however, with pinkish, bright little flowers and dark glossy leaves. Possibly because of its unusual name, sanicle was believed to have been associated with St Nicholas who was one of the earliest saints to be connected with medicine.

The drug is taken either from the basal rosette of leaves or from the rhizome. These contain substances with bland astringent activity. Sanicle was used by early herbalists as a vulnerary 'to heal green wounds speedily', both for man and beast. Today preparations based on the herb may be used internally for intestinal disturbances and as a blood purifier, and also as a vulnerary and an astringent to strengthen the tissues.

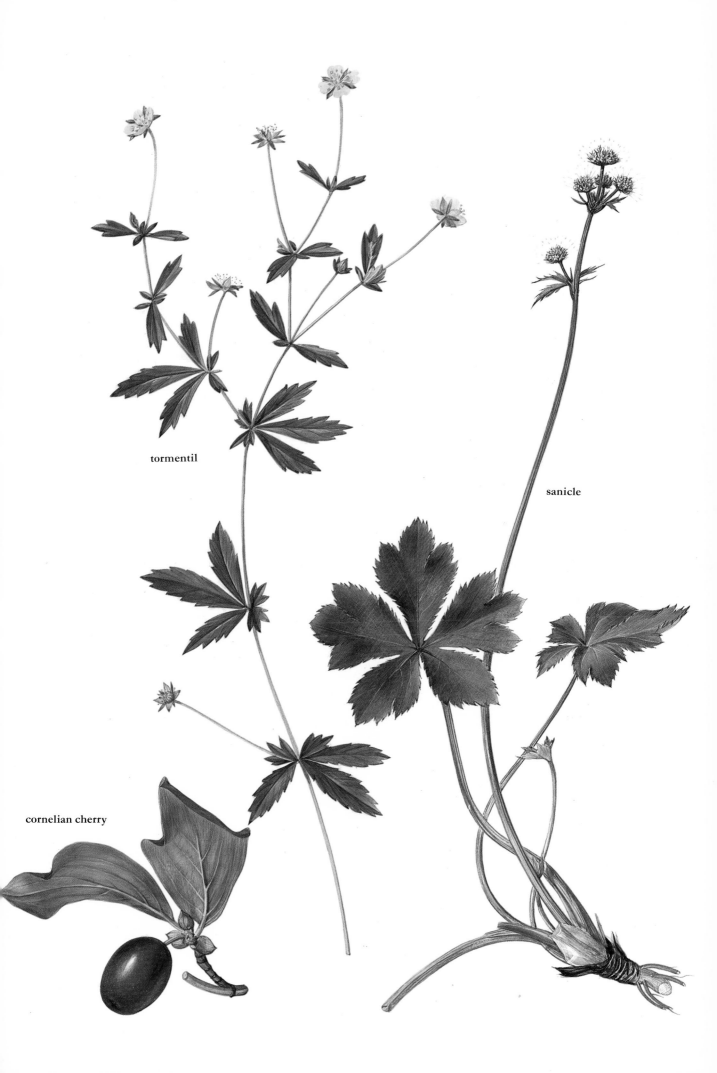

tormentil

sanicle

cornelian cherry

Arbutus
Oak galls
Salad burnet

The **Arbutus** (*Arbutus unedo*), of the Ericaceae, is a very large shrub typically found in the Mediterranean scrubland, but also growing profusely throughout the Mediterranean basin, the Canaries, Mexico, south-west Ireland and the southern United States. Because of the beauty of the leaves and fruit it is often cultivated as an ornamental, and even in localities that have quite severe winters it may be planted in exposed positions. The arbutus has been known since ancient times; the dead hero Pallas was laid on a litter of its flowering branches.

The deep green, leathery leaves contain properties which can be used in urinary antiseptics and antirheumatics. Their tannin content is valued as an astringent and diuretic. The acidulous sweetish fruits resemble warty berries which accounts for the plant's other name of strawberry tree, by which it is generally known in France, especially in Languedoc where it is grown mainly for the distilling industry. A famous liqueur, *creme d'arbouse*, is made from the berries and is believed to be a good digestive. In Spain, Italy and Algeria wines and spirits are also distilled from the fruits, which, when ripe are sweet and fleshy with a slightly acidulous after-taste. In France a jam is manufactured from them.

Oak galls are the curious excrescences found on the twigs of *Quercus infectoria*, caused by certain insects, members of the genus *Cynips*, puncturing the leaf-buds and laying their eggs. Other trees similarly infected are the beech and the dog rose.

Oak galls are prized both commercially and pharmaceutically. *Cynips gallaetinctoriae* produces the galls used in the ink and colouring industries. The high tannin content of these galls, as much as 50 per cent, gives them astringent properties valuable in pharmacy. In parts of the United States the black oak gall (*Dryoscosmus deciduus*) is used as animal feed for poultry, cattle and sheep. In the seventeenth century oak galls were used to dye women's hair black, and were mentioned in early herbals as being 'good to staunch bleeding in any place' if they were first burnt and then quenched in a mixture of wine and vinegar. There are more than 700 Cynipid galls in the oak family in North America alone, despite their natural enemies. The oak pill gall is a target for birds, and squirrels are particularly fond of the oak apple.

Salad burnet (*Poterium sanguisorba*) is one of the prettiest wild herbs to be found. Its botanical name comes from the Greek *poterion*, meaning a drinking cup, and is indicative of one of the plant's earliest uses as an addition to wines and other beverages. It has a delicate cucumber flavour. It was said by early physicians to 'clear the heart and drive away melancholy.' In Tudor times it was planted along the borders of garden paths so that its gentle fragrance would rise up when it was trodden on. The Pilgrim Fathers took salad burnet, or pimpernel as it is also called, with them to the New World.

Of the Rosaceae, salad burnet is a medium-sized plant growing to about a foot high, and is widely diffused across Europe, Asia and North Africa. It is a herbaceous perennial which prefers dry, calcareous soils, and grows in meadows, fields and uncultivated lands like railway banks. The drug is derived from the entire plant, and contains tannin and a saponin, similar to the properties of *P. officinale*. Both have astringent action, and are used as a tonic. The young leaves can be used like watercress as a delicious addition to summer salads.

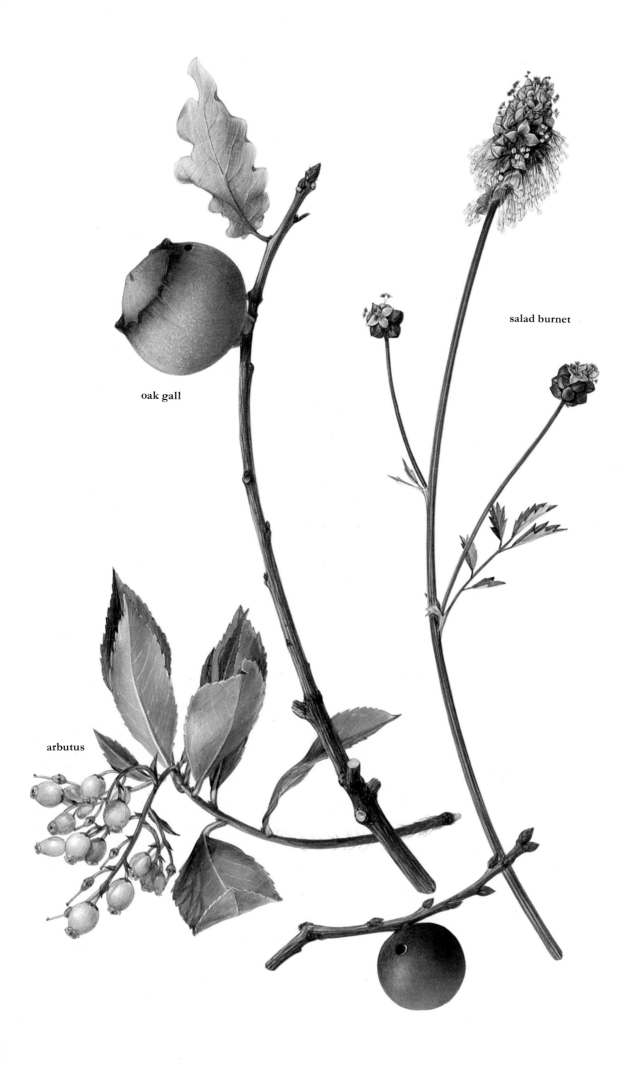

oak gall

salad burnet

arbutus

White dead-nettle
Purple loosestrife

Despite its common name, **White dead-nettle** (*Lamium album*) is not a member of the Urticaceae, but a Labiate. In mediaeval times the plant was known as white archangel, and its flowers were baked with sugar to make a pudding called sugar roset. The sixteenth-century herbalist, Gerard, prescribed the distilled water of white archangel 'to make the heart merry, to make a good colour in the face, and to refresh the vitall spirits.'

The drug is derived from the entire flowering plant, although some authorities claim that it comes only from the corollas. The fresh plant emits a dreadful smell which disappears on drying. According to Pliny it was this fearful scent that kept gardens free of snakes. It is a herbaceous perennial which flowers from May to August along roadsides and on wastelands, and is so prolific that Culpeper observed ironically that 'they grow almost every where unless it be in the middle of the street.' The properties contained in white dead-nettle make it a useful astringent. It is particularly efficacious in arresting haemorrhage, and in the treatment of various conditions such as leucorrhoea (the whites) and amenorrhoea (cessation of menstruation). It may also help older persons with poor circulation resulting in inflammation of the prostate gland or of the urethra. In veterinary medicine it is used by pigeon breeders to cure intestinal troubles in their birds. Two other species, red archangel and yellow archangel, have similar properties to *Lamium album*, but in smaller quantities.

Purple loosestrife (*Lythrum salicaria*) or salicaria, so called because of its slight resemblance to a willow, is a large herbaceous plant growing to 2–5 feet high, over most of the north temperate zones, including Great Britain and Australia. It likes river banks, ditches and marshy ground, and flowers during high summer from June to August. It belongs to the Lythraceae. The drug is provided by the flowering tops although all the green parts of the plant contain a glucoside, tannin and pectin. Its astringent qualities have been known and appreciated since antiquity and it was also burnt to drive away gnats and other insect pests. Both Pliny and Dioscorides believed that if garlands of purple loosestrife were hung around the necks of oxen at the plough it would appease any unruliness which they might feel. Such was the versatility of the herb that it was also employed for some hundreds of years as a hair dye, for those who wished to be blond. During the seventeenth century the plant fell into disuse, and it was only some two hundred years later that it was officially recognized as an antidiarrhetic and antidysenteric. Today its antibacterial qualities are valued in the treatment of amoebic dysentery. It may also be used as a douche to allay vaginal irritation, and as a haemostatic. Herbal industries manufacture an extract of salicaria for use as an antidiarrhetic.

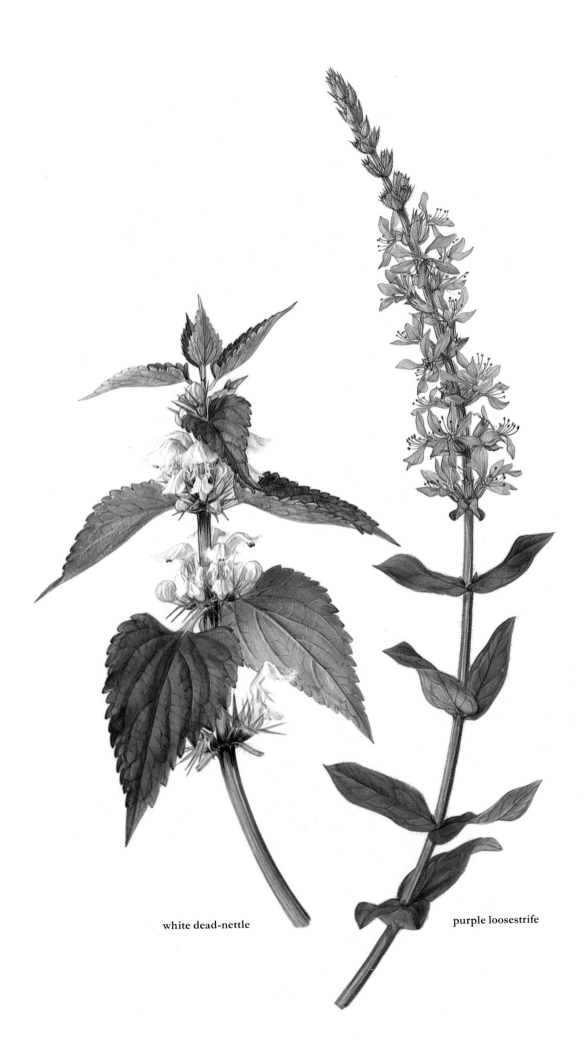

white dead-nettle purple loosestrife

Squirting cucumber
Madder
Common buckthorn
Alder buckthorn

Elaterium, which is obtained from the **Squirting cucumber** (*Echallium elaterium*), has been prized since ancient times: Theophrastus, Dioscorides and Hippocrates all wrote of the virtues of the leaves and roots as a purgative and emmenagogue. When the fruit is ripe the seeds are squirted violently out from the hole left where it has dropped from the stalk, which is what gives it its generic name, from the Greek *ekballein*. The specific adjective *elaterium*, which also means 'to cast out', refers to the predominant medicinal action of the plant as a purgative. This member of the Cucurbitaceae is widespread around the Mediterranean, but probably originated in the Orient as far away as India. Pharmaceutically the sediment from the juice of immature fruits is used; this drug is commonly known as white elaterium or English elaterium, and is in the form of a yellowish powder. The active principle contains elaterin which causes it to be a drastic hydragogue cathartic. It should be administered with the utmost caution, therefore, as even the slightest overdose would cause nausea, vomiting and diarrhoea.

Two plants of the Rubiaceae share the common name of **Madder**, *Rubia cordifolia* which is indigenous to India, and a European species, *R. tinctorum*, also known as dyer's madder, because it had once provided a glucoside called alizarine, the ancient dye of the East. When alizarine began to be produced artificially for industrial use madder was almost forgotten. On a limited scale the roots and rhizome are employed pharmaceutically and in herbal medicine for their tonic and astringent action, to stimulate biliary secretion and intestinal peristalsis.

Gerard in his *Herball* (1597) wrote of several kinds of wild madder; Goose grasse; our Ladie's Bedstraw and Soft Cliver among them. Decoctions of madder were given to people who had 'fallen from high places' and were suffering from internal injuries. Early physicians called these remedies 'wound drinks'. Culpeper recommended applications of the bruised roots and leaves as a beauty treatment to remove freckles.

Common buckthorn (*Rhamnus cathartica*) is a shrub belonging to the Rhamnaceae, found in Europe, western Asia and Algeria. The shoots often develop spiny tops in age, and in some countries it is called *Spina-Christi* from the belief that Christ's crown of thorns was woven from its branches. It has many other names: Rhine berry; highwaythorn; herba-stellaris and sanguinaria.

The mature berries which must be picked in late autumn, contain the drug which is violently purgative. In Victorian days unfortunate children were dosed with *Syrup of Buckthorn*, a vile mixture unsuccessfully disguised with ginger and sugar. The berries have an extremely unpleasant taste, and if they are kept in the home they should be carefully labelled. Although not actually poisonous they can cause vomiting, severe abdominal pain and diarrhoea if eaten by mistake. The unripe berries provide a yellow dye. The mature berries are also used in veterinary medicine as a cathartic. In the sixteenth and seventeenth centuries herbalists recommended buckthorn as a certain cure for warts.

Alder buckthorn (*R. frangula*) also belongs to the Rhamnaceae, and is a deciduous shrub or small tree growing to 18 feet in height, found in Europe, North Africa, Asia Minor and the Caucasus and Siberia. The drug is derived from the bark of the tree and is collected in the spring. Although milder than either the aloe or rhubarb, it is considered to be an excellent purgative with a prolonged effect which makes it useful in the treatment of chronic constipation. In these cases it is often used in place of cascara sagrada (*R. purshiana*) whose prolonged use may lead to intestinal irritation. It is usually taken in the form of a liquid extract. The bark is known medicinally as frangula bark. At one time its charcoal was in great demand for gunpowder-making.

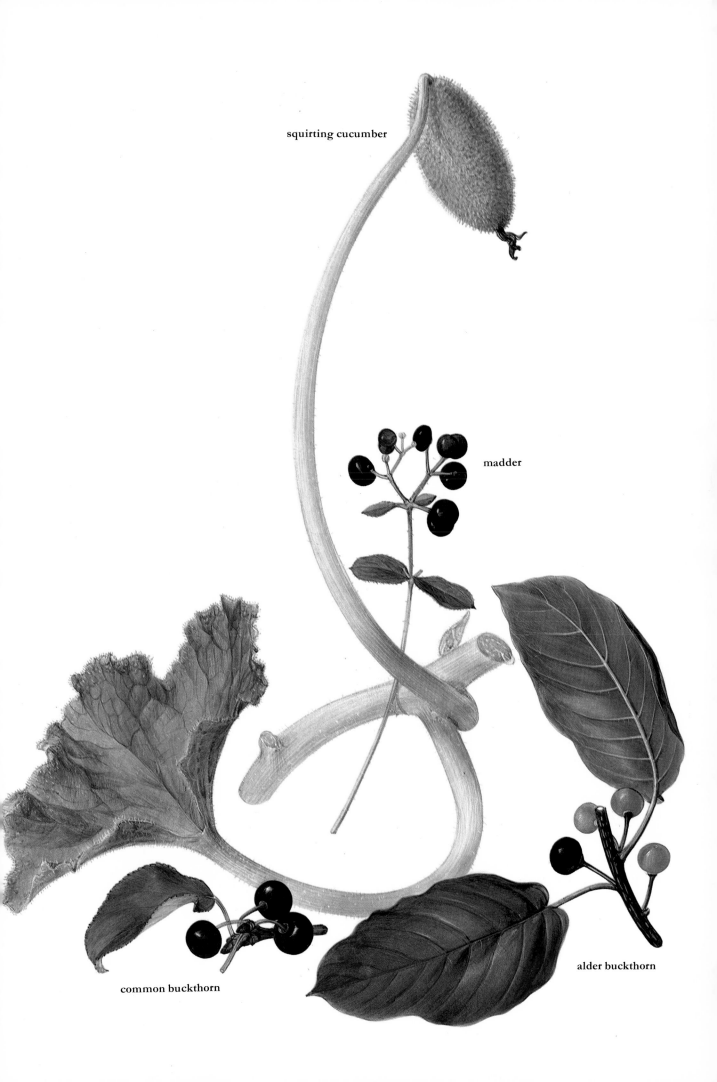

squirting cucumber

madder

alder buckthorn

common buckthorn

Convolvulus
Pokeweed
Castor oil plant

The root and green part of the larger bindweed or **Convolvulus** (*Convolvulus sepium*) have a purgative and cholagogic action. The basic active principle is derived from a gum resin similar to that of *C. scammonia*, which is also used in pharmacy. This resin increases peristalsis in the small intestine, at the same time affecting the activity of the large intestine. Convolvulus is a member of the Convolvulaceae which comprises at least 200 species. Its other names are morning glory and bindweed. *C. sepium* is native to Europe and the United States, and is one of the most common weeds to be found in either continent, although it is sometimes grown as an ornamental. Pliny in his *Historia Naturalis* likened the convolvulus to the lily: 'for whiteness they resemble one another very much, as if Nature in making this flower were a learning and trying her skill how to frame the Lilly indeed' (Bk xxi, ch. 10).

Pokeweed (*Phytolacca decandra*) owes its generic name to two words: *phyton*, the Greek for 'plant', and *lakka*, the Arabic word for 'coloured', referring to the purplish shade of the fruit. Pokeweed is known in some country districts as pigeon berry or red-ink plant. It is a herbaceous perennial, native in the warmer regions of America, especially Florida; Africa; and Asia. The active ingredients are taken from the roots and contain a bitter resin and a saponin with emetic and purgative properties. Pokeweed is also used in the treatment of chronic rheumatism and arthritis. The berries, which are pleasant tasting and were at one time used to colour wine, have similar properties which may prove toxic if taken in excessive doses.

Seeds of the **Castor oil plant** dating back to 4000 BC have been found in ancient Egyptian tombs, but it is thought that its usage dates back even further. The use to which it was put is uncertain but it may have provided oil for lamps, a practice which was confirmed by Herodotus some centuries later. Today castor oil is known as a purgative, but this medicinal role is fairly recent in Europe, going back only to the eighteenth century. The plant's scientific name comes from the Latin meaning 'a tick', *ricinus*, a parasite the castor seed is supposed to resemble. *Ricinus communis* belongs to the Euphorbiaceae and is a half-hardy herb growing to a height of 3–5 feet which flowers in July. It originated in tropical Asia, possibly India, but is now cultivated all over the world, and in some places has run wild. The drug comes from the seed which contains a high percentage of a fatty oil that gives it its purgative action, as well as sugar, resins, an alkaloid called ricinine, and a very poisonous albumin called ricin, which does not however, pass into the oil and can be extracted under cold pressure. Castor oil has a gentle action especially beneficial in cases of constipation due to inflammation of the abdominal organs. The seeds are extremely toxic. If eaten they cause a burning sensation in the mouth, and two or more will cause ricinism, that is, gastro-enteritis with congestion of the liver, and jaundice, and this will be speedily followed by death.

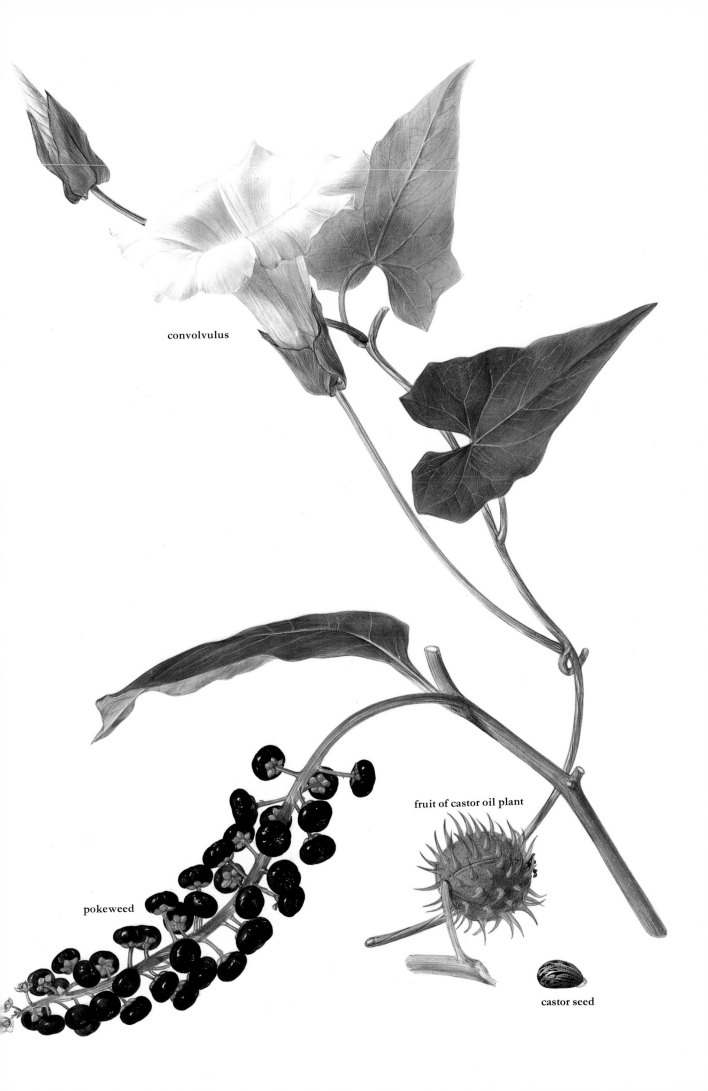

convolvulus

pokeweed

fruit of castor oil plant

castor seed

Aristolochia
Bryony
Spindle tree

Aristolochia is a genus of about 300 species of woody vines or herbs of the Aristolochiaceae. It is widely distributed over the warm and temperate regions of the world. In antiquity the aristolochia was highly prized medicinally. Its name, *aristos*, meaning 'best', and *lokheia*, 'child-birth', is evidence of its supposed usefulness in aiding parturition. The old name of *A. clematitis* was birthwort. Pliny recommended it to cleanse and beautify the teeth, and Disocorides mixed it with wine as a cure against the bites of serpents. Today, Virginian snakewort (*A. serpentaria*), which may have been the species written of by Dioscorides, is valued for its aromatic-stimulant root. It grows in the eastern United States.

The part of aristolochia used in pharmacy is the rhizome. Its chief components are malic and tannic acids, resins and a crystalline alkaloid called aristolochine which is highly toxic. Care should be taken in the use of aristolochia because of its drastic purgative action.

Bryony (*Bryonia dioica*) is a climber of the Cucurbitaceae. It is another plant known since ancient times for its medicinal properties. Dioscorides called it white vine because of its pale colour in contrast to the dark, shiny black bryony (*Tamus communis*; *v*. p. 50) known as black vine. Hippocrates also mentions it. In the fourteenth century its juice was mixed with deadly nightshade and used as an anaesthetic. Two centuries later Culpeper, describing it as 'a furious martial plant', that is, under the dominance of Mars, strongly advised that it be left alone by all except experienced physicians, as 'needing an abler hand than most country people have.' Its other name of English mandrake gives an indication of the danger of using it unwisely.

The active principles are contained in the large, fleshy roots which should be gathered before May when the plant flowers. The drug consists of two bitter glucosides, an essential oil, pectin and resins. Bryony's main action is as a drastic purgative which may be irritating to the digestive tract mucosa. Pharmaceutically bryony is manufactured as a tincture to allay coughing, and is a useful expectorant in cases of asthma and whooping cough. Homoeopathic pharmacies sell a tincture which is believed to cure chilblains. Slight overdoses of bryony are likely to cause congestion of the pelvic organs and serious disturbances of the haemorrhoidal and menstrual flow. The plant grows very rapidly, and is sometimes used as an ornamental to cover ugly fences, but it is thought by medical circles to be inadvisable to cultivate.

The **Spindle tree** (*Euonymus europaeus*) belongs to the Celastraceae. It is a small deciduous shrub or tree growing to 25 feet high, and easily recognizable by its strange red fruits which are half-round and four-lobed, and have given it the name of priest's biretta in some continental countries. Unfortunately, these fruits which are highly toxic, are very attractive to children. Even three or four can act as a drastic purgative on an adult, and to a child may prove fatal. The most important active principles are contained in the bark, but are also present in the roots and fruits. Primarily there is a glucoside which increases intestinal peristalsis, but can also cause a certain amount of colonic pain if taken indiscreetly. Pharmaceutical products of *Euonymus* have a mild laxative action. Altogether there are about 120 species of *Euonymus*, natives of Europe, Asia, Australia and North and Central America.

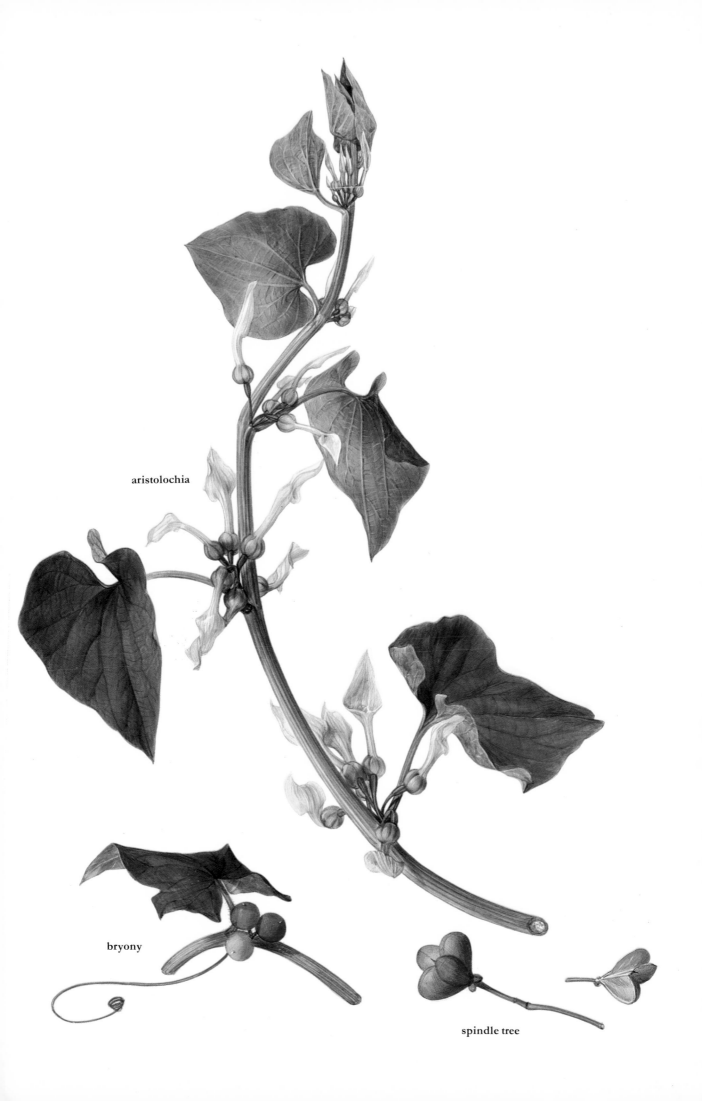

aristolochia

bryony

spindle tree

Foxglove
Yellow foxglove

The **Foxglove** (*Digitalis purpurea*), of the Scrophulariaceae, is a beautiful wayside plant found growing in profusion on heaths, in hedges and in woods throughout central Europe, especially Hungary and the Harz mountains. Today it is so renowned as the source of the drug digitalin that it seems hardly believable that its value was unrecognized by the ancients, and that the discovery of its beneficial effect on heart cases was made only in the seventeenth century. However, both the purple and the yellow foxglove (*D. ambigua*) have been used for many hundreds of years for their cleansing effects. It is recorded in an Anglo-Saxon herbal as *Foxes glofa*, and is praised highly by Culpeper who prescribed a mixture of the juice of the bruised leaves with honey or sugar 'to cleanse and purge the body both upwards and downwards.' He claimed that foxglove could remove obstructions from the liver and spleen, cure falling sickness and King's evil (tuberculosis of the skin), and heal 'a scabby head'. But Gerard, only about half a century earlier, while admitting that the plant had 'a certaine kind of clensing quality joyned therewith' added that 'yet are they of no use, neither have they any place amongst medicines, according to the Antients.' It was included in the *British Pharmacopoeia* in the seventeenth century, when its cardiotonic action was discovered, and in 1775 an Englishman named William Withering began to use digitalin as a diuretic in cases of dropsy. In Italy the bruised leaves had been employed for some time to heal fresh wounds, and made into poultices to reduce swellings.

Some pharmacopoeias claim that the drug comes only from the leaves, but it is also obtained from the seeds. The plant is a biennial, blossoming in the second year, and dying after the dispersal of the seeds. The leaves for the manufacture of the drug are picked at the beginning of the second growing year at the moment of flowering; they have a pleasant perfume which becomes really fragrant after drying. Their active ingredients consist of three cardiac glucosides; digitoxin; gitoxin and gitalin, as well as digitonin and other saponins, enzymes and organic acids. Digitalin's beneficial action on the heart includes a toning effect and a slowing of the pulse; it regulates the working of the cardiac muscle while relieving disorders caused by obstructed circulation, such as congestion and oedema. Near toxic doses are needed however, and sometimes cause side effects like gastrointestinal upsets, so that it is important that the drug be used only under medical supervision.

In addition to *D. purpurea* there is a small group of related species commonly called **Yellow foxglove**. Their botanical names are *D. ambigua*; *D. lutea*; *D. ferruginea* and *D. micrantha*. They have similar properties to the purple foxglove. *Digitalis* is derived from the Latin *digitus*, 'finger'. The plant has many country names including Fairy thimbles, and the more sinister Dead men's bells, alluding to its poisonous nature. In French country districts it is called *Gants nostre dame*. The name foxglove is said to be a corruption of 'Folks glove', referring to the fairies or little folk.

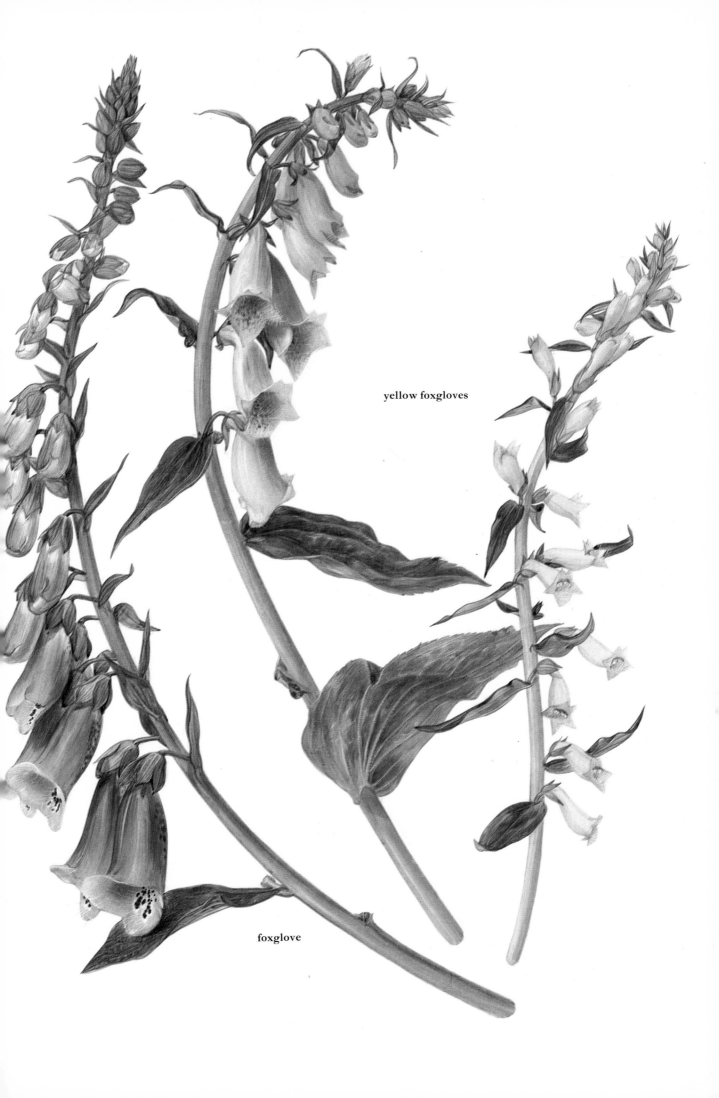

yellow foxgloves

foxglove

Lily of the valley
Oleander
Hawthorn

Lily of the valley (*Convallaria majalis*), of the Liliaceae, contains valuable therapeutic properties similar to that of the foxglove, but less toxic and therefore without dangerous cumulative effects. The drug comes from the entire plant; the flowers are picked when in full bloom during May; the leaves in June and July, and the rhizomes are dug up in autumn when all the leaves have died. Lily of the valley contains the glucoside convallarin and a glycoside, convallatoxin. Another glucoside, obtained only from the dried flowers, is convallamarin. The plant is now employed as a cardiac stimulant and diuretic, but early herbalists found many uses for it. Gerard had the most extraordinary remedy for gout, using the May lilly as it was then popularly called: 'The floures of May Lillies put into a glass, and set in a hill of ants, close stopped for the space of a moneth, and then taken out, therein you shall find a liquor that appeaseth the paine and griefe of the gout, being outwardly applied . . .' Culpeper was more restrained in his use of the plant, simply distilling it with wine to restore speech to those struck by the dumb palsie, or various mental afflictions. The May lily grows in shady woods in parts of Britain and Europe, northern Asia and the Allegheny mountains of North America.

Lily of the valley has several local names, one being Our Lady's Tears because it flowers in May and is therefore associated with the Virgin Mary. Wordsworth in *The Excursion* caught the essence of its beauty: 'That shy plant . . . the lily of the Valley/That loves the ground, and from the sun withholds/Her pensive beauty.'

The toxic qualities of the **Oleander** were recognized by the ancient Greeks long before its therapeutic action was discovered. Pliny described its beautiful roselike flowers and poisonous nature, and Gerard called it 'a small shrub of a gallant shewe.' It is a shrub of the genus *Nerium* and flourishes in the Mediterranean, preferably where the climate is rather humid. All parts of the plant contain toxic active principles. In pharmacy the leaves, which exude a poisonous milky liquid, are used, and must be gathered between May and July. More rarely the bark and immature fruits are also employed. The drug acts as a cardiotonic and diuretic, and is a brachycardiac agent. Its action is similar to that of digitalis, but milder, and like lily of the valley, it does not have a cumulative effect. It contains two glycosides, neriin and oleandrin, which are highly toxic. Not all patients can tolerate preparations based on oleander and it should only be taken under medical supervision. Used externally however, it is unlikely to cause harmful side effects, and is useful against scabies and various forms of lice. The symptoms of poisoning from oleander are depression and nausea; bloody diarrhoea, weakened pulse and eventual paralysis.

To most people the **Hawthorn** (*Crataegus oxyacantha*) evokes poetic rather than pharmaceutical allusions. Proust was haunted all his life by the beauty of the hawthorn way at Illiers, and Shakespeare preferred its 'sweeter shade' to that of a king's rich canopy. In religion too, it was important, the staff of Joseph of Arimathea supposedly having been cut from the Glastonbury thorn which flowers in December as well as in spring. The hawthorn, of the Rosaceae, is native of Europe, western Asia and Siberia, and North Africa. It was known in ancient times and has been variously described by Theophrastus, Dioscorides and Mattioli. When the Romans occupied Britain they used hawthorn hedges for the enclosure of land because of its compact growth, but it only began to be cultivated as a park and hedge plant in the seventeenth century. It varies greatly in height from 4 to over 20 feet.

The drug is derived chiefly from the flowers, which are gathered when the inflorescence starts to open. It has antispasmodic and sedative properties, especially useful in cases of cardiac disturbances of nervous origin. There is no problem of accumulation. The fruits or haws are sometimes used in liquid form as a cardiac tonic. In the early sixteenth century it was thought to be good against dropsy and 'inward paines' as well as being applied externally to draw out thorns and splinters. Swinburne described the effect the first sight of may blossom has on many people when he wrote: 'In hawthorn-time the heart grows light' (*The Tale of Balen*).

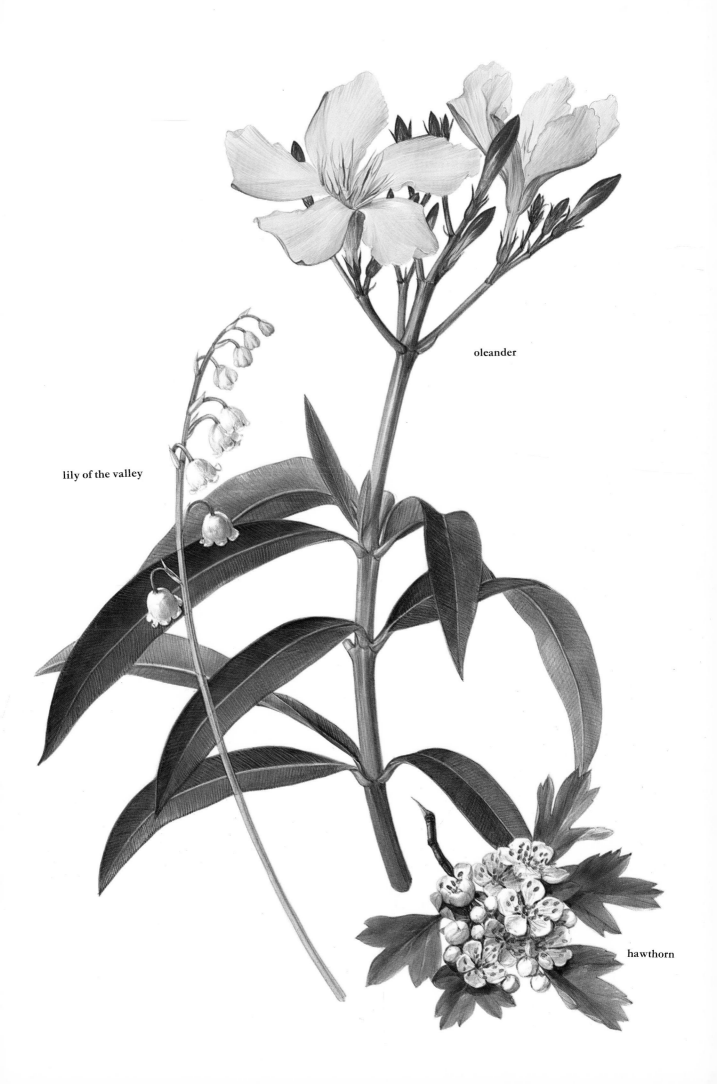

oleander

lily of the valley

hawthorn

Squill
Pheasant's eye

Squill (*Urginea (Scilla) maritima*), called scilla in pharmacy, is a plant with a bulbous root belonging to the Liliaceae. It grows wild along the Mediterranean coasts, but can be found at elevations of 3000 feet. The two British species, however, *S. autumnalis* and *S. verna*, are confined to coastal regions. The two most important varieties in medicine are the white squill and the red squill. They are differentiated by the size of their bulbs, that of the red squill reaching the proportions of a melon, while that of the white squill is only as big as a medium-sized onion. They can weigh as much as 3–4 pounds. The drug is found in the bulb which is collected in August, prior to flowering. After the dry membranous outer scales have been removed the fleshy portion is cut into slices and dried. It is then prepared as syrups, vinegars or other fluid extracts, as a cardiotonic with an action similar to that of lily of the valley or pheasant's eye, but its use is declining as its cumulative effect on the intestines is still uncertain. Squill contains a crystalline glycoside scillarin-A, as well as an amorphous mixture of glycosides called scillarin-B. In addition red squill provides an anthocyanin colouring matter. In India *U. medica* is used in pharmacy in the same way as the European species.

Squill is one of the medicinal herbs whose use can be traced back over many centuries. Theophrastus and Pliny recommended it as a diuretic, and Dioscorides advised its use in cases of dropsy and asthma. Albertus Magnus (*c.* 1193–1280) prescribed it as an emmenagogue. Its action on the heart was finally discovered in the eighteenth century. Red squill is now chiefly employed as a rat poison. Some species such as the bluebell (*S. nonscripta*) are cultivated as garden plants.

Pheasant's eye or winter adonis, the local names of *Adonis vernalis* of the Ranunculaceae or crowfoot family, is another herb with a basically digitalis-like action. It is a herbaceous perennial indigenous to the mountains of France, Spain and central Europe, but is no longer found in Italy, except rarely, in remote districts. About twenty species of Eurasia are known, some of which are annuals, such as *A. annua* (illustrated) and *A. aestivalis*; these annuals are often known as summer adonis. The drug is obtained from the entire plant and is collected before the flowering stage. It contains various glucosides such as adonidin and adonin, as well as adonitol. Formerly adonidin was used as a local anaesthetic. Early herbalists believed pheasant's eye to be efficacious in helping sufferers from dropsy. It can be used in heart cases needing prolonged, slow treatment, being alternated with digitalin, and as a diuretic to reduce oedemas caused by cardiac insufficiency.

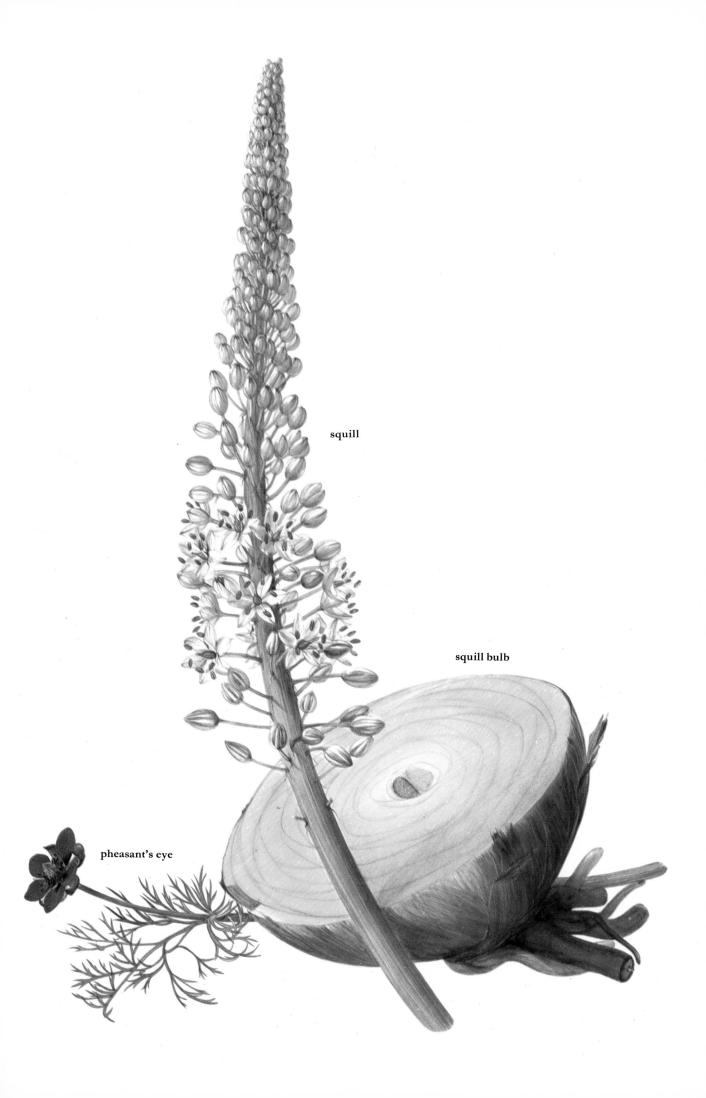

squill

squill bulb

pheasant's eye

Broom
Witch hazel

Broom or genista (*Cytisus scoparius*) is a modest-sized bush with evergreen branches having prickly spines and a strong scent of almonds. It is found in most of the temperate regions of Europe and Asia, and has become naturalized in North America. Its flowers are a beautiful and vivid yellow, which sometimes causes it to be confused with gorse. It belongs to the Papilionaceae, which includes such useful species as peas, beans and liquorice. The drug comes from the young branches, which have a nauseatingly bitter taste. They are collected before the flowers appear, and are then tied up in bunches to be dried. They contain sparteine and other alkaloids, and scoparin and scoparium. The seeds have similar properties. In the past the principal component, sparteine, was used as a cardiovascular restorative, but today the drug is chiefly used as a diuretic because of the scoparin content, and to help kidney and liver afflictions. Culpeper used to boil the young branches in oil for a concoction that would not only kill lice in the head, but also cure pains in the side. Henry VIII was said to have drunk vast quantities of the distilled water of broom against indigestion, presumably caused through overeating.

As well as being a powerful protection against witchcraft, broom was used by housewives in the Middle Ages for sweeping out their houses, hence the common name. The Plantagenets took their family name from the Latin *planta genista*, and Geffroi le bel, husband of the English queen Matilda, wore a sprig of it in his hat. In France the buds are sometimes pickled and used instead of capers.

The great Yorkshire scholar Alcuin (*c.* 735–804), who taught Charlemagne, grew broom outside his cell to house his nightingale, but unfortunately it did not afford enough protection, as recorded in his poem: 'Whoever stole you from that bush of broom/I think he envied me my happiness,/O little nightingale. . . .'

Witch hazel (*Hamamelis virginiana*) was given its familiar name through the custom of using its branches as divining rods. As its botanical name shows, it is a native of the United States, and belongs to the Hamamelidaceae. It is a small deciduous shrub, sometimes cultivated as an ornamental. The drug comes from the leaves and bark which contain tannin and an essential oil, and is used as an astringent and haemostatic, either in suppositories or in the form of extracts. It is prepared as ointments and lotions as a styptic and antiseptic, and is also believed to be beneficial in the treatment of haemorrhoids, phlebitis, congestion, dysmenorrhoea and menopausal disturbances. It is not widely cultivated in Great Britain.

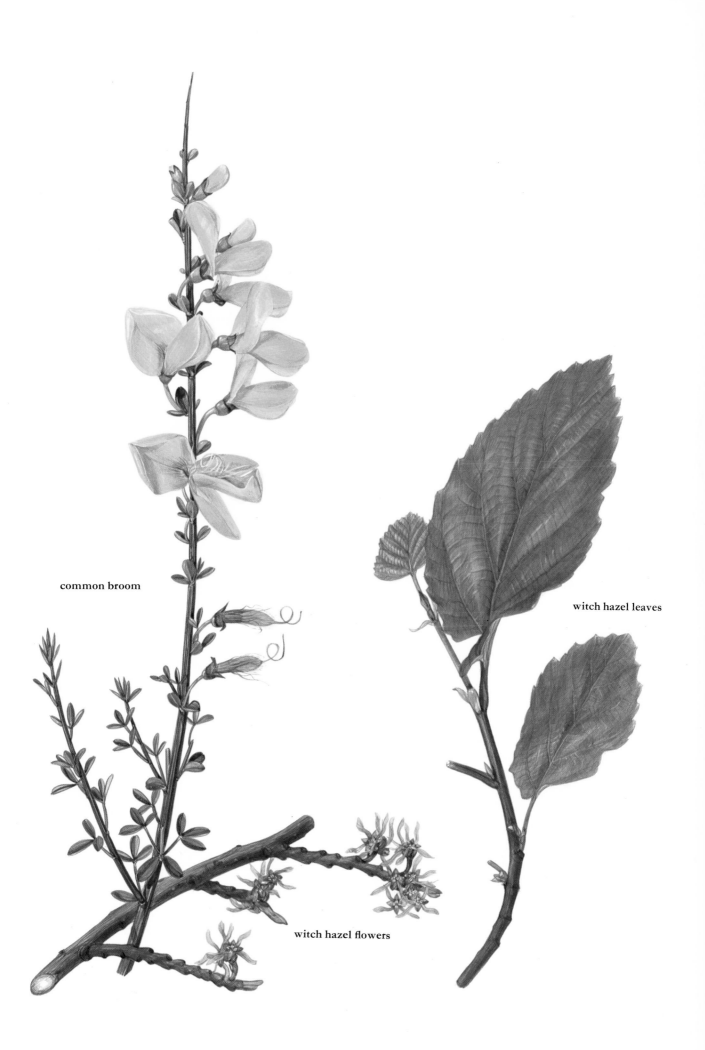

common broom

witch hazel leaves

witch hazel flowers

Motherwort
Aconite

'There is no better herb to take melancholy vapours from the heart, and to strengthen it; it makes mothers joyful, and settles the womb, therefore it is called **Motherwort**.' So wrote Culpeper in his *English Physitian and Complete Herball* (1633) of *Leonurus cardiaca* of the Labiatae. It is found in the temperate zones of Europe and Asia, but is rare in Great Britain, although it is occasionally seen in country gardens where it may have been cultivated long ago for its therapeutic qualities. *Wort* is the Saxon word for a medicinal herb, and proves that motherwort has been used in healing since mediaeval times. *Mother* shows that it was employed for female disorders. Today it is used as a nerve tonic and sedative to allay the pains of angina pectoris, especially after childbirth. In the seventeenth century and earlier, it was given to epileptic patients in the hope of calming them.

The drug is obtained from the herb after flowering, and has been recognized as a stachydrine. It contains various glycosides, tannins, resins, saponins and some organic acids.

Aconite has been known since ancient times as one of the most lethal poisons in existence. The most deadly is the Indian *bikh*, which comes from *Aconitum ferox*. According to the nineteenth-century *Brewer's Dictionary* aconite 'is properly the herb wolfsbane; but commonly used in poetical language for poison in general.' Aconite belongs to the Ranunculaceae and is a herbaceous perennial common in central Europe and Asia. *A. napellus* is used in pharmacy. The drug is provided by the roots and, according to some authorities, also by the leaves. The most important of its alkaloids is aconitine. The drug is rarely used internally as safe doses are ineffective, and effective doses are toxic, causing giddiness, confusion, weakness and lethargy. Aconite was used in the treatment of heart disease, hypertension and sthenic fevers, slowing the heart rate, and slightly lowering the blood pressure. Today its greatest value is as a painkiller against neuralgia and rheumatism. It is manufactured as both an ointment and a liniment, but even externally must be used very carefully, and never when cuts or small cracks occur in the skin, as this may cause accidental poisoning. The root has sometimes been fatally mistaken for horseradish. When poisoning has taken place the patient's stomach should be washed out and he should be kept as warm as possible.

Long ago archers tipped their arrows with aconite to kill both men and beasts. Avicenna (980–1037) was said to make the victim eat a mouse that had been fed on *A. napellus*, but Antonio Guanerius, a famous doctor in Pavia, disputed this, claiming that no mouse would eat aconite, and that the translation from the Arabic had been wrong, and Avicenna must have prescribed flies that had crawled over the plant's leaves. The dose was twenty flies.

Gerard thought that a certain cure was another plant which he called *Antithora*, and he commended the 'fatherly care' of God in providing 'a conqueror and triumpher over this plant so venomous.'

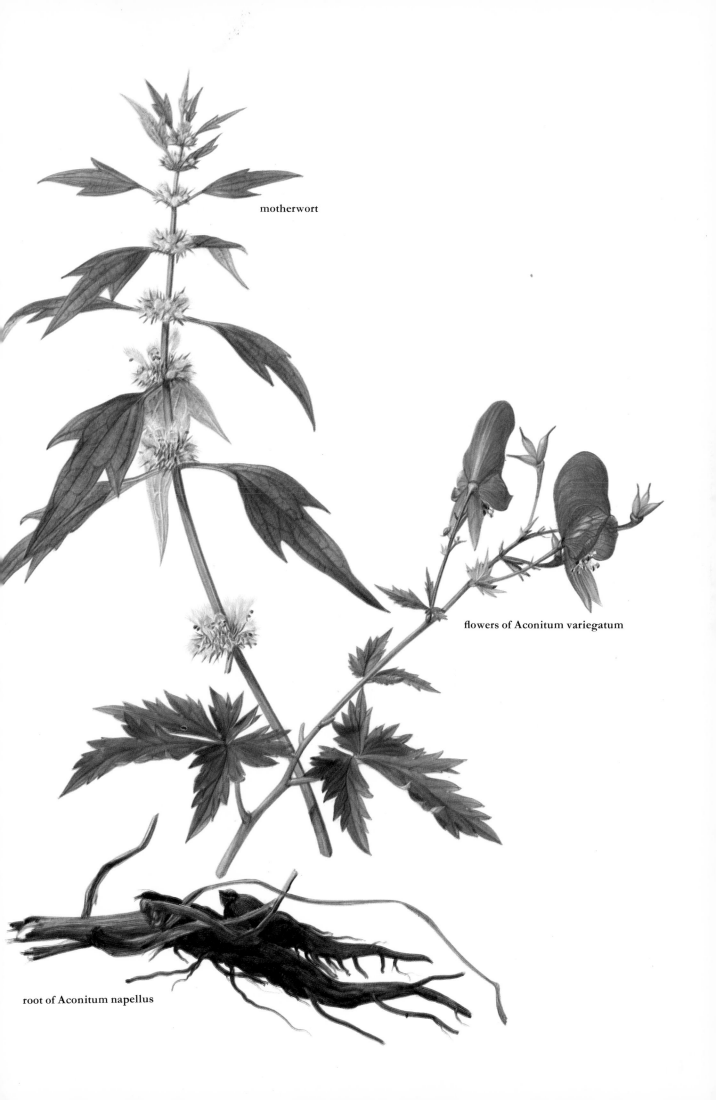

motherwort

flowers of Aconitum variegatum

root of Aconitum napellus

Mistletoe
Olive

Mistletoe (*Viscum album*) is generally better known for the Christmas custom of kissing beneath its branches than for its therapeutic qualities. This amorous tradition is said to come from an ancient Norse legend which relates how Balder, the god of peace, was slain by the blind god Höder with an arrow made of mistletoe. The other gods restored Balder to life, and, to avoid further trouble with mistletoe, gave it into the care of Freya, the goddess of love. Of the Loranthaceae, mistletoe is a parasitical plant living off apple trees, poplars, willows, limes and others, and, rarely, the oak. It has no contact with the ground, and is propagated by birds who eat the viscous white berries. The American species, *V. flavescens*, which is similar to *V. album*, is found on the red maple and the tupelo in Florida, Texas and Mexico, and in parts of Missouri and New Jersey.

The magical uses of mistletoe go back to the Druids and even further. It has been identified as the Golden Bough that opened the door to the Underworld for Aeneas and the Sibyl. The Druids used it for their religious rites when they found it growing on an oak, which doubled its magical powers. They cut it with a golden sickle which symbolized the sun, and caught it in a cloth before it could touch the ground. It is now believed that the Druids employed mistletoe therapeutically as a cure for sterility and epilepsy, and as an antidote to poisons. These ancient beliefs are justified by the pharmaceutical use of the plant at the present time. Its active principles only began to be appreciated in the nineteenth century. The leaves and young branches contain the glutinous substance viscin, gum and tannin, which have marked hypotensive and diuretic properties. The drug acts as a vasodilator and antispasmodic, and is recommended for hypertension, arteriosclerosis, chronic nephritis and internal haemorrhage. In some cases of cardiac asthma and whooping cough it is believed to be effective. The apple orchards of Normandy produce a particularly large mistletoe crop for commercial purposes. Most English mistletoe comes from the apple orchards of Herefordshire.

As well as providing the best alimentary oil in the world, the **Olive** (*Olea europaea*) can also be employed as a demulcent and bland laxative due to the presence of a bitter glycoside and a fixed oil consisting chiefly of olein. It has a high vitamin content. Duodenal and gastric ulcers may also be treated with preparations made from the olive's leaves.

The origins of the olive are unknown, but go far back into antiquity. It is recorded as having been cultivated by the Egyptians in the seventeenth century BC, and was certainly known to the Semitic peoples in 3000 BC. It was grown on Crete around 3500 BC, and eventually reached Europe from Egypt via Greece. The ancient Greeks prized the oil as a luxury and anointed their bodies with it. The Romans also considered the olive to be a valuable crop. It grew wild in south-central Asia and along the eastern shores of the Mediterranean. The Jesuits, great scholars and gastronomes, took the olive to California and Mexico along with their religious teachings. South Australia now produces a considerable crop.

There are two forms in southern Europe; the oleaster (*O. europaea* var. *oleaster*) which is typical of temperate zones near the sea, and the cultivated form, *O. europaea* var. *sativa*. The olive can grow to a great age; some trees are reputed to be over 1000 years old.

Pharmacologically the drug is provided by the leaves, and may be used in the treatment of certain forms of hypertension, and for its hypoglycaemic action. The oil is often used in soaps, ointments and liniments, and has a soothing action. The olive symbolizes 'peace' and it was an olive leaf or branch that Noah's dove took to him in the Ark. Even Milton showed approval of the olive in *Paradise Regained*: 'See there the olive grove of Academe,/Plato's retirement, where the Attic bird/Trills her thick-warbled notes the summer long.'

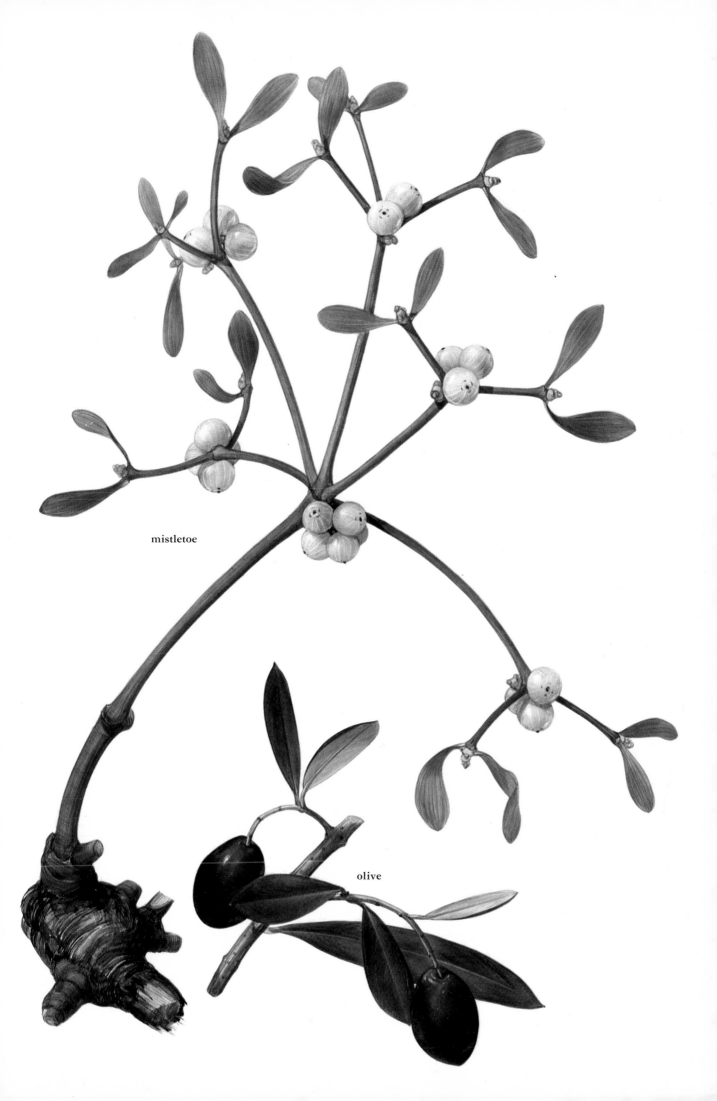

mistletoe

olive

Common mallow
Marsh mallow
Hollyhock

The blue or **Common mallow** (*Malva sylvestris*) is of the Malvaceae, a family of plants possessing no unwholesome qualities at all. It is diffused throughout Europe and western Asia, Siberia and North Africa. Many of the species are tropical or sub-tropical. In medicine the mallow's importance is unfortunately more of historical than current interest as, despite its benign qualities, its pharmacological use is declining. The emollient properties of mallow's leaves and flowers may be useful in relieving inflammation of the digestive tract and urinary organs. Applied externally as poultices, they reduce inflammations and swellings. The dwarf mallow (*M. rotundifolia*) has similar medicinal action, and its leaves may be eaten raw in salads, or cooked as spinach.

According to Culpeper, both the mallow and the **Marsh mallow** (*Althaea officinalis*) were possessed of so many healing properties, that they were practically cure-alls. This belief in their curative powers had existed since ancient times. *Althaea officinalis*' name comes from the Greek *althaino*, 'I cure', and it may have been the *althea* which Hippocrates recommended so highly for healing wounds. Dioscorides, Theophrastus and Pliny all described marsh mallow's uses, both externally and internally, and in his Capitularies Charlemagne ordered its cultivation. Renaissance herbalists used marsh mallow to cure coughs, sore throats, stomach troubles, gonorrhoea, leucorrhoea and toothache. No other plant could have been necessary. Today, although it is listed in all pharmacopoeias, it is rarely employed in pharmacy. However, in certain country districts where the knowledge of herbs persists, the roots are still boiled with honey to make a soothing decoction that alleviates sore throats and bronchial complaints. Sometimes the plant is used in an ointment which is believed to help chilblains and chapped hands. The flowers and leaves also possess a large amount of mucilage. They may be picked in summer at the moment of flowering, and dried in the shade. The roots should be dug up when autumn comes; scraped free of their cork-like outer covering and dried. Marsh mallow is still sometimes used for gastritis, enteritis, dysentery, bronchial catarrh and coughs, as well as in a gargle to treat throat and mouth infections, just as it was in times past.

'Flaunts the flaring hollyhock' writes Austin Dobson in *A Garden Song*, and gives a vivid picture of this tall and stately plant with its large, bright flowers that caused Gerard to call it Outlandish Rose, or *Rosa ultramarine*. The **Hollyhock** (*Althaea rosea*) is another member of the Malvaceae, believed by various authorities to have originated in such farflung places as China and the Lebanon. Hollyhocks do not grow wild; even in the sixteenth century Gerard wrote 'These Hollihockes are sowne in gardens, almost every where, and are in vaine sought elsewhere.' The plant has similar properties to marsh mallow. The active ingredients have calming and soothing powers, and are believed to be helpful in relieving coughs, and also gastritis, enteritis and cystitis. The roots provide a starch flour with a very high nutritive content. A purple dye is obtained from the flowers. Culpeper recommended the hollyhock to prevent miscarriages, help ruptures and to kill worms in children. Despite its versatility this plant too, has lost its popularity in medicine. At the end of the nineteenth century it was almost wiped out in Europe by the fungus *Puccina malvacearum*. However, it survived to grace country gardens and serve home-herbalists.

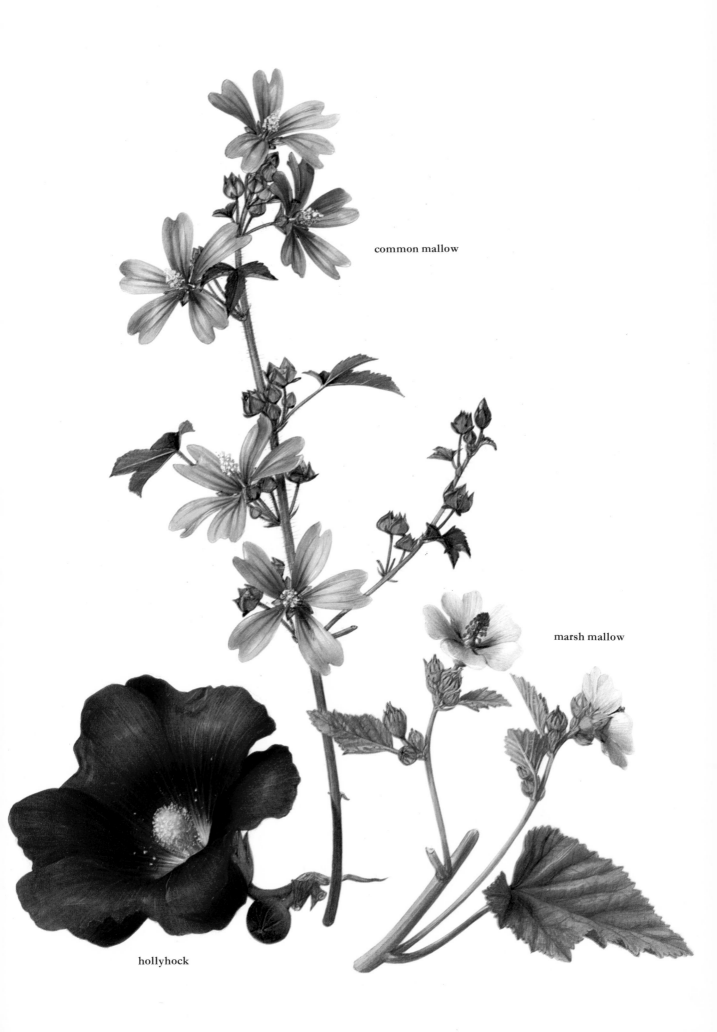

common mallow

marsh mallow

hollyhock

Cowslip
Violet
Iceland moss
Lung lichen

According to Gerard the **Cowslip** is known botanically as *Primula veris* 'because they are among those plants that doe floure in the spring, or because they floure with the first.' This elegant little flower has many country names, the most common being paigles, which is believed to come from the Anglo-Saxon for keys, the pendant flowers symbolizing St Peter's bunch of keys. Two other names for cowslip are the Keys of Heaven and Our Lady's Keys.

Early herbalists claimed that users of this plant would become beautiful. Culpeper, who held that every plant was under some astronomical domination, wrote 'Venus lays claim to this herb as her own . . . and our city dames know well enough the ointment or distilled water of it adds to beauty, or at least restores it when it is lost.' It was believed to remove wrinkles and freckles, and used with linseed oil, would heal burns. From very ancient times it was used for its soothing effect against fits and convulsions, and today is still employed in pharmacy as an antispasmodic and sedative. The active ingredients are contained in the flowers, which are gathered during May and June when in full bloom. Cowslip wine is still a popular home-made drink in the country, although its original use was as a cure for insomnia. The cowslip is no longer easy to find in the countryside and is one of the many victims of urbanization.

One of the best-loved of all wild flowers is the **Violet** (*Viola odorata*) which has probably more romantic and poetic associations than any other flower except the rose. Even some old pharmacopoeias list some species for their fragrance and beauty, and scarcely mention their therapeutic value. Galen (*c.* AD 130–*c.* 200), the great Greek physician, knew the violet for its emollient and expectorant properties, which are similar to, but less powerful, than those of ipecacuanha. The drug comes from the flowers, and contains mucilage, a special alkaloid and a blue colorant. Commercially violet petals are candied for confectionery and pastry-making.

The Greek poet and doctor Nicander, who lived in the second century BC, claimed that his countrymen called the violet *Ion* because the flower was given to Jupiter by the Nymphs of Ionia. Another theory is that it was so called after Io, beloved of Jupiter, whom he turned into a cow. Violets sprang from the earth for her food. Gerard believed that the violet's delicate beauty brought to men's minds 'the remembrance of honestie, comlinesse, and all kindes of vertues.'

Through the ages various lichens have been recommended by men of such repute as Dioscorides, Pliny and Mattioli, but it is more likely that these were the sleep-inducing mosses found on trees such as the cedar, poplar and pine, and not **Iceland moss** (*Cetraria islandica*), the foliaceous lichen found growing in grass and moss in northern and central Europe, North America and Siberia. Of the Parmeliaceae, *Cetraria* has been known for many centuries as a cure for all kinds of chest ailments and was even believed, at one time, to be capable of curing tuberculosis. In the eighteenth century both Linnaeus and Scopoli still used prescriptions of Iceland moss to treat chest diseases. *Cetraria* contains the carbohydrate complexes lichenin and isolichenin, and the bitter principle cetrarin. The drug is made from the dried thalli which is collected in spring or autumn. It is used as a bitter tonic, and as a flavouring for nauseous medicines.

Another lichen, which may well have been known to Dioscorides and Pliny, is **Lung lichen** (*Sticta pulmonaria*) which grows on tree trunks in most parts of the world. There is today little demand for it, although it may be used as a substitute for Iceland moss. An extract can be made from it which is thought to be beneficial for bronchial complaints and coughs.

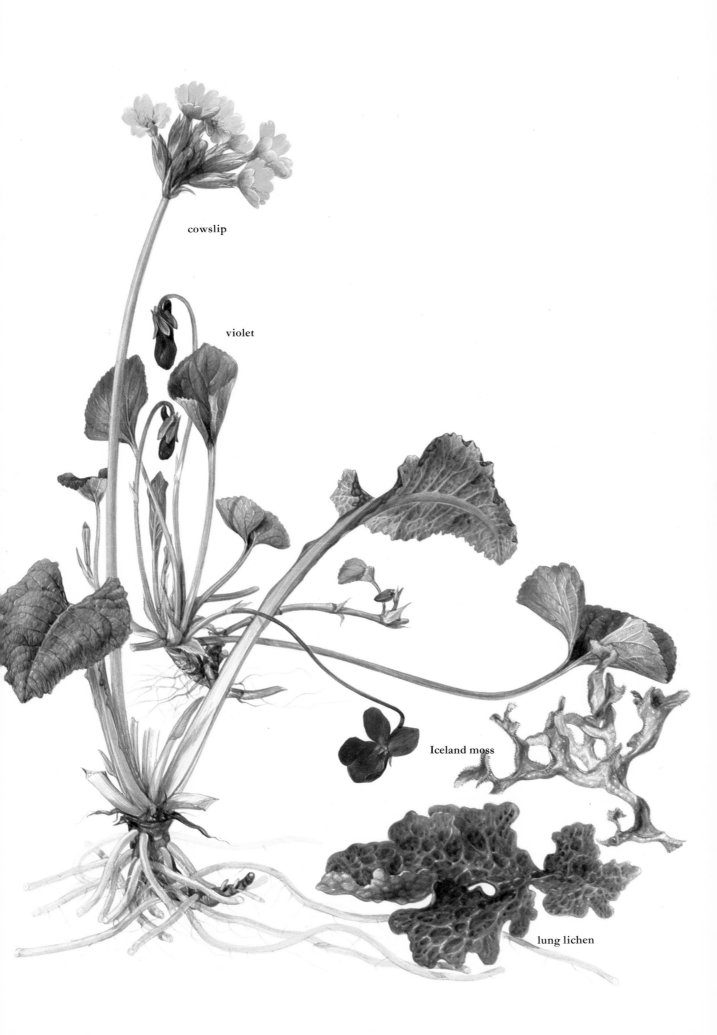

cowslip

violet

Iceland moss

lung lichen

Lungwort
Soapwort
Lime

The etymology of both the botanical and common names of **Lungwort** (*Pulmonaria officinalis*), of the Boraginaceae, indicates its medicinal use. It was the German Paracelsus (*c.* 1490–*c.* 1541) who first developed the *Doctrine of Signatures* which claimed that all plants must be associated either by appearance, smell or habitat, with the disease it was said to heal. Therefore lungwort, whose white-spotted leaves resemble lungs, was declared to be the proper cure for chest troubles. This reputation has lasted through the centuries. Nicholas Culpeper recommended it for 'boiling in pectoral drinks' and also gave it to victims of yellow jaundice. In herb medicine today infusions or decoctions of the leaves are used to treat inflammation of the bronchial tubes, and the plant is also gaining a reputation as a sudorific. Some of the properties contained in the leaves are mucilage, saponins, tannins and carotene.

Another plant known since ancient times for its curative powers, is **Soapwort** (*Saponaria officinalis*) of the Caryophyllaceae. This herb was known to early herbalists as bruisewort. Mediaeval Arab physicians prescribed it for leprosy and various skin complaints. It was also used in those times to make a soapy lather which would take out greasy spots from clothes and cure the itch. The dried leaves and the roots are rich in saponins, a very small quantity of which makes water soapy. If the leaves are soaked for a short time they will yield an extract which may be used as a sudorific, a remedy against rheumatism, and to purify the blood. It is more widely used on the continent than in the British Isles or the United States.

The **Lime** tree or linden has aroused admiration for its kindly and beneficial action for hundreds of years, as shown by the testimonies of Theophrastus, Pliny and Galen, and it enjoys the same high reputation to this day. The bark, sap and foliage were all thought to be good for the treatment of leprosy, abscesses and falling hair, but today the active ingredients are obtained only from the flower.

The generic name *Tilia* includes several species which are divided into two groups: those with single flowers: the common lime (*T. vulgaris*); the broad-leaved lime (*T. platyphyllos*); and the small-leaved lime (*T. cordata*), which provide the drug *tilia officinalis*, and the double-flowered limes: the American species *T. americana*, which is known on that continent as the linden tree, and *T. argentea* from which the medicament silver lime is made. The active ingredients contained in the inflorescence consist mainly of mucilage; carotene; the glycoside tiliacin; an essential oil; malic, tartaric and acetic acids and some vitamin C. The lime is useful for its diaphoretic and antispasmodic properties, but is more widely known as a soothing herb tea, called in France *tilleule*. It was this brew into which Proust dipped his *madeleine*, thus evoking all the nostalgia of his childhood and inspiring his masterwork *A la recherche du temps perdu*.

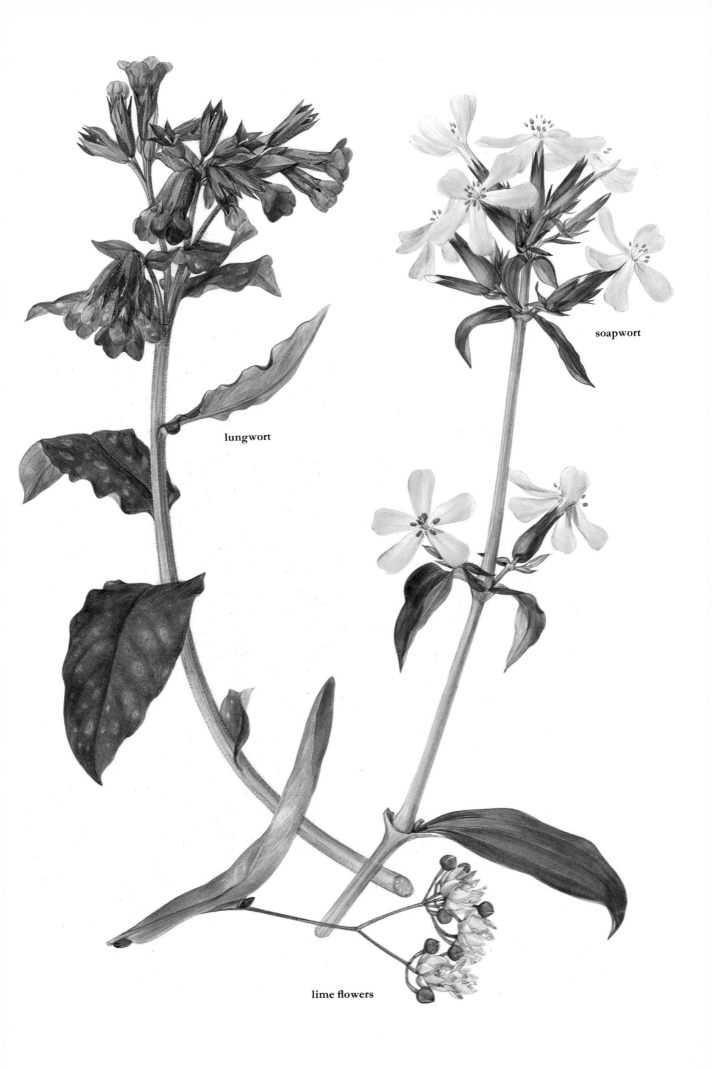

lungwort

soapwort

lime flowers

Elecampane
Corn poppy
Wild pansy

There is a legend which tells how the beautiful **Elecampane** (*Inula helenium*) sprang forth from the earth after Helen of Troy's tears had fallen there. Its name is believed to be a corruption of Helen or Elena. This lovely but rare plant is of the Compositae, and grows in damp fields and hedgerows in Europe and Asia. It has been grown in 'physick gardens' since Anglo-Saxon times, and was a favourite with mediaeval and Elizabethan herbalists for the sweetmeats which were made from the candied roots, as well as for its therapeutic properties. The roots contain inulin and should be taken up in autumn when it is most abundant. Today, as in times past, elecampane is used to treat pulmonary ills; bronchitis, bronchial asthma and whooping cough. It is also a beneficial diuretic, sudorific and blood purifier. Nicholas Culpeper thought highly of this plant, writing in his herbal: 'it resists poison, and stays the spreading of the venom of serpents, as also putrid and pestilential fevers, and the plague itself.'

A field of wheat scattered profusely with scarlet poppies evokes all the heat and stillness of a summer's day. The field or **Corn poppy** (*Papaver rhoeas*) is widely diffused across the temperate zones of Europe and Asia, and North Africa. Although it does not contain morphine as does *P. somniferum*, it has nevertheless been used for many centuries as a mild sedative. Etymologically *papaver* comes from the Celtic word *papa*, meaning pap or porridge, and refers to the Celtic custom of mixing poppy juice with gruel to send crying babies off to sleep. The ancient Egyptians, as long ago as 1500 BC, are recorded as using poppy seeds in baking for their aromatic flavour, and this practice survives today. Virgil mentioned the poppy in one of his *Eclogues*, and it was used as a flavouring in ancient Roman cooking.

The drug is made from the flower petals which must be laid out to dry as soon as they are collected, before they lose their colour. Robert Burns captured the evanescent quality of this frail plant in *Tam o' Shanter* when he wrote: 'But pleasures are like poppies spread:/You seize the flow'r, its bloom is shed . . .' The flowers contain alkaloids including protopine and rhoeadin, which have no morphine-like activity; mucilage and a colouring matter, while the seeds are rich in oil. In France an edible oil called *olivette* is obtained from these seeds and is used like olive oil. The corn poppy is used in pediatric medicine as a mild sedative, and to ease the chest in bronchitis, whooping cough and similar ailments.

The little **Wild pansy** (*Viola tricolor*) which owes its scientific name to the mixed colours of its corolla, is known to poets and country dwellers by many other names, the most beautiful of which must be heartsease and love-in-idleness. The name pansy is derived from the French *pensée*, for thought, and much great poetry has been inspired by this theme.

The pansy, which is of the Violaceae, is found growing across Europe, Asia and North Africa, preferring hilly pastures and fairly high ground. Elsewhere it has been naturalized and cultivated to produce various ornamental species. Its medicinal properties were well known in antiquity as shown by the writings of Hippocrates, Dioscorides, and the Arab and mediaeval physicians. The drug is usually extracted from the flowers, although the entire plant contains active ingredients including sugars, tannin, saponins, traces of violine and a glycoside known as violaquercitrin. The flowers are made into cough extracts and syrups, and the whole plant can be used in preparations for treating acne and other skin eruptions such as milk scab in small babies. Early herbalists also made use of the pansy in syrups and decoctions to cure venereal diseases.

Shakespeare mentioned the pansy only once, but in unforgettably beautiful lines: 'Pray, love, remember: and there is pansies, that's for thoughts.' (*Hamlet*, iv, 5.)

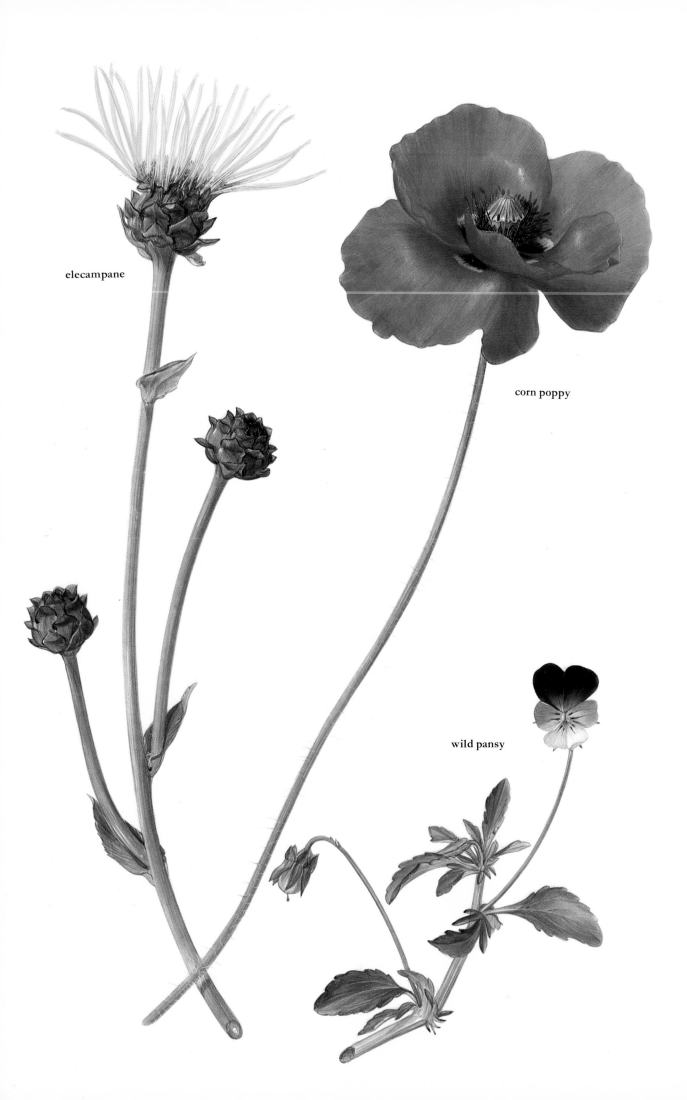

elecampane

corn poppy

wild pansy

Pines

The Phrygian nature goddess Cybele, changed her faithless lover, the young shepherd Atys, into a **Pine**, and Zeus, to comfort her, promised that the tree would be ever green. When Cybele's cult reached Greece in the fifth century BC she was identified with Rhea, and the Greeks dedicated the pine to many of their own gods, including Pan, Neptune and Bacchus. They even flavoured their wine by putting pine cones into the vats, and the modern Greek wine *retsina* still has a resinous taste. The ancient Romans prized the Italian stone pine (*Pinus pinea*) for its edible seeds which are eaten to this day under the name of *pignons*, as a dessert or in cooked dishes. The resins from both pines and firs were known to the Ancients as shown by the writings of Virgil, Ovid, Pliny, Horace and Propertius. Essential oil of turpentine is said to have gone into the making of Greek Fire which was used in early warfare by the Byzantines and the Crusaders.

There are many members of the genus *Pinus* of the Pinaceae. The wood of various species is used in boat building, mining, agricultural appliances, and particularly in Scandinavia, the USSR and Canada, for building houses. Rope is made from the inner bark. The stone pine of Siberia (*P. cembra*) which also grows extensively in the Alps, has edible seeds with abundant oil which is expressed for use as food and in lamps. The Scots pine (*P. sylvestris*) which in Britain is found only in the Highlands, except where it is cultivated, and in Scandinavia and Lapland where it flourishes, produces large quantities of turpentine for commercial and pharmaceutical use. Preparations made from the bark can be fermented with sugar to produce spruce beer. Its roots are a source of tar which has been found to be very efficacious for some skin diseases which have not responded to other treatment. In the United States a syrup of tar used for scrofulous diseases enjoys a high reputation. The Scots pine can attain a height of 120 feet, but an even more magnificent tree is the Corsican pine (*P. larico*) which can grow to 150 feet. It is found in many Mediterranean countries besides Corsica and is valued chiefly for its timber.

In the United States pines are divided into two types: hard and soft. One of the largest species is the sugar pine (*P. lambertiana*) which grows mainly in California. This is one of the 'soft' pines, and has large seeds which the American Indians used to eat after they had been pounded and baked. The timber is used in furniture making. Another Californian soft pine is the nut pine (*P. edulis*). It is more widely distributed than the other species, and has large tasty seeds which are sold commercially. The most important of the 'hard' varieties is the longleaf pine (*P. palustris*) which is the chief timber-producing pine of the southern and south-eastern United States, and also yields great quantities of turpentine, tar and colophony. America is today the most important source of resin and turpentine. Colophony is an oleo-resin which is distilled to extract turpentine. The residue, after distillation, is used in pharmacy to make ointments, liniments and plasters, but it has a wider use in the manufacture of linoleum, varnish, waxes and soap. At one time turpentine oil was used against intestinal worms, but this practice is now considered to be dangerous and out of date. When it is necessary to use the oil internally it is usually added to hot water and the vapours are inhaled, although for this purpose terebene, which is prepared from oil of turpentine, has been found to be better. It is very good in the treatment of nasal catarrh. The bark of the white pine (*P. strobus*) is used in cough treatments. Pumiline, or dwarf pine oil, is extracted from young pine branches. It is pleasantly aromatic and is used like turpentine. The maritime pine (*P. pinaster*) is the source of Bordeaux turpentine. Great quantities come from France, although this species has been cultivated in England since the sixteenth century. It flourishes in most north Mediterranean countries.

The English poet Abraham Cowley (*c.* 1618–1667), recalls the sad legend of this commercially valuable tree: 'This plant a lovely boy was heretofore,/Belov'd by Cybele, upon whose score/He sacrific'd to chastity, but now/His fruit delaying Venus now excites,/His wood affords the torch which Hymen lights.'

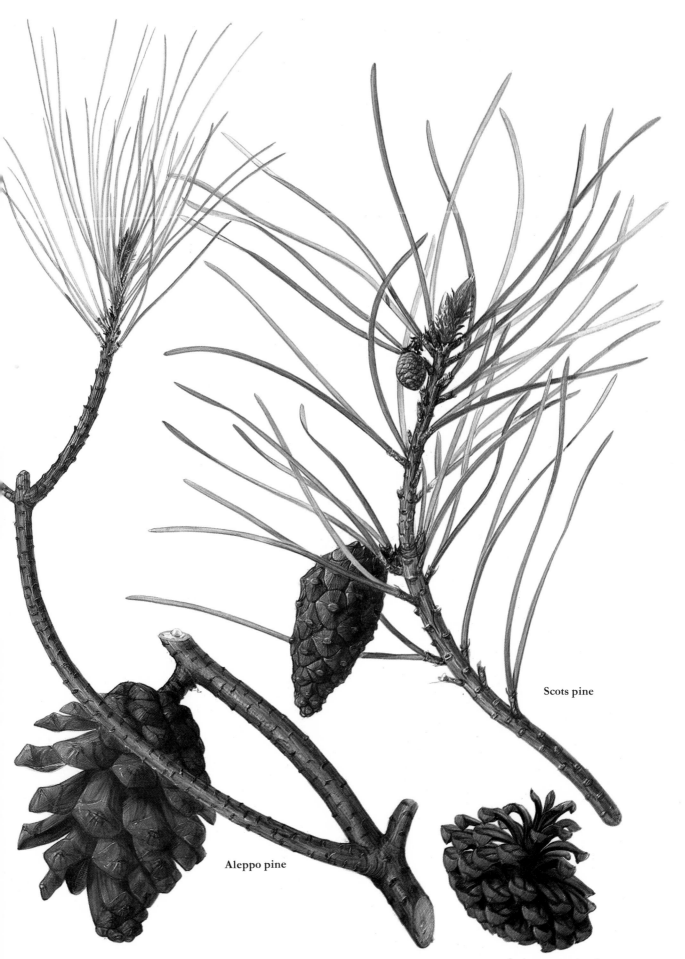

Scots pine

Aleppo pine

Swiss mountain pine

Grindelia
Ephedra
Lobelia

Grindelia (*Grindelia robusta* [illustrated], *G. humilis, G. squarrosa, G. camporum*) is a herbaceous perennial of the Compositae. It is indigenous to the south-western United States and likes wet marshy ground. It can be easily cultivated in small gardens as an ornamental, and is grown in large quantities for commerce. The drug is derived from the leaves and the sticky resinous flower heads which give the herb its common name, gum plant. Grindelia principally contains resins, tannins and a trace of volatile oil. The dried leaves and flower heads are used in preparations for hay-fever, spasmodic asthma, whooping-cough and bronchial disturbances. The resin is believed to be efficacious in the treatment of chronic cystitis accompanied by a discharge of mucus, because it can be eliminated by way of the kidneys. Grindelia has also been found to be an antidote for poison ivy and is now mainly used in the form of a lotion for dermatitis caused by *Rhus toxicodendron*.

About 40 species of the genus **Ephedra** are diffused throughout Europe, Asia and Africa. Under the name of *ma-huang, Ephedra sinica* and *E. equisetina* have been used as a febrifuge and cough mixture in Chinese medicine for over five thousand years, but despite this ancient knowledge ephedrine has only come into general use in the twentieth century. Other species are the Indian and Pakistan *E. gerardiana* and *E. nebrodensis*, and the European *E. distachya* and *E. fragilis*. The drug, which is derived from the branches, is collected in autumn when the amount of alkaloid present is more abundant. It is the presence of ephedrine and pseudoephedrine which makes this plant a valuable vasoconstrictor and cardiac stimulant. Ephedrine's action is more prolonged, but less intense than that of adrenaline, and it may be taken orally. It has a wide range of clinical uses; it is given in hay-fever, asthma, nocturnal enuresis, laryngospasm in children, urticaria, articular rheumatism, and is used in ointments as a decongestant for severe colds, and as an eye-lotion.

Lobelia (*Lobelia inflata*) is named after the botanist Matthias de Lobel, who became private physician to King James I. It is indigenous to the United States and Canada and is found in meadows and marshy ground. Parkinson in his *Paradisus* (1629) says: 'it groweth neere the riuer of Canada, where the French plantation in America is seated.' Lobelia is also called Indian tobacco, probably because it was used by American Indians. At the end of the eighteenth century Cutler published an account of lobelia describing the giddiness and pains in the head which were the result of chewing the leaves. At the beginning of the nineteenth century it was introduced into Europe, and was first used in pharmacy in 1829 by Reece. The entire plant is used, dried and in flower. It contains numerous alkaloids, the most important being lobeline; organic acids and oils. It is used in the treatment of chronic bronchitis and spasmodic asthma. Injections of lobeline hydrochloride have been used to resuscitate new-born babies.

Lobelia may be toxic in large doses, and will cause nausea, vomiting, trembling and sweating. Another species, *L. tupa*, contains the same alkaloid, lobeline, as *L. inflata*. The leaves of *L. tupa* are smoked for their narcotic effect by the Mapuche Indians in Chile. Their name for it is devil's tobacco.

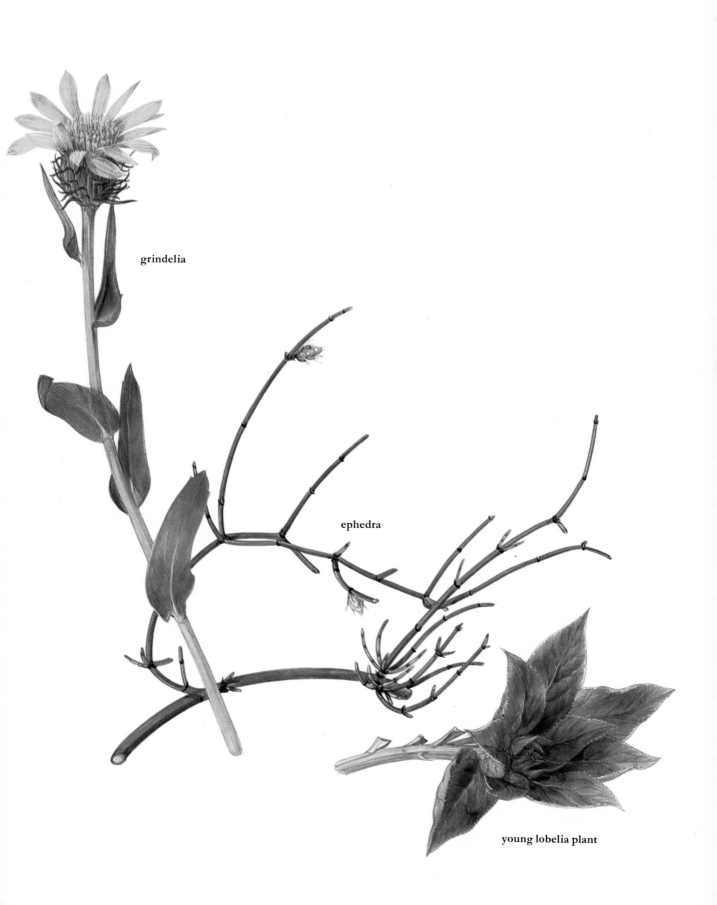

grindelia

ephedra

young lobelia plant

Coltsfoot
Wall mustard

Coltsfoot (*Tussilago farfara*) has many country names all of which refer to the unusual formation of the scape: horse-hoof; bull's foot; foal's wort; but the name Son before Father indicates its strange way of growing as the brilliant yellow flowers bloom as early as February, but the leaves do not appear until May. The plant's botanical name comes from the Latin *tussis*, a cough, as for hundreds of years herbalists have used the leaves to give relief to coughs, and called the herb coughwort. Culpeper wrote that 'the fresh leaves, or juice, or syrup thereof, is good for a hot, dry cough, or wheezing or shortness of breath.' Coltsfoot is widely diffused across Europe, Asia and North Africa in all kinds of waste places, ditches and railway embankments wherever the soil is heavy and damp. The leaves are covered on the underside with a thick, soft white down. In some English country districts it is believed that goldfinches use it to line their nests, and one hopes that they do. After the leaves have been collected, usually in June or July, this down is stripped off and the leaves are then tied into small bunches and dried. They are tonic and demulcent because of their mucilage, and are made into cigarettes and herbal tobacco for asthmatic sufferers. They are also used in cough mixtures, pastilles and cold cures, and relieve chronic coughs, bronchitis and catarrh. A preparation to help clear skin eruptions can sometimes be found in health shops. At one time Syrup of Coltsfoot was included in the *British Pharmacopoeia*. Coltsfoot seems to have enjoyed a higher reputation in France than anywhere else, and was even used as the insignia of *pharmacies*. Even today it can still be seen on the walls or windows of French chemists.

This bright little plant has been vividly described by Richard Mant, Bishop of Down, Connor and Dromore (1776–1848): 'O'er scaly stem, with cottony down/O'erlaid, its lemon-colour'd crown/Which droop't unclosed, but now erect,/The coltsfoot bright develops, deck't/Ere yet the unpurpled stalk displays/In dark green leaves . . .'

A more domesticated plant than coltsfoot, but with similar properties, is **Wall mustard** (*Brassica tenuifolia*), a herbaceous perennial of the Cruciferae. Like coltsfoot it abounds on wasteland, ruins and walls. It is also known familiarly as rocket but must not be confused with garden rocket (*Eruca sativa*), which it resembles in some ways. Wall mustard may be used in spring salads to give a slightly aromatic flavour, or the leaves can be cooked in the water in which they have been rinsed in the same way as spinach. Like other members of the Cruciferae this rocket contains sulphurated glucosides, and the juice of the fresh plant may be drunk as an expectorant to aid catarrh. The leaves have stimulant, diuretic, antiscorbutic and revulsant properties.

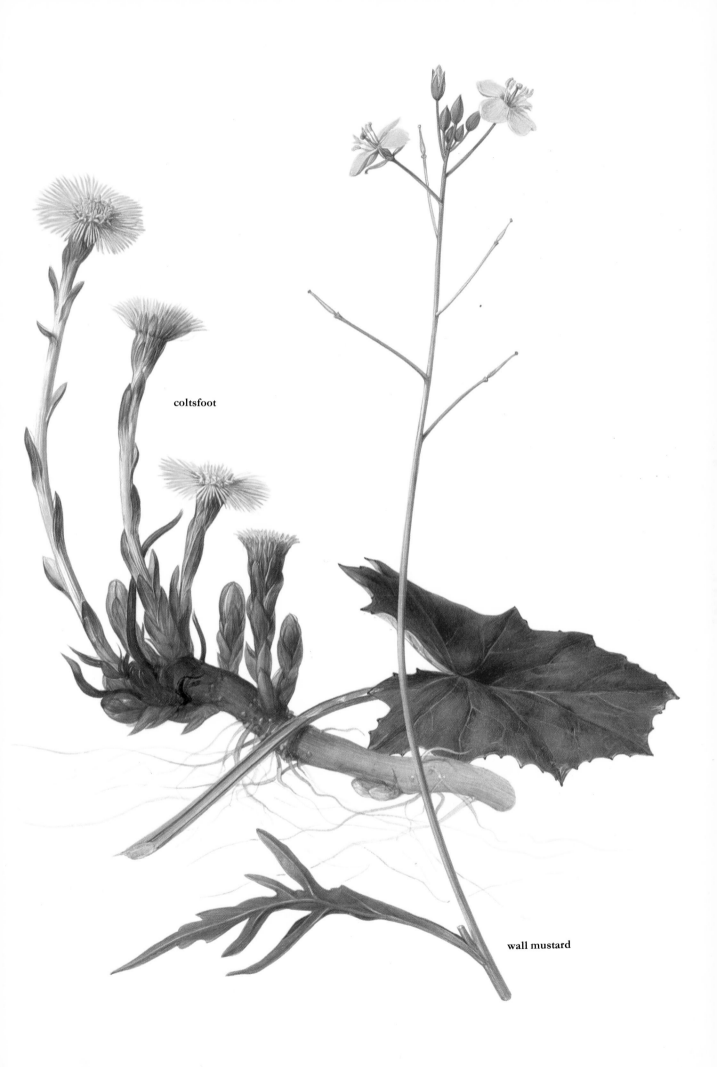

coltsfoot

wall mustard

Ground Ivy
Eucalyptus
Bignonia catalpa

Ground ivy (*Nepeta hederacea*) is a pretty plant with mauvish blue flowers. It bears no resemblance at all to ivy. Its country names, Gill-go-over-the-ground, Robin-run-in-the-hedge and cat's-foot, give a better picture of this little herb which sprawls in profusion over hedges and fields. At one time it was used in brewing in place of hops to clear the beer, and so earned the name of alehoof. For hundreds of years ground ivy has been esteemed as a cure for catarrh and colds, and was made into a herb tea mixed with honey or sugar to disguise its dreadfully bitter taste. In the sixteenth and seventeenth centuries it was sold in London's streets and 'Gill tea' was one of the familiar cries of London. In the days of Queen Elizabeth I herb women in the markets hawked it as Gill-by-the-ground. Gerard mixed it with other herbs and used it as an eye lotion equally efficacious for humans and cattle. He praised the plant highly, claiming that it removed 'any griefe whatsoever in the eies, yea although the sight were nigh hand gone: it is proved to be the best medicine in the world.' He also recommended it 'against the humming noyse and ringing sound of the eares, being put into them, and for them that are hard of hearing.' He was referring to the catarrhal symptom of 'singing' in the ears. It was widely believed for some centuries that the constant use of ground ivy would eventually cure hardness of hearing. If sniffed up the nose the juice or powder could relieve catarrhal headaches, and although it is no longer official in the *British Pharmacopoeia* it is thought to help sufferers from indigestion. The leaves provide the drug and are gathered throughout the spring and summer as the flowering period is long.

One of the most enormous trees in the world is the **Eucalyptus** which is indigenous to Australia and Tasmania. It can reach a height of 250 feet, and has pinkish white flowers which grow either singly or in clusters. The leaves contain oil glands and have an antiseptic smell with germ-killing properties. The huge wide-spreading roots act as a sponge in draining marshy areas which have previously been breeding grounds for malarial mosquitoes. For this reason several species of this member of the Myrtaceae were introduced into western Europe at the beginning of the nineteenth century and planted in coastal and wet regions where malaria was prevalent, and eventually the land was reclaimed and made habitable.

The best-known species is the blue gum tree (*E. globulus*) which is fast-growing, and provides the oil used in pharmacy for the treatment of malaria and typhoid, and against poisonous germs in general. Eucalyptus oil tastes of camphor and has a high cineol content. The fresh leaves are more efficaceous than the dried. They are collected in summer and those that are dried are kept sealed in the dark. Because of the presence of tannin eucalyptus has a tonic and astringent action. A tincture of the leaves is used to treat asthma and chronic bronchitis, and as an antiseptic in respiratory, uro-genital and intestinal infections. Pastilles, sprays and asthma cigarettes are manufactured from the dried leaves. *E. citriodora* provides the lemon scented oil used in the perfume industry. It contains the aldehyde, citronellal.

There are about 650 species in the Bignoniaceae family which are mainly trees, shrubs or twining plants. In medicine the **Bignonia catalpa** (*Catalpa bignonioides*) is valued for its expectorant and antiasthmatic properties, due to the presence of a bitter principle, catalpine, which is found in all parts of the plant, including the large showy flowers. The fruit can be made into a drink which speedily brings relief in cases of whooping cough and spasmodic asthma. This catalpa is native to the United States and flourishes in tropical regions. It was introduced into southern Europe in the sixteenth century. It may also be used as a febrifuge, astringent and antiseptic, and is one of the most decorative of all 'the kindly fruits'.

100

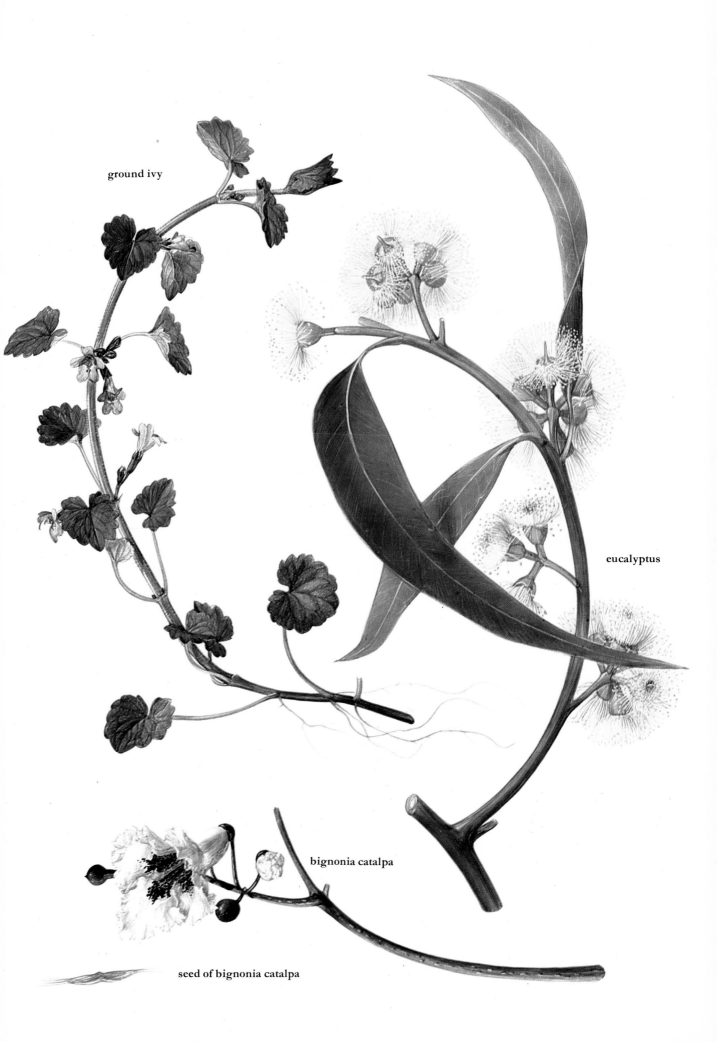

ground ivy

eucalyptus

bignonia catalpa

seed of bignonia catalpa

Milkwort
Hart's tongue fern

Throughout many centuries members of the genus *Polygala* have been utilized as expectorants, emetics, stimulants, sialogogues, to relieve nervous affections of the eye and to cure snake bites. The best known medicinal species are **Milkwort** (*Polygala vulgaris*), Senega snake root (*P. senega*) and *P. amara* which is the most rare of the three and, in Britain, is confined to the north of England. Senega snake root was believed to be an antidote to the stings and bites of venomous insects and reptiles, and was named after the Indian tribe which used it. It is prolific in western Canada and parts of the United States, especially Virginia, hence its alternate name of Virginian snakeroot. The Ancients credited it with similar but much stronger, powers to that of ipecacuanha. It should not be used when inflammation is present. Homoeopaths rate it highly as a cure for double vision, blepharitis and lacrimation. *P. amara* which is found in European Alpine regions, contains bitter principles which make it a useful bitter tonic.

Milkwort was said to promote milk in wet-nurses as evidenced by its common name. In the fifteenth century it was known as Rogation-floure or Procession floure, because it was at the height of its flowering in Rogation week, and the young girls who walked in the religious processions made garlands and nosegays of milkwort. Because of its importance in these processions Rembert Dodoens (1517–1585), Gerard's chief source, called it *Flos Ambarvalis*, but the herb women in Cheapside sold it as hedge hyssop, either mistakenly because of the plants' resemblance to each other, or through cupidity, milkwort being more difficult to find. Galen, Dioscorides and Theophrastus all knew this herb's virtues. The flowers, which smell of methyl salycilate, are used with the base of the stems, but sometimes the entire flowering plant is employed. Milkwort is recommended as an expectorant in the treatment of bronchitis and asthma, and as an emetic. However, if too large a dose is taken, nausea, vomiting and gastric irritation may result.

'The distilled water is very good against the passions of the heart' wrote Culpeper of the **Hart's tongue fern** (*Scolopendrium vulgare* or *Asplenium scolopendrium*), and it also stopped hiccoughs. Hart's tongue fern belongs to the Polypodiacea, and likes damp and shady locations, growing at the mouths of caves and wells and in rock fissures, in most of the northern hemisphere. The large distinctive leaves contain tannins and mucilage which give them diuretic, expectorant and astringent properties. An infusion of the fronds may be recommended for bronchial catarrh.

Ferns have always been believed to have the power to make people invisible. This is because they bear no flower and the seeds on the back of the frond are not readily seen. Paracelsus gave further credence to this belief in his *Doctrine of Signatures*, and even Virgil's name for ferns was *filicem invisam*. The fact that this superstition endured for so long may have been because of the complicated procedure required to work the spell. The seeds could only be collected on St John's Eve (June 23), and then had to be passed among no fewer than twelve pewter plates. They were then worn inside the shoes of the person who wished to be invisible. If carrying a pile of heavy pewter plates to the spot where the fern grew was not a deterrent it was quite possible that the seeds would roll away in the darkness. But it was far more likely that the devil would come by and steal them.

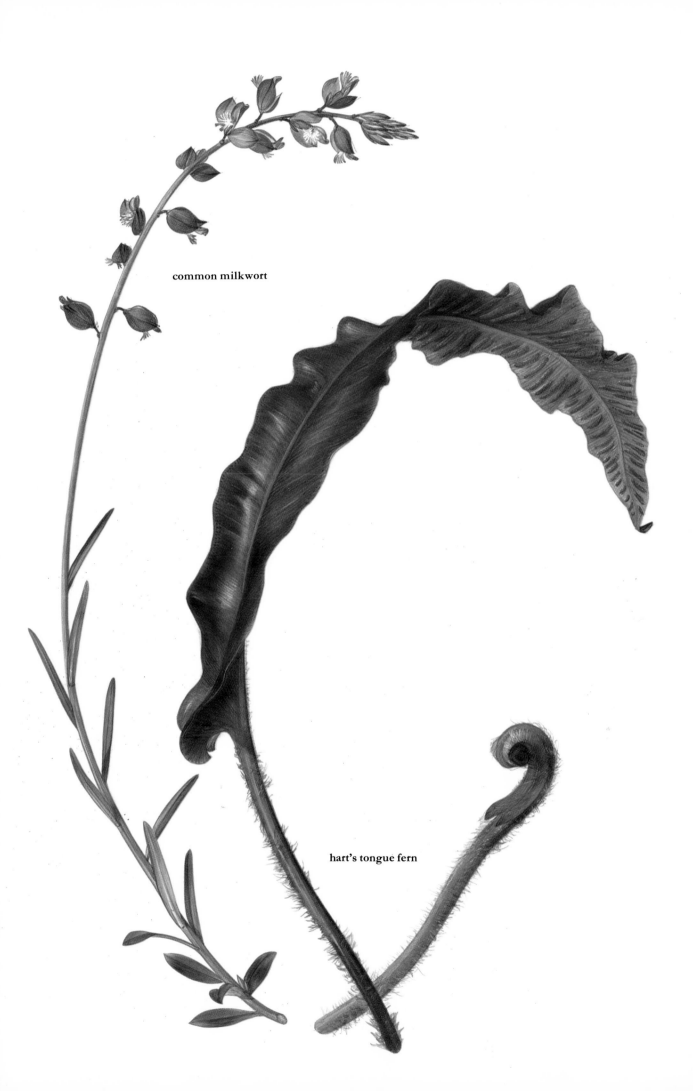

common milkwort

hart's tongue fern

Ivy
Liquorice
Wild thyme

In the Middle Ages **Ivy** (*Hedera helix*) formed part of the 'soporific sponge', a foul mixture of hemlock, mandrake, poppy, lettuce and other herbs, poured onto a sponge and held under the patient's nose as an anaesthetic. The victim could not have failed to pass out after sniffing such a combination of evil smells. Ivy is a liana belonging to the Araliaceae, and is credited with strong antiseptic properties. It was used to ward off the plague. It is also thought to have some influence on the brain, and is used in homoeopathic medicine against depression caused by inter-cranial pressure. In mediaeval England liquid was left to steep in cups made of ivy wood and then drunk to benefit the spleen. The leaves contain saponins, rutin and a balsamic resin. They are manufactured into an ointment which is believed to bring relief to swollen feet and to cure corns. The berries are eaten by many birds for whom they provide food throughout the winter, but are poisonous to man. However they can be made into an infusion to help rheumatic sufferers. Culpeper prescribed the yellow berries of *H. chrysocarpa* 'against the jaundice and a drunken surfeit.' Ivy has sudorific, diaphoretic and discutient properties. It belongs to Bacchus.

Liquorice was known to the ancient Egyptians and the Chinese, as well as to the ancient Greeks. Dioscorides recommended the juice in cases of hoarseness and heartburn, and in the form of an ointment or *pomatum* for the dressing of wounds. Culpeper employed it against dropsy and claimed that it 'excelled Spanish juice'. He may have been referring to Spanish broom (*Genista juncea*).

The drug comes from the roots and stolons, and contains a sweet principle called glycyrrhizin, vitamin B and many other substances which give it cough-preventing, expectorant and antiseptic properties. A sweet pectoral drink can be obtained by infusing the root. Solidified liquorice is sold in sweet shops in the form of cylindrical sticks or Pontefract cakes or their imitations. Chaucer (*c.* 1340–1400) gives it particular mention: 'Then springen herbes grete and smale,/The licoris and the Setewale (valerian).'

Sir Francis Bacon (1516–1626), Lord Chancellor of England and a most knowledgable gardener, had a special fondness for **Wild thyme** (*Thymus serpyllum*). In his *Essays* he wrote: 'But those which perfume the air most delightfully, not passed by as the rest, but being trodden upon and crushed, are three: that is, burnet, wild thyme, and water-mints. Therefore you are to set whole alleys of them, to have the pleasure when you walk or tread.'

Wild thyme has been valued by herbalists for many centuries. According to the *Doctrine of Signatures* it was under the dominion of Venus, and therefore good for helping nervous disorders. A tisane was drunk to allay giddiness and headaches. It was said by Culpeper to be 'a certain remedy for that troublesome complaint, the nightmare.' Even earlier it was used as a kind of incense or insecticide to fumigate rooms and keep away troublesome insects. Its name is derived from a Greek word meaning to fumigate. Today, because of its valuable oil, thymol, it is used in medicine to help bronchial and intestinal disorders, and as an antiseptic and expectorant. It is also one of the most popular domestic herbs for flavouring.

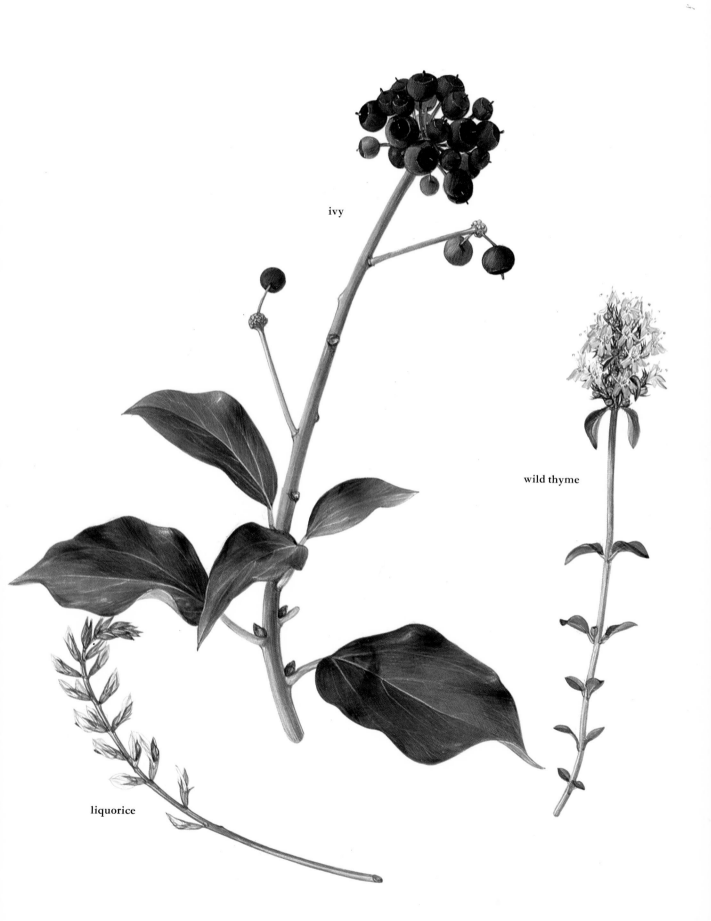

ivy

wild thyme

liquorice

Passion flower
White willow
Hop

In his great *Dictionary* Dr Johnson (1709–1784) defines the **Passion flower** (*Passiflora incarnata*) thus: 'A flower. The passion-flower or Virginian climber; the first of these names was given it by the Jesuits, who pretended to find in it all the instruments of our Lord's passion.' This belief still survives; the crown above the petals represents the crown of thorns; the stamens, the wounds; the ovary is the sponge soaked in vinegar; the three styles are the three nails, and the five sepals and five petals symbolize ten of the Apostles, Peter who denied, and Judas the betrayer, being left out.

The drug is provided by the branches, flowers and leaves which must be collected before the fruits appear. A fluid extract of the leaves is employed as a sedative and antispasmodic. The drug contains alkaloids, glucosides, flavonids and bitter principles, and is used to combat insomnia and anxiety states, and as a hypotensive. The edible fruit of this species is called maypop; other species produce passion fruit, also called grenadilla or granadilla.

Spenser's 'willow worn of forlorn paramours' (*Faerie Queene*) has been an emblem of sorrow and mourning for many centuries. Shakespeare, Herrick, Thackeray and many other poets have symbolized grief with garlands of willow, yet this same tree, particularly the **White willow** (*Salix alba*), has brought relief and comfort to sufferers from pains and fevers. The bark of *S. alba* was the only source of salicylic acid until the beginning of the twentieth century. It has great medicinal value, especially in the treatment of rheumatism, and became the main ingredient of aspirin after German chemists had learned how to synthesize the acid, just prior to the First World War. The drug is provided by the bark of the branches when they are two to three years old. It has tonic and astringent properties. As well as its use in rheumatism it is helpful in debility of the digestive organs and fever. The white willow grows in damp shady places and along river banks throughout most of Europe. The black willow (*S. nigra*) is found in the southern United States, and is valued as a nerve sedative because it leaves no depressing after-effects. It relieves ovarian congestion and has a calming effect on nervous excitement. In country medicine the willow is still used as an animal emetic. A branch is held in the mouth of a cow which may be suffering from flatulence after eating too much wet clover.

The **Hop** (*Humulus lupulus*), of the Cannabinaceae, was introduced into England by the Dutch in the reign of Henry VIII. It was used in pharmacy for its sedative action and soon ousted ground ivy (alehoof) in the clarifying of ale, a practice which originated in Italy. The first part of its botanical name refers to the type of soil it prefers as shown by Thomas Tusser (1524–1580) in his treatise on *June's Husbandrie*. He gives clear instructions for its cultivation: 'Choose soil for the hop of the rottenest mould,/Well doonged and wrought, as a garden plot should:'. *Lupulus* comes from the Latin *lupus*, 'a wolf', and describes the hop's ability to strangle everything in its path in the same way as a wolf devours its prey. Tusser approved of the hop's use in brewing: 'The hop for his profit I thus doe exalt,/It strengtheneth drinke, and it favoureth malt;/And being well brewed, long kept it will last,/And drawing abide, if ye draw not too fast.' John Evelyn (1620–1706) in *Pomona* strongly disagreed: 'Hops transmuted our wholesome ale into beer, which doubtless much altered our constitutions. This one ingredient, by some suspected not unworthily, preserves the drink indeed, but repays the pleasure with tormenting desires, and a shorter life.'

In ancient times the hop was not used medicinally, and Pliny knew it only as a food. The tips are still cooked and eaten as a substitute for asparagus. However, Paracelsus, Mattioli and Avicenna, knew of its tonic, sedative and mildly hypnotic action. The drug is provided by the female inflorescences which contain humulon: an antibacterial substance, and lupulin; humulene, and two bitter principles, humalone and lupulinic acid, and tannin. Because of their sleep-inducing perfume hops are made into pillows, and are therefore the safest sedative in the world. When George III was suffering so terribly from porphyria and being treated as a lunatic by his physicians, he at least had the comfort of sleeping on a hop-pillow. During the nineteenth century hops were used to calm nervous disorders. They have antiseptic, aromatic, diuretic, narcotic, tonic and stomachic action.

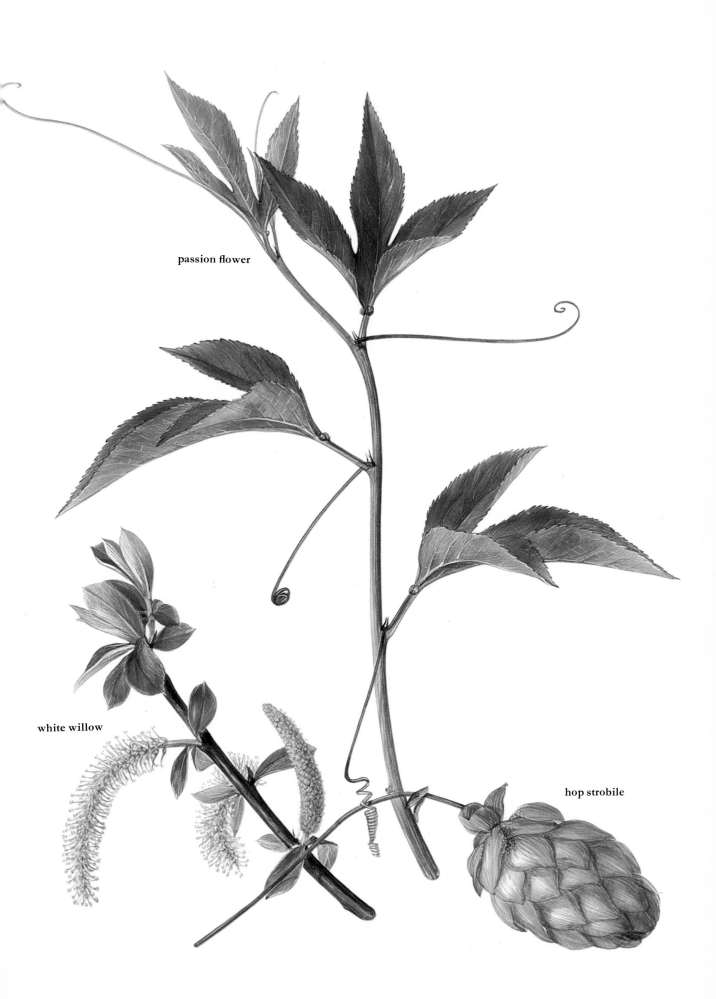

passion flower

white willow

hop strobile

Butterbur
Lavender
Valerian

Butterbur (*Petasites officinalis* or *Tussilago petasites*) got its common name from its large soft leaves which were used for wrapping up butter. Its botanical name *Tussilago* refers to its pectoral qualities which it shares with its close relation coltsfoot. Herbalists have always esteemed butterbur as a heart strengthener because, according to the *Doctrine of Signatures*, it is under the dominion of the Sun. Culpeper called it 'a cheerer of the vital spirits' and used the roots against plagues and pestilences because of their sudorific action, and mixed them with wine in a decoction to prevent wheezing. Butterbur was also used as a beautifying astringent by ladies of quality. In his *Herball* Culpeper claims that 'The powder of the roots taketh away all spots and blemishes of the skin. It were well if gentlewomen would keep this root preserved to help their poor neighbours.' Dioscorides and Galen prescribed the leaves and rhizome made into an ointment for ulcers and sores, but it was only in the middle of the twentieth century that its value in regulating blood pressure began to be appreciated.

Lavender (*Lavandula vera*), more than any other herb, evokes the nostalgia of summer days and herbaceous borders in cottage gardens. Great sentiment is attached to it, perhaps because it recalls times past when small bags of the dried herb were kept in linen closets for the 'blanched linen, smooth and lavender'd' that Keats wrote of in *The Eve of Saint Agnes*, and living was more gracious.

Provence is famous for its lavender which grows wild all over the countryside. The Romans scented their baths with it, and its botanical name is thought to be derived from the Latin *lavare*, to wash. Virgil mentions lavender in the *Bucolics* and the *Georgics*. Since ancient times it has been valued as a nerve medicine and digestive. Gerard prescribed it as good for 'a light migram . . . and them that use to swoune much' and to 'helpe the panting and passion of the heart.' However he also cautioned against drinking the distilled wine 'for by using such hot things that fill and stuffe the head, both the disease is made greater, and the sick man also brought into daunger.' In some cases it could even cause death. Shakespeare in *The Winter's Tale* is referring to the habit of chewing lavender in the lines: 'Here's flowers for you;/Hot lavender, mints, savory, marjoram.'

The fresh flowering tops of the plant yield an oil which is widely used in medicine and perfumery. That of the English lavender is more esteemed than that of the continental species, and they vary greatly in strength and fragrance. The drug contains active ingredients with a sedative and antiseptic action making it useful for healing wounds and easing coughs, as well as aiding the digestion, promoting the flow of bile, relieving flatulence and inducing sweat. It is included in the *British Pharmacopoeia*.

Because of its tremendous curative powers the great wild **Valerian** (*Valeriana officinalis*) was given the name of All-heal. It was also known as Drunken Sailor in certain ports because witches employed it as an aphrodisiac. References to *V. phu*, which is native of Alsace and Dauphiny, can be found in Dioscorides and Pliny, but this is the garden valerian and not the great wild species which is so highly valued in pharmacy. *V. officinalis* is indigenous to Europe and Siberia. It was distilled in the monastries as a medicine as the term *officinalis* proves. *Valerian* comes from the Latin *valere*, 'to be well'.

The roots are rich in volatile oil. Valerian's fame spread, especially during the Middle Ages, and it was prescribed for a variety of illnesses from tuberculosis to gout and poisonous snake bites. At the end of the sixteenth century a Neopolitan, Fabio Colonna, claimed to have been cured of epilepsy by valerian. Other epileptics followed his example, apparently with good results. Valerian acts as a sedative on the whole nervous system. Its action is not strong nor of long duration as its components are easily eliminated through the kidneys. The roots have antispasmodic, anodyne, diuretic, hypnotic, antiperiodic, carminative, nervine, stimulant and vermifugal action. In Catholic countries the herb is dedicated to the Virgin Mary and known as Blessed herb. Its old name was Setewall and it is mentioned by Chaucer as such. This name is still current in the North of England. Gerard declared that 'no broths, pottage or physicall meats are worth anything, if setwall were not at an end.'

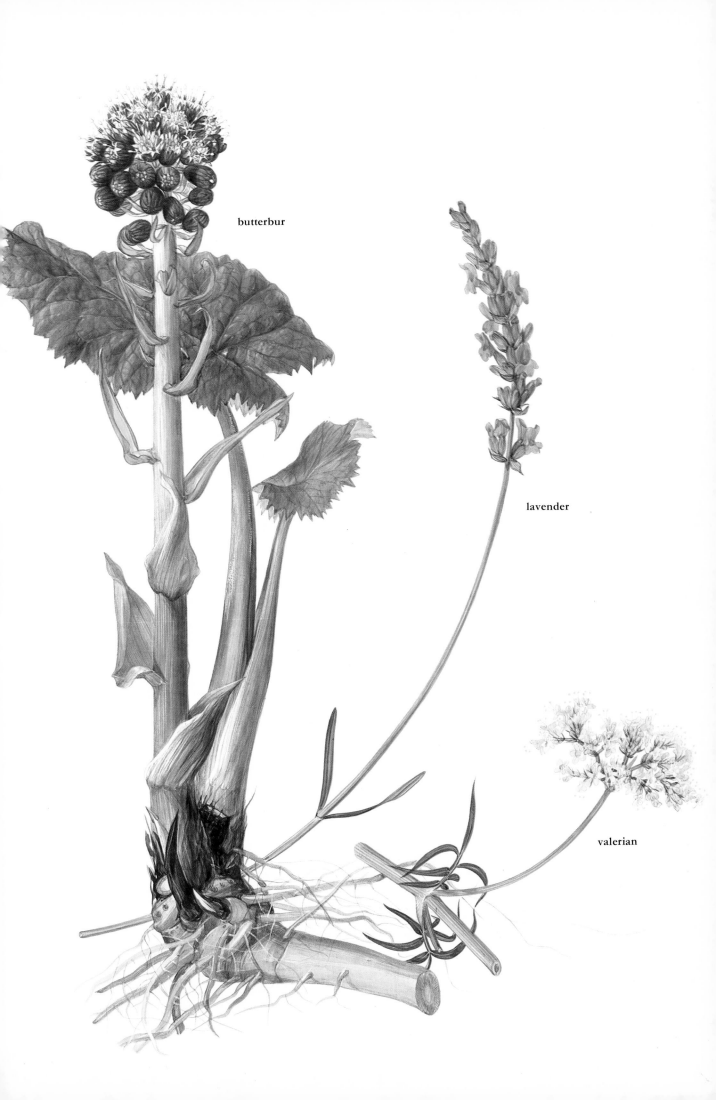

butterbur

lavender

valerian

Red valerian
Bastard balm
Lemon verbena

The **Red valerian** (*Centranthus ruber*) has escaped from cultivation and is now naturalized on banks, crumbling walls and rocks in coastal regions, although it may still be grown as an ornamental. Of the Valerianaceae, this herbaceous perennial is native of the Mediterranean but flourishes in southern England, the Midlands and eastern Ireland. It flowers between June and August.

The botanical name of the plant comes from the Greek *kentron*, 'a spur', and *anthos*, 'a flower', referring to the spurred flower. The drug is obtained from the rhizome which resembles a huge radish and has a characteristic odour. It is believed to be helpful in hysteria and nervous disorders because of its sedative and antispasmodic properties. Robert Burton (*c.* 1576–*c.* 1640) in his *Anatomy of Melancholy* wrote: 'Melissophyllon, Balm, hath an admirable virtue to alter melancholy, be it steeped in our ordinary drink, extracted, or otherwise taken.' He was praising the **Bastard balm** (*Melittis melissophyllum*), a member of the Labiatae which grows in shady woods in temperate regions throughout Europe and the British Isles. Despite its beautiful white flowers patched with reddish-purple, it grows only in the wild state and is not cultivated. This herb should not be confused with snapdragon (*Antirrhinum majus*) whose flowers are similarly formed.

The old country name for bastard balm was Butter and Eggs. Its botanical name comes from the Greek *melissa*, a honeybee. Bees are very attracted to the flowers. The whole herb, which emits a strong distinctive odour, is used. It has sedative and antispasmodic action, and is useful as a diuretic and antiseptic in disorders of the urinary tract. Infusions may be safely given to babies, elderly people and those with delicate constitutions suffering from nervous disorders.

Lemon verbena (*Lippia citriodora*), of the Verbenaceae, has been highly regarded for its delicate refreshing scent since very ancient times. It is named after the Italian botanist Augustino Lippi (1678–1701) who died violently in Abyssinia. The cultivated verbena is probably derived from wild species found in Brazil and Argentina, which found their way to North America and Europe. It is often grown as an ornamental pot herb, and the dried leaves may be used in the same way as lavender to give a pleasant fragrance to linen and clothes.

The leaves, which should be collected before the plant flowers, are used in medicine. They contain an essential oil rich in citral, terpenes and glycosides. The drug is helpful in disorders of the nervous system because of its antispasmodic action. It is also an effective antiseptic. Made into a tisane it aids the digestion. This tisane is so popular in France where it is known as *verveine odorante*, that it is served in bars and cafés.

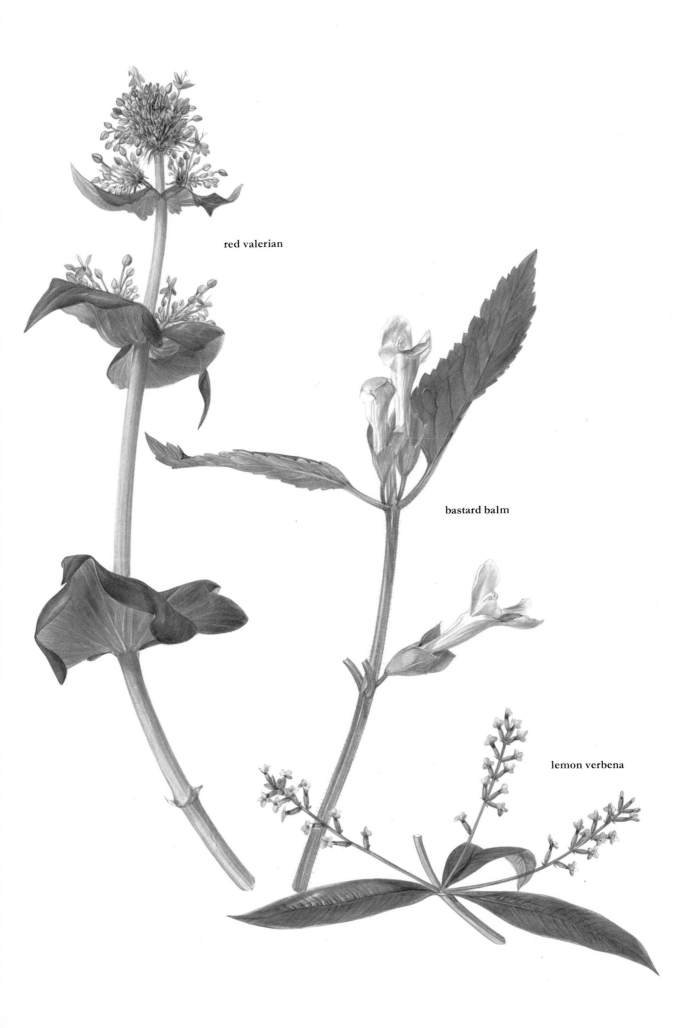

red valerian

bastard balm

lemon verbena

Cherry laurel
Bitter almond

Cherry laurel (*Prunus laurocerasus*) is a small tree with shiny evergreen leaves. Originally from western Asia, this little tree is now extensively cultivated as an ornamental throughout western Europe and the United States. Unfortunately it is often overpruned which prevents it from blossoming, but if allowed to grow freely it flowers abundantly from April to June, and produces large crops of black drupes which bear a slight resemblance to the olive. Cherry laurel belongs to the Rosaceae, and is planted in woods and copses where it sometimes regenerates.

At one time the fresh leaves were official in the *British Pharmacopoeia*, and in the Middle Ages the tree was grown in the 'physicke' gardens of herbalists and monasteries. The leaves should be gathered between June and August when they contain a higher proportion of the drug. When rubbed, the fresh leaves give out a characteristic smell of bitter almonds, but this scent is lost when they are are dried. On hydrolysis the leaves yield hydrocyanic acid. A solution known as Cherry Laurel Water is distilled from the fresh leaves and used as a mild carminative and sedative, especially helpful for nervous coughs and respiratory and circulatory spasms.

For culinary purposes the fruits are used on the Continent to flavour various creams, but as they contain a large amount of prussic acid great care should be taken. In Italy during the nineteenth century there was a report of several people suffering from poisoning after eating desserts or sweets over-generously flavoured with *laurocerasus*. The plant is nevertheless used commercially in the distillation of a delicious liqueur.

'And it came to pass, that on the morrow Moses went into the tabernacle of witness; and, behold, the rod of Aaron for the house of Levi was budded, and brought forth buds, and bloomed blossoms, and yielded almonds' (*Numbers*, xvii, 8). The almond is mentioned many times in the Bible and has been prized since antiquity. Hippocrates and Theophrastus both knew the 'Greek nut' as it was named by the Romans. Those growing on Naxos were said to be the best, according to Athenaeus in his *Deipnosophistai*. The Greeks ate five or six **Bitter almonds** (*Prunus amygdalus* var. *amara*) before dining in the belief that their drying nature expels moisture and therefore provokes thirst. Sweet and bitter almonds grow trees of the same species, but have very different properties; amygdalin is absent from the sweet almond (*P. amygdalus* var. *dulcis*).

The almond belongs to the Rosaceae and is native of Barbary. Today it is extensively cultivated in California, North Africa and around the Mediterranean, especially in Italy, Provence and Languedoc. Both the sweet and the bitter almond provide a delicate oil which constitutes more than half their weight, and is used in soothing emulsions as a mild laxative and a dressing for burns, and also in perfumery and the distilling industry. The bitter almond is more prized in medicine. It contains, besides the oil, emulsion, sugar, mucilage and ash. The ash contains potassium, calcium and magnesium phosphates. The almond's sedative and antispasmodic properties make it useful in the treatment of nervous coughs, insomnia and diseases of the respiratory organs. Almond milk has a reputation for reducing fever and, of all the vegetable oils, almond oil has the least acid reaction.

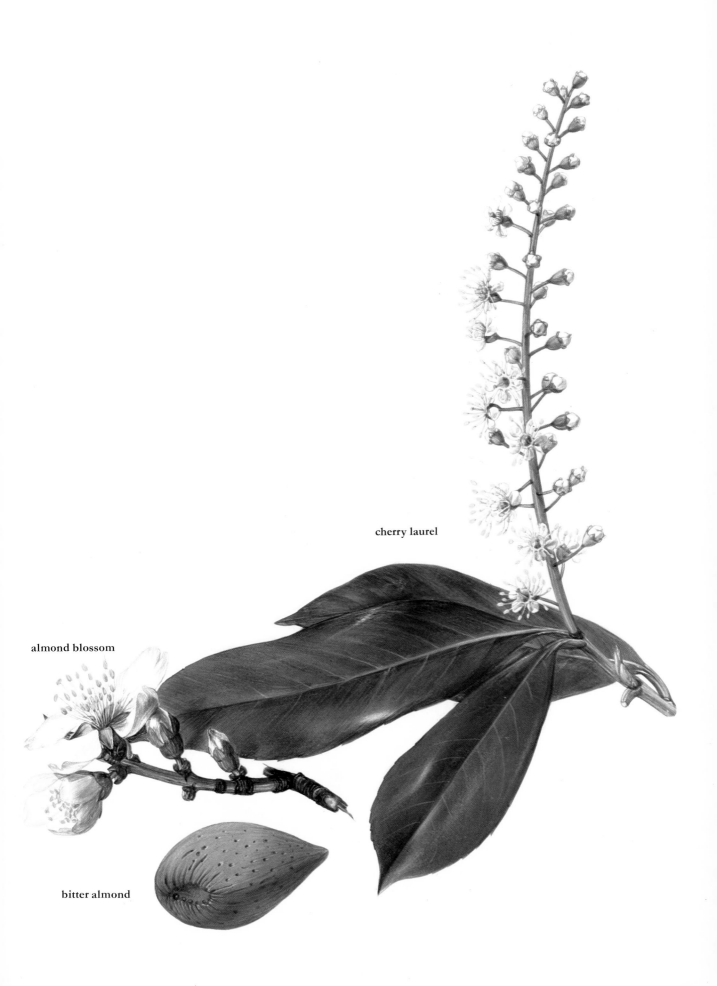

cherry laurel

almond blossom

bitter almond

Anemones

'Anemone or Wind-floure, is so called, for the floure doth never open it self but when the wind doth blow, as Pliny writeth: whereupon it is named of divers, *Herba venti*: in English, Wind-floure.' So wrote John Gerard in the sixteenth century, on the controversial subject of the name **Anemone**, which may derive from the Greek *anemos*, 'wind': the reason has caused speculation for centuries.

This large genus of Ranunculaceous plants grows wild throughout most temperate regions, but is easy to cultivate from seed. Since ancient times the anemone has been valued for its therapeutic propertes. Dioscorides named three species: *A. nemorosa*, *A. stellata* and *A. coronaria*. He prescribed their external application for ulcers and inflammations of the eye; Pliny believed them to be equally effective against toothache and swollen gums. *A. coronaria*, the beautiful poppy anemone, is thought to be 'the lily of the field' in the New Testament. It is still employed medicinally in many countries although its use is dying out in Britain. The pasque-flower (*A. pulsatilla*) has been known to Chinese physicians for thousands of years, and the roots and flowers are still esteemed as a cure for many ailments from dysentery to madness. In homoeopathic medicine the 'wind-flower' is used appropriately for emotional people whose moods change rapidly from elation to deep depression, and who are prone to changeable psychosomatic illnesses which can cause them real distress. The root was held to have a strong influence on the brain and the sympathic nervous system, and to be helpful in cases of nervous prostration, Homoeopaths still find these treatments effective, as do the Chinese. The anemone is also believed to bring relief to sufferers from pains in the joints, especially the extremities; varicose veins, uticaria, asthma, nervous headaches, amenorrhoea, gastric upsets, uterine malfunctions and acute prostatitis. The root can be used in the form of a tincture or extraction, and the leaves are sometimes made into an ointment. Gerard, referring to the root, wrote: 'All the kinds of Anemones are sharp, biting the tongue, and of a binding facultie.'

The American pulsatilla (*A. ludoviciana*), the European pulsatilla (*A. pratensis*) and *A. pulsatilla* are sources of anemonin and iso-anemonic acid which are employed as alteratives and depressants. The yellow wood anemone (*A. ranunculoides*) and the blue anemone (*A. appennina*) are also used medicinally, although to a lesser extent, and in some parts of the United States where the tradition of folk medicine still flourishes, *A. hepatica* is thought to be a beneficial tonic for the liver. Because of their colour and shape the leaves are known as liver leaves. They have demulcent and vulnerary properties, and until the late nineteenth century were used to treat patients in the early stages of tuberculosis.

Many legends are attached to this bright flower which is said to have first sprung from the blood of Adonis, killed by a wild boar.

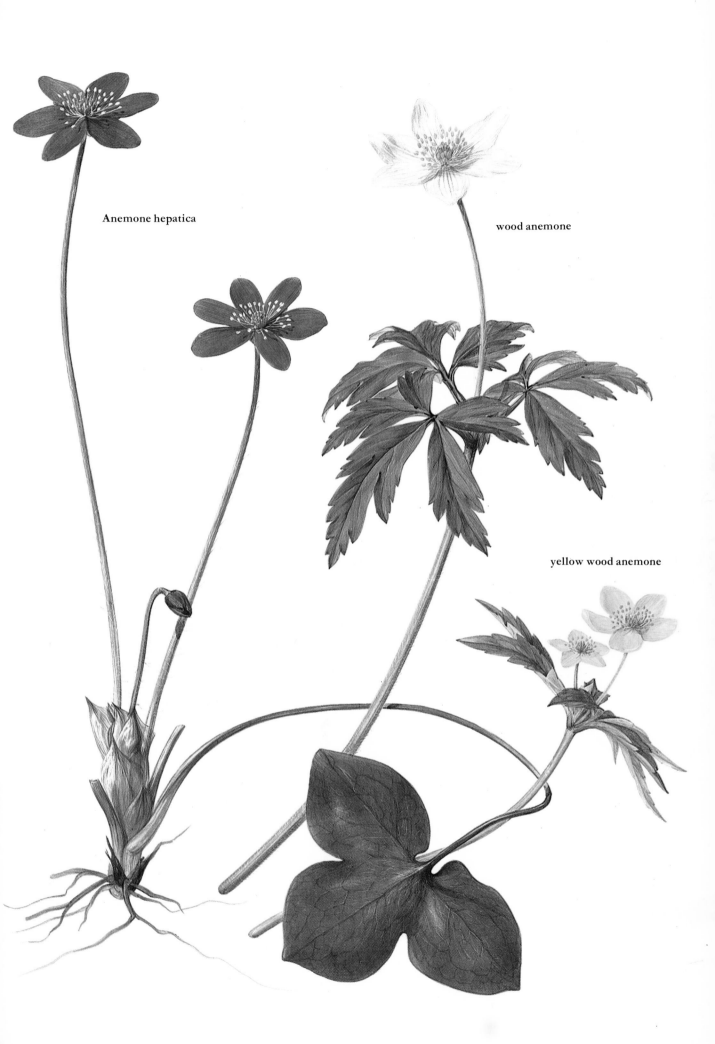

Anemone hepatica

wood anemone

yellow wood anemone

Cow parsnip
Coca
Clove

Cow parsnip (*Heracleum sphondylium*) is a common member of the Umbelliferae which grows profusely in damp marshy places such as meadows and ditches, and is very appetizing to cattle. Another of its many common names is hogweed. Botanically it is named after Hercules, one of whose Twelve Labours was to drive the cattle of Geryon across Europe. Cow parsnip contains an essential oil and is used as a nerve sedative, anti-hysteric and analgesic. Some people are allergic to the plant and may develop irritating rashes. In parts of Russia the young shoots are cooked and eaten in the same way as asparagus, and in Poland the seeds and leaves are made into a very potent beer.

In the twelfth century the Incas in Peru prized **Coca** (*Erythroxylon coca*) so highly that it was kept exclusively for the use of chieftains and priests, and the plant was worshipped as a divinity. Today Peruvian Indians chew the leaves to allay hunger and fatigue, and regard coca as an economical foodstuff. In its natural state it has a stimulating effect similar to that of coffee or tea, but its alkaloid cocaine, when isolated, is an addictive and dangerous drug, despite the habit of Sherlock Holmes.

Coca is cultivated in Peru, Bolivia and Java. In medicine it was one of the early local anaesthetics, but is chiefly used now in ear, nose and throat surgery. Sometimes, in the form of a tincture or liquid extract, it is given to convalescents. Cocaine acts directly on the central nervous system and the higher levels of the brain, and gives the user a feeling of tremendous energy. In the sixteenth century the Spanish invaders gave the Inca miners coca leaves to enable them to work endless hours producing gold. In twentieth-century Bolivia where miners still work for extremely low wages, they are kept going on coca leaves. At one time in the United States, coca was one of the ingredients used in Coca-cola, but in 1904 this practice was made illegal. In South America coca is used in a wine and a liqueur, and is even made into little cakes.

The **Clove** (*Eugenia caryophyllata*) which is associated in the minds of many people with such mundane things as apple-pie or toothache, has an exotic history. As early as 260 BC the Chinese were using cloves medicinally. They were introduced into Europe sometime in the fourth century and were one of the treasures brought back by Marco Polo from his travels. For several hundred years they were a very expensive commodity.

The clove tree is believed to be indigenous to China, and is now cultivated extensively in the Moluccas, Zanzibar and Pemba. At the beginning of the sixteenth century the Portuguese held the Spice Islands, but in 1605 they were routed by the Dutch, who held the monopoly on cloves; as they did with nutmeg; even going so far as to destroy all the trees on their native islands, and cultivating them on Amboyna and a few small neighbouring islands. However, in the mid-eighteenth century the French, who resented the high price demanded by the Dutch, managed to introduce clove trees into Mauritius, and by the start of the nineteenth century cultivation was under way in Sumatra, Cayenne, Zanzibar, Pemba and Madagascar.

The drug comes from the flowers which are picked in bud and sun-dried. They are aromatic and spicy, and contain a volatile oil, tannin and caryophyllin. Oil of cloves is used as a stimulant, antiseptic, aromatic, antispasmodic, carminative and flavouring agent. In dentistry it is used as a local analgesic, and in folk medicine cloves are chewed to allay toothache. Oil of cloves is employed externally as a rubefacient and can be mixed with olive oil as a mild analgesic. The bark of the tree, which is highly aromatic, is also used pharmaceutically.

Domestically the clove has many uses: a béchamel sauce gets its delicate flavour from an onion stuck with a few cloves, and no hot punch is complete without an orange or lemon decorated with cloves, bobbing on its surface.

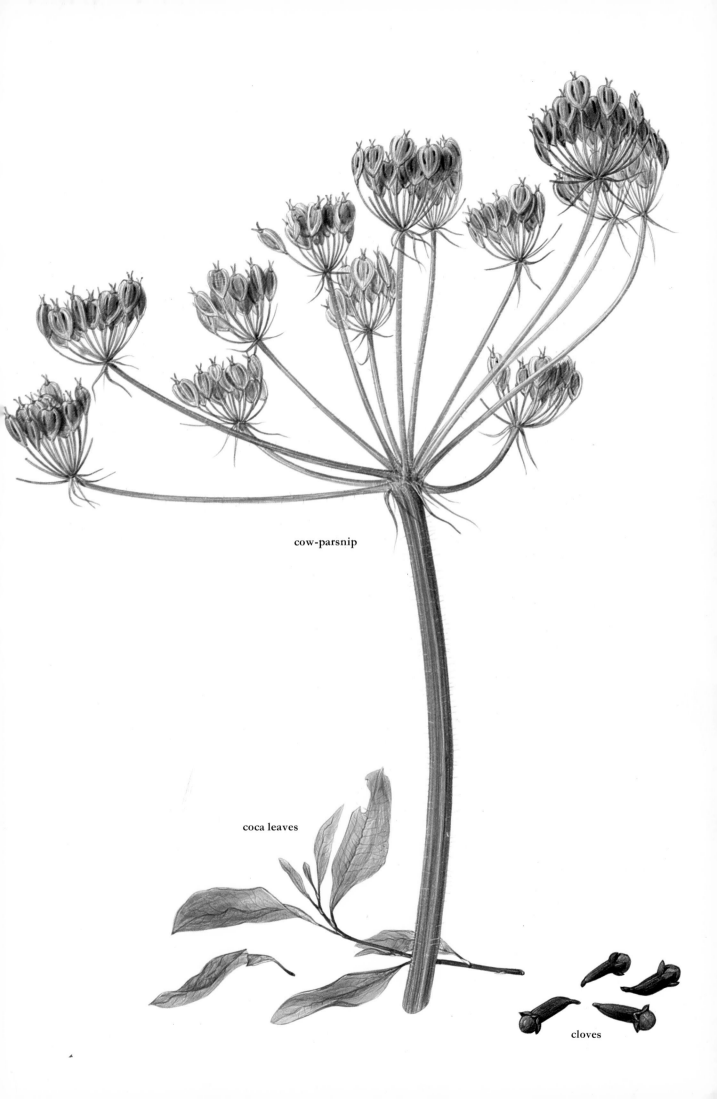

cow-parsnip

coca leaves

cloves

Chaste tree
Waterlily
Rue

The **Chaste tree** (*Vitex agnus-castus*), as its name implies, has a reputation for preserving chastity. Pliny describes how each year Greek matrons covered their beds with its branches to kill their husbands' lust and promote the fertility of the newly sown corn, on the festival of Thesmophoria. The plant's botanical name is derived from the Greek *hagnos* and the Latin *castus*: both meaning 'chaste'. It is dedicated to Juno and to Aesculapius. The drug is obtained from the leaves, inflorescence and fruit, and although employed occasionally as an anaphrodisiac, is mostly used for certain eye conditions, and as a poultice. The tree also possesses digestive, emmenagogic and soporific properties.

Shelley's 'floating water lilies broad and bright,/which lit the oak that overhung the hedge,/With moonlight beams of their own watery light' are also plants whose chief function in early medicine was to preserve chastity. The white **Waterlily** (*Nymphaea alba*) is named for the water nymphs. Its other names are water rose, Nenuphar and candock. It grows in marshy rivers, streams and lakes in most parts of Europe and the United States, and is cultivated as an ornamental in many garden pools. The rhizome contains the active ingredients; tannin, starch, resin, gallic acid, tartaric acid, mucilage and ammonia. It is used as an anaphrodisiac, astringent, demulcent and anodyne.

Waterlilies of many colours are found in the tropics. The beautiful blue waterlily is indigenous to Egypt, and a plant with glowing red flowers is common in the East Indies. The yellow waterlily found in England is known as 'brandy-bottle' because of its brandy-like perfume. All varieties are used in medicine. Herbalists employ the white and yellow species for skin inflammations, boils, ulcers and tumours. The plant may be given both internally and externally. Carolus Linnaeus, the great eighteenth-century Swedish botanist, believed that the waterlily rose out of the water at seven o'clock each morning, and opened its bloom to the sun. At four o'clock in the afternoon it would close its petals and sink down to repose again on the surface of the water.

'They sayen the stolen sede is butt the bestte.' So says an early fifteenth-century herbal about **Rue** (*Ruta graveolens*) which was believed to grow far better when it had been stolen from another garden. Its power against evil was thought to be so great that it was known as 'herb of grace'. Not only did it keep away the plague but the devil as well, and since ancient times was used as an antidote against every kind of poison from toadstools to snake bites. Gerard said of rue, 'When the Weesell is to fight with the serpent, shee armeth her selfe by eating Rue, against the might of the serpent.' In the Middle Ages it was one of the herbs in the nosegays carried by the rich when they went out-of-doors, as a protection from 'evill aires' and the vermin they might catch from importunate beggars.

Rue was introduced into England by the Romans. It was famous for preserving the eyesight, and was said to promote second sight, perhaps by acting on the Third Eye. Herbalists use it to help eyestrain and disorders of the eyes. Its other virtue was as a preserver of chastity. According to the early mediaeval *Schola Salernitana*, 'Rue maketh chaste: And eke preserveth sight;/Infuseth wit and putteth flies to flight.'

Rue has a bitter taste, and is never used in cookery, but this bitterness could be lessened, so Pliny said, through the great friendship which exists between rue and the fig-tree. The best rue for 'physicks' was that which had been planted under a fig-tree, especially, of course, if it had previously been stolen. The fig imparted some of its own sweetness to the rue, which 'prospered nowhere so well as under the fig.'

Dioscorides recommended rue for bleeding noses, and Gerard wrote in his herbal: 'the juice of Rue made hot in the rinde of a pomegranat and dropped into the eares, takes away the paine thereof.' Rue is mentioned in many Saxon leech books. It was said to bring relief to all parts of the body: the nerves; the head; the bowels and the stomach.

Its most important constituent is a crystalline body called rutin. The United States Department of Agriculture found that rutin was very effective in treating high blood-pressure, and it also helps to harden the bones and teeth. It comforted the heart as well, as shown by Shakespeare's gardener, who, pitying the Queen's sorrow, says: 'Here did she fall a tear; here, in this place/I'll set a bank of rue, sour herb of grace' (*King Richard II*).

118

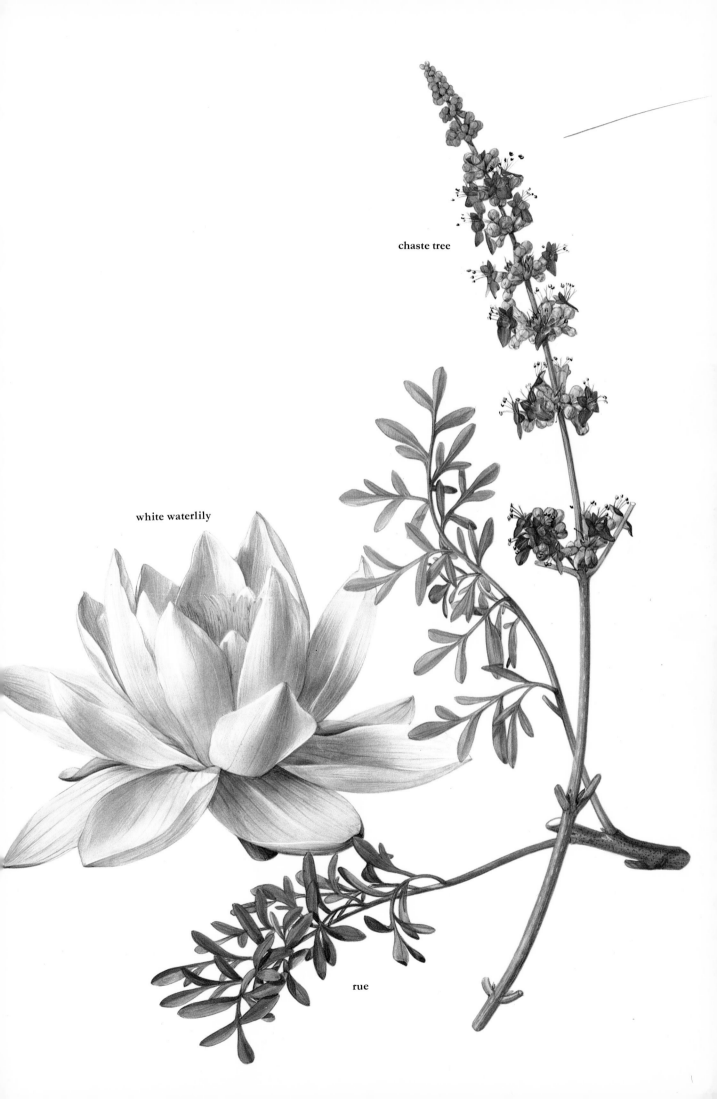

chaste tree

white waterlily

rue

Thornapple
Henbane
Deadly nightshade

Jupiter, according to the *Doctrine of Signatures*, governs the **Thornapple** (*Datura stramonium*) and it was therefore used against epilepsy, fits and madness. All parts of the plant are narcotic and the evil uses to which it has been put in the past account for its old name of Devil's apple. In Russia thieves and murderers stupified their intended victims with a concoction made of the ground seeds, and young girls were procured for prostitution. The therapeutic value of the thornapple however, has been appreciated by physicians in both the Old and New Worlds. Avicenna, the eleventh-century Arab physician, wrote about the thornapple's medicinal virtues, and the Spaniard Nicholas Monardes in his herbal (*c*. 1564) mentions the seeds sent to him from Peru, with commendations for its curative powers from both the Spaniards and the Indians.
Its common names are Peruvian apple and thorny apple of Peru. In the United States it is known as Jimson weed. Today the plant flourishes practically everywhere in the world except the Arctic, and is a common weed in some regions.
The leaves contain the drug. The presence of hyoscyamine and atropine give it antispasmodic, anodyne and narcotic action, similar to that of *belladonna*. Although the dried leaves and stalks may be used in a mixture for asthma cigarettes, it is extremely unwise to use this plant except under medical supervision as it is highly toxic. When properly administered, preferably in homoeopathic form, it may be used to relieve skin eruptions, haemorrhoids, hysteria and neuralgia. In the sixteenth century the wife of a merchant, Mistress Lobel of Colchester, was struck by lightning. It is recorded that she was saved by a preparation of *Datura stramonium* 'when all hope was past'.
Henbane (*Hyoscyamus niger*) has earned its common name from the lethal effect it has on poultry. It was widely used as a sedative by the ancient Egyptians, Babylonians, Greeks and Romans, and in the Middle Ages was one of the ingredients of the dreaded 'soporific sponge'. In the twentieth century a drug containing hyoscine known as 'Twilight sleep' was administered to women in labour and those suffering from nervous breakdowns. In ancient times the plant was used 'against the phrenzy of madness' especially when the patient was believed to be possessed by a demon. All parts of the plant are poisonous and toxic doses will produce aggression, suspicion and other manic symptoms. Prescribed under medical supervision it is helpful in overcoming shocks to the nervous system. It has antispasmodic, anodyne and hypnotic action. Pilgrims, before starting on their journeys, put leaves of henbane in their shoes to alleviate weariness, and a decoction of the leaves in a footbath relieves aching feet. Henbane's deadliness is vividly described by the ghost of Hamlet's father: '. . . thy uncle stole,/With juice of cursed hebenon in a vial/And in the pouches of mine ear did pour/The leperous distilment; whose effect/Holds such an enmity with blood of man . . .'
After the mandrake, **Deadly nightshade** (*Atropa belladonna*) is probably more associated in the layman's mind with witchcraft than any other plant. According to folklore the devil himself tends it as its country names indicate: Devil's herb and enchanter's nightshade. The botanical name *Atropa* comes from the Greek *Atropos*, one of the three Fates who held the shears with which to cut the thread of man's life. Until the Middle Ages the plant was known as *Dwale*, Scandinavian for sleep or trance.
The leaves and roots of deadly nightshade are an important source of atropine and scopolamine. Scopolamine is thought to have caused delusions of flight in witches some centuries ago when they anointed their bodies with an ointment containing *belladonna*. During the Renaissance Italian ladies dropped the juice into the eyes to exaggerate their size by dilating the pupils. From this custom comes the name *belladonna*. Today the plant is used in ophthalmology for its mydriatic action. It is also anodyne, antispasmodic, diuretic, sedative and lactifuge, acting particularly on the heart, nervous system and muscles. Hahnemann (1755–1843) the founder of homoeopathy, used *belladonna* against scarlet fever and erysipelas. However, the plant is one of the most dangerous in the countryside, and should never be used for home medicine. It can cause loss of speech, convulsions and hallucinations. Its virtues however, assure its inclusion in the *British Pharmacopoeia*.

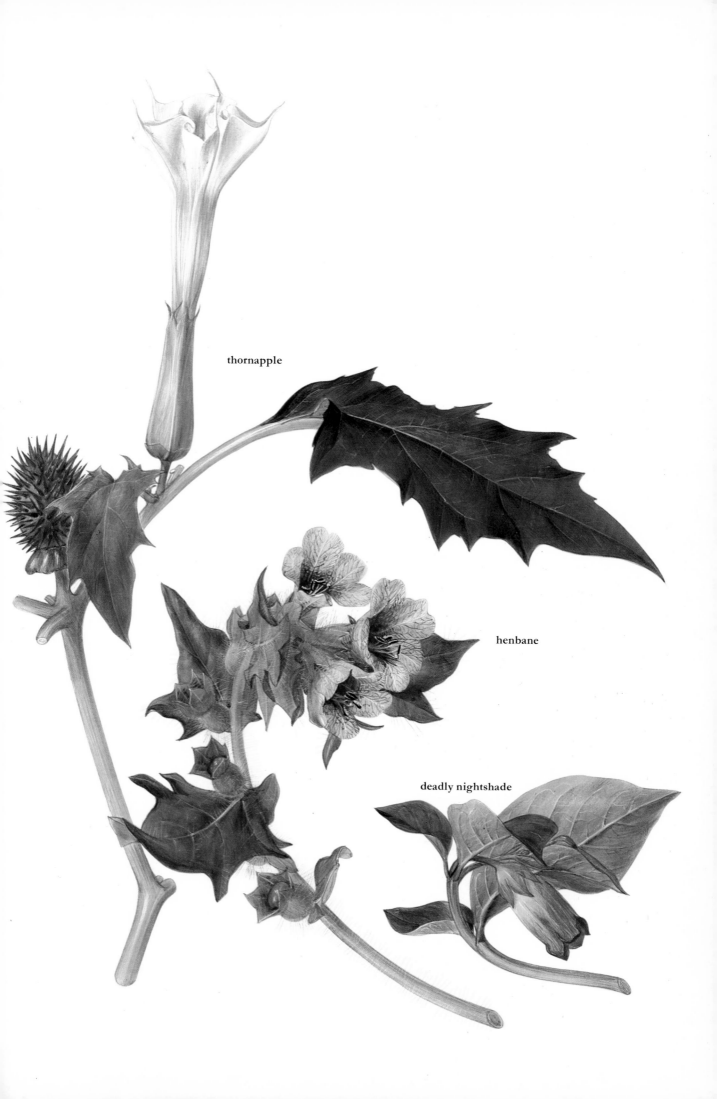

thornapple

henbane

deadly nightshade

Spanish chestnut
Indian hemp
Black nightshade

'It were as needless to describe a tree so commonly known as to tell a man he had gotten a mouth.' So Nicholas Culpeper in his seventeenth-century *Herball* did not trouble to give a description of the chestnut tree. The genus *Castanea*, of the Fagaceae, includes four species; the American chestnut (*C. dentata*), the Chinese chestnut (*C. mollissima*), the Japanese chestnut (*C. crenata*) and the best known, the **Spanish chestnut** (*C. sativa*), which is widely used as a food for both man and beast, and in medicine. Culpeper praised its nourishing fruit but warned that if too many were eaten 'they make the blood thick, procure headache, and bind the body.'

The drug is provided by the leaves which have tonic and astringent properties. It helps to ease respiratory complaints and persistent coughs, and, in conjunction with other drugs, is particularly successful against whooping cough. In many European countries dried chestnuts are ground into flour and substituted for cereals to make bread, soup and other foods. It is especially popular in Corsica where chestnut fritters called *castagnacci* are a staple food. Sometimes they are flavoured with pine kernels or aniseed. Commercially the Spanish chestnut is made into a sweet paste to be used in desserts, or an unsweetened purée which may be eaten as a vegetable in place of boiled chestnuts. The American chestnut produces nuts which, although small and greyish, have a particularly sweet flavour. In many forests in the United States the trees grow to heights of 100 feet or more. The chestnut has been esteemed for its flavour since antiquity. The Greek poet Alcaeus (*c.* 600 BC) wrote that 'The Arcadians were chestnut-eaters' (*Fragment* no. 86).

Indian Hemp (*Cannabis sativa*) is one of the few plants to be more usually referred to by its botanical name *cannabis*. It is also known as marihuana, grass, pot, hashish, bhang, dagga and a variety of other terms. Its cultivation for its hallucinogenic resins goes back thousands of years. As early as 2737 BC marihuana was included in the pharmacopoeia of the Chinese Emperor Shen Nung. It was used in ancient Scythian funeral rites, and seeds have been found in funerary urns dating back to the fifth century BC. The name hashish may have been passed down by Marco Polo, who, in 1271, came across a band of ferocious robbers near the Caspian Sea. They were called *ashishins*, hence the modern word 'assassin', and consumed great amounts of cannabis to increase their daring. 'Hashish' has been thought to be derived from their name.

The use of Indian hemp in Africa is widespread, and in the northern part of the continent is the social equivalent of the western custom of offering a drink. Its use in the United States has increased so much that it is said to be responsible for the drop in the rate of alcoholic consumption, and legally, its possession is now a misdemeanour and no longer a felony.

In pharmaceutical doses marihuana has been found helpful in certain cases of mental illness and depression. It is said to be non-addictive and no more harmful than alcohol, but it should be remembered that, in excess, alcohol can be totally destructive. Medical opinion is divided on the subject of Indian hemp. Culpeper, who records it as being 'cultivated in many countries', lists it as a cure for mundane afflictions such as colic, bleeding noses, jaundice, and even to 'draw forth earwigs or other living creatures.'

Black nightshade (*Solanum nigrum*), of the Solanaceae, is a common weed in the British Isles; its stalks and berries have been used in medicine since the time of the ancient Romans. The plant has mildly narcotic soothing properties and is employed as a sedative and analgesic to treat skin diseases where painful itching occurs, and to relieve colic and asthma. In the Middle Ages it was given to patients before surgery as recorded by Theodorus, Bishop of Cervia.

Black nightshade drives its botanical name from the Latin *solamen* which means 'soothing'. Its common name comes from the colour of its berries, although occasionally species are found with yellowish or carmine fruits. Early herbalists recommended a decoction of the berries 'gargarised . . . against swellings and impostumations of the throat . . .' Despite its soothing virtues it would be extremely unwise to eat the berries.

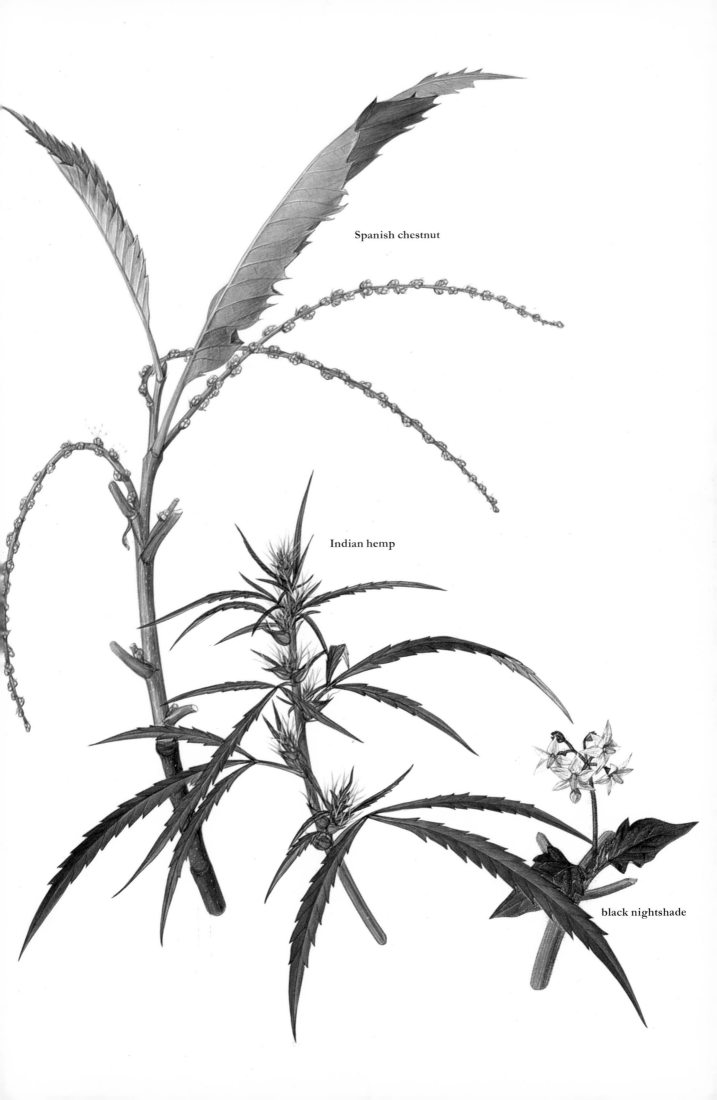

Spanish chestnut

Indian hemp

black nightshade

Corydalis
Opium poppy

Unlike other members of the Fumariaceae, *Corydalis cava* is always known only by its botanical name **Corydalis**, and does not have a common English name as do the yellow, purple and climbing corydalis. Corydalis is derived from the Greek *korydallis* meaning 'crested lark', and refers to the flowers which have spurs like those of larks. This plant is quite rare; it grows wild in fields and meadows and blooms in April and May. The drug of this *recherché* species is obtained from the hollow tubers which are the size of walnuts. Its chief alkaloids are corydaline and bulbocapnine which are sometimes employed for their narcotic and sedative action against chorea and other diseases characterized by muscular tremors. As an anaesthetic bulbocapnine may be used in place of morphine, but it must be remembered that large doses may cause convulsions and death.

The **Opium poppy** (*Papaver somniferum*), according to the *Doctrine of Signatures*, belongs to the Moon, which is fitting, for it induces sleep and turbulent dreams. There is a legend that Buddha, not wanting to fall asleep, cut off his eyelids and where they fell upon the earth a plant sprang forth bearing beautiful mauve petals, and this is how the opium poppy was created. One of its earliest mentions as a sleep inducer and opiate was found on Sumerian baked clay tablets dating back to *c.* 3500 BC. The ancient Greeks, who believed that sleep was a divine healing gift, celebrated the poppy in their art using the flower heads and capsules to decorate jewellery, household utensils and coins. Images of their gods were crowned with poppies, and it was dedicated to the god of death Thanatos, and to his brother Hypnos, the god of sleep, and to Hypnos' son Morpheus, the god of dreams. Native to Europe and western Asia, the poppy spread to India and China. There is a popular but erroneous belief that opium addiction began in China, but until the nineteenth century the opium poppy was cultivated there only as an ornamental and the import of opium was forbidden by the Chinese government. Opium is extracted from the unripe heads. Cuts are made in the capsules with a many-bladed knife so that the white juice or latex escapes. As it dries it turns brown and is scraped off and formed into little cakes. The principal constituent is the alkaloid morphine, and there are smaller amounts of narcotine, papaverine, thebaine and other minor alkaloids. This poppy is official in the *British Pharmacopoeia* for its use in sedative drugs for coughs and colds, and for external inflammation. The seeds, which do not contain the drug, are used in confectionery and baking to flavour cakes and bread, a practice which dates back to the ancient Egyptians. Homer, Virgil, Aristotle and the elder Pliny all esteemed the poppy as a medicine, although Hippocrates, while recommending poppy wine as therapeutic, warned against poppy milk. Despite this early knowledge of opium addiction Avicenna, the celebrated Arab philosopher and physician, died of opium intoxication in 1037. Thomas De Quincey in his *Confessions of an English Opium Eater* gives the addict's view: 'Thou hast the keys of Paradise, O just, subtle, and mighty opium!'

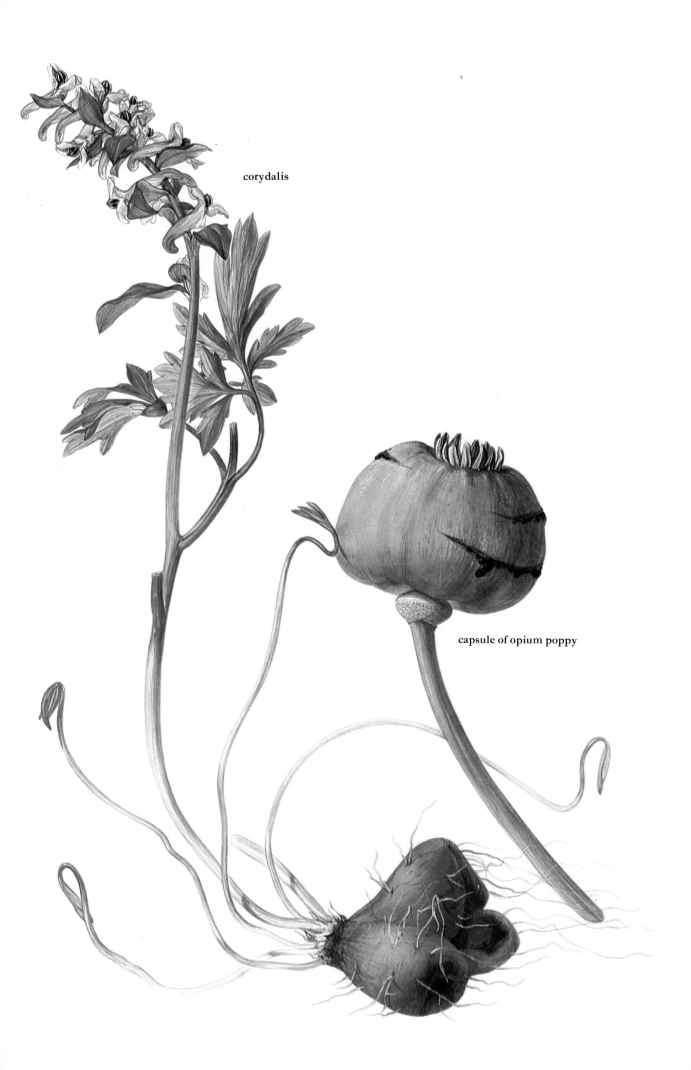

corydalis

capsule of opium poppy

Coffee
Tea
Kola nuts

'They have in Turky a drink called coffee, made of a berry of the same name, as black as soot, and of a strong scent, but not aromatical; which they take as hot as they can drink it. This drink comforteth the brain and heart, and helpeth digestion.' So wrote Sir Francis Bacon in one of the earliest descriptions of coffee. 'A Turky merchant' Mr Daniel Edwards, brought his Greek servant Pasqua back to England especially to make his coffee. Pasqua set up as a coffeeman in 1652, opening the first coffee house in London which achieved immediate popularity.

Coffee (*Coffea arabica*) is indigenous to Abyssinia. Its first cultivation is traced to Arabia. It was so highly prized by Muslims that it was drunk during prayers in the mosques, even in the Holy Temple at Mecca. The first man ever to drink coffee was said to be the Mufti of Aden in the ninth century, and a description of the shrub by Avicenna has survived from that time. However, it was scarcely known in Europe until the early seventeenth century. Pietro della Valle introduced it into Italy in 1615; and Thévenot to Paris in 1647, but it did not become popular in France until twenty years later when Suleiman Aga, Ambassador of the Sublime Porte to the Court of Louis XIV, followed the Turkish custom of offering it to visitors. It became the rage among the courtiers to drink it, especially as it remained rare and expensive. Having founded the East India coffee trade in 1690 when they began growing coffee in Java, the Dutch thought that they had yet another monopoly, but a Frenchman named Desclieux, braved incredible dangers to take a small coffee shrub to Martinique. It flourished and seedlings were sent from there to French Guiana and Brazil, and to Desclieux goes the honour of having introduced coffee into the Western Hemisphere. In many countries coffee was a controversial subject. Some German doctors tried to get a law passed forbidding women to drink it as they believed it caused sterility. J. S. Bach wrote his *Coffee Cantata* supposed to be women's reply in its defence. Coffee, which has a direct effect on the cortex of the brain, is widely drunk by people whose work is mental rather than physical, to relieve weariness and keep their minds alert. The best varieties come from Arabia, Martinique and Réunion Island.

Dr Johnson (1709–1784) 'with tea amused the evening, with tea solaced the midnight, and with tea welcomed the morning.' The cultivation of **Tea** (*Thea sinensis, Camellia thea*) in China and Japan goes back to prehistoric times, but its cultivation in India and Ceylon only began in the nineteenth century.

The Dutch introduced tea into Europe early in the seventeenth century, and in 1644 the Earls of Arlington and Ossory brought it to England where their ladies showed other women of quality how to use it. Its price was sixty shillings a pound and it remained costly until about 1707 when it became possible for 'the lower classes of people' to drink it.

Culpeper spoke highly of it: 'Green tea (*Thea viridis*) (*Camellia viridis*) is diuretic, and carries an agreeable roughness with it into the stomach, which gently astringes the fibres of that organ, and gives such a tone as is necessary for a good digestion: the Bohea (black tea) is softening and nutritious, and proper in all inward decays. Strong tea is prejudicial to weak nerves, but is salutary for violent headache and sickness occasioned by inebriation.' Much has been written against tea and coffee, but the great physician Sir William Roberts (1830–1899) claimed that the drinking of tea, coffee and cocoa produced an upward change in the mental calibre. Many intellectuals would seem to agree with this. Sydney Smith, Canon of St Paul's (1771–1845) speaks from the heart: 'Thank God for tea! What would the world do without tea? How did it exist? I am glad I was not born before tea.'

Approximately one hundred tons of **Kola nuts** (*Cola nitida*) are imported into the United States each year to be used in cola drinks which are not considered by most people to be stimulants. *C. nitida* however, contains 2% caffeine besides traces of tannin and theobromine. Native to tropical Africa, *C. nitida* is now cultivated extensively in the American tropics and other parts of the world. The natives of all these countries either chew the nuts or boil them to make a drink, to stave off hunger and fatigue. The nuts are also known as cola seeds, bissy nuts and gooroo nuts. The kola is a member of the Sterculiaceae and is used in pharmacy as a general tonic and nerve stimulant.

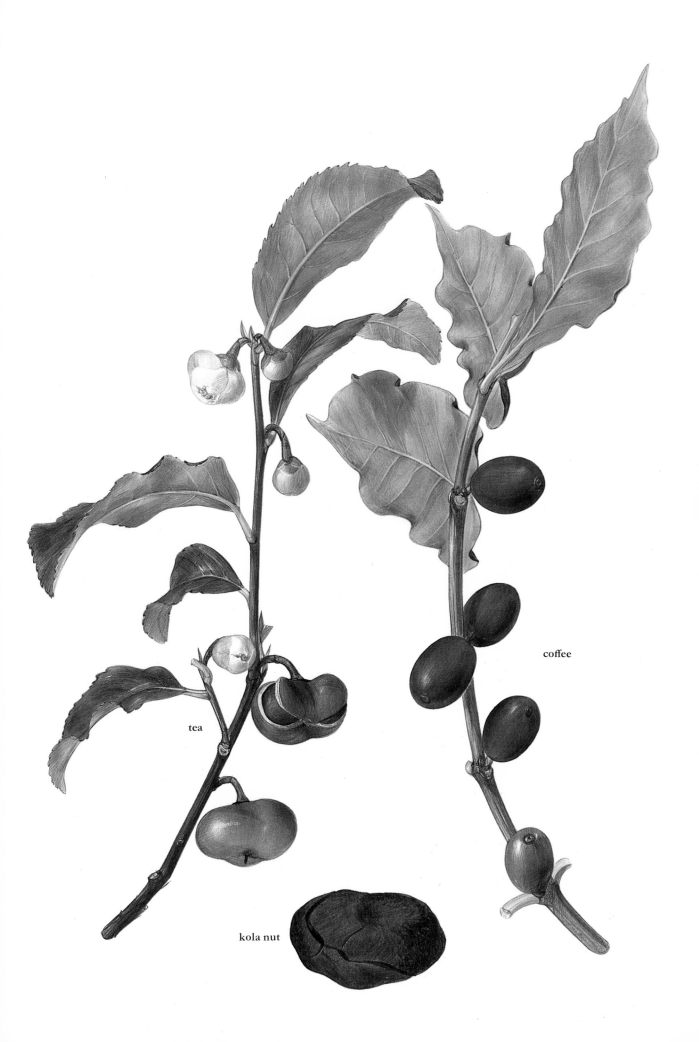

coffee

tea

kola nut

Plantain
Rest-harrow
Woodruff

Plantain (*Plantago major*) is a little plant whose many virtues more than compensate for its lack of beauty. For thousands of years it has been universally employed against various ailments. In ancient China it was thought to promote fertility and cure wasting diseases; Alexander the Great took it for his raging headaches, and, throughout the centuries, Dioscorides, Pliny, Galen, Chaucer and Culpeper all recommended it for healing wounds, assuaging tertian and quartan fevers, and curing bites from 'madde dogges'. Abraham Cowley (1618–1667) in his verses described its action: 'Her nature is astringent, which grate hate of her among blood letters does create.' In the United States it is still known as snakeweed from the belief that it can take away the pain of bee stings and cure the bites of snakes and scorpions. It appears in Anglo-Saxon books of remedies and was used in the famous medical school in Salerno.

Several species of plantain exist: *P. major*, which is properly called Great plantain; buck's horn plantain (*P. coronopus*); ribwort plantain (*P. lanceolata*); hoary plantain (*P. media*) and *P. psyllium* which has no common name and yields psyllium, a demulcent used for intestinal irritation. Most species have similar action. The seeds were once a well-known remedy for diarrhoea and dysentery, and the leaves, which contain a mucilage similar to linseed, were made into a decoction with diuretic and cooling properties. Today it is an anodyne for earache and toothache, and the seeds are still used for dysentery and haemorrhoids. They are safer to use than medicinal parafin because they do not irritate the mucous membranes of the intestines but strengthen the tissues and restore tone. The young leaves are sometimes eaten in salads.

The generic name is derived from the Latin *planta*, meaning 'sole of the foot'. In the Antipodes the plant is known as Englishman's foot from the legend that wherever an Englishman treads the plantain springs up. Another old tale relates how a young girl waited a long time by the roadside for her lover, but he never came, and eventually she was changed into this wayside plant and it earned its other name of waybroad.

Rest-harrow (*Ononis arvensis*) and prickly rest-harrow (*O. spinosa*) are members of the Leguminosae, subfamily Papilionaceae. Their old country name was cammock. The two species are often confused although it is *O. spinosa* which is valued in pharmacy for its diuretic and emollient action. The plant has enormous roots which may grow to half a yard in length, and have given it its common name because they are believed to have the power to break the plough if it gets caught in them. These huge roots provide the drug which contains saponins, tannin, citric acid and essential oil. It is soothing to the urinary tract and remedial for nephritis and in dissolving kidney stones. Its reputation for curing gravel and stone goes back to ancient Rome when it was mentioned by Pliny and Dioscorides. Pier Andrea Mattioli (1500–1577), the Italian physician and botanist, used the bark of the root mixed with wine as a cure for renal diseases and to aid the liver. The young shoots can be cooked as a vegetable. In remote regions of the Jura the plant is said to have a supernatural power that can make horses cast their shoes.

Woodruff (*Asperula odorata*) is a small country plant of the Rubiaceae. It prefers the undergrowth of beech woods where it grows thickly enough to form a carpet underfoot. It is found throughout Europe and western Asia, and flowers in May and June. Its old names were woodrowel and squinancy. In Culpeper's day, apart from its restorative qualities, it was thought to be a mild aphrodisiac: 'It is nourishing and restorative, good for weak consumptive people: it opens obstructions of the liver and spleen, and is said to be provocative to venery.' The bruised herb was laid on fresh wounds and cuts.

The drug is obtained from the entire plant which must be collected just before or during flowering. When the plant is dried it smells like new-mown hay due to the presence of coumarin. Its action is sedative, antispasmodic and mildly hypnotic, and it may be used to treat insomnia in people with delicate constitutions such as the aged and convalescents.

It is an essential part of a delicious summer drink popular in Europe for two or three centuries. The main ingredients today for May Wine would be a bottle of hock, a glass of sherry, sugar, strawberries and a few sprigs of woodruff thrown in an hour before serving.

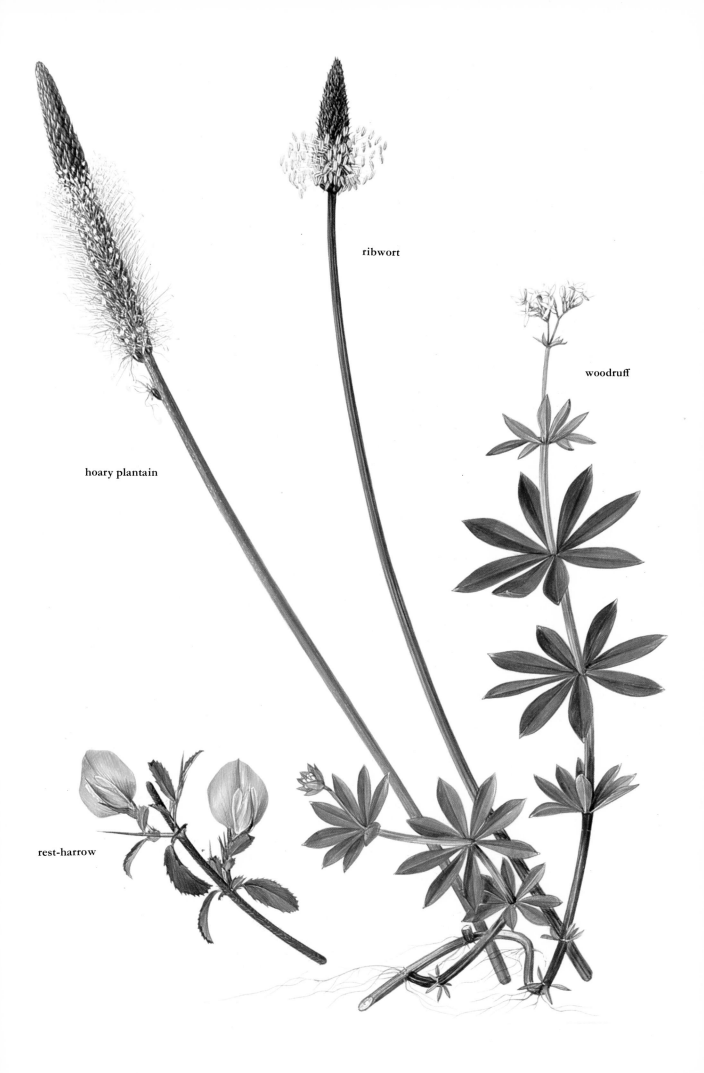

hoary plantain

ribwort

woodruff

rest-harrow

Butcher's broom
Asparagus
Pellitory of the wall

Butcher's broom (*Ruscus aculeatus*) earned its generic name from the practice long ago of scrubbing butchers' chopping blocks with bunches of the twigs tied together. It is a curious plant with tiny scale-like leaves. What, at first, seem to be the leaves are actually flattened branches. The large scarlet berries are responsible for its other local names of knee holly and box holly. Quite often it grows in the vicinity of real holly in woods and on cliffs. The young shoots may be cooked and eaten in the same way as asparagus. Its bitter roots are one of the ingredients of the famous Five Roots Liqueur, of which the others are fennel, celery, asparagus and parsley. The roots possess diuretic and aperitive properties and are manufactured into drugs for kidney and liver complaints. At one time the plant had many uses in folk medicine; it was thought to be helpful for jaundice, headaches, menstrual pains and chest ailments. Culpeper also advised: 'The decoction of the roots drank, and a poultice made of the berries and leaves being applied are effectual in knitting and consolidating broken bones or parts out of joint.' But he added a warning: 'The more of the root you boil the stronger will the decoction be: it works no ill effects, yet I hope you have wit enough to give the strongest decoction to the strongest bodies.'

Asparagus (*Asparagus officinalis*) which has always been one of the most expensive vegetables in any country, grows wild in abundance on sea cliffs and sand all over the British Isles, on Atlantic and Mediterranean coasts and in temperate regions all over Europe and the United States. Its botanical appellation *officinalis* shows that it was cultivated for its therapeutic virtues hundreds of years ago in monasteries and physic gardens. The rhizome and roots are used in medicine: their constituents are asparagin, albumen, sugar, resin, and other substances, with diuretic, sedative and mildly aperient action. Asparagus has been found helpful in anaemia, obesity, some forms of dropsy, nasal catarrh, heart trouble and those with insufficient diuresis. According to early herbalists a decoction of the roots of 'sperage' held in the mouth was said to ease toothache and stiffness in all the joints and sinews, especially in the lower parts of the body.

The ancients knew asparagus both as a gastronomic delicacy and as a medicine, but it was only in the reign of Louis XIV of France that it became popular in Europe when the Sun King himself brought it into vogue. Not until the time of William and Mary did the present-day English custom of eating asparagus with the fingers and using finger-bowls come into use. Previously it had been eaten with a spoon. King William, with an Orangeman's dislike of waste, insisted that his courtiers ate all the asparagus including the inedible woody stem. Those who did not were not given a second helping.

Pellitory of the wall (*Parietaria officinalis*), as both its generic and botanical names imply, is found growing in the crevices of old walls in most temperate zones of Europe and the British Isles. For many centuries it has been included in pharmacopoeias for its demulcent properties. It contains abundant potassium nitrate and is diuretic and refrigerant. It helps diseases of the bladder and kidneys and is good for certain kinds of dropsy. Old books of husbandry also recommend it for getting rid of weevils if corn is placed with it. Early face-creams contained pellitory, and it was believed to 'comfort the body'. A very old remedy for this purpose entails sitting for two hours in three gallons of milk in which sprays of pellitory, rosemary, nettles and violets have been immersed.

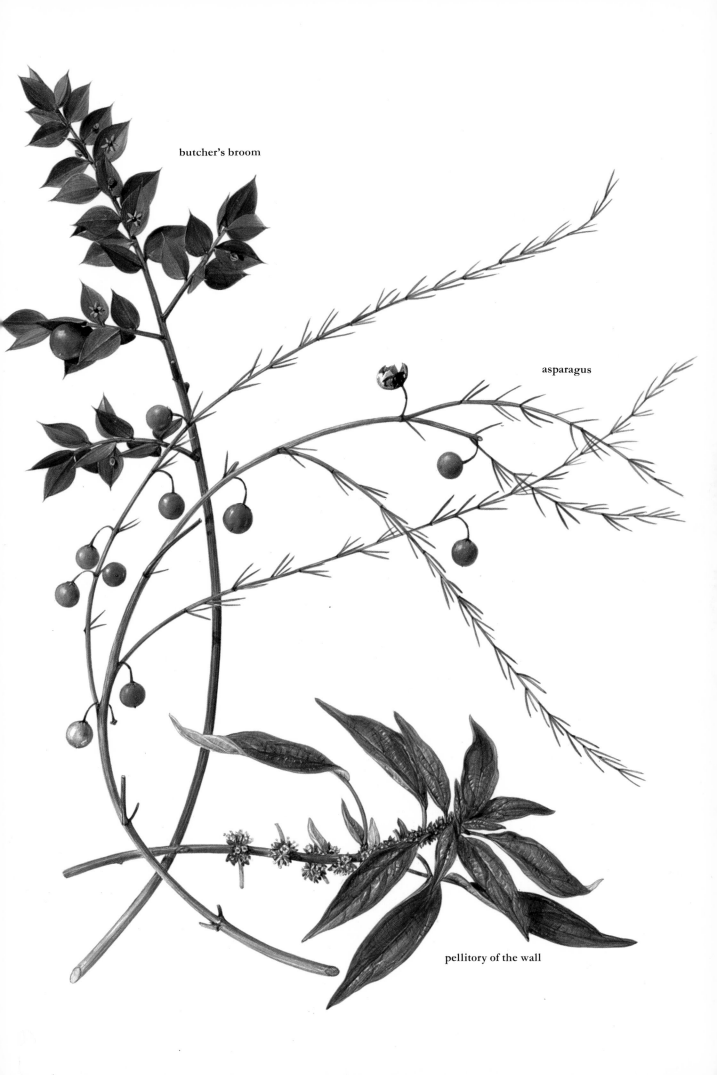

butcher's broom

asparagus

pellitory of the wall

Borage
Chinese lantern

'Ego borago gaudia semper ago' : 'I, Borage bring always joys.' This was Pliny's recommendation for **Borage** (*Borago officinalis*), beloved of physicians and herbalists because it was believed to make men merry and joyful, and to drive away sadness. For this reason Pliny called it *Euphrosinum*. This member of the Boraginaceae is a garden escape which may be found growing wild on waste ground in all temperate zones. Its flowers, which resemble brilliant blue stars, appear in June and July. The young leaves are used to flavour salads, vegetables and summer drinks, and in some parts of France the flowers are cooked as fritters. Gerard wrote that 'The leaves and floures of Borrage put into wine make men and women glad and merry, driving away all sadnesse, dulnesse, and melancholy.'

The herb contains potassium, calcium and other mineral salts, and has diuretic, antispasmodic, febrifuge, demulcent and emollient action. Its saline content makes it a useful restorative helpful to the blood and all the organs of the body. In Tudor times herbalists believed that 'a syrrup made of the floures of Borrage comforteth the heart, purgeth melancholy, and quieteth the phrenticke or lunaticke person.' Culpeper recorded the herb as flowering 'near' London 'as between Rotherhithe and Deptford by the ditch side.' Its ornamental flowers made it a popular motif in needle work and it can be seen in many examples of early embroidery. Today, as well as being valued for chest and throat complaints, it may still be taken as it was in ancient times 'to defend the heart'.

One of the most unusual and pretty plants, and one which often appears in illustrations to fairy stories, is the **Chinese lantern** (*Physalis alkekengi*) or winter cherry. Its delicate lacy calyx does resemble a little lantern especially when it has started to decay and its bright red fruit can be seen gleaming inside it. Like borage, the Chinese lantern is a garden escape and grows on waste ground, although it is often cultivated in gardens as an ornamental. It flowers between June and August. It is native to Mexico and is a member of the Solanaceae or nightshade family. The juicy berry is slightly acid but agreeable to the taste and quite high in vitamin content. They are usually eaten raw, and have mainly diuretic properties. They are known to some children as 'dewdrops'.

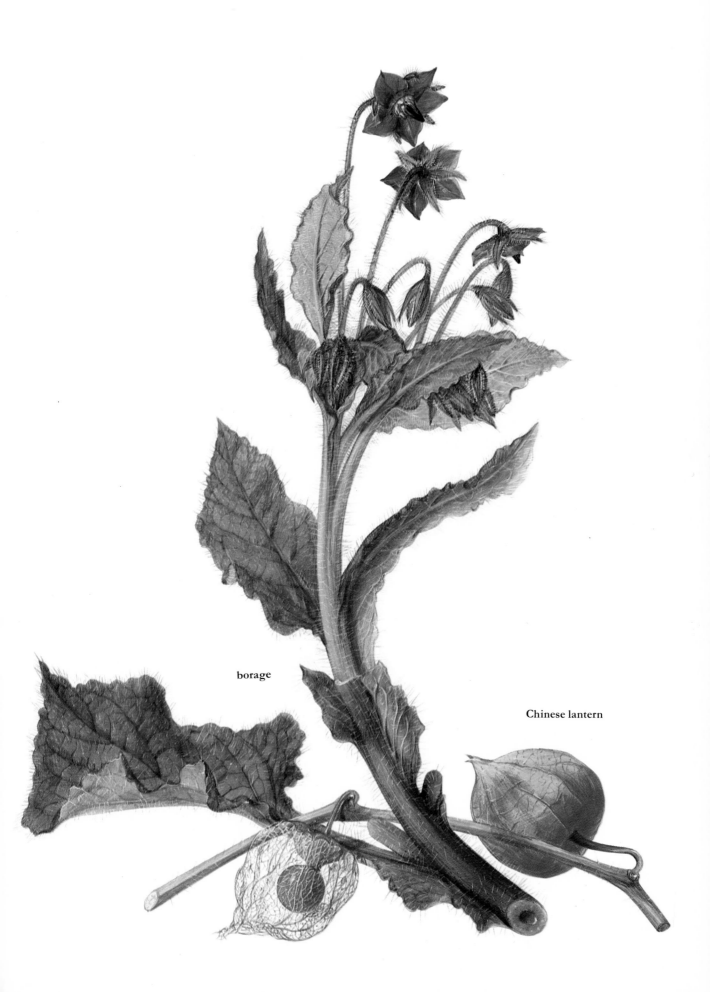

borage

Chinese lantern

Couch grass
Rusty-back fern
Elder

Cats and dogs are well aware of the virtues of **Couch grass** or creeping twitch (*Agropyron repens*) as, when they are ill, they will eat it in preference to any other grass in the fields. Physicians and herbalists since remote times have also been aware of the therapeutic properties of this grass, which, because of its long, creeping entwined roots, is the farmers' bane, as these are almost impossible to eradicate. It is these roots that are curative. However, even Gerard made allowances: 'Although that Couch-grasse be an unwelcome guest to fields and gardens, yet his physicke vertues do recompense those hurts.'
Couch grass is used for kidney and bladder ailments, and is so important to the French with their preoccupation with their inner organs that it even has a place in the *Larousse gastronomique*, under *Chiendent*. This, in fact, is another but very similar species, dog's tooth couch grass (*Cynodon dactylon*). The rhizomes of both grasses have diuretic and demulcent action. *C. dactylon* contains starch in addition to sugars, mannitol and triticin. The roots are collected in spring and autumn and are washed and dried after the tops have been removed. The word 'couch' is derived from the Anglo-Saxon word meaning 'holding on to life'.
Rusty-back fern (*Ceterach officinarum*) is a small fern native to Europe and western Asia, belonging to the Polypodiaceae. It likes growing in narrow cracks in old walls and on ruins. In the eighteenth century the leaves were official in some pharmacopoeias, as its botanical name indicates. These leaves or fronds contain tannin, mucilage and a bitter substance which imparts a vile taste to the drug; it can however be disguised with flavourings such as peppermint or aniseed. Infusions made from the fern have diuretic, bechic, expectorant and astringent properties. They are particularly helpful to sufferers from dysuria (difficulty in passing urine) when oxalic acid is present, and to prevent colic caused by kidney stones.
The **Elder** (*Sambucus niger*) is probably the most necromantic tree in the world. Not only was it unthinkable for a witch of any standing not to have an elder in the garden; quite often they actually lived in it, and country folk rarely chopped down this tree for fear that the branches would drip blood, the witch having been hacked in error, with disastrous consequences for the woodsman. From this old belief stem others: that the elder should never be planted too near the house, nor used as firewood, nor to make a cradle. If it is ever necessary to prune the elder it is wise to apologize to it first. It was used in many spells, and is the tree that Judas is said to have hanged himself from, although in Mediterranean countries the Judas tree (*Cercis siliquastrum*) has this distinction. Elder flowers cooked with gooseberries impart a most delicious flavour of muscatel.
Every part of the elder is useful. The leaves are mixed with linseed oil to make an external emollient application called green oil of elder, and they are also used in insecticides; the distilled water of the flowers known as *Aqua sambuci* is an astringent used in eye and skin lotions; the flowers also go into drugs for bronchial troubles, influenza and colds, and the berries, which are said to encourage longevity have, since ancient times been made into a 'port' wine. They make excellent jams, especially when mixed with apples, and are used by naturopaths in a cosmetic wash believed to be able to rejuvenate the skin. The active principle of the bark is a soft resin and an acid which is identical with valeric acid. There are also traces of many other substances such as salts, chlorophyll and tannic acid. The leaves contain the glucoside sambunigrin and the alkaloid sambucine. The *Larousse gastronomique* contains a recipe for elderberry gourilos. The woody outer casing of the stalks is pared away, and they are then cooked in the same way as endive stumps: half a cup of water and the juice of a quarter of a lemon with three ounces of butter to one pound of stalks.
Another member of the Caprifoliaceae is the dwarf elder (*S. ebulus*) which rarely grows to more than three feet. One of its country names is ground elder. A decoction of the root produces urination, making it very helpful in the treatment of dropsy. The leaves used as poultices relieve swellings and inflammations. The dwarf elder is said to grow near or in battlefields and to spring up where blood has been shed.

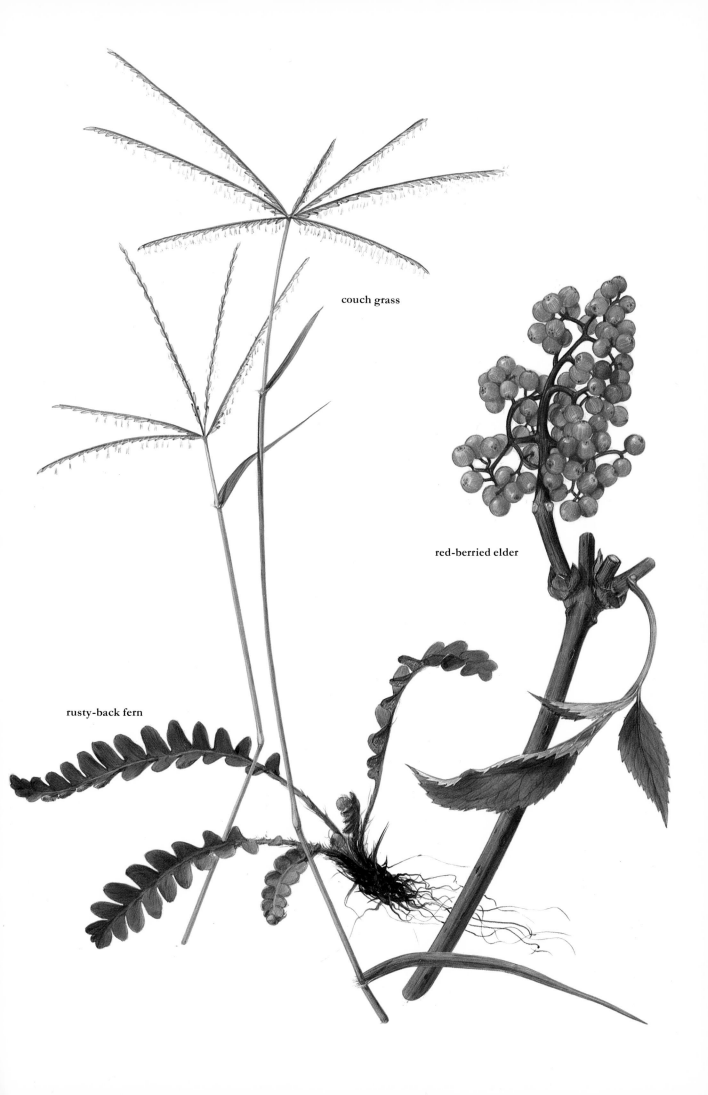

couch grass

red-berried elder

rusty-back fern

Bearberry
Cowberry
Golden rod
Juniper

Bearberry or beargrape (*Arctostaphylos uva-ursi*) was entered in the *British Pharmacopoeia* in 1788, and has remained there for the drug provided by the leaves, called arbutin, which is valuable in kidney diseases and digestive troubles. The leaves are gathered in early autumn and dried quickly so that they do not lose their dark green colour. Bearberry is found mostly in Scotland and the north of England, growing on heaths and mountainsides. This pretty little member of the Ericaceae is often catalogued under the more simple name of *uva ursi*.

The Ericaceae or heath family contains four very similar species: the red whortleberry or **Cowberry** (*Vaccinium vitis-idaea*); the bilberry (*V. myrtillus*), also known as blueberry and whortleberry (*v.* p. 152); the bog whortleberry (*V. uliginosum*); and the cranberry (*V. oxycoccus*). Gerard was much taken with the cowberry because 'they make the fairest carnation colour in the World . . . Indian *Lacca* is not to be compared thereunto', although he did not advise eating them. Later, Culpeper lamented the fact that the whortleberries, both red and black, were not more used in herbalism, thus confirming Gerard's scant information on them. The drug is contained in the leaves, which are hypoglycaemic, and have diuretic and antiseptic properties. These plants are widespread in Europe and are usually found on pasture land. The cowberry is mentioned in a gruesome Breton legend which tells of a young girl, Kermaris, who had both her arms cut off. By bathing in water in which cowberries had been steeped (how she gathered them without arms is part of the story) her arms miraculously grew again and she lived happily ever after.

Golden rod (*Solidago virgaurea*) has been a favourite with herbalists for many centuries. Arnald of Villanova (*c.* 1240–1311), the Catalan doctor and theologian, recommended it for curing calculus (stone in the bladder) and later Gerard prescribed 'this admirable plant' for healing wounds. Mocking the English for paying half a crown an ounce for imported golden rod when it grew wild in abundance on Hampstead Heath 'even as it were at our townes end', Gerard points the truth of the proverb: 'Far fetch't and deare bought is best for Ladies.' Culpeper claimed that it was 'inferior to none, both for inward and outward use.'

The flowers and leaves are used in medicine. Apart from its diuretic properties golden rod relieves hay-fever, which it also causes with its abundant pollen. Only one species grows wild in England but in the United States almost eighty species are to be found. Another name for this inestimable plant is Aaron's rod, an allusion to its great powers.

In his *De Re Rustica* Cato mentions the berries of **Juniper** (*Juniperus communis*) as the base of a wine with diuretic properties. This was possibly a forerunner of *Vin de Genièvre*, an aromatic, stimulating, bitter medicinal beverage made of juniper berries and absinthe in the Gâtais district of France. Juniper is also used in the distillation of gin, and is an excellent addition to marinades, sauerkraut and stuffings for guinea fowl and other game birds. In pharmacy the leaves and fruit are used for their carminative, stomachic, antiseptic, stimulant and diuretic action. They contain volatile oil, wax, resin, ligrin, salines, gum and sugar. Juniper stimulates the heart and kidneys and is helpful in certain forms of dropsy and digestive complaints. It is also used in veterinary medicine.

In Scandinavian countries the branches are burnt as a disinfectant. According to Culpeper there was nothing juniper could not cure or aid; its properties included healing leprosy, strengthening the brain, and procuring appetite when it was lost.

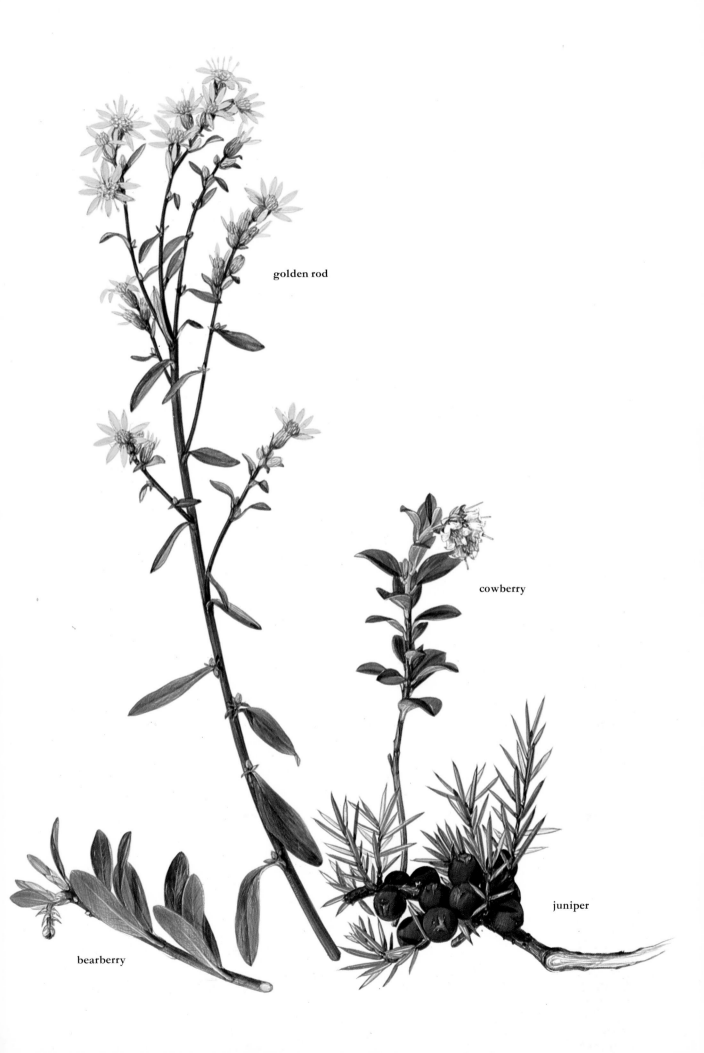

golden rod

cowberry

juniper

bearberry

Maize
Lycopodium
Herb mercury

Maize (*Zea mays*) or Indian corn has been cultivated by American Indians for thousands of years. It is probably indigenous to Peru, where it was known as *sara*. Maize never reverts to the wild and, unlike other cereals, cannot propagate itself but is dependent upon cultivation. In the sixteenth century it was introduced into France, indirectly through the Spanish invaders of Peru. It flourishes particularly well in wine-growing districts. From the top of the leafy bracts enclosing the grains emerges a silky tassel or beard. It is this corn silk which is used as a diuretic and demulcent; it has antiseptic properties. It contains maizenic acid, sugar, resin, fixed oil, mucilage and salts. Maize is the staple grain in Central America, Mexico and southern Africa. In the United States 90% is used as animal feed. The leaves are used for wrapping the 'whacking white cheroot' of Burma.

The most popular way of serving it for human consumption is 'on the cob' covered with butter. For this purpose it is either baked or boiled, but if boiled, salt should not be added until serving as it toughens the kernels. A teaspoonful of sugar should be put into the boiling water to bring out the corn's delicate flavour. Gerard's opinion of *Z. mays* was low: 'it is of hard and evill digestion, a more convenient food for swine than for men.' The only variety grown in England has pale gold seeds, but in America the grains may be red, chocolate brown or black. The Indians reverenced *Z. mays*, and the ritual of husking the maize has been described by Longfellow in *Evangeline*: 'In the golden weather the maize was husked, and the maidens/Blushed at each blood-red ear, for that betokened a lover.'

Lycopodium (*Lycopodium clavatum*) belongs to the Lycopodiaceae. Its country name is club moss although it is not a moss but possesses long creeping stems with forked branches and very thin leaves. The entire herb is employed for its diuretic action. The spores provide a light mobile powder which was used for coating pills, as a dusting powder and as a diluent in snuffs. In Poland and the USSR the spores are collected on a commercial basis. Lycopodium today is used in the form of a tincture for many urinary complaints. Because of its essential oil it is often employed in the theatre to simulate explosions; it produces a vivid flame and some smoke. The American ground pine (*L. complanatum*) has similar action and uses.

Herb mercury (*Mercurialis annua*) was so named in honour of Mercury, the messenger of the gods. It is a member of the Euphorbiaceae, and can thrive anywhere, springing up out of heaps of rubbish on waste ground or clustering around fruit trees in orchards. It varies in height from a few inches to three feet or more. The drug is obtained from the entire herb. It has diuretic and laxative action and is sometimes used to interrupt the secretion of milk. The leaves and stalks, particularly, are aperitive and mollifying. A diuretic decoction once popular in folk medicine was Mercury honey, but it is not advisable to experiment with this plant in the home. Homoeopathic preparations, however, have been found helpful. Early herbalists recommended the juice for removing warts.

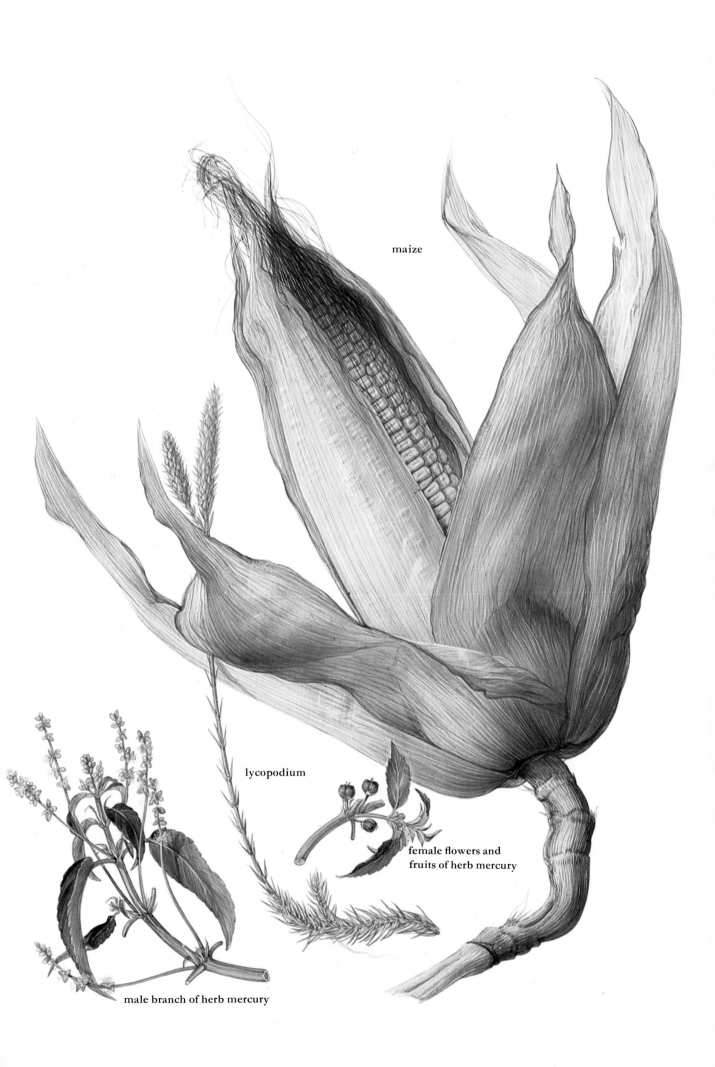

maize

lycopodium

female flowers and
fruits of herb mercury

male branch of herb mercury

Everlasting
Horsetail
Meadowsweet

The genus *Helichrysum* is so called for the perpetual radiant yellow of some of its species, e.g. *H. italicum*; the name comes from the Greek *helios*, 'sun', and *khrysos*, meaning 'golden'. Many other plants are also known as **Everlasting** flowers, including the cudweeds (*Gnaphalium*). The Romans put the downy leaves and stems into pillows and mattresses as a substitute for feathers, but the plants were also used medicinally in very early times. Pliny recommended the everlasting flower as a cure for quinsies and mumps with the certainty that there would never be a recurrence of either disease. The entire plant is used today for its astringent, pectoral and discutient action. In homoeopathy everlasting is recommended for some forms of sciatica, and is an excellent gargle. It is also useful for cramp in the feet and legs, and for stiffness of the joints in all parts of the body, either if the herb is rubbed on the affected parts, or if a decoction is drunk. Everlasting grows in most parts of Europe and America. Some of the cudweeds are to be found in Africa and the Levant. The plant, which symbolizes unceasing remembrance, is to be seen in large quantities in French cemeteries, where it is fittingly called *immortelle*. The French, who are too realistic to pay overmuch attention to death, give this plant to their dead because the flowerheads retain their colour throughout the winter without needing to be replaced.

The **Horsetail** (*Equisetum telmateia*), described by Culpeper as 'but knotted rushes, some with leaves and others without', belongs to the sole surviving family and genus of an order of plants that can be traced back in fossils to the Carboniferous period, about 390 million years ago, when the earth was covered with forests of gigantic horsetails. They are closely allied to ferns and bear no flowers. Their Latin name derives from *equus*, 'horse', and *saeta*, 'bristle', referring to the bristly appearance of the jointed stems. They grow in temperate northern regions, and are believed to be a favourite food of reindeer. In the seventeenth century this plant was known as 'scouring rush' because of the enormous quantity of silica it contains. It was used for scouring pewter, to which it gave a very fine finish, and in some remote districts it is still used for cleaning saucepans.

The presence of silica makes horsetail of inestimable value in the treatment of the eyes. It is also made into strengthening medicines for the heart, lungs and kidneys because of its diuretic and astringent action, and brings relief to sufferers from dyspepsia. Cardinal Newman (1801–1890), on a visit to Scotland, was struck by the distinctive appearance of a mass of horsetails growing in a little fir-wood. He described it as: 'a magic scene, created by the fairies for their especial use and pleasure. It was a forest in miniature, and a forest of surpassing beauty.'

Pretty little **Meadowsweet** (*Filipendula ulmaria*) is deservedly known in many countries as Queen of the Meadows, for there is nothing noxious about this plant at all. The Druids venerated it for its many domestic and medicinal uses. In the *Knight's Tale* Chaucer, who knew it as meadwort, gives it as one of the ingredients of a drink called Save. John Parkinson (1567–1650), who held in turn the offices of Apothecary to James I and King's Herbalist to Charles I, recorded that: 'Queene Elizabeth of famous memory did more desire it than any other herbe to strewe her chambers withall.' It was the early custom to cover floors with rushes and herbs, both to give some warmth underfoot, and to keep away smells and infection. Gerard extolled this herb, saying that 'the smell thereof makes the heart merrie, delighteth the senses: neither does it cause head-ache . . .' Meadowsweet was often used for flavouring drinks and a very good beer was, and still is, made from it. The leaves and flowers are used in the manufacture of certain vermouths. If they are left to infuse in wine or hydromel (a sort of mead made from honey and water) they impart a very refreshing flavour. The plant's action is astringent, diuretic, aromatic, tonic and sudorific. The entire herb is used and is particularly useful for treating diarrhoea in children. It helps the stomach, bowels and blood, and will cure skin eruptions and soreness of the eyes.

A form of meadowsweet beer may be made by boiling two ounces each of dried meadowsweet, agrimony and dandelion in six gallons of water for 20 to 30 minutes. Strain and add two pounds of sugar to the water with half a pint of barm or yeast. Leave it to stand for twelve hours in a warm place, and then bottle.

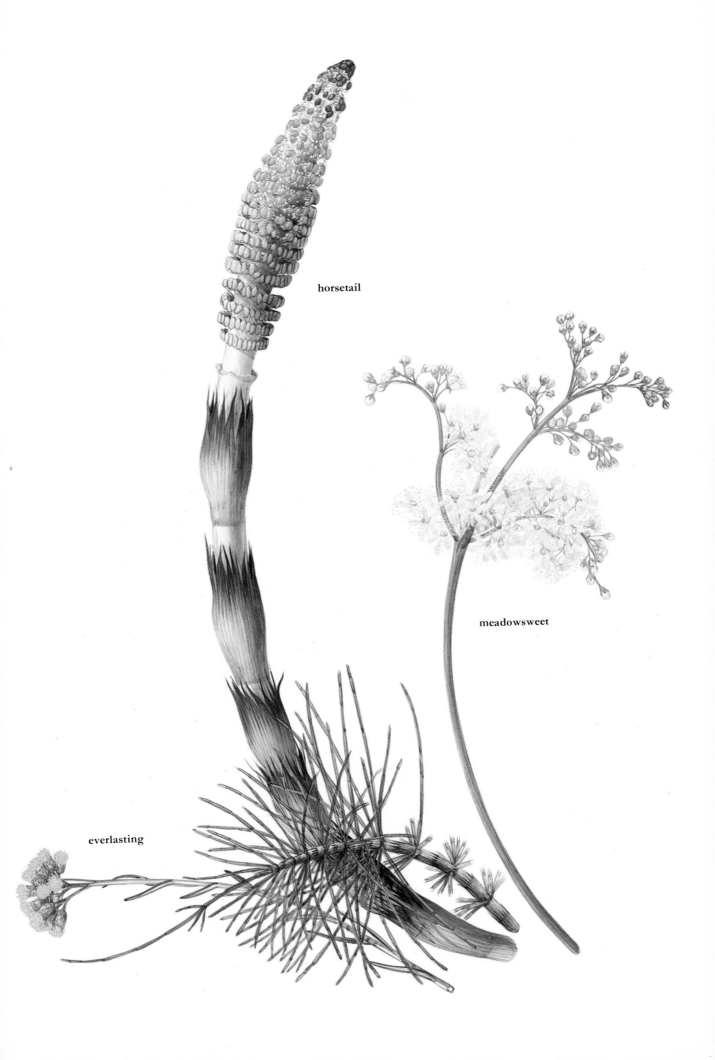

horsetail

meadowsweet

everlasting

Fumitory
Maidenhair fern
Woody nightshade

The 'lace-leaved lovely/Foam-tuft **Fumitory**' of Gerard Manley Hopkins is in fact a small, grey, frail and unobtrusive herb called *Fumaria officinalis* because early herbalists believed it to have sprung without seed from the earth's vapours: hence its name, from the Latin *fumus terrae*, 'smoke of the earth'. This little herb has been cultivated since ancient times as a medicine and cosmetic. It was believed to drive away melancholy, a disease of the time, to judge by the many herbs cultivated for that purpose. It grows in Europe, the United States, Iran, Nepal, Australia and South Africa. The herb and the leaves are used. Their constituents include fumaric acid and an alkaloid called fumarine, identical with corydaline (*v.* p. 211). Fumitory has diuretic, diaphoretic, alterative, aperient, anthelminthic and tonic action. It is excellent for liver derangement, being one of the old visceral tonics. It cures skin complaints and an infusion of the leaves was applied by ladies of quality to remove freckles. Pliny, who believed that its name came from its power of making the eyes water as smoke does, recommended it for restoring sight. American fumitory (*F. indica*) has the same action but is much stronger.

Maidenhair fern (*Adiantum capillus-veneris*) is known also as Venus's hair, a name believed to have been given to it by the early Latin *Herbal of Apuleius* in reference to its water-repelling properties, an attribute shared by Venus who rose, bone-dry, from the sea. It is possible that this name is much older as maidenhair was used in pharmacy many centuries ago. It originated in Afghanistan, the Himalayas and Iran, but now grows plentifully almost everywhere except Scotland. Because of its stimulant, demulcent and tonic action it is thought to be helpful in asthma and various pulmonary troubles. It is good for the liver, and some herbalists believe it to prevent baldness. The ashes, mixed with vinegar and olive oil and rubbed into the scalp, have been said to cure alopecia.

An addition to many punches, both hot and cold, in Georgian and Victorian times, was capillaire, the chief ingredient of which is maidenhair fern. To make it, it is necessary to infuse two ounces of the fresh plant in boiling water for ten hours. It should then be strained and added to a syrup made of three pounds of granulated sugar and three pints of water. Stir in two tablespoons of orange-flower water (available at chemists) and after a few minutes remove from the fire. Strain well and when cold bottle for use. The corks should be sealed. Capillaire is an excellent addition to summer drinks such as Sherry Cobbler and Cool Tankard.

Woody nightshade (*Solanum dulcamara*) belongs to the same genus as the potato, the tomato (in some classifications) and the aubergine, but is not quite so innocuous. Although it is less toxic than its relation deadly nightshade (*v.* p. 120), it should be taken only under medical supervision. The berries could be particularly harmful to children. Another name for the plant is bittersweet, because of the bitter-tasting twigs with their sweetish aftertaste. Woody nightshade is often mistaken for *belladonna*.

One of its ancient names was felonwort; *felon* meaning 'abscess'. The berries were cut open and bandaged over the sores. This practice is still in use where folk medicine is popular. Bittersweet has been used since at least Roman times, its botanical name *solanum* coming from the Latin *solamen*, 'comfort, solace', referring to its soothing narcotic properties. Its purple flowers and bright yellow stamens resemble those of the sweet potato. Its green berries turn orange and then red when ripe. The active ingredients are found in the stalks: they are an alkaloid solanine, an amorphous glucoside dulcamarine, starch, resin, sugar and gum. Its action is alterative, and it particularly affects all the organs of the senses. It is very helpful in skin diseases and rheumatism and in bringing relief to paralysed limbs. It also helps hay fever. The only other native British species of this genus is the black nightshade (*S. nigrum*; *v.* p. 122).

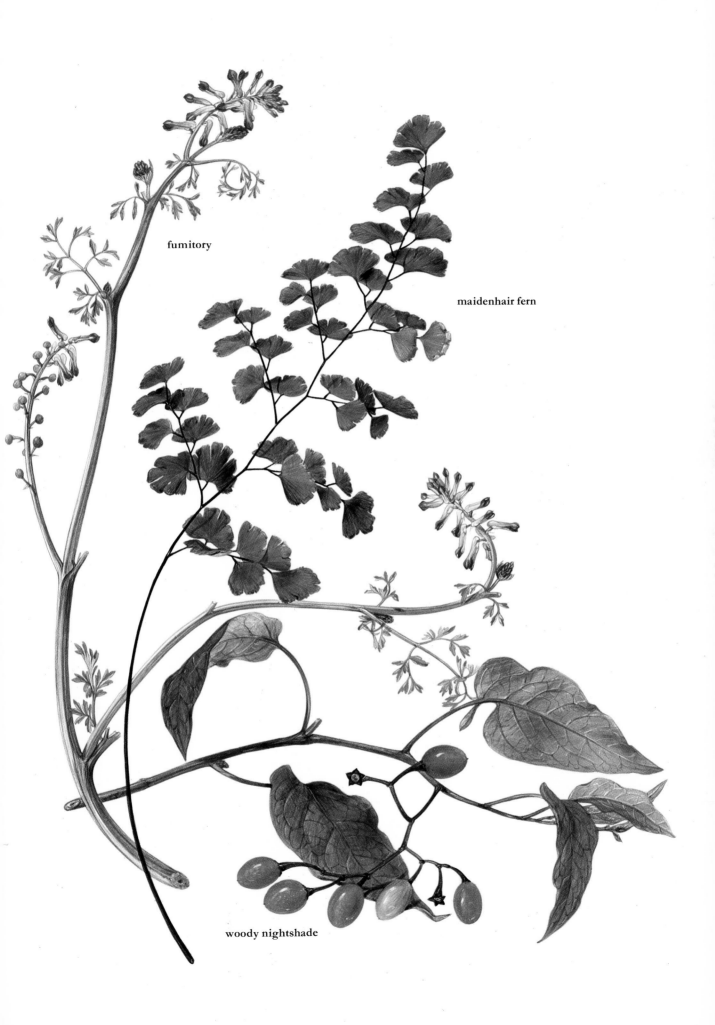

fumitory

maidenhair fern

woody nightshade

Shepherd's purse
Barberry

The insignificant little **Shepherd's purse** (*Capsella bursa-pastoris*) was once considered to be the most valuable member of the wallflower family by herbalists who have employed it for hundreds of years to stop internal bleeding from the stomach, uterus, kidneys and lungs, and also for external bleeding. Today it is used as a uterine haemostatic in cases of painful menstrual flow. The herb relieves the ache of joints swollen by rheumatism if it is put into a hot bath or applied externally as a poultice. It has antiscorbutic, tonic, diuretic and stimulant action due to the presence of bursinic acid and an alkaloid bursine. Shepherd's purse, like the plantain (*v.* p. 128), has travelled far and wide, following the Pilgrim Fathers to the New World, and going wherever man has gone, with the exception of the tropics. Its specific name has come from the resemblance of its fruits to the little leather pouches once carried by shepherds. In Ireland it is called Clappedepouche, and its other English familiar names are Mother's heart and St James' herb. Even wild birds love this plain little weed for the taste of its seeds which are also used commercially in birdseed mixtures.

'Conserve of Barbarie: quincies as such,/With sirops that easeth the sickly so much.' This reference to the **Barberry** (*Berberis vulgaris*) was made in 1573 in the *Good Housewife Physicke*. The dried bark of the plant contains the alkaloid berberine; all plants that have this alkaloid are valuable medicinally. It is used as a bitter tonic, sometimes in conjunction with quassia (*v.* p. 178), and it has been found helpful in many illnesses: jaundice, catarrh, gall complaints and also diabetes because it allays the thirst which often accompanies that condition. Barberry is employed as an antihaemorrhagic, the best results being obtained by mixing the fluid extract with fluid extract of cypress and Garus elixir. The bark, root and berries are all used in pharmacy; the berries contain malic and citric acids and tannin. In Nepal the dried berries of another species *B. aristata*, are eaten in place of raisins. Barberry is also known as jaundice berry, woodsour, pepperidge and maiden barber.

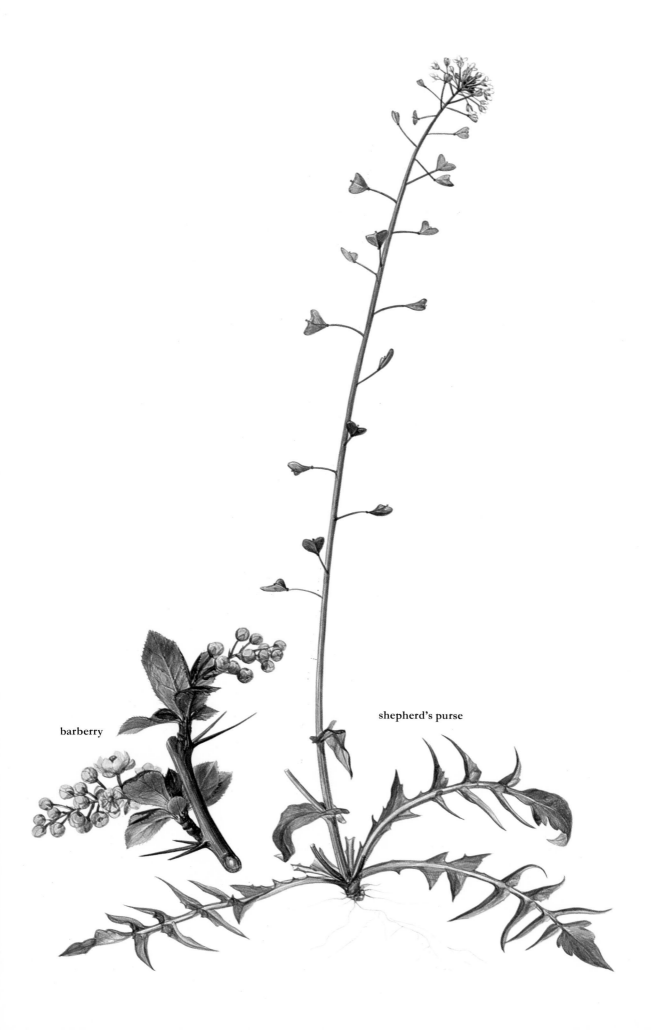

barberry

shepherd's purse

German chamomile
Groundsel
Tansy

German chamomile (*Matricaria chamomilla*) is one of the group of soothing plants that, made into a tisane and slowly sipped, acts as a sedative on the nervous system, cures digestive troubles and helps remove headaches and neuralgia. *M. chamomilla* is sometimes known as bachelor's buttons because of the appearance of the little flowerheads which contain the plant's healing properties: a bitter principle, coumarins, mucilage and, most important, a volatile oil with a sedative, carminative and tonic action. This herb will also give relief to smarting eyelids and cure earache and ringing in the ears. Roman chamomile (*Anthemis nobilis*; *v*. p. 156) is used in the form of bitters to soothe bad digestion. It is more popular in Britain than German chamomile, which is widely used on the Continent. The root of Spanish chamomile (*A. pyrethrum*) was once a cure for toothache.

This plant's generic name comes from the Latin *matrix*, 'womb', and in mediaeval times referred to the mayweed which was a specific herb for affections of the uterus. The chamomiles, mayweeds and feverfews are apt to cause confusion because of their superficial resemblance. They have all been used since ancient times by great doctors such as Hippocrates and Dioscorides. The chamomile was a favorite 'strewing' herb for covering floors because of the pleasant scent which emanates from the crushed plant when it is trodden on. Today it is often grown on crazy pavements in gardens for the same purpose. This herb is sometimes incorrectly called 'camomile'.

'*Dioscorides* saith, That with the fine pouder of Frankincense it healeth woundes in the sinues' writes Gerard in his *Generall Historie of Plantes*. Dioscorides must have often needed this remedy for the Roman troops to whom he was army physician. **Groundsel** (*Senecio vulgaris*) is another little weed whose humble appearance belies its healing properties. It was used chiefly for female complaints, as an emmenagogue and for painful menstruation, and for women suffering from anaemia due to excessive menstruation. In Elizabethan times 'the leaves stamped and strained into milke and drunke, helpe the red gums and frets in Children.' For pharmaceutical purposes the entire plant, except for the root, is used. Care should be taken however as groundsel contains the alkaloid senecione and is toxic, which is the reason for its waning popularity. It should be taken only under proper medical supervision.

Groundsel's generic name is from the Latin *senex*, 'old man', either because it soon dies, or for the white fluff of the fading flowerheads. Its common name is derived from the Anglo-Saxon *groundeswelge*, 'ground-swallower', from its habit of spreading everywhere.

A third member of the Compositae is **Tansy** (*Tanacetum vulgare*), which has rather sepulchral associations. Linnaeus in his *Flora Suecica* of 1775 records that tansy, which was regarded as a specific for intestinal worms, was used in Europe, and also in some parts of New England, in winding-sheets and shrouds. Sometimes, even, the plant was rubbed on the corpse to discourage worms. It is believed that this is how the plant got its name, which is derived from the Greek *athanasia*, 'immortality'.

The dried herb is still used as an anthelminthic, and also as a tonic. The leaves and flowerheads contain tanacetin, a bitter principle and tanacetone. These constituents are toxic; so it is not advised to use tansy in home medicine. The plant possesses sudorific, carminative and emmenagogic properties: it has a direct action on the uterus and was an old remedy against miscarriage. Some centuries ago it was worn inside the shoes to prevent ague.

Tansy has been used in traditional Easter cakes and puddings, to which it imparts a yellow colour as well as a flavouring. 'Tansies' were eaten in remembrance of the bitter herbs of the Jews at the Passover, and may indeed have tasted like them, as one old writer has described Tansy pudding as 'a nauseous dish'.

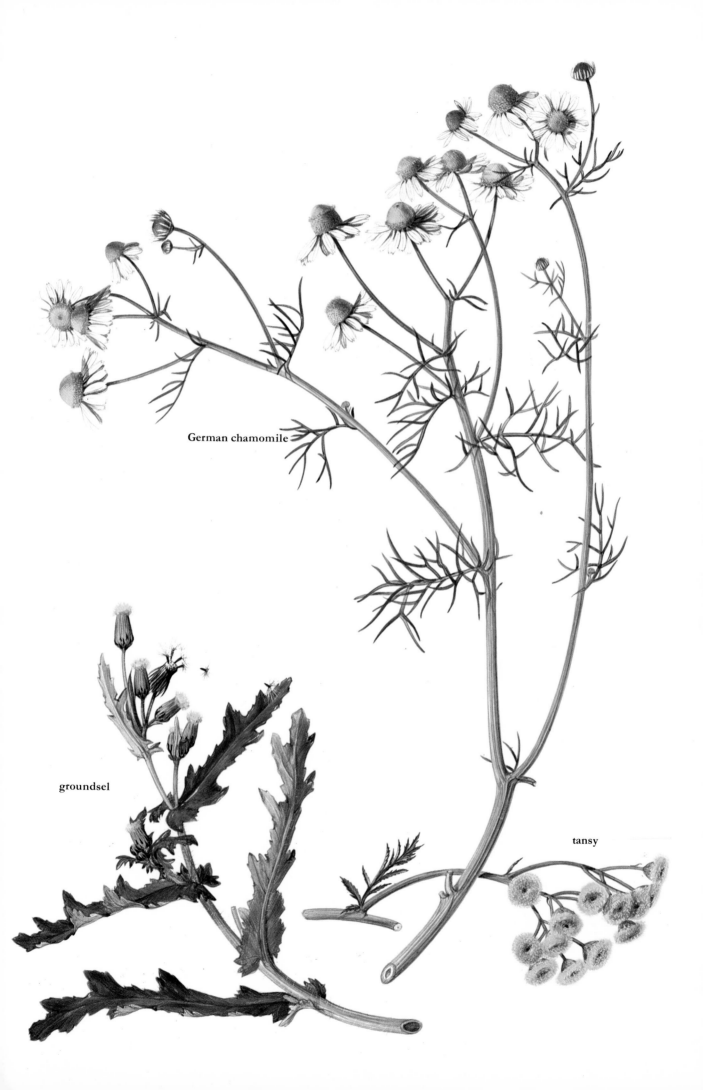

German chamomile

groundsel

tansy

Guelder rose
Ground pine
Yew

'. . . white as annunciating angels, and breathing a fragrance of lemons.' This is how Marcel Proust described the **Guelder rose** (*Viburnum opulus*), tall vases of which stood in Madame Swann's drawing-room. Chaucer also described this flower which he called the Gaitre-berry tree. He advised eating the berries raw, but they are very sharp and would be unpalatable to today's more sophisticated tastes. In Canada they are cooked like cranberries, and one of the plant's other names is high bush cranberry. Children call it the snowball tree. The guelder rose was first cultivated by the Dutch in Europe, and it is from Holland, known as Gueldersland, that it has received its English name. The wild variety produces berries, but the cultivated varieties do not. In Siberia the berries are distilled into a spirit.

The drug is derived from the dried bark, which is reputed to have a depressant action on the uterus that is due to the presence of an essential oil. It is recommended for the treatment of menopausal disturbances and is used in gynaecology. Herbalists employ the guelder rose for asthma and to relieve cramp in the extremities because of its fast action. Another species, the black haw (*V. prunifolium*), is used in pharmacy for the presence in the root and stem of salicin and a volatile oil.

The guelder rose usually blooms in bitterly cold weather, as Proust remarks in *A la recherche du temps perdu*.

The **Ground pine** (*Ajuga chamaepitys*) has many common names, among them Herb ivy, field cypress and yellow bugle. It does not, in fact, resemble the other bugles of the genus *Ajuga*. In pharmacy the herb is used for its diuretic and emmenagogic properties. It is considered by herbalists to be an excellent remedy for rheumatic pain and gout, and it is recorded that the Emperor Charles V was cured of gout after only eight weeks of taking an infusion of ground pine. It makes a refreshing mouthwash and gargle, and has been successful in treating some forms of dropsy.

The **Yew** (*Taxus baccata*) was a most useful ingredient in witches' spells as demonstrated by Shakespeare's Third Witch in *Macbeth*, when she threw into the cauldron 'slips of yew/Sliver'd in the moon's eclipse.' Yew trees are commonly planted in churchyards, possibly because of their association with immortality due to the great age they can attain; one yew in Derbyshire is believed to be about 2000 years old. Because the wood was used for making bows there is a theory that it was to protect the trees from damage by cattle (and also to save the cattle from being poisoned by the leaves), churchyards being well fenced. This theory is unlikely as the best wood for bows came from foreign yews. The tree's generic name comes from *toxos*, 'bow, arrow'.

All parts of the tree are poisonous except the berries, but even these have been known to cause death. A tincture of the leaves is used in homoeopathy for night sweats. It is not advised to take this plant in any form except under medical supervision. It has a strong influence on the brain. Gerard scoffed at the superstitions connected with the yew, and admitted to having eaten the berries when he 'was yong and went to schoole' but Thomas Johnson, his first editor in 1636, was more cautious and added in his edition of the *Herball*: 'Divers affirme that in Province in France, and in most hot countries, it hath such a maligne qualitie, that it is not safe to sleepe or long to rest under the shadow thereof.'

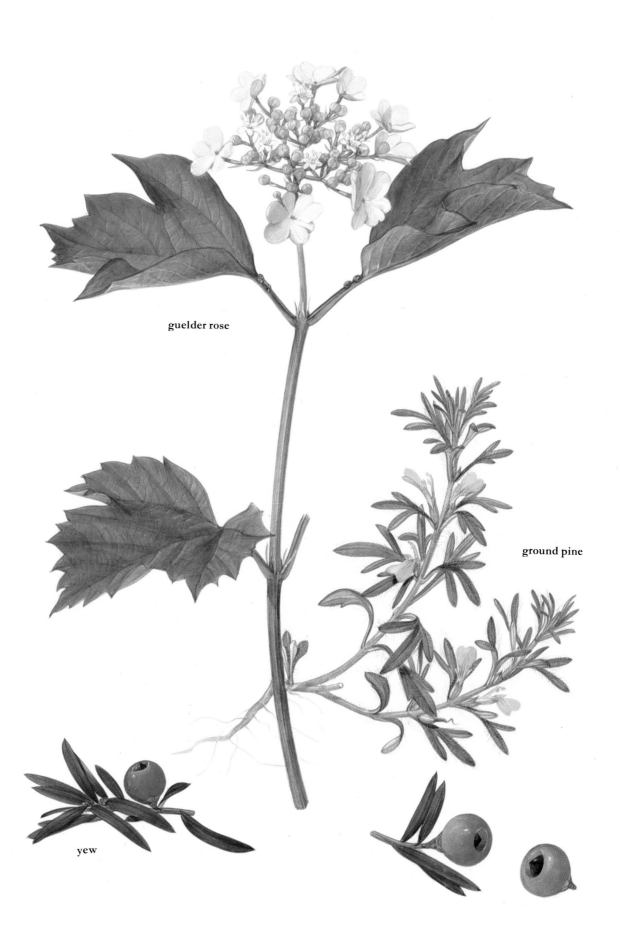

guelder rose

ground pine

yew

Savin
Wallflower
Ergot of rye

'Fatal Sabina, Nymph of Infamy' was how Abraham Cowley (*c.* 1618–1667) referred to **Savin** (*Juniperus sabina*), but he was alluding to the malpractices in which the plant was used by reason of its specific action on the uterus and the male genitalia. This is why savin is also known as Devil's tree and magician's cypress.

The fresh or dried young shoots provide the drug. Their constituents are an essential oil, gallic acid, resin, potassium salts and other substances. The plant has emmenagogic, diuretic and alterative action. Herbalists put the leaves into a versatile ointment which removes warts and cures baldness. The most beautiful specimens of savin are found in Greece, where it attains the size of a tree and bears deep purple fruit.

There is a Scottish legend that the **Wallflower** (*Cheiranthus cheiri*) was first seen on the wall of a castle from which a young girl had fallen to her death while trying to elope with her lover. The derivation of its generic name is obscure, one theory being that it comes from the Greek *kheir*, 'hand', and *anthos*, 'flower': this refers to the mediaeval custom of carrying small bunches of wallflowers when going out-of-doors, as a protection against germs and smells.

The flowers, seeds and stems are used in medicine. The seeds contain myrosine, and the plant has emmenagogic and tonic action. It is used for uterine and liver disorders, for enlarged glands and to purify the blood. It has a specific action on the muscles and sinews. Paracelsus in the *Doctrine of Signatures* prescribed the wallflower for jaundice, and Culpeper recommended the yellow wallflower as being the best for medicine. He used a conserve of the flowers 'as a remedy both for the apoplexy and palsy'.

Ergot of rye (*Claviceps purpurea*) is the resting stage of a parasitic fungus which attacks some cereals. It sometimes grows in the ovary of the rye (*Secale cereale*), breaking down the rye protein. It should be employed in medicine only for its active constituents: the groups of alkaloids known as ergotoxine, ergotamine and ergometrine, the last having a direct effect on the pregnant uterus, increasing the strength of the contractions.

If eaten, even for a short time, rye flour which has been contaminated with ergot produces a pathological condition known as ergotism. This terrible disease causes the victims to feel as though they are literally on fire and they suffer from strong hallucinations such as being pursued by wild beasts. Very often these hallucinations drive them insane. Constriction of the blood vessels eventually causes gangrene, especially of the legs. Pregnant women invariably miscarry. A case of ergotism in the present time occurred in a French village during 1951, when the local baker unknowingly used contaminated flour with the result that almost the entire village died. One young girl believed she saw geraniums growing out of her arms. In the Middle Ages ergotism was not recognized as a disease and victims were thought to have become possessed by demons. The Order of St Anthony was founded to take care of them.

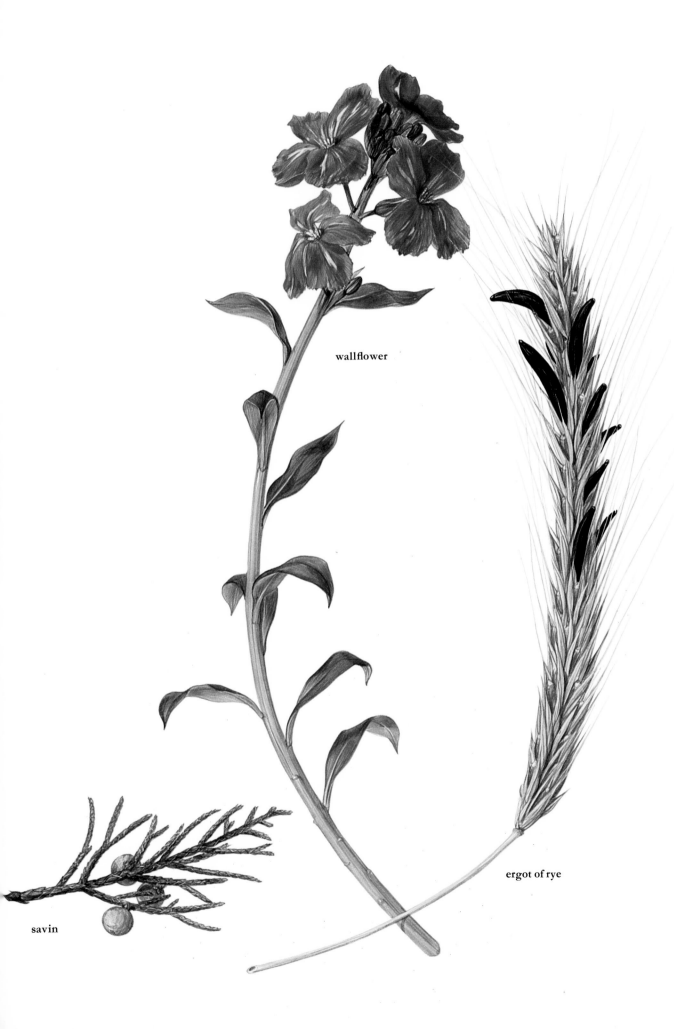

wallflower

ergot of rye

savin

Onion
Nettle
Bilberry

A bunch of **Onions** (*Allium cepa*) hung outside the door would absorb the infection of the Plague and the inhabitants would be saved. So it was believed in the Middle Ages, and it is recognized that the sulphur contained in the onion acts as a strong disinfectant. Since very early times this vegetable has been esteemed as a food and a medicament. The Romans made great use of it, and the ancient Egyptians worshipped it as a symbol of the Universe. Today in Egypt, the onion is an extremely popular dish; the Egyptian varieties contain a large amount of saccharine.

The bulb is used in pharmacy to help catarrh, hay-fever, nasal discharge, smarting eyes and earache. Eaten in sufficient quantities, especially baked or boiled, the onion is believed to help ward off colds in winter, and also to induce sleep and cure indigestion. It has diuretic, stimulant, expectorant and antiseptic properties. In the fifteenth century the juice was mixed with vinegar to make a cosmetic wash for removing freckles and spots. Queen Elizabeth I's surgeon William Clowes, used onion juice to cure burns caused by gunpowder. Before him Ambroise Paré (1517–1590) had used it to heal gunshot wounds. The onion is one of the most stimulating flavourings in cookery, particularly if eaten raw, as attested in his *Recipe for Salad* by the Reverend Sydney Smith (1771–1845): 'Let onion atoms lurk within the bowl,/And, scarce-suspected, animate the whole.'

'Tender-handed stroke a nettle,/And it stings you for your pains;/Grasp it like a man of mettle,/And it soft as silk remains.' These *Verses Written on a Window* by Aaron Hill (1685–1750) state a fact, although few people would care to put it to the test. The **Nettle** (*Urtica dioica*) is mentioned in the works of all the most celebrated ancient writers on medicine: Nicander (probably second century BC) said it was an antidote against the venomous qualities of hemlock, toadstools and quicksilver; Apollodorus (third century BC) recommended it as a counterpoison for henbane and the bites of serpents and scorpions; and Pliny, at the beginning of the Christian era, prescribed the nettle's own juice to cure its stings, a remedy still employed by homoeopaths. This herb is one of the most highly valued in domestic medicine for the varied illnesses and hurts it can ease. It is reputed to help gout, asthma, tuberculosis, and, applied externally, heals burns. Country people make it into wine or beer and drink it as a tea. Because of the iron, protein, sodium and lime contained in the nettle, it is an excellent addition to cattle fodder and poultry food.

Before World War II vast quantities were imported into Britain from Germany. During the war there was a drive to collect as much of the home-grown nettle as possible; the dark green dye obtained from the plant was used for camouflage, and it was also used medicinally. The Roman nettle (*U. pilulifera*) originally came to Britain with the invading Roman army. The soldiers planted the seeds to keep themselves warm: they flogged their legs and arms with nettles to keep their circulation going. Before cotton began to be imported, people spun flax from the fibres. Hans Andersen wrote a story of a princess whose eleven brothers were changed into swans. To break the spell she had to weave eleven coats out of nettle-fibre and throw one over each swan. There were not sufficient nettles, and so the youngest prince was left with a swan's wing in place of one arm.

Nicholas Culpeper (1616–1654) thought highly of the **Bilberry** or whortleberry (*Vaccinium myrtillus*) and tried to promote the greater use in 'physic' of both this plant and the red whortleberry or cowberry (*v.* p. 136). The leaves are hypoglycaemic and contain flavonoids and tannins, also an ash rich in manganese. The berries are used in confectionery and in cooking, usually in pies and tarts: a lot of sugar is needed. Bilberries contain vitamins A, C and P.

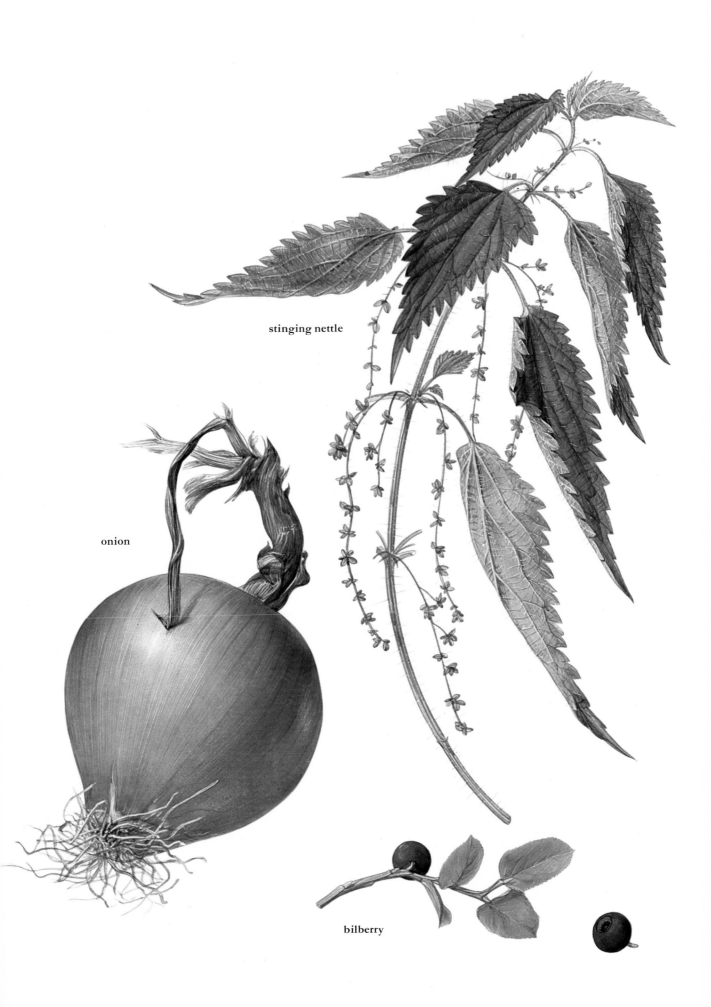

stinging nettle

onion

bilberry

Galega
Star anise
Fennel

Galega (*Galega officinalis*) is better known to most people by its country name of goat's rue, but in pharmacy and in homeopathy it is always referred to by its generic name. Its country name comes from the old belief that goats will give more milk if they feed on this herb. It belongs to the Papilionaceae, a subfamily of the Leguminosae. Galega is a native of Italy but flourishes in most temperate parts of Europe including Britain.

The drug comes from the entire plant, including the flowers. It has hypoglycaemic and galactogenic action and is taken in the form of an infusion. Early herbalists in the sixteenth and seventeenth centuries prescribed goat's rue for mild and serious complaints: a footbath for persons tired with overwalking, and in a decoction to cure smallpox. In the north of England it was used in place of rennet to make cheeses. The flowers contain an acidity which is got through distillation, and in some districts it was known as cheese-rennet.

The aromatic Chinese or **Star anise** (*Illicium verum*) must not be confused with the Umbelliferous aniseed (*v.* p. 42). It is named for the decorative shape of its fruit, which makes an agreeable tisane. It is also known as the yellow-flowered starry aniseed tree of China. The Chinese have been using it medicinally for centuries, especially for rheumatism and lumbago, and many Chinese dishes are seasoned with it. The nightwatchmen of Japanese temples burnt star anise as a chronometer to denote when the bells should be rung.

The seeds and oil are used in pharmacy for their stimulant, carminative, galactogenic, diuretic and digestive action. The constituents are a volatile oil, mucilage, resin, saponin, proto-catechnic acid, cane sugar and a little ash. An excellent remedy for acute nasal catarrh is made from star anise. It is also widely used in the liqueur industry. *I. floridanum*, the red-flowered aniseed tree, is a native of Florida and has similar properties but is not so much used.

'Crabs, salmon, lobsters are with Fennel spread/That never touched the herb till they were dead' said *The Art of Cooking* in 1700. To most people **Fennel** (*Foeniculum vulgare*) is better known as the finest herb for flavouring fish dishes, than as a medicinal plant. Yet it has been used for its curative properties since ancient times, being especially valued as a restorer of lost eyesight, and, so it was believed, having the power to remove cataracts. The ancient Greeks gave it to their Olympic competitors to increase their strength while preventing them from putting on weight. Culpeper, centuries later, wrote: 'It is much used in drink to make people more lean that are too fat' and in some countries where herbal medicine is still practised, fennel is made into soups, or eaten as a vegetable, by people trying to slim. The Greek name for fennel is *marathron*, which may come from *maraino*, 'I grow thin'. In the eighteenth century the peeled stalks were eaten like celery, to induce sleep.

The fruits and roots are used for their galactogenic, carminative, stimulant and diuretic action. Fennel is believed to have originated in Syria and the Azores, but it will grow in almost any soil, especially where there is plenty of sun. It is a benevolent herb, all parts of it being agreeable to the stomach. It is thought to impart strength and courage. In the Middle Ages supernatural powers were attributed to fennel which was believed to drive away evil spirits. In early times therapeutic doses of fennel oil had been observed to cause hallucinations and a form of madness resembling epilepsy. Used as a seasoning, appreciable quantities of the oil are not absorbed into the system, but oil distillates should only be taken under medical advice.

154

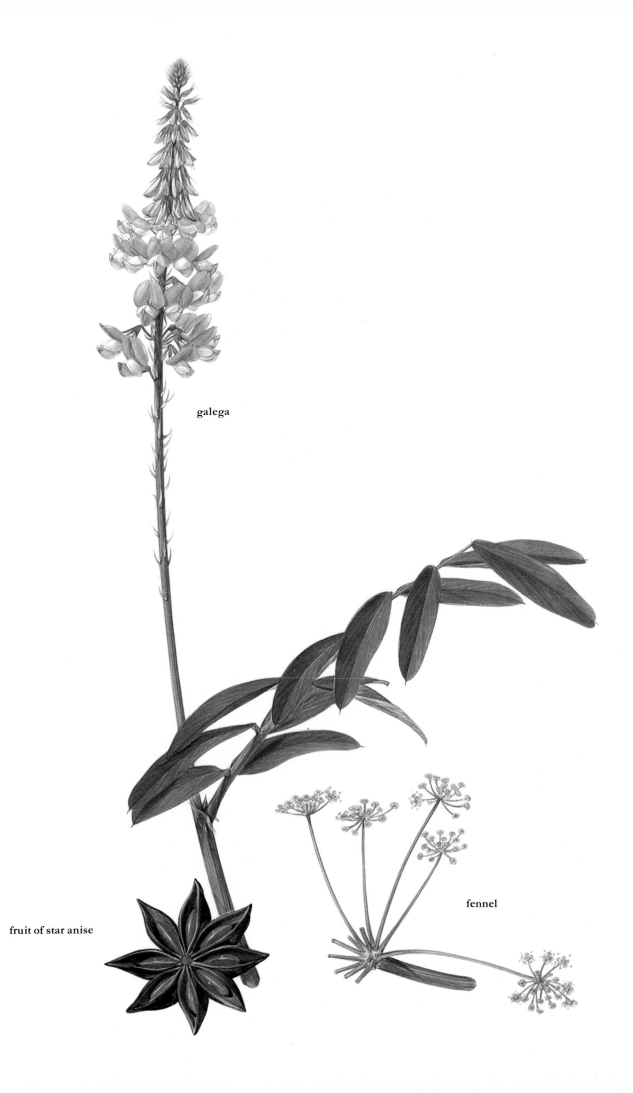

galega

fruit of star anise

fennel

Walnut
Comfrey
Roman chamomile
Yellow chamomile

'A woman, a dog and a walnut tree, the more you beat them the better they be.' This proverb goes back at least to the time of Ovid (43 BC–c. 17 AD), who wrote a poem, *Nux*, on man's ingratitude towards a tree which provides him with such valuable wood and fruit. The **Walnut** (*Juglans regia*) was appreciated in the ancient world for its nutritive and medicinal properties, and was known as Jupiter's nuts or Jove's acorns because men believed that when they were eating acorns at the earth's beginning, the gods were feasting on nuts. Walnuts are reputed to promote love: the custom of throwing nuts at weddings dates back to ancient Greece. Nevertheless, the walnut has an evil reputation, especially in remote parts of Italy. Demons are said to inhabit walnut trees and to dance around them at night.

The leaves contain the drug, and must be collected early in the summer, without any leaf-stalk; they must then be dried quickly in the shade so that they do not turn brown. Sufferers from skin eruptions that have not yielded to any other treatment have been cured by tinctures of the leaves or bark which have astringent action. Homoeopaths use a tincture of the leaves for cutting wisdom teeth. Since very early times all nuts have had the reputation of keeping the arteries soft. Culpeper wrote in his *Herball*: 'the kernals when old and therefore more oily – heal wounds of the sinews, gangrene and carbuncles' and: 'stays the falling of the hair, and makes it fair, being anointed with oil and wine.' Before him, Paracelsus in the *Doctrine of Signatures* had prescribed the oil from the nuts as being good for the scalp and hair. The rind and oil make a stain used in furniture making. Artists, too, use the oil for mixing their paints.

Unlike fennel, walnuts are fattening. They are excellent pickled, and eaten with cold meat. It is said that one tree will not fruit without another; so it is usual to see two trees planted near each other.

Comfrey (*Symphytum officinale*) is another ancient healing herb known to the Greeks and Romans. Its old name was knitbone; the leaves, made into poultices, were believed to help sprains, swellings and bruises. The term *officinale* denotes that this plant was cultivated in monastery gardens in the days when monks were the only physicians the common people had recourse to. Comfrey was reputed to suppress bleeding, and was used for bronchial and other inflammatory complaints. Old herbalists made an infusion to relieve colds and bronchitis: a pint of boiling water was poured on to an ounce of the dried leaves and left to stand for 30 minutes at least. It was then strained for use. At one time comfrey was used for fodder, but it is not as popular with farmers today as it once was.

Roman chamomile (*Anthemis nobilis*) is so called because of the belief that the invading Romans brought the seeds with them to Britain. It is another member of the comforting group of chamomiles (*v.* p. 146) which so many people find soothing, drunk in the form of tisanes or tea. *A. nobilis* has bitter-tonic properties and is an excellent remedy for indigestion. It reduces inflammations and acts as an antispasmodic and emmenagogue.

The **Yellow chamomile** (*A. tinctoria*) possesses very similar properties to *A. nobilis*, and may be used in its place. When carpets were perquisites of the rich alone, and most people had bare floors of stone or wood, the chamomile was a popular strewing herb. When it was trodden on, it gave off a fresh sweet scent which was a comfort in those insanitary times.

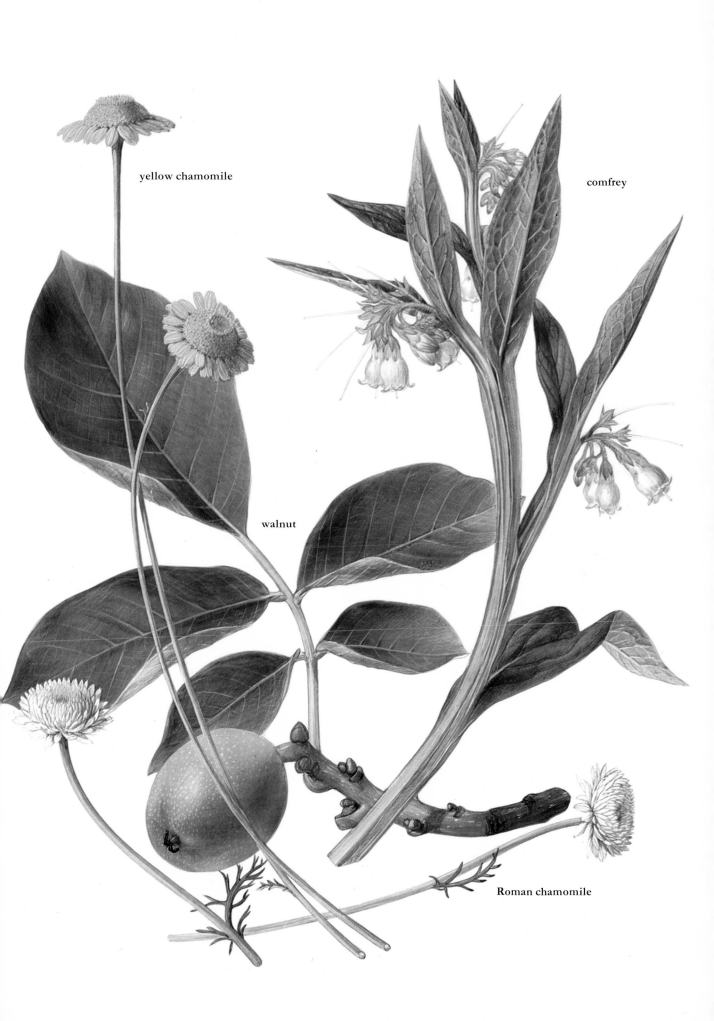

yellow chamomile

comfrey

walnut

Roman chamomile

Betony
Myrtle
Marigold

Betony (*Stachys officinalis*), which for centuries has been held in high esteem by all the greatest doctors, is now ignored by everyone except herbalists. This is because it yields no indication of its therapeutic value to modern analytical methods. In ancient Greece they said: 'Sell your coat, and buy betony', and Antonius Musa, physician to the Emperor Augustus, wrote a book devoted entirely to this herb, which has tonic, aperitive, carminative and healing properties. Turner, Parkinson, Gerard and Culpeper have spoken highly of betony, Gerard writing in his herbal: 'Betony is good for them that be subject to the falling sicknesse, and for those also that have ill heads upon a cold cause. It maketh a man to have a good stomacke and appetite to his meate.'

The drug is largely concentrated in the leaves. Varicose ulcers and sores of various kinds may be healed by the application of poultices. Betony is highly recommended by herbalists for insomnia, and pains in the head from whatever cause. The early Latin *Herbal of Apuleius* spoke for all those who know betony: 'It is good whether for man's soul or for his body; it shields him against visions and dreams.'

Myrtle (*Myrtus communis*) is dedicated to Venus who rose out of the waves, because it flourishes better near the sea than anywhere else. It is still the custom in many European countries for brides to wear wreaths of myrtle, symbolizing love and constancy. In the sacred Eleusinian mysteries the high priest and the initiates were crowned with myrtle, but it has a dual character. After its later dedication to Mars it became debased and the symbol of unchaste desire. Wine in which myrtle leaves had been steeped was said to become more potent and to encourage sensuality. Chiefly the leaves, but also the fruit, which is a many-seeded blue-black berry, are used in pharmacy, their content of tannin, essential oil, resin and a bitter principle giving them astringent, antiseptic and haemostatic action. As a nerve sedative and stimulant to the mucous membranes, *M. communis* is highly recommended.

'The Marigold floureth from Aprill or May even untill Winter, and in Winter also, if it bee warme. The Marigold is called *Calendula*: it is to be seene in floure in the Calends almost of every moneth': thus Gerard explains the botanical name of **Marigold** (*Calendula officinalis*), which men believed could be seen on the Calends, or first day, of every month throughout the year. These flowers are the 'marybuds' of Shakespeare, the prefix 'mary' coming from the belief that they were worn by Our Lady. In India, which may have been the marigold's country of origin, the gods and goddesses adorning the temples are crowned with wreaths of marigolds.

This beautiful and kindly herb is full of goodness: medicinal properties are present in the entire plant, particularly in the petals, which are made into ointments for cuts, burns, bruises and sores. Marigold, in the form of an infusion, soothes red, watery eyes, gives relief in bronchial ailments, helps combat anaemia, induces perspiration in fever, and is prescribed in cases of amenorrhoea and dysmenorrhoea. In the sixteenth century in many countries, but especially Holland, grocers and spice-sellers had barrels filled with the dried petals, which were sold in large quantities for use in drinks, broths and possets, and for medicaments. The fresh petals, sprinkled on salads, give a piquant flavour. An old recipe for marigold cheese required the milk of seven cows, and the cream from the milk of seven more cows. Of the plant mixed with other herbs, Fletcher (1579–1625) wrote: 'These for frenzy be/A speedy and a sovereign remedy,/The bitter wormwood, sage and marigold.'

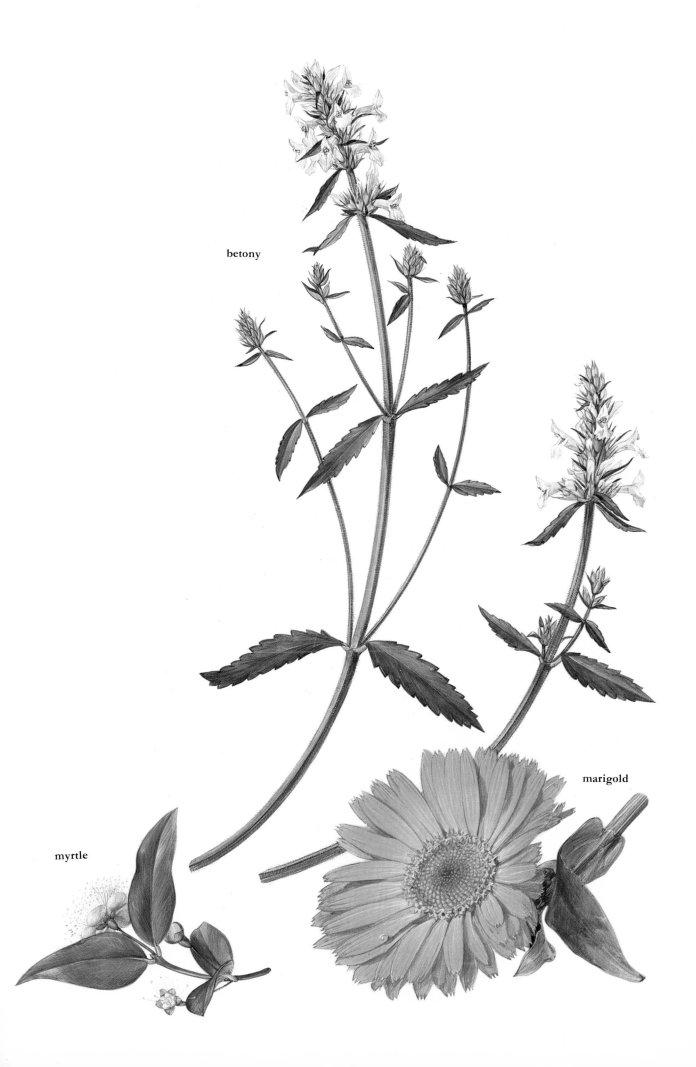

betony

marigold

myrtle

Burdock
Birch
Toad-flax

'By its leaves or seed you may draw the womb which way you please, either upward by applying it to the crown of the head in case it falls out; or downwards in fits of the mother, by applying it to the soles of the feet; or if you would stay it in its place apply it to the navel, and that is one good way to stay the child in it.' This was one of the uses to which the seventeenth-century herbalist Nicholas Culpeper put the **Burdock** (*Arctium lappa*), which he also knew as clot-bur from the thorny flowerheads whose hooked points cling to any person or animal that touches them. These burrs gave the plant its botanical names, from the Greek *arktos*, 'bear', after the burrs' fancied resemblance to a bear, and the Latin *lappa*, 'burr'.

Burdock is common on waste ground, in ditches and on roadsides, growing in most parts of Europe and northern Asia. Every part of the plant is useful in pharmacy: seeds, flowers, leaves and root, which have alterative, diaphoretic, antiscorbutic, astringent, diuretic and hypoglycaemicizing action. The herb influences the sebaceous and sweat glands, and is valuable in uterine displacements and for purifying the blood; it clears up eczema, acne, boils and dandruff. If the stalks are picked before flowering they can be stripped of their rind and boiled like asparagus. They should be eaten with a little butter. Burdock's country names are beggar's buttons or love's leaves.

The **Birch** (*Betula alba*) symbolizes good fortune and kindness, and the return of spring. To the herbalist it is a purifier of the blood, a tonic and stimulant, and a pain-killer. The birch tree can grow to a height of 20 metres (65 feet) and is found in North America, Russia, Scandinavia, parts of Germany and in places where the climate is rather cool. The drug is derived from the bark and the leaves. Birch oil, obtained from the bark, is useful for skin affections such as eczems, and as a skin tonic and blood cleanser. The leaves contain tannin, betulin, mucilage and a volatile oil, with diuretic and stimulant properties. In Sweden poultices of the leaves are applied to ease rheumatic pains, and the Chinese use a decoction of the bark for jaundice and bilious fevers, and as a tonic for the middle-aged and elderly. Birch twigs are used in sauna baths. Pliny (*c*. AD 23–79) claimed that the books of Numa Pompilius which were buried with their author in 700 BC, had been written on birch wood.

Practically all parts of the **Toad-flax** (*Linaria vulgaris*) contain active principles. Its constituents include two glucosides, linarin and pecto-linarin; linarosin; linarium; antirrhinic acid; mucilage; sugar and tannin, giving it an astringent, hepatic, antiscorbutic, detergent and predominantly diuretic action. One of the plant's old names was urinals, because of its powerful diuretic effect. In the form of an ointment it can cure boils, haemorrhoids and fistulae, and as an infusion it has been recommended for illness involving the urinary tract, jaundice and dropsy. Toads are said to be fond of sheltering under the leaves, but the prefix 'toad' may ultimately derive, not from this, but from a misreading as *bufonis* ('toad's') of the Latin *beneficus*, 'useful'. The ivy-leaved toad-flax (*L. cymbalaria*) has similar properties, and adds a pungent cress-like flavour to salads.

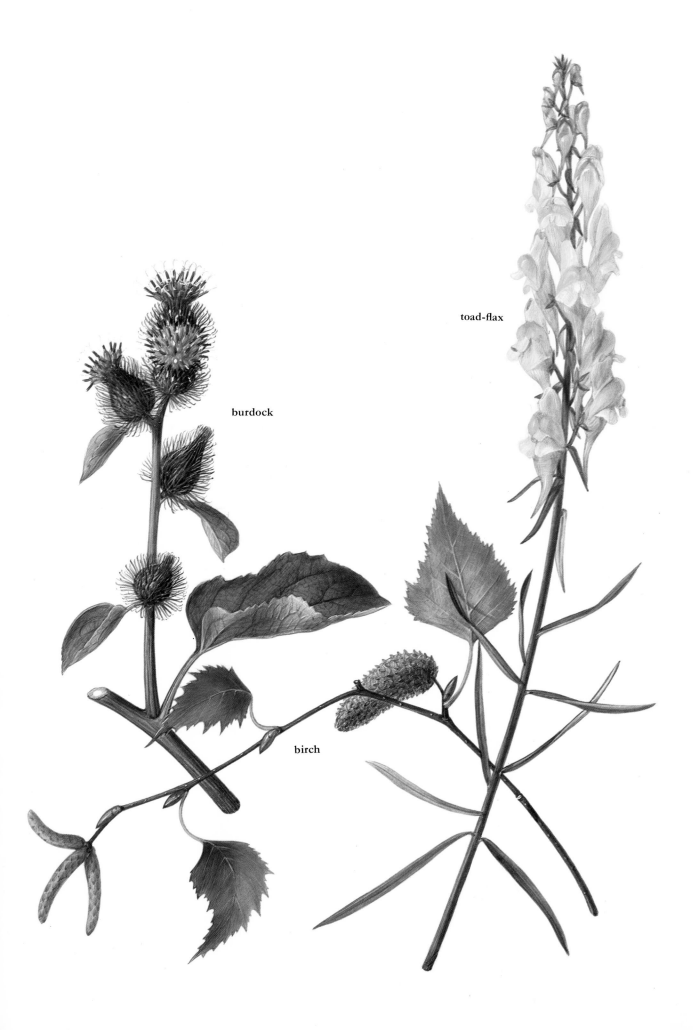

burdock

toad-flax

birch

Mezereon
White hellebore
Spotted hemlock

Mezereon (*Daphne mezereum*) is more usually known by its generic name Daphne, after the nymph who, fleeing from the amorous Apollo, metamorphosed into this shrub of the Thymelaeaceae, recognized by herbalists as a valuable plant for the organs of the senses. Mezereon is rarely seen in the British Isles, and is seldom found wild. It is usually cultivated, both for the beauty of its shining leaves and poisonous little scarlet drupes, and for its medicinal virtues. Theophrastus, Dioscorides and Galen all recommended this plant, but Mattioli, in the sixteenth century, cautioned his contemporaries against its toxicity. The drug comes from the bark, which is torn from the shrub in long strips: it should only be used under medical supervision and preferably in homoeopathic form. A concoction of the bark is helpful in cutaneous diseases, and is thought to relieve certain forms of rheumatism. Mezereon is used by herbalists for ciliary neuralgia, especially following operations, hay-fever and post-nasal adenoids. In China *D. odora* and *D. Geukwa* are cultivated for their flowers, leaves and roots, which are used for fevers and skin complaints. *D. mezereum* should not be confused with spurge laurel (*D. laureola*); both are powerfully irritant and may prove fatal in large doses. Mezereon is no longer included in the *British Pharmacopoeia*.

'This strong medicine made of white Hellebor, ought not to bee given inwardly unto delicate bodies without great correction; but it may bee more safely given unto country people which feed grosly, and have hard tough and strong bodies.' Despite Gerard's sanction, country people, however tough, would be ill-advised to take **White hellebore** (*Veratrum album*). This plant, which is not related to the true hellebores, is another medicinal herb which may be dangerous in the wrong hands, and should be used only on the advice of a doctor. The active constituents are contained in the rhizome, which is collected in the autumn and dried. In the Middle Ages the *Veratrums* were known as remedies for 'falling sicknesse, phrensies, sciatica, dropsies, poison, and all cold diseases that be of hard curation, and will not yield to any gentle medicine.' Today this 'very harsh medicine', as Culpeper referred to it, is known to act on the cardiovascular and respiratory systems, and the nervous system. Used externally, it has an anaesthetic effect, and also makes a good sneezing agent. Even in Elizabethan times the powdered root was used as snuff. Culpeper knew this species as Indian poke.

The **Spotted hemlock** (*Conium maculatum*) grows plentifully along roadsides, ditches and meadows in most parts of Europe and the United States, and may reach a height of two metres (six to seven feet). It is one of the most poisonous plants in existence, and can be recognized by its vile, foetid smell and smooth spotted stems: these spots are called by country people 'the marks of Cain'. Hemlock has strong associations with witchcraft, and the dead stalks rattling in the wind at summer's end are known in some remote districts as kricksies. The plant contains three alkaloids: conia, coniine and conhydrea, which give it sedative, antispasmodic and narcotic action. The effect of the drug is to paralyse the muscles. It is another herb for the organs of the senses: it helps corneal ulcers, excessive lachrymation and paralysis of the ocular muscles, as well as defective hearing and polypus of the nose, and is included in the *British Pharmacopoeia*. Other poisonous members of the parsley family are water hemlock and water dropwort. Hemlock's ancient evil reputation stems in part from its use as the executioner of kings and philosophers. Socrates died of a draught of hemlock in 399 BC; Plato has left a description of that serene death which makes it seem probable that other herbs had been mixed with the hemlock, which, on its own, would throw the victim into a frenzy of madness. Its name may come from the Greek word for 'a top', from the resemblance of that toy's whirling motion to the appalling giddiness produced in a human brain by a poisonous dose. The Romans added opium to hasten death. Keats was certainly ignorant of the dreadful effect of hemlock when he wrote in his *Ode to a Nightingale*: 'My heart aches and a drowsy numbness pains/My sense, as though of hemlock I had drunk.'

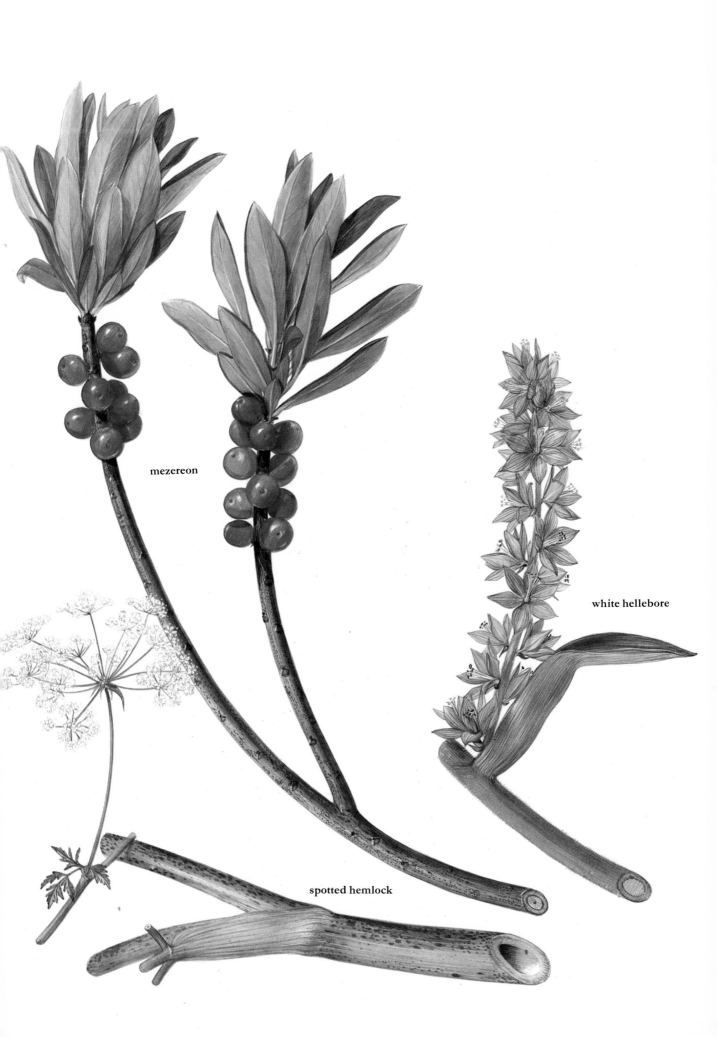

mezereon

white hellebore

spotted hemlock

Periwinkle
Herb Robert

'Fresh pervenke rich of hue' was Chaucer's vivid description of the **Periwinkle** (*Vinca major* or *V. minor*), whose brilliant little blue flowers may be seen blooming at any time of the year, no matter how cold the climate. Sir Francis Bacon (1561–1626), giving instructions on how to have a beautiful garden even in mid-winter, desired 'periwinkle, the white, the purple and the blue'. This herb is thought to be an escape from the physick gardens of monasteries where it was grown for its astringent properties. The active principles are contained in the leaves, which are collected when fully grown and dried on wire trays in a warm place. The lesser periwinkle (*V. minor*) is favoured by herbalists today as a tonic, and as a cure for intestinal complaints. Mixed with other herbs, it may help diabetics, and is a useful remedy for skin diseases, especially those affecting the scalp. It is still employed by herbalists to treat uterine haemorrhage, and at one time was valued as a cure for diphtheria. Culpeper and his contemporaries preferred the larger periwinkle (*V. major*), especially as a cure for nightmares. Magical properties have been attributed to the periwinkle: it was believed that if a husband and wife ate the leaves together, it would bind them more closely to one another. This superstition may be connected with the plant's name, over which there is some controversy. 'Periwinkle', comes either from the Latin *pervincire*, 'to bind closely', or from *pervincere*, 'to overcome'. This could refer either to the practice of binding the legs with the trailing stems to relieve muscular cramp, or to the plant's recognized astringent properties which helped to overcome internal bleeding. The oleander (*v.* p. 76) is of the same family, the Apocynaceae, some members of which are highly poisonous.

Herb Robert (*Geranium robertianum*), with its soft velvety leaves, is one of the numerous species of the genus *Geranium*, all of which are benevolent with no poisonous principles. Its other, less attractive name is Stinking cranesbill. It flourishes in Europe and the United States. The American cranesbill grows in shady locations from Newfoundland to Manitoba, and as far south as Georgia and Missouri. Herb Robert has an ancient reputation as a vulnerary and may still be applied to all cuts and wounds. It is also used externally for tumours, and internally for various ulcers. *G. masculatum*, which grows in the United States, has been found to lessen the vomiting that accompanies gastric ulcers. The drug comes from the herb and leaves and has styptic, tonic and astringent action. A good mouthwash and gargle may be made from the flowers. Gerard, in the sixteenth century, cured himself of a rupture with powdered *G. molle*. Culpeper commended herb Robert 'to stay blood, where or however flowing'. Its common name is linked to the eleventh-century saint, Robert, Abbot of Molesme.

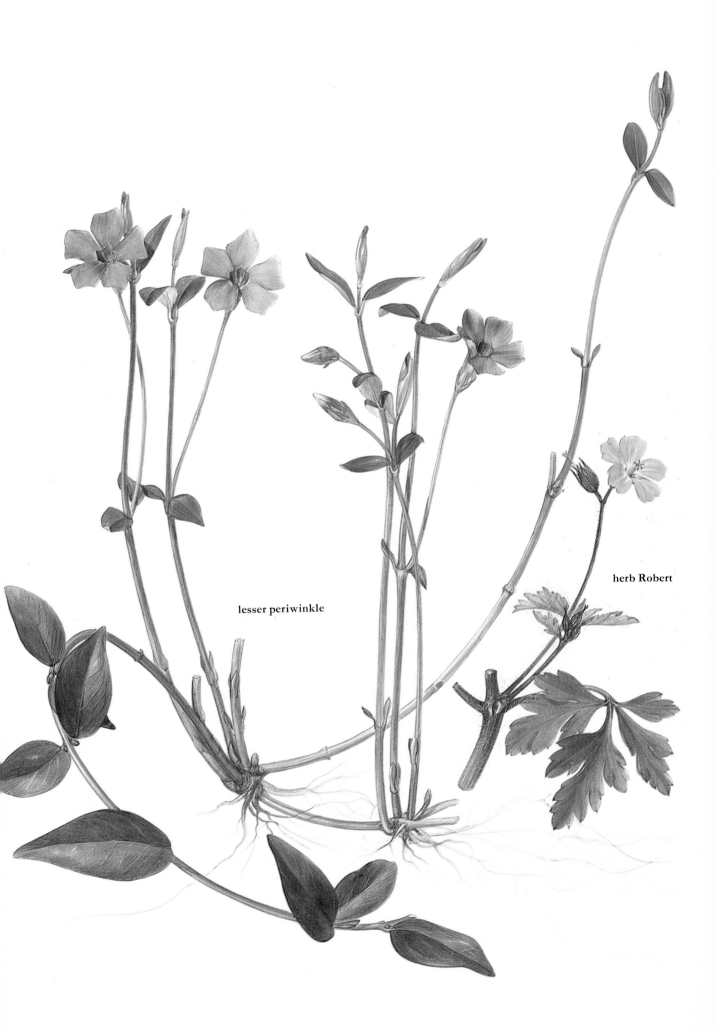

lesser periwinkle

herb Robert

Persicarias
Yarrow

There are several species of **Persicaria** which are valued by herbalists, but shunned by animals, as, according to Linnaeus, the great Swedish botanist (1717–1778), all animals refuse to eat these plants. *Polygonum hydropiper*, the water pepper, known colloquially as arsemart or smartweed, grows in most parts of Europe and in Russian Asia, as far as the Arctic region. *P. lapathifolium*, the pale persicaria, and *P. persicaria*, the persicaria, have similar properties to the water pepper and all are utilized pharmaceutically for their hypotensive, diuretic, diaphoretic, astringent and emmenagogic action. According to the *Doctrine of Signatures* persicaria has an affinity with the liver, and was an ancient cure for gravel, jaundice, haemorrhoids, uterine derangements and varicose veins. Externally, it was applied to chronic ulcers and for toothache. The fresh plant must be used: an infusion of the leaves in a hot bath has been known to bring relief to sufferers from rheumatism. In parts of the United States where folk medicine continues to flourish, this remedy is still used. The persicarias did not arrive in England until the beginning of the eighteenth century, but could be said to have got off to a noble, or at least aristocratic start, being first grown by the Duchess of Bedford in 1707.

Yarrow (*Achillea millefolium*), for all its rather dingy appearance, derives its generic name from the mighty Achilles, who, following the instructions of the wise Centaur Cheiron, staunched the wounds of his soldiers with this herb: hence its country name staunch-wound. It is also commonly called milfoil, meaning 'a thousand leaves', and nose-bleed because its astringent properties quickly arrest bleeding. There is an old superstition which still lingers in remote parts of Britain and the United States: young girls tickle their nostrils with sprays of yarrow; if their noses start bleeding, this proves the fidelity of their lovers: 'Yarroway, yarroway, bear a white blow;/If my lover loves me, my nose will bleed now.' This is possibly not a very reliable form of love-divining.

The name yarrow is derived from the Anglo-Saxon *gaerwe*. The commonest forms of the plant have greyish-looking white flowers, but sometimes a variety with pink or, more rarely, deep rose flowerheads may be found; possibly these plants are garden escapes. Since ancient times yarrow's medicinal virtues have been recognized. The Greeks employed it as a vulnerary, especially for haemorrhages, for which it is still prescribed in homoeopathy and herbal medicine. It may also be used as a tonic and stimulant and to subdue feverish colds. Its antispasmodic properties are helpful in epilepsy and hysteria, and it can ease the discomfort of haemorrhoids and boils. In pregnancy yarrow can be comforting when the varices are painful and the temperature is high.

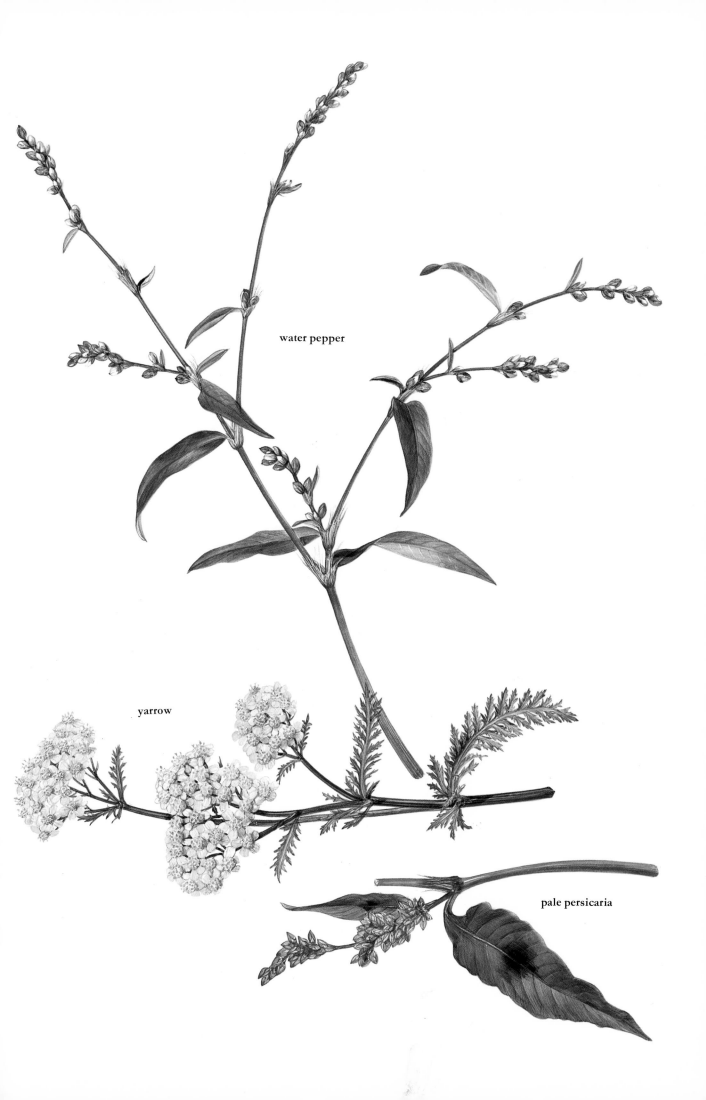

water pepper

yarrow

pale persicaria

Solomon's seal
Madonna lily
Arnica

Solomon's seal (*Polygonatum officinale*) was another herb put to good use by that renowned army doctor Dioscorides, who wrote of the virtues of the root for closing up fresh wounds and healing broken joints. The plant's name derives either from its power to 'seal' wounds or from the appearance of the rhizome, which is covered with large nodules, some of which resemble seals. Another species, *P. multiflorum*, which is more common in the British Isles, has similar properties. About a hundred years after Dioscorides, Galen (*c.* 130–200) warned against taking either plant internally, but Gerard, in the sixteenth century, commenting on Galen's caution, mentions 'the vulgar sort of people in Hampstead, which Galen, Dioscorides, or any other that have written of plants have not so much as dreamed of;' who actually drank the crushed roots in ale as a cure for broken bones. However, it appeared to be effective, and was equally successful with the same 'vulgar people's' cattle that had broken joints. In Italy, Gerard's contemporary Mattioli wrote of a cosmetic wash obtained from the roots with which Italian women 'scoured their faces from Sunneburning, freckles, morphew [scurf on the face], or such deformities of the skin'. Gerard, displaying some male chauvinism, wrote that the root 'while it is fresh and greene, and applied, taketh away in one night, or two at the most, any bruise, blacke or blew spots gotten by fals or women's wilfulnesse, in stumbling upon their hasty husbands fists, or such like.' The reputation of Solomon's seal has endured: in the form of compresses or decoctions, the pounded rhizome is used in modern medicine for contusions, bruises and whitlows.

Jupiter laid the infant Hercules against Juno's breast while the goddess slept. As the child drank, some drops of the ambrosial milk were spilt: those that fell on the heavens were transformed into the Milky Way, and from those that reached the earth there sprang up the **Madonna lily** (*Lilium candidum*). This flower has always been associated with purity in both the pagan and the Christian worlds. Its cultivation goes back many thousands of years: the ancient Egyptians prized it for its beauty and medicinal virtues; the bulbs were made into a form of bread, and are still used in this way in some Eastern countries. Parkinson, Gerard, Culpeper and before them the monk-physicians all used the madonna lily as a remedy for swellings, burns, cuts and bruises, and this practice persists today. The drug is contained in the bulbs. In the form of a decoction, *Lilium candidum* has numerous properties, including diuretic, emmenagogic and antiuricaemic. The lily is the only rival that the rose accepts.

Leopard's bane, called more prosaically **Arnica** (*Arnica montana*) by botanists and herbalists, has always been recognized as an extremely useful herb for external application to all injuries. It may be taken internally but it is recommended that only homoeopathic doses should be used, as the plant is toxic. Arnica's common name comes from its power to kill animals. Sometimes it is erroneously known as wolf's bane, but this name refers to a species of aconite. Arnica grows in mountainous regions in the Alps, the Apennines and the Pyrenees. The drug is provided by the flowers, leaves and roots; the flowers have more arnica than the roots, but no tannin. The plant has discutient, stimulant, diuretic, antiseptic and vulnerary action. It came to Britain in the eighteenth century and was grown in many physic gardens.

Gerard in his *Herball*, recounts how the Swiss naturalist Konrad Gesner (1516–1565), 'a man in our time singularly learned, and a most diligent searcher of many things' took two drachms of arnica on an empty stomach, and then wrote to his friend Adolphus Occo, telling him he was well. Hermann Boerhaave (1668–1738) however, in his history of plants, continues the story: within an hour of writing his letter, Gesner was dead. The cause was not specified.

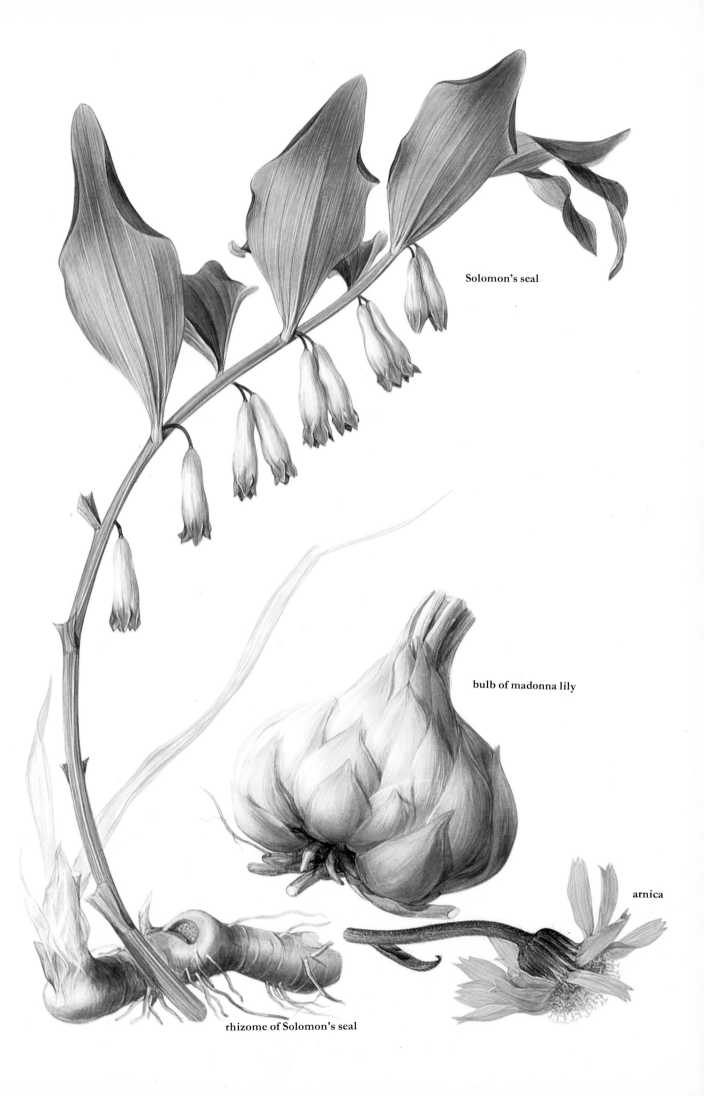

Solomon's seal

bulb of madonna lily

arnica

rhizome of Solomon's seal

Agrimony
Columbine
St John's wort
Terebinth

Agrimony (*Agrimonia eupatoria*) is another herb named botanically after King Mithridates Eupator, a great herb-collector, especially of poisonous species, which he took in small prophylactic doses to such good effect that he was eventually unable to end his life by poison. The plant's generic name is Greek and may refer to its supposed power of removing cataracts. It has been known to remove certain films from the eyes, and is employed in homoeopathy and herbal medicine in various eye treatments. Agrimony, or church steeples as it is also called, has vulnerary, febrifuge and astringent action, and at one time was included in the London *Materia Medica* as a certain cure for ague. Long before that, it appeared in Anglo-Saxon herbals under the name *garclive* as a remedy for wounds, warts and snake-bites. Today it is still popular with herbalists as a blood-purifier and liver tonic, a freshener of the breath, a soporific and for the eyes. In the sixteenth century Gerard made a decoction of the leaves 'for them that have naughty livers'.

Columbine (*Aquilegia vulgaris*) has many country names: dove's foot, blue starry and granny's nightcap. It is an old home remedy for sore throats, and was formerly given to children suffering from liver complaints. The Italian physician and botanist Pier Andrea Mattioli used it for obstructions of the spleen in the sixteenth century. The greatest champion of columbine was St Hildegarde, Abbess of Rupertsberg, who mentioned it in her *Physica Sacia* (1097) and used it extensively for swollen glands. She made columbine a popular medicinal plant throughout Germany. It has diaphoretic and resolvent action, relieves palpitations, and prevents loss of consciousness; the fresh juice is helpful in clearing up ulcers and boils. Some herbalists know this herb as *Aquilegia*, but others call it *Herba Leonis*, or 'the herb wherein the Lion doth delight'.

Whoever treads on **St John's wort** (*Hypericum perforatum*) after sunset will be swept up on to the back of a magic horse which will charge around the heavens until sunrise before depositing its exhausted rider on the ground. This herb, otherwise, is so beneficial that its other name is grace of God. 'Wort' is Anglo-Saxon, meaning 'a medicinal herb', but the use of 'grace of God' goes far beyond this time, and the plant was universally known. In England it cured mania; in Russia it gave protection against hydrophobia; and the Brazilians knew it as an antidote to snake-bite. It was the herb always called upon to cure madness, especially if the patient was thought to be possessed by a devil, and was collected on every St John's Eve (23 June) to be hung in the house to ward off evil spirits. Hypericon oil, which is made from the inflorescence and leaves, is helpful for all kinds of wounds, especially those that are deep. When he was physician to the Roman army, Dioscorides made great use of this herb, which is known as 'the arnica of the nervous system' for its great effect in lessening pain and acting as a tonic on the mind and body. It is particularly effective after operations; for the after-effects of shock; and for spinal concussion and other injuries of the spine. It helps brain-fag, neurasthenia and melancholia. The flowers are put into gargles and infusions for chest complaints; at one time the aromatic, resinous fragrance and bitter taste of these flowers made them popular in the liqueur industry. The herb's action is aromatic, astringent, nervine, and expectorant. Blood-red spots are said to appear on the leaves on 29 August, the day on which St John was beheaded.

The turpentine tree is the name by which the **Terebinth** (*Pistacia terebinthus*) is often known, conjuring up a picture of a shrub from Lewis Carroll's Wonderland. Incisions are made in the bark to obtain a greenish fluid used in the preparation of ointments and plasters, called Chian, Scio or Cyprus turpentine. Two other species are *P. vera*, which yields the pistachio nut, and *P. lentiscus*, which provides mastic. In India this is combined with salep as an aphrodisiac. Terebinth had more domestic uses in the sixteenth century: 'Here grows melampode [the black hellebore] everywhere,/And terebinth, good for goats' (Spenser, *Shepherd's Calendar*).

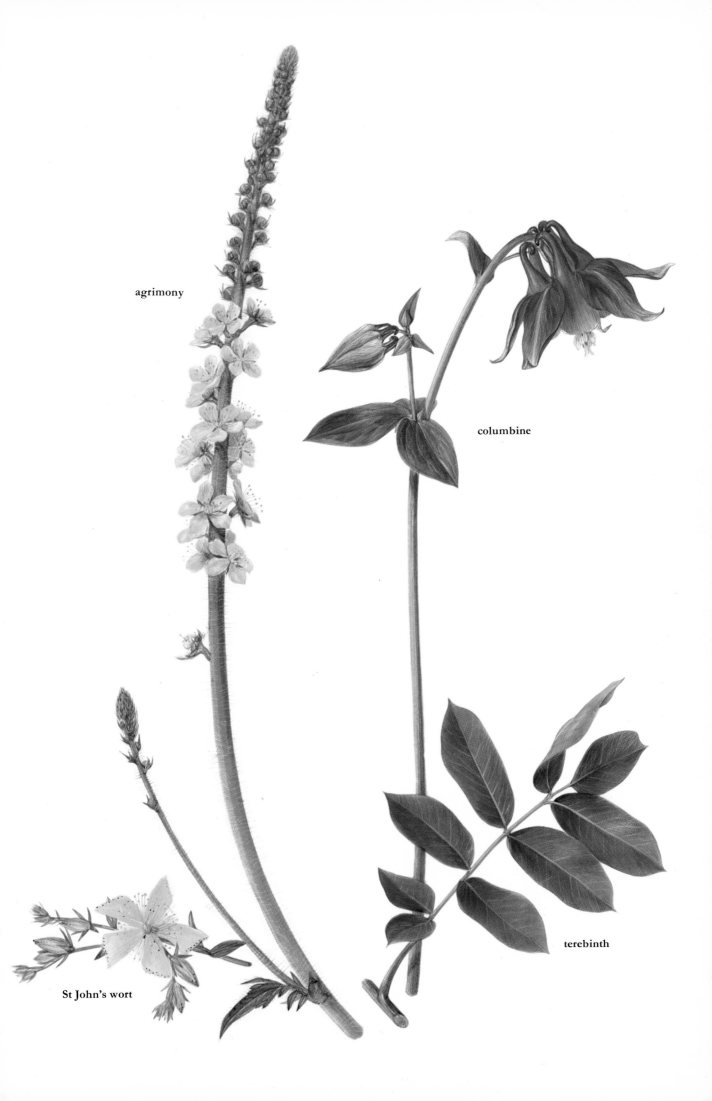

agrimony

columbine

terebinth

St John's wort

Lesser celandine
Ranunculi
Poplar buds

The **Lesser celandine** (*Ranunculus ficaria* or *Ficaria ranunculoides*) is engraved on Wordsworth's tomb because he so loved its 'glittering countenance' which appears long before winter is over. This plant is a member of the Ranunculaceae or buttercup family, and is not related to the greater celandine (*v.* p. 176), which belongs to the poppy family. It has astringent and healing properties: the *Doctrine of Signatures* recommends it for haemorrhoids because of the shape of the tubers on the roots, and this practice is continued today in herbal medicine; hence its other name, pilewort. This herb is beneficial to the veins generally, and may also cure polypi of the nose if sniffed up the nostrils. Culpeper believed the lesser celandine to be a cure for King's evil (tuberculosis of the skin): 'The very herb borne about one's body next the skin helps in such diseases, though it never touches the place grieved; let poor people make mind of it for these uses.' Because it is believed by certain country folk to close its petals punctually every day at five o'clock, this little herb is also known as five o'clock flower.

There are many species of **Ranunculi** of diverse form and habit, growing in most parts of Europe. The name of the genus *Ranunculus* is derived from the Latin *rana*, 'frog', and refers to the preference of some of these plants for damp, marshy locations. They are all toxic, with an acrid juice. *R. velutinus* is a native of Italy. *R. sceleratus*, the celery-leaved crowfoot, is extremely acrid, and should be employed only in homoeopathic tinctures; it is beneficial for defects of the tongue. The bulbous buttercup (*R. bulbosa*) is a counter-irritant and may be used for various skin eruptions. The ranunculi are indigenous to Iran, Turkey and the Levant. They were one of the fruits of the Crusades, brought over to France by Louis IX, and spreading to the rest of Europe. Toxic doses will result in stomach irritation and diarrhoea, and eventually convulsions. Gerard's words of warning should be heeded with regard to this group of plants: 'they require a very exquisite moderation, with a most exact and due maner of tempering, not any of them are to be taken alone by themselves, because they are of a most violent force . . .'

Galen, in the second century AD, recommended the use of **Poplar buds** to treat inflammations of all kinds. They are still in use today, forming an essential part of an ointment used for haemorrhoids, burns, scalds and boils. At one time the bruised buds were added to fresh butter which was then left in the sun to melt, and used by peasant women in China to give a sheen to their hair. This practice could not be emulated in the West, where it is more common to wear hats. The juice of the leaves is used in herbal medicine to relieve the pain of earache, and the bark of the black poplar (*Populus nigra*), the hybrid black poplar (*P. canadensis*) and the white poplar (*P. alba*) may all be substituted for Peruvian bark (cinchona), as these may be tolerated where the latter is too strong. In Norway, bread is made from the bark. The black poplar is dedicated to Proserpina and the white to Hercules. The white poplar has been used medicinally by American Indians for many centuries; it is given by modern herbalists for debility, especially where accompanied by diarrhoea.

P. tremula, the aspen, is said to tremble incessantly even on a windless day, because it is associated with the accursed poplar tree from which Christ's cross was made.

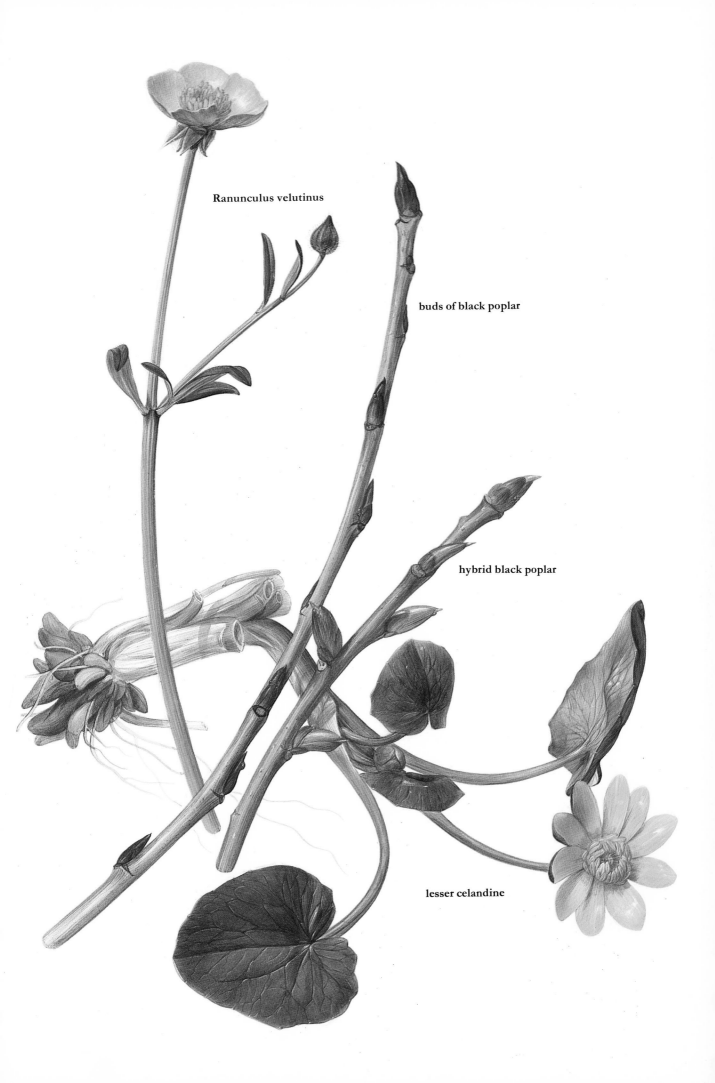

Ranunculus velutinus

buds of black poplar

hybrid black poplar

lesser celandine

White horehound
Horse chestnut
Cypress

'Here horehound, 'gainst the mad dog's ill by biting, never failing': Michael Drayton (1563–1631) gives this remedy for hydrophobia. If **White horehound** (*Marrubium vulgare*) is worn inside the shoes, dogs will not bark as the wearer goes by. It was included in Hippocrates' list of 'simples' nearly 500 years before Christ, and physicians have been using it ever since for its bitter-tonic, diuretic, stimulant and expectorant action. It is particularly useful for bronchial troubles and digestive complaints, especially in the form of a tisane, and may safely be given to consumptives. Long ago in East Anglia it was brewed as Horehound ale.

In ancient Egypt the priests called this plant 'the seed of Horus'. Its generic name comes from the Hebrew *marrob*, 'bitter juice', and refers to its use, mentioned in the *Mishna*, as one of the five bitter herbs at the feast of Passover. Its specific name *vulgare* is rather misleading, as white horehound is not nearly so easy to find as the name implies.

No one seems to know for certain why the **Horse chestnut** (*Aesculus hippocastanum*) is so called. James I's apothecary, Parkinson, said that the Turks used the nuts to cure broken-winded horses, but this seems an unlikely theory. It was, however, the Turks who brought the horse chestnut to the European mainland. The first physician to mention it was Pier Andrea Mattioli in the sixteenth century, who noted it as a cure for malarial and intermittent fevers. Today decoctions of the bark are used to treat haemorrhoids and varicose veins, and homoeopaths employ it for sensitive nasal passages, coated tongues and pharyngitis. It is a useful medicine for a distended abdomen, having a specific action on the capillary circulation of the lower bowel.

France and Britain welcomed the horse chestnut with the greatest enthusiasm, and it was widely planted in both countries as an ornamental tree, for its immense size and the beauty of the flowering 'candles'. It will grow in almost any kind of soil and adapts easily to varying climatic conditions.

The **Cypress** (*Cupressus sempervirens*) is a funereal tree associated with mourning and remorse. The Greeks and Romans, and also the Persians, planted cypress trees near their temples, and it was dedicated to Apollo and other deities. Ovid tells the story of the young man Cyparissus, beloved of Apollo, who accidentally killed a pet stag and, overwhelmed with grief, begged the gods to let his remorse last for ever; he was changed into a cypress, and the tree became a symbol of the immortal soul.

The ancients had a more cheerful use for this gloomy tree, flavouring their wine with it, because of its fragrance. Its balsamic resin has a marvellously curative effect on diseased lungs and, when burnt, soothes the mucous membranes of the nose. Early physicians sent patients with lung diseases to the island of Candia (Crete), which was so thickly populated with cypress trees that their aromatic perfume acted as a balsam in the same way as pine. In allopathic medicine the fruit is used: it is gathered just before ripening and dried. Its powerful styptic and disinfectant action, and balsamic properties make it useful as an astringent and a vasoconstrictor for haemorrhoids and varicose veins.

The most beautiful cypresses are found in Italy, where they give the countryside its characteristic appearance. Some of the trees are believed to be over 3000 years old. The wood is incorruptible: no insect can attack it, and for this reason the doors of Saint Peter's were originally made of cypress wood in the reign of the Emperor Constantine before being replaced by bronze ones in the time of Pope Eugenius II.

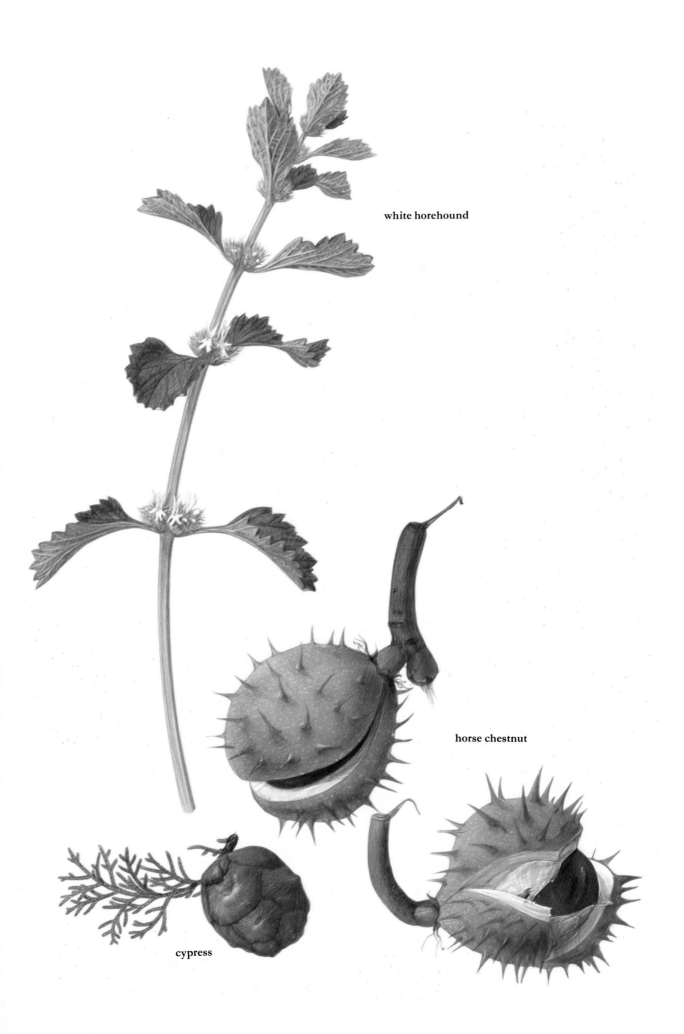

white horehound

horse chestnut

cypress

Meadow saffron
Celandine
Rose periwinkle

The local name for **Meadow saffron** (*Colchicum autumnale*) is Naked Ladies; the flowers are without foliage, appearing long after the leaves have died, and this, with their pale lilac colour, gives them a strange naked aspect. *Colchicum* is often known as autumn crocus although it is in no way related to the real crocus. Its generic name is believed to come from Colchis, an area in the Black Sea region of Georgia where the plant originates. The seeds and corm are used for the extraction of a toxic alkaloid colchicine, which has been valued as a pain-killer since very early times. It is also a specific for gout. In homoeopathic medicine it is a herb for the eyes: it helps dimness of vision after prolonged reading; spots before the eyes; visual acuity and sharp pains behind the eyes. It is also used in homoeopathy to clear up certain skin eruptions.

Because it is poisonous to livestock as well as to humans, meadow saffron has been virtually exterminated in parts of Britain. In other regions where it is cultivated for use in pharmacy and grows profusely, the small corms are replanted quickly to ensure another crop. They are difficult to dig up, often being 10 inches below the ground. Gerard's comments on this herb should be heeded: 'The roots of all sorts of Mede Saffron are very hurtfull to the stomacke, and being eaten they kill by choking as Mushromes do, according unto *Dioscorides*, whereupon some have called it *Colchicum strangulatorium*.'

The **Celandine** or greater celandine (*Chelidonium majus*) is no relation of the lesser celandine (*v.* p. 172), and belongs to the Papaveraceae or poppy family. Its generic name has aroused as much controversy as its common name. Pliny claimed that it came from the Greek *chelidon*, 'a swallow', because it is with the juice of this plant that swallows open the eyes of their unfledged young. Gerard denies this upon the earlier authority of Aristotle who points out that certain birds have eyes which 'do afterwards grow againe and perfectly recover their sight.' Another theory, also refuted by Gerard who caustically comments: 'it may be found all the yere' is that the swallows arrive when the flowers start to bloom and leave again when they die. Whatever the real reason for celandine's botanical name, one of its local names is Swallow wort.

When any part of the plant is broken an acrid, sticky yellow juice with an unpleasant smell exudes. Paracelsus in his *Doctrine of Signatures* took this as a sign that the plant had an affinity with the liver, and was good for jaundice and all liver complaints. It is a useful purgative and aid to the digestion, and a soothing eye lotion is made from the herb. The latex in the plant is used pharmaceutically to remove warts and soften callouses. Celandine has an old reputation as a tooth-losener. Queen Elizabeth I, who had very bad teeth (the Spanish ambassador in a report home, likened the queen's teeth to pearls, black ones) refused to let a badly aching tooth be pulled. One of the Court physicians suggested dropping the juice of celandine into the hollow of the tooth, which was done. The queen found she was able to remove it with her fingers quite easily.

Some scientists affirm that, in the wrong hands, **Rose periwinkle** (*Catharanthus roseus*) presents 'the possibility of untold horrors'. This beautiful little flower, with its romantic names, is a most dangerous plant. In recent years much research has been done on its numerous alkaloids which are found in scarcely any other plants, and make it likely that rose periwinkle may be anti-diabetic, and may also inhibit cancerous tumours because of the presence of vinblastine and vincristine. In Madagascar, the home of *Catharanthus* from where it gets its other name, Madagascar periwinkle, it is used for skin diseases and to treat diabetics.

In the United States where this herb proliferates like a weed, it was noticed that patients being treated with *Catharanthus* suffered from side effects: hallucinations and a state of euphoria. In parts of the States the dried leaves are smoked like 'pot'. The debilitating effects of getting 'high' on *Catharanthus* are very terrible: severe muscle deterioration which results in ataxia; loss of hair and a sensation of burning all over the body. There is also a reduction in the white blood cell count which leaves the individual vulnerable to a variety of germs. This herb must never be used in home medicine.

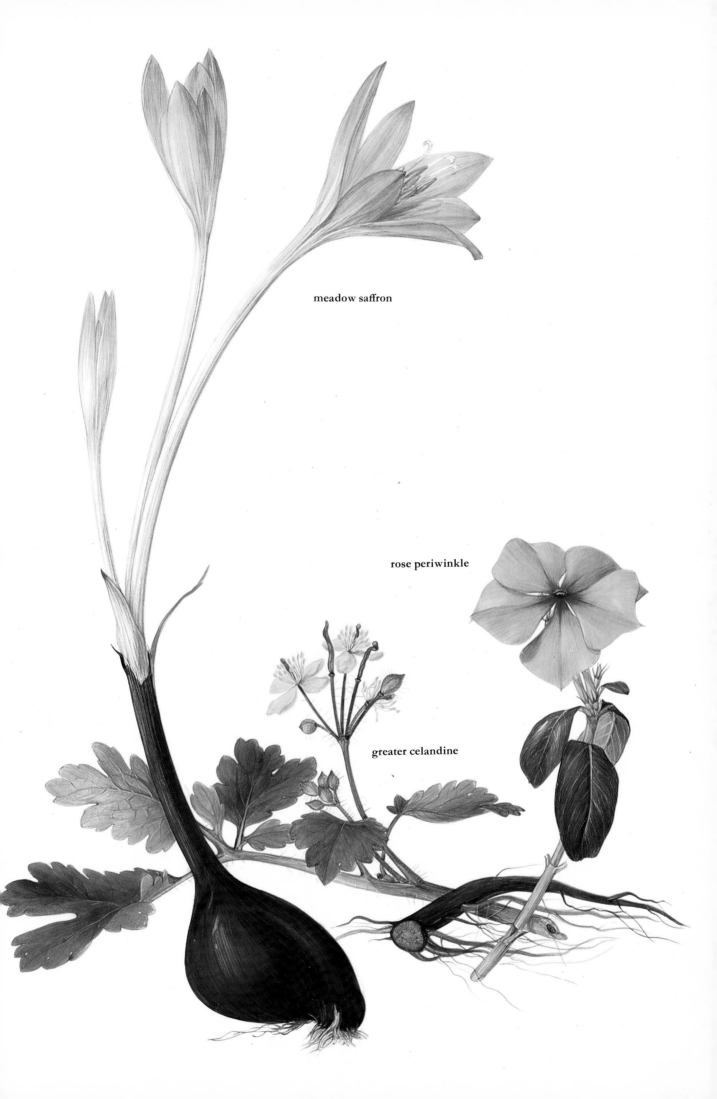

meadow saffron

rose periwinkle

greater celandine

Pyrethrum
Thuja
Quassia

The chemical constituents of **Pyrethrum** (*Chrysanthemum cinerariaefolium*) are employed mostly in the manufacture of insecticides and pest-killers. The plant is indigenous to Dalmatia but is cultivated commercially in many parts of the world. The flowerheads contain the active principles which, although death-dealing to insects, are quite harmless to men and animals. Herbalists have found the roots to be a remedy for certain fevers. They are hot and promote a flow of saliva which aids the digestion. Pyrethrum is also used as an anthelminthic.

In China the **Thuja** (*Thuja occidentalis*), like the cypress (*v.* p. 174), faces West when all the other trees face East, and so is a symbol of chastity. The Chinese use the leaves for parasitical skin diseases and to stop haemorrhages of all kinds. This member of the cypress family is native of Canada and grows wild as far south as Virginia and Carolina. It arrived in France in the reign of Francois 1er and came to England at the end of the sixteenth century. Hermann Boerhaave successfully treated dropsy with it, but it was the founder of homoeopathy, the German doctor C. F. S. Hahnemann (1755–1843), who discovered its full importance; a single homoeopathic dose is effective for three weeks in dealing with all the organs of the senses. Thuja has been found helpful in ciliary neuralgia, chronic inflammation of the ear, chronic scleritis, iritis, nasal polypi, catarrh and pyorrhoea. This 'tree of life' known as Arbor vitae, will also cure tissue degeneration and urinary diseases, and has emmenagogue, anthelminthic, aromatic and astringent action. Thuja must not be used in home medicine as it is very toxic.

The name **Quassia** is given to the bitter tasting wood chips from two closely related trees, *Quassia amara* and *Picrasma excelsa*, which are used in medicine, for flavouring tonic wines and aperitives, and in brewing. One of the best stomach bitters in the world, especially indicated for extreme inactivity of the digestive organs, is obtained from *Q. amara*. Early herbalists kept cups carved from quassia filled with water which soon soaked up the bitterness of the wood and provided a tonic which stimulated the gastric juices and sharpened the appetite. Quassia is excellent for alleviating digestive complaints and for dyspepsia; it promotes the gastric, intestinal, hepatic and renal secretions, and also has anthelminthic and febrifuge action. Like Peruvian bark (cinchona) it can restore energy to the debilitated and may be tolerated in cases where Peruvian bark may not. Brewers sometimes use it as a substitute for hops, and it may be added to marmalade to accentuate the flavour.

The extract is used with sugar to make fly-papers and is also made into an effective insecticidal spray. The best quassia comes from Jamaica.

Bitter ash and bitter damson are other names for this tree. It was the Swedish botanist Linnaeus, who named it quassia in honour of Gramen Quasi, a negro slave who used the bark to cure fevers. Quasi was given his name (the West African *Kwasi*) because he was born on *Kwasida*, the first day of the week.

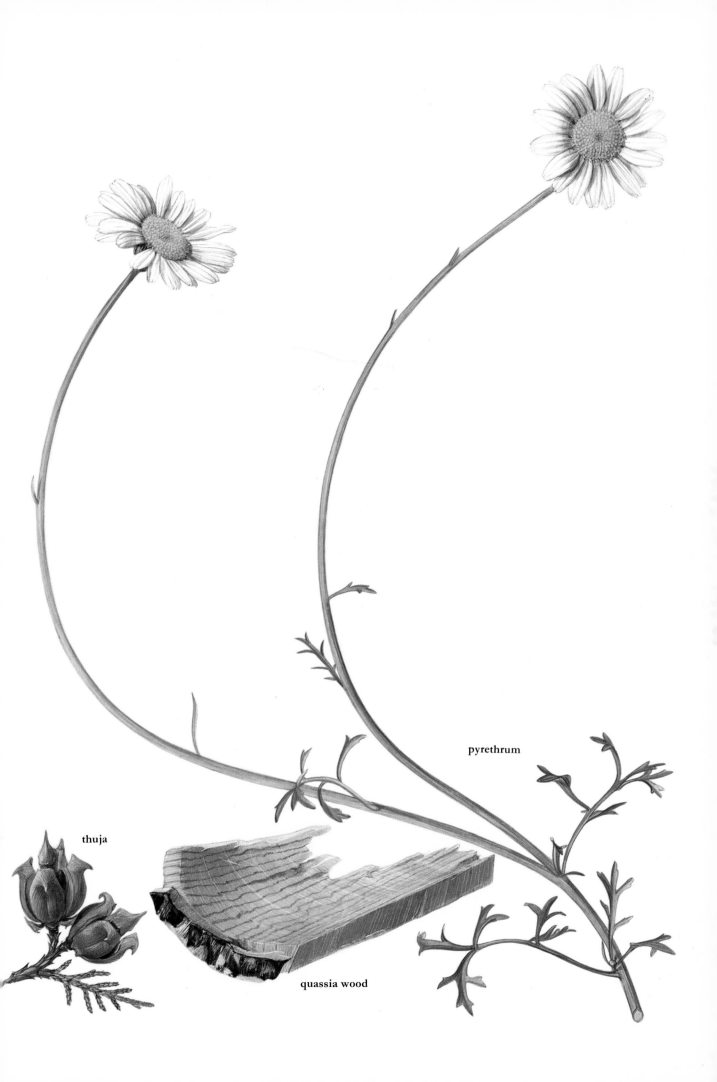

thuja

quassia wood

pyrethrum

Appendix

Glossaries

Bibliography

Index

Appendix | Digestive System

p. 16   **Holy thistle**

The holy thistle (*Cnicus benedictus*) is an annual herb of the family Compositae found in dry situations, particularly in coastal regions of the Mediterranean. It reaches a height of about one metre (over 3 feet) and has an erect, angular, reddish and hairy stem. The leaves are tough, sinuately lobed, bordered with thorny teeth; on short petioles or sessile and decurrent on the stem. The flowerheads, which open in late spring, are solitary and are surrounded by an involucre of scaly bracts. All the florets, up to 20 in a flowerhead, are tubular and have yellow corollas veined with violet. The whole plant, excepting the larger stems, is used and is characterized by having a very bitter taste. The plant contains flavonoid glycosides, a bitter principle called cnicine, and a little essential oil. It has long been valued in the form of an infusion as a bitter tonic, diuretic and febrifuge. More recently it has been recommended for Maltese fever. It is used in homoeopathy.

Star thistle

The star thistle (*Centaurea calcitrapa*) is an annual or biennial herb of the family Compositae which is fairly common on waste ground by the sea throughout Europe but relatively rare in England. It is sometimes covered with cottony down, grows to one metre ($3\frac{1}{4}$ feet) in height and has pinnatifid radical leaves which form a prickly rosette. The upper leaves are small and linear. The flowerheads are solitary and almost globular, with an involucre of prickly bracts; the florets are purple. The plant has a reputation as a bitter tonic and febrifuge, and, like holy thistle, contains a bitter principle. It may be taken as an infusion.

Holly

The common holly (*Ilex aquifolium*) is an evergreen shrub or tree belonging to the family Aquifoliaceae. It is common in hedges and woods in most parts of Europe. It has persistent leaves which are sparse, short-stalked, coriaceous and a shining green in colour. The lamina is elliptical to oval, with a wavy margin having coarse, very prickly teeth. The small flowers are white, often unisexual, and are clustered in the axils of the leaves. The fruit is a globular drupe, usually bright red in colour but sometimes yellow. The drug is derived from the leaves, which contain caffeotannic acid and other constituents which require further investigation. An infusion made from them is said to have tonic properties. The berries, however, are poisonous and produce purgation and vomiting. The South American species *Ilex paraguensis* contains caffeine and the dried leaves form maté or Paraguay tea, which is now widely used as a beverage in both Europe and the Americas.

p. 18   **Wall germander**

The wall germander (*Teucrium chamaedrys*) is a member of the family Labiatae. It is a perennial herb up to 20 cm (8 inches) high with a hairy stem, rarely branched. The glossy dark green leaves are opposite and deeply dentate. The flowers, which grow in unilateral verticillasters, have reddish-purple corollas about a centimetre (0·4 inches) long. The flowering tops are used as a bitter tonic and digestive in the form of an infusion. The constituents include a bitter principle, tannin, ursolic acid and a trace of essential oil.

Common centaury

The common centaury (*Centaurium erythraea* or *Erythraea centaurium*) belongs to the family Gentianaceae. The plant is commonly found on dry pastures, beside field paths and on sea-cliffs. It is an annual or biennial, averaging 20 to 30 cm (8 to 12 inches) in height, with an erect stem branching out towards the top. The radical leaves are ovate and form a rosette, while those growing from the stem are sessile, disposed in pairs, and oblong-linear. Flowering is from May to September, the pink or red flowers being clustered into a forked cyme or panicle. The flowering tops are used, generally in the form of an infusion, as a remedy popular since antiquity with tonic, stomachic, febrifuge and sedative properties. Centaury contains a bitter glycoside, alkaloids and much mineral matter. It is also used in veterinary medicine and in homoeopathy, and enters into the composition of vermouths.

Balm

Balm (*Melissa officinalis*) is a member of the family Labiatae, fairly common in hedges, along the banks of streams and in more or less shady situations. In southern England it is often an escape from gardens. It is a perennial herb, 30 to 80 cm (1 to $2\frac{1}{2}$ feet) high, with

182

opposite, oval, petiolate leaves of a deep green colour, reticulately veined and crenate at the margin; the upper leaves have shorter petioles. The flowers grow as axillary cymes in groups of three to twelve and have a corolla twice as long as the calyx. As buds they have a yellowish tinge, but later turn white. When fresh, especially if rubbed between the fingers, the plant gives off a pleasant lemony fragrance, whence it is often known as lemon balm. The flowers and leaves contain an essential oil, tannin and resins. The oil contains citral and citronellal, which give the lemon-like odour. Infusions, herb teas, syrups and so on prepared from balm have antispasmodic and sedative as well as digestive, stomachic and sudorific qualities. The oil distilled from the fresh plant is used in the manufacture of liqueurs and perfumes. Fresh balm leaves are used for flavouring fruit salads and iced drinks, and form a suitable ingredient for *pot-pourri*.

p. 20

Pepper

Pepper (*Piper nigrum*) belongs to the family Piperaceae. The shrub originated in India and is also cultivated in other tropical countries. The cultivated 'pepper-vines' are usually supported on poles and kept pruned to a modest height to facilitate collection of the fruits. The plant has alternate, petiolate leaves with two to three large veins on each side. The flowers are not very conspicuous and are grouped in spikes. The fruits are small drupes which in some species of *Piper*, e.g. that yielding 'long pepper', fuse into an elongated cone. Our common pepper consists of individual fruits. Three varieties are commercially available: 'green pepper', which is harvested when immature and kept in boxes; 'black pepper', also harvested immature, but dried; and 'white pepper', which is the mature fruit macerated or fermented so as to remove the outer pericarp. Pepper contains essential oil, the alkaloid piperine, and resin. The aroma is due to the oil and the pungency of the other constituents. Pepper has a stimulating action on the digestion and is used in cooking to flavour various dishes.

Saffron

The saffron (*Crocus sativus*) belongs to the family Iridaceae. It probably originated in western Asia and is now cultivated in Mediterranean countries such as Spain, France and Italy; it was formerly cultivated in England and gave its name to Saffron Walden. It is a herbaceous perennial with a fleshy corm from which long, narrow grooved leaves emerge in September. During the summer the plant is entirely dormant. At flowering, in October, the leaves are 4 to 5 cm ($1\frac{1}{2}$ to 2 inches) long, but they continue to grow during the winter and the following spring. The flowers have a perianth with a long thin tube. Each has six violet petal segments and three stamens. The style is divided into three stigmas and it is the stigmas and the tops of the styles which provide the drug. Saffron contains a coloured glycoside, crocin; a bitter glycoside, picrocrocin; carotenoid pigments; and safranal, which is responsible for its odour. It is used in folk medicine as a stomachic in the form of an infusion, and also employed in cooking as a colouring and flavouring agent, e.g. in curries and, particularly in Cornwall, for saffron cakes.

Ginger

Ginger (*Zingiber officinale*) belongs to the family Zingiberaceae. It is a perennial reed-like plant with a fleshy rhizome which when sun-dried produces the drug. It has been grown in India from the earliest times and subsequently introduced into Africa and the West Indies. The two main commercial forms are the coated and the scraped, the former bearing some or all of its original corky outer coat. Ginger contains essential oil in which are terpenes, zingiberene and other substances which give ginger its aroma. The pungency is due to a series of phenols known as gingerol.

Cinnamon

Cinnamon (*Cinnamomum zeylanicum*) belongs to the family Lauraceae. Much cinnamon is obtained from cultivated plants grown in Ceylon (Sri Lanka). Its production is labour-intensive and may be briefly described as follows: the young tree is first cut down to form a stool. The shoots which develop on this are allowed to grow for about eighteen months, being kept straight by pruning. They are then cut when about three metres (10 feet) long. The thin bark is removed and its outer corky layer removed by careful scraping. The resultant paper-thin pieces of inner bark are packed inside one another. During careful drying in the shade the pieces contract and form a compound quill (*v.* illustration). Originally 42 inches (just over a metre) long, these are cut into 'cigar lengths' for retail sale. Barks known as Saigon and Chinese cinnamon are derived from other species of *Cinnamomum* and are markedly different from the above, being thicker pieces of bark, not packed within one another and often bearing most of their original cork. Cinnamon is used as a flavouring agent and carminative; its mild astringency is due to tannin. The odour and flavour are due to essential oil which contains cinnamic aldehyde and the phenol eugenol. This oil is a powerful germicide.

Garden thyme Thyme or garden thyme (*Thymus vulgaris*) is a small shrubby member of the family Labiatae, with creeping stems, commonly found wild in the Mediterranean region but cultivated over a much wider area. Many of the thymes are hybrids with other species, for example lemon-scented thyme, which owes its characteristic odour and taste to citral. Thyme has erect branches, bearing opposite, very small lanceolate leaves on short petioles. The leaves are fairly hairy on their under surfaces and are rich in oil-containing glandular hairs. The flowers are grouped in whorls and grow in the axils of leaf-like bracts. The corolla is pale rose in colour, more rarely white, with an entire upper lip and a three-lobed lower one. The drug consists of the aerial parts. Thyme is widely used as a pot herb and in aromatic liqueurs. It has stimulant and antiseptic properties and contains an essential oil in its glandular hairs. This oil contains thymol and carvacrol.

Horseradish The horseradish (*Cochlearia armoracia*; other names include *Nasturtium armoracia*), of the family Cruciferae, is a native of southeastern Europe but is now found wild in many parts of western Europe, where it is also cultivated; a related species, also found in Britain, is *C. officinalis*, scurvy-grass. Horseradish is a herbaceous perennial with a thick rootstock which tapers into a very long root. The radical leaves which arise in the spring are petiolate and up to 30 cm in length (nearly a foot); they have a sinuate-dentate margin. The aerial stem, up to a metre ($3\frac{1}{4}$ feet) high, bears much smaller, deeply toothed leaves. The small white flowers are borne in numerous racemes. The constituents of horseradish closely resemble those of black mustard (*v.* below) and the grated fresh root is used as a condiment in the form of horseradish sauce. It can also be used, like mustard, in the form of a poultice or plaster. Both horseradish and the related scurvy-grass have anti-scorbutic properties.

White mustard The white or cultivated mustard (*Sinapis alba* or *Brassica alba*) belongs to the family Cruciferae. It is an annual herb growing in waste places throughout Europe, occasionally as an escape from cultivation. Its stems are rather robust and branching, reaching 70 to 80 cm (around $2\frac{1}{2}$ feet) in height. It has pinnately lobed leaves, the upper lobe often being the largest. The flowers, each with four yellow petals, are in racemes. The fruits are siliquas about 2 cm (0·8 inches) long with a flattened, often curved beak, each containing three seeds. These are spherical and yellowish, with a minutely wrinkled surface. White mustard seeds contain mucilage and the glycoside sinalbin which, when the seeds are crushed and moistened, reacts with an enzyme (myrosin) to produce an oil with a pungent taste. As the oil is only slightly volatile, the odour is not very marked. Black and brown mustards, from *Brassica nigra* and other species (not illustrated), contain a similar glycoside, sinigrin (also present in horseradish; *v.* above), which produces a more volatile oil which therefore has both odour and pungency. This explains the difference between English and Continental table mustards. In addition to its use as a condiment, mustard may be useful in some cases of poisoning, to produce vomiting. Mustard plasters and poultices are now much less used than formerly.

Gentians The yellow gentian (*Gentiana lutea*) belongs to the family Gentianaceae and provides most of the gentian root of commerce. It is a perennial herbaceous plant, native to mountain pastures of central France, the Jura and Vosges and similar districts. It has a large cylindrical rhizome from which branch large roots. The crown produces up to four aerial stems which bear oval, stalked, light green leaves with longitudinal veins that are sunken on the upper surfaces and protruding from the lower. The flowering stems carry numerous yellow flowers in the axils of the leaves. The fruits are capsules. The drug is derived from the rhizomes and roots and after collection is usually allowed to ferment before being dried and used.

Gentiana asclepiadea or willow gentian, one of the so-called minor gentians, is widespread in the woods and glades of the Alps and Apennines, and is a smaller plant than the yellow gentian. It produces slender drooping stems and tubular-campanulate flowers of an attractive blue colour. The roots are only about 1 cm (less than half an inch) in diameter, whereas those of the yellow gentian may be 4 cm ($1\frac{1}{2}$ inches) or more.

Gentiana acaulis, often known to gardeners as gentianella, is a gentian found in Alpine and northern Apennine meadows. It is a herbaceous perennial with a basal rosette of leaves from which arises a single flower with a tubular-campanulate corolla, deep blue in colour. The entire plant of gentianella is employed for use as a bitters, especially in liqueur manufacture.

All these gentians, of which *Gentiana lutea* is the most popular, have a stomachic and appetite-stimulating effect and are commonly used in bitter tonics and in liqueurs. They contain a number of bitter glycosides; and sugars such as gentianose, gentiobiose and sucrose.

p. 26 **Rhubarb** Medicinal rhubarb or Chinese rhubarb consists of the rhizomes of *Rheum palmatum*, belonging to the family Polygonaceae. It is a large perennial herbaceous plant which grows in the mountains of Tibet and northwest China. It has a robust rhizome with short branches and large leaves; these have a thick cylindrical petiole and a very large lamina deeply divided into three to five lobes which in turn are laciniate. The flowering stems are two to three metres ($6\frac{1}{2}$ to 10 feet) high. Other species are grown in Europe for medicinal use but are less valued than the Chinese rhubarb; these include *Rheum rhaponticum* (English garden rhubarb), *R. undulatum* and various hybrids. They are also large perennial herbs, but with flattened petioles and leaves with an entire lamina and undulate margin. The petioles are often stewed and eaten as a fruit. Rhubarb rhizome is used as a bitter stomachic and purgative, and also in liqueur manufacture. In folk medicine an infusion or a rhubarb wine can be used. Rhubarb contains a wide variety of purgative anthraquinone derivatives, but purgation is followed by an astringent effect produced by phenolic substances such as glucogallin, gallic acid and catechin.

Bay laurel The bay laurel or sweet bay (*Laurus nobilis*) is a bush or shrub belonging to the family Lauraceae. It is the laurel of the ancients and should not be confused with the cherry-laurel (*v.* p. 112), a member of the rose family. Bay laurel has evergreen leaves of rather variable form, but generally lanceolate. It is a dioecious plant, flowering in early spring. The female plants produce abundant fruits in the form of glossy black ovoidal drupes. Either the leaves or the fruits may be used. They have a cholagogic and stimulant action, and are often employed in cooking. In home medicine an infusion of the leaves can be used, sweetened to taste.

p. 28 **Aloes** The product used medicinally as aloes consists of the evaporated juice which drains from the leaves of various species of *Aloe* when these are cut transversely. Different commercial varieties are obtained from different geographical sources and species, e.g. Cape aloes from *Aloe ferox*, West Indian aloes from *A. barbadensis*. There are about 180 different species of *Aloe* (family Liliaceae): herbs, shrubs or small trees. The leaves are very fleshy, strongly cuticularized and generally prickly at the margins. The inflorescence consists of spikes of white, yellow or red flowers. Aloes contains purgative glycosides, collectively known as 'aloin', and purgative resins. It is seldom presented alone and is not recommended for internal use without medical advice. Having an intensely bitter taste, it was formerly used to discourage children from biting their fingernails. It is an ingredient of the well-known Friars' Balsam.

Lemon The lemon (*Citrus medica* var. *limon* or *C. limon*) belongs to the family Rutaceae, subfamily Aurantioideae. It is a small evergreen tree up to five metres (16 feet) high, originating in India, and now very widely cultivated in, for example, Italy, Spain, California, South Africa and Australia. The flowers are white, with petals occasionally veined with rose, and highly scented. The fruit is a particular type of berry called a hesperidium; the fleshy part is divided into segments. The pulp is very rich in citric acid and ascorbic acid (vitamin C) and the juice is used as a vitaminized drink. The rind or peel contains an essential oil rich in the terpene limonene; the aldehydes citral and citronellal; and the ester geranyl acetate. The peel also contains flavanone colouring matters and vitamin C. Lemon juice is used as a flavouring and for its anti-scorbutic properties. The peel is an aromatic bitter which has various culinary uses, e.g. as candied peel or in marmalade. An infusion of lemon, often with honey added, is a common domestic remedy.

Capsicums Capsicums or red peppers are botanically unrelated to black pepper (*v.* p. 20). They are obtained from several species of *Capsicum* (family Solanaceae), but there are many cultural varieties and botanists find it difficult to agree on the number of species and varieties. Generally speaking, the fruits (chillies) derived from *Capsicum minimum* and *C. frutescens* are smaller and more pungent than those derived from *C. annuum*. The smaller fruits, e.g. from Africa, are elongated, not more than 3 cm (1.2 in) long; they are used in pickles and, when powdered, as Cayenne pepper. The Hungarian *paprika* is a mild race of *Capsicum annuum*, whilst the even larger 'sweet' peppers come from *C. annuum* var.

grossum. The pungency of capsicums is due to a phenolic substance, capsaicin; other constituents are vitamin C and carotenoid pigments. Capsicums are used as condiments and vegetables. They are often employed externally as counter-irritants in the form of ointments, plasters or medicated cottonwool.

p. 30	**Rosemary**	Rosemary (*Rosmarinus officinalis*) belongs to the family Labiatae, from which so many essential oils are obtained. It occurs wild in Italy on seashores, cliffs and slopes; elsewhere it is cultivated or naturalized. It is an evergreen, branched shrub up to 1·5 metres (5 feet) in height, with scented, linear entire leaves which are green and glabrous above but white and very hairy below. In Italy its flowering period lasts from the winter through to the following autumn. The flowers are borne in spikes and have a campanulate calyx with a bifid inferior lip and a three-toothed superior one; the corolla is pale blue with two lips, the superior being bilobate and the inferior trifid. The glandular hairs of the leaves contain the oil of rosemary, the constituents of which include terpenes, cineole, borneol and bornyl acetate. Rosemary also contains flavone pigments, a depside, a bitter principle and triterpenoids. It is used as a flavouring and a digestive; the oil is used in perfumery and as an antiseptic, particularly in veterinary practice.
	Boldo	The boldo (*Peumus boldus*) belongs to the family Monimiaceae. It is a shrub or small tree reaching a maximum height of five to six metres (16 to 20 feet), native to Chile. It has perennial, opposite leaves on short petioles, elliptical or oval in shape, rough to the touch, aromatic, and up to 6 cm ($2\frac{1}{2}$ inches) long. The boldo has dioecious flowers, borne in small corymbs and appearing at the end of winter or in spring. Boldo leaves are used in the form of an infusion as a biliary stimulant. They contain the alkaloid boldine, and an essential oil.
	Artichoke	The horticultural artichoke (*Cynara scolymus*) was derived by cultivation from *C. cardunculus*, the wood artichoke, a Composite found wild in southern Europe, North Africa, Madeira and the Canary Islands. The artichoke is widely cultivated; it is a herbaceous perennial, about a metre (over 3 feet) high, with pinnatisect, fairly long radical leaves and shorter cauline leaves. It flowers in the summer; the flowering scapes bear one or two flowering heads which are covered with fleshy bracts (the edible parts) of a dark green colour, changing to violet. The bracts are occasionally spiny, sometimes not. The flowers are tubular, with a long blue corolla. The cauline leaves constitute the drug. The active principles are polyphenols, the chief being cynarine, flavonoids and enzymes, particularly a very active oxydase. Besides being used as a vegetable, the artichoke is employed for its biliary stimulant, digestive and diuretic properties. Various preparations such as wines, tinctures and pills are made.
p. 32	**Garlic**	Garlic (*Allium sativum*), a member of the family Liliaceae not found in the wild state, is widely cultivated for its strong flavour and aroma. It is a perennial plant with linear greyish-green leaves, producing globular heads of white or reddish flowers. It has a bulb divided into oblong bulblets or 'cloves', wrapped in a single integument. The active ingredient of the drug extracted from the bulb is an essential oil containing glycosides which decompose to give volatile sulphur compounds; other constituents are sugars, pectin, vitamins A, B_1, B_2, B_3 and C. Applied externally, garlic acts as a counter-irritant. Taken internally, it has antiseptic, diuretic, hypotensive and vermifugal properties. It is widely used in cooking and as a condiment.
	Sage	Sage (*Salvia officinalis*), of the family Labiatae, grows wild in Italy and is cultivated throughout most of Europe. It is a shrubby, profusely branched plant up to 80 cm (over $2\frac{1}{2}$ feet) in height, with stems that are woody near the base and herbaceous above. The lower leaves are petiolate and oblong-lanceolate, the upper ones sessile, smaller, and acute to acuminate; they have a rough, reticulate surface, light in colour and hairy below. The purple flowers grow in terminal spikes. Sage has a strongly aromatic odour and taste. Its essential oil contains a terpene ketone and other terpene derivatives. Sage is much used as a flavouring and is particularly useful for its preservative antioxidant action. It is a favourite domestic remedy and, besides acting as a tonic and digestive, has antiseptic properties.

| | Clary | Clary or clary sage (*Salvia sclarea*) grows wild in most parts of Italy. It is a perennial herb with large triangular-ovate, petiolate leaves which are very hairy. In the verticillate flowers that form the rather sparse panicles, the upper lip of the corolla is purple, the lower one whitish. The whole plant has a strong odour which is due to the essential oil; this oil, which is used in perfumery, contains linalol and its esters. Clary is a popular domestic remedy and is sometimes added to wines. |

p. 34   **Meadow sage**

The meadow sage (*Salvia pratensis*), a member of the family Labiatae, is common in Europe but found in only a few parts of England. It is a perennial plant with an erect stem up to 45 cm (18 inches) in height. The radical leaves are ovate to oblong, wrinkled and toothed; the stem leaves few and narrow. The flowers, which have a blue or blue-violet corolla, are arranged in vertical whorls, forming a terminal spike. The drug is obtained from the flowers and contains substances with properties similar to those of sage and clary (*v.* above).

Hemp agrimony

Hemp agrimony (*Eupatorium cannabinum*) is most frequently found in wet grassy or wooded sites; it belongs to the family Compositae. It has a perennial rootstock and erect stems a metre or more (over 3 feet) in height. The leaves are opposite, short-stalked and palmately lobed with three to five lanceolate segments, coarsely toothed. The flowers are grouped in composite corymbs; the individual florets are all tubular. They have a pleasant odour and a rose-purple or white corolla with a five-toothed margin. Hemp agrimony has cholagogic and laxative properties, which are more marked in the rhizome than in the leaves. Both are used medicinally in the form of an infusion. They contain bitter principles, sesquiterpene lactones and a little essential oil. The rhizome also contains inulin.

Sweet fern

Common polypody or sweet fern (*Polypodium vulgare*) is a fern belonging to the family Polypodiaceae. It is fairly common and can be found on walls, cliffs or rocks and at the foot of old trees. Its form is essentially that of a tufted rhizome, of creeping habit, covered with scales. The fronds which arise from this rootstock are 10 to 30 cm (4 to 12 inches) long, oblong-lanceolate, with linear lanceolate segments which are joined at the base. On the underside of the fronds, in two rows parallel to the median vein, are large round sori, brown in colour and lacking an indusium. The rhizome of polypody is used in popular medicine as a purgative and vermifuge. Its constituents require further investigation but probably resemble those of male fern (*Dryopteris filix-mas*), a member of the same family (*v.* p. 56).

p. 36   **Dandelion**

The dandelion (*Taraxacum officinale*) is among the most widely diffused of all the Compositae. Meadows, hedgerows, grassy banks and waste land from sea level to high hills are starred with this little plant. It is a rather polymorphous perennial. The large vertical rootstock continues into a thick tap-root; on this arises a rosette of more or less deeply dentate leaves with hollow ribs. The yellow ligulate florets form solitary heads supported on hollow, erect leafless stalks larger than the leaves. All parts of the dandelion contain a branched system of latex tubes from which a milky juice exudes when the plant is broken. In the USSR a related plant, *Taraxacum kok-saghiz*, is grown commercially for the production of rubber. European dandelion root contains up to 25% of the carbohydrate inulin which is a characteristic constituent of the Compositae. It also contains resins, latex, triterpenoids and bitter principles; one of the bitter principles is probably identical with the lactucopicrin found in chicory (*v.* below). The leaves, which are often used in salads, are rich in vitamins B and C. Both root and leaves are diuretic and aperient.

Chicory

Wild chicory or succory (*Cichorium intybus*) is another plant of the family Compositae, common in pastures and on waste land, roadsides and escarpments. It is an annual, biennial or perennial herb rather more than a metre (well over 3 feet) in height. Like the dandelion, it has a large rootstock and tap-root. Its hairy, branching stem rises from a rosette of leaves rather variable in shape, lanceolate to spathulate with margins ranging from dentate to runcinate. The sessile flowerheads, grouped in threes and fours, consist of an involucre made up of two series of bracts and some fifteen bright blue, more rarely pink or white, florets with a five-toothed ligule about 2 cm (0·8 inches) long. Under cultivation the wild chicory has been modified into a number of types. One of these is mainly grown for chicory root, and another (Witloof or endive) for its leaves. Chicory roots lifted from the ground and later forced develop the crisp white leaf buds known as chicons. Blanching reduces the bitter taste of both endive and chicons. Chicory contains much inulin and bitter substances such as lactucopicrin. It is used as a domestic remedy for its bitter-tonic and diuretic properties. Dried and roasted chicory root is used as an addition to, or in place of coffee and was much drunk in Europe during both World Wars.

p. 38	**Aubergine**	The eggplant or aubergine (*Solanum melongena*) belongs to the family Solanaceae. It is a tender annual plant with oval petiolate leaves which are often spiny along the veins. It has solitary violet flowers and large globular or elongated fruits in the form of berries. The white or violet fruits are widely grown for culinary purposes in both Europe and America. Italian writers credit the fruits with diuretic and cholagogic properties, but analysis shows them to contain little but the anthocyanin colouring matters, caffeic acid, choline and trigonelline.
	Buckbean	The buckbean or marsh trefoil (*Menyanthes trifoliata*) belongs to the family Gentianaceae. It is an aquatic perennial herb with a long creeping rhizome and long-stalked leaves, inserted in the apex of the rhizome, which are subdivided into three leaflets. The flowers have a five-toothed calyx and a white corolla tinged with red. The fruit is a subglobular capsule. The leaves and flowers are used. Like other members of the gentian family, the buckbean contains bitter principles, one called menyanthine, with other substances such as betulinic acid and colouring matters. In popular medicine it is used as a bitter tonic, febrifuge and laxative. In large doses it is purgative and emetic.
	Vanilla	Vanilla (*Vanilla planifolia*) belongs to the family Orchidaceae. It is a perennial herbaceous epiphyte, growing by means of white, fleshy adventitious roots. The leaves are equally fleshy, shiny and glabrous. The vanilla orchid is a native of Mexico, where it is pollinated by very long-tongued insects; in countries such as Réunion, the Seychelles and Tahiti where vanilla is cultivated, such insects are absent and the flowers have to be hand-pollinated. The fruits (pods) are collected when the colour changes from green to yellow. They are then subjected to a lengthy process of fermentation and drying during which they become almost black in colour and changes take place in the constituents which result in white crystals of vanillin being deposited on the surface. The fresh fruits contain several glycosides, one of which, glucovanillin, decomposes during curing into vanillin and glucose. The other glycosides decompose in a similar way. Vanilla pods are used as a flavouring in cooking and as an addition to chocolate. A tincture or essence made from the pods is more expensive but has a better odour and taste than one made only from vanillin. The latter can be obtained more cheaply by chemical means, for example from the eugenol present in oil of cloves.
p.40	**Seville orange**	The Seville or bitter orange (*Citrus aurantium* var. *bigaradia* or *amara*), of the family Rutaceae, is a strong-flavoured orange grown quite extensively in Italy, Spain and elsewhere for the sake of its leaves, flowers and fruit. It is a tree less than ten metres ($32\frac{1}{2}$ feet) high with spiny branches and glossy green, oval, very aromatic leaves growing on long, winged petioles. The flowers have five white, highly fragrant petals, and are arranged in small terminal cymes. The fruit looks like an ordinary orange but has very bitter, sour pulp and peel. The leaves are made into a bitter tonic and an antispasmodic remedy, while the flowers, picked before they open, are used for flavouring. Far more important is the bitter orange peel, which contains a high-quality essential oil with tonic, digestive and stomachic properties. This oil contains limonene and terpene alcohols which are both in the free state and as esters. The flowers contain a quite different essential oil which is used in perfumery.
	Angelica	Garden angelica (*Angelica archangelica* or *A. officinalis*) is an Umbelliferous herb that grows in moist, shady situations in northern and eastern Europe. It is a perennial about two metres (over 6 feet) tall with a large rhizome and a striated branching stem bearing

large irregular, serrate bi- or tripinnatisect leaves. The greenish-white florets are disposed in a compound umbel of 20 to 30 rays; the fruit is an angular oblong cremocarp marked by three conspicuous ridges. Long cultivated for confectionery, both fruit and roots yield an essential oil greatly valued in the perfumery, cosmetic and distillery industries; this contains phellandrene and furocoumarins. The young petioles are often candied with sugar and used in confectionery.

Wild cherry The sour cherry illustrated is among the many varieties derived from the wild cherry *Prunus cerasus*, of the family Rosaceae, which has a drupaceous fruit, pale pink to amber in colour and pointed at the tip. Sour cherries contain vitamin C; their colouring is due to anthocyanin glycosides. Their chief medicinal virtue lies, however, in the juice from the pulp, which, in the form of a syrup, is used to disguise the taste of disagreeable medicines.

Raspberry The wild raspberry (*Rubus idaeus*), of the family Rosaceae, is found in woods throughout Europe and Asia, and is widely cultivated for its fruit. It has a perennial creeping rootstock. The leaves are pinnate, composed of three to seven ovate, dentate leaflets which are green above but covered with a whitish down on the lower surface. The flowers have white or pale pink petals. The fruits (raspberries) are composed of numerous dark red drupelets having a pleasant taste and a delicate fragrance. Raspberry juice, which is rich in vitamins B_1 and especially C, as well as containing a number of salts, is used in the pharmaceutical industry to make certain medicinal products more palatable. The leaves contain tannin and are sometimes used in the form of an infusion as an astringent gargle.

p. 42 **Peppermint** Peppermint (*Mentha piperita*) belongs to the family Labiatae. Among the mints there are many species, varieties and hybrids. Peppermint is generally regarded as a hybrid between *Mentha aquatica* (water mint) and *M. viridis* or *M. spicata* (garden mint or spearmint). Also grown in England is *Mentha pulegium*, the pennyroyal. All the mints have square stems, creeping rhizomes and flowers arranged in verticillasters. The black variety of peppermint, commonly grown in England, has purplish stems and leaves; the leaves are petiolate, up to 8 cm (over 3 inches) long, and have an acute apex and a serrate margin. The flowers, arranged in spikes, are purple. The plant has an aromatic odour and taste which is due to the essential oil contained in the numerous glandular hairs. This oil varies in composition with its source, and English, American and Japanese peppermint oils each have their own characteristics. All, however, contain terpenes and the alcohol menthol, which is present both in the free state and as esters. The herb also contains flavonoid colouring matters, a bitter principle and triterpenoids. Besides being a source of the oil and menthol, peppermint is used as a carminative and flavouring agent. Its leaves make a pleasant change from the ordinary garden mint for making mint sauce.

Hyssop Hyssop (*Hyssopus officinalis*), of the family Labiatae, occurs in Italy and elsewhere in dry, stony places. It is a small bushy herb up to 60 cm (nearly 2 feet) high. The stem is woody near the base and carries small, opposite lanceolate leaves. The flowers are arranged in verticillasters, and each has a bluish-purple two-lipped corolla. All parts have a strong aromatic odour which is due to the essential oil contained in the glandular hairs; and a warm, slightly bitter taste. The leaves and flowering tops are used in the form of an infusion as a stimulant and expectorant. Hyssop contains essential oil, ursolic acid, oleanolic acid and flavone glycosides. It is widely cultivated for use as a pot herb.

Aniseed The aniseed (*Pimpinella anisum*) is an annual of the family Umbelliferae. It originated in the Middle East and is now cultivated throughout the Mediterranean area. It bears pinnately divided leaves and small flowers arranged in compound umbels, which are without bracts. The fruits are about 6 mm ($\frac{1}{4}$ inch) long, greyish-brown and pear-shaped: they are slightly hairy and have a characteristic aromatic odour and taste. The fruits contain both essential oil and fatty oil. The essential oil (oil of anise) contains up to 90% of anethole; its composition is almost identical with the oil obtained from the star anise (*Illicium verum*; v. p. 154), which belongs to an entirely different family, the Magnoliaceae. Aniseed has a carminative action, the fruit being used in an infusion. Oil of anise is much used in liqueurs, confectionery and perfumery.

Cardamom The cardamom (*Elettaria cardamomum*), a member of the family Zingiberaceae, occurs in two varieties, var. *minuscula* and var. *major*. The fruits illustrated are those of the *minuscula* variety, which is widely cultivated in Ceylon (Sri Lanka) and southern India. The plant is reed-like, up to four metres (13 feet) high, and bears large elongated leaves which arise from a rhizome. The aerial stems bear racemes of flowers and the capsular fruits. The latter are rounded or somewhat triangular and have three chambers each containing

189

numerous seeds which have a pleasant odour and a pungent taste. The essential oil of the seeds contains terpinyl acetate and cineole. Cardamom seeds are widely used, particularly in the East (for curries) and in Scandinavia (for flavouring cakes). The oil from the seeds of the larger-fruited var. *major*, which grows wild in Ceylon, is mainly used in liqueurs. The relatively small quantities of cardamom used in pharmacy are employed as flavouring agents and carminatives.

p. 44   **Iris**

Of the many species and varieties of *Iris* (family Iridaceae), those usually regarded as sources of the drug are *Iris florentina*, *I. germanica* and *I. pallida*. *Iris florentina*, which has bluish-white flowers, is probably a form of one of the species with bluish-purple flowers (*v.* illustration). The plants are perennials with fleshy rhizomes. The latter, scraped free from cork and slowly dried, gradually develop their characteristic odour and are known as 'orris root'. The leaves are sabre-like, and the flowering stem, up to a metre ($3\frac{1}{4}$ feet) in height, usually bears from three to six large flowers. Orris root is sometimes used in the form of a decoction as a diuretic and expectorant, but its main uses are in liqueur manufacture and perfumery. An essential oil present in orris contains irone, a substance with an intense violet odour; as orris is used in dusting powders for babies, these are sometimes called violet powders.

Sweet sedge

The sweet flag or sweet sedge (*Acorus calamus*) is an aquatic perennial herbaceous plant, belonging to the family Araceae. It has a flattened branching rhizome up to 2 cm (0·8 inches) in diameter, carrying numerous roots from which the sword-shaped leaves arise. In spring, the triangular stem bears simple erect inflorescences with a leaf-like spathe; the inflorescence is composed of a large number of single inconspicuous flowers. Sweet flag contains a bitter principle and an essential oil, one component of which is a substance called asarone. The root has long been used as a digestive and diuretic, and enters into the composition of some liqueurs and perfumes. There is recent evidence that asarone has insecticidal properties.

p. 46   **Orchid tubers**

The tubers of various orchids (family Orchidaceae) have been employed medicinally but are now little used except as described below. Various species, such as *Orchis morio* (the green-winged orchid; *v.* illustration), have tubers which were formerly imported into England from Turkey under the name of salep. The most important constituents of such orchid tubers appear to be abundant mucilage, starch and traces of volatile oil. These give the powdered tubers the property of forming a thick, slightly scented jelly with water. Their powder is so used, particularly in the Levant, in various foods and drinks (juleps), ice cream and confectionery. Of the species employed, *Orchis morio* has a thick stem up to 20 cm (8 inches) high and spherical or ovoid tubers; the tubers of *O. mascula*, *O. militaris* and *O. purpurea*, as well as those of plants belonging to some other genera of the same family, are used in the same way. British readers, however, are earnestly requested not to make such use of any British wild orchid, many species of which are rare and endangered.

p. 48   **Dog rose**

The dog rose (*Rosa canina*), of the family Rosaceae, is widely distributed in Europe and Asia, but is confined to the northern part of Africa. It is a shrub not more than two to three metres ($6\frac{1}{2}$ to 10 feet) in height, typical of hedgerows and thickets, producing robust branches equipped with hooked prickles enlarged at the base. Its leaves are composed of five to seven oval or elliptical leaflets with dentate margins. The solitary flowers, arranged in corymbs, have pale pink or white petals. The scarlet ovoid fruit, known as a hip, is formed by the swollen receptacle and contains very hairy achenes with an acid, pungent but quite agreeable flavour.

Sea buckthorn

The growing area of the sea buckthorn (*Hippophae rhamnoides*), belonging to the family Elaeagnaceae, is limited to temperate Europe and Asia. It is fairly common near rivers and on escarpments and detrital soil. It is an intricately branched, prickly shrub three to four metres (10 to 13 feet) tall with nearly sessile, entire, linear-lanceolate, alternate leaves which are green on the upper surface and silvery-reddish below. The small flowers are inconspicuous; the orange berry (a pseudo-drupe) is formed from the perianth, which develops into a covering for the membranous pericarp. The fruits of both the dog rose and the sea buckthorn contain a high percentage of vitamin C and thereby possess antiscorbutic properties.

Blackcurrant

The blackcurrant (*Ribes nigrum*), of the family Saxifragaceae, grows in cool, shady places and woods, especially in mountain areas. It is a shrub about two metres (over 6 feet) in height, without prickles. The leaves, when rubbed, emit a distinctive aromatic smell; they are large, stalked and palmately lobed with three to five lobes, dentate at the margin and downy on the lower surface. The deep pink flowers hang in loose racemes which, at the height of summer, bear the juicy, sweetish black currants. Pharmacologists are concerned with the leaves and fruits, which have refreshing, tonic, diuretic and depurative properties.

p. 50   **Black bryony**

Black bryony (*Tamus communis*) is a member of the family Dioscoreaceae. It is fairly widespread in Britain, growing in hedges, scrubland and thickets. The plant is a perennial, climbing by means of its striated twining stems, which grow clock-wise. The leaves are alternate, petiolate and cordate in shape with an acuminate apex; they are occasionally lobed. The flowers are dioecious and arranged in axillary racemes; they are very small and yellowish-green in colour. The fruits are very conspicuous red berries, about 1 cm (0·4 inches) in diameter, each containing three to six globular seeds. The drug consists of the fleshy root, which contains poisonous principles (not fully investigated), probably of the saponin type. It is rarely used internally, but has emetic and purgative properties. Used externally, in poultices, it is said to be very effective for treating bruises.

Asarabacca

Asarum or asarabacca (*Asarum europaeum*) belongs to the family Aristolochiaceae. It is sometimes known as European snake-root to distinguish it from Canadian snake-root (*Asarum canadense*). It grows in beech and alder woods in the Alps and Apennines; it is rare in Britain. Although it is mentioned in classical writings and official in some pharmacopoeias to the end of the nineteenth century, recent writers make special mention of its poisonous properties and recommend that it should not be used without medical advice. Asarum is a herbaceous perennial with a creeping rhizome, brown in colour and bearing short, thin branches, each of which has two long-stalked leaves, coriaceous and kidney-shaped, with pubescent veins and margins, green on the upper surface and yellowish-green below. The flowers are small, purple and solitary, carried on a short peduncle; they appear between March and June, and have little or no ornamental value. The rhizomes and leaves, which constitute the drug, contain asarine, essential oil, resin, tannin and starch; allantoin, a ureide found in other plants such as comfrey, was isolated from asarum in 1966. These substances, particularly the essential oil, which has a pleasant camphorated aromatic odour, have powerful emetic and, in smaller doses, purgative and expectorant qualities. Recent researches on other members of the Aristolochiaceae (but not asarum) have found alkaloids and anti-tumour properties.

p. 52   **Black hellebore**

The black hellebore or Christmas rose (*Helleborus niger*) belongs to the family Ranunculaceae. It is a perennial herb, typical of mountain woods, with a short creeping rhizome from which arise a small number of leaves with long petioles. The leaves are divided into five to nine segments and have a partially serrated margin; they are deep green in colour, leathery in texture. Hellebore flowers in the winter, sometimes around Christmas, and produces flowering stems 10 to 20 cm (4 to 8 inches) high, carrying one or two large flowers with a perianth composed of five white sections tinted on the outside with rose. Between the numerous stamens and the perianth is a series of green nectaries. The fruits are follicular. The drug is derived from the rhizome and has emetic, revulsive and sternutatory properties.

Green hellebore	The green hellebore or bear's-foot (*Helleborus viridis*) is also a perennial herb of woods, hedges and thickets. The leaves, borne on a much longer stalk than those of black hellebore, are larger but much more indented and less leathery in texture. During the winter and on into the spring, the plants produce numerous flowering stems, taller than those of *Helleborus niger*; the perianth sections are greenish. The uses of green hellebore are more or less the same as those of black hellebore. A similar plant, the stinking hellebore (*Helleborus foetidus*; not illustrated), may be distinguished by its drooping, purple-edged flowers and unpleasant smell.
Winter aconite	The winter aconite or cock's foot (*Eranthis hyemalis*) also belongs to the Ranunculaceae. It is a small herbaceous perennial which produces its flowers at the end of the winter, before its leaves. The flowers, of a fine lemon yellow, are composed of five to eight sepaloid petals; the true petals, as often occurs among the Ranunculaceae, are transformed into nectaries. Each flower produces a variable number of follicular fruits. The leaves are palmatisect. The entire vegetative period of the plant is rather brief. The rhizome resembles the hellebores in its action. Like them, this plant is toxic.

p. 54

Wormwood	*Artemisia absinthium*, the absinth or wormwood plant, is a perennial of the family Compositae, found in waste places. It grows to about a metre (over 3 feet) in height and has petiolate, bi- or tripinnate lower leaves, smaller and less incised upper ones. The yellowish, hemispherical flowers grow in large terminal panicles. Leaves and flowerheads supply the drug, which is used in infusions, tinctures and medicated wines with stomach-tonic, digestive and febrifugal properties, effective also as vermifuges and emmenagogues. The essential oil has been used to flavour vermouths and liqueurs, including the notorious absinthe.
Pomegranate	The pomegranate (*Punica granatum*) belongs to the family Punicaceae. It is a small tree or shrub, four to five metres (13 to 16 feet) high at the most, with an erect trunk covered with bark that is reddish at first, later grey. The rigid, spiny branches bear lanceolate leaves, alternate or occasionally clustered. The flowers are solitary as a rule, but sometimes appear in twos and threes; a short pedicel carries the bright red corolla. The pendant spherical fruit has a very woody pericarp and ends in a little crown formed of the old calyx. It is divided internally by membranous pale yellow septa into irregular loculi containing polyhedral seeds with a gelatinous garnet-red outer covering; in the centre is a woody kernel. The fruit has a pleasant sweet-sour taste. As a medicinal plant, the pomegranate has taenifugal and astringent qualities, present in practically the entire plant. At one time the rind of the fruit was used, but it is now considered more advisable to use the bark, especially the root bark. Its remedial properties are due to several alkaloids, principally pelletierine, which has a strong vermifugal action, and to gallotannic and punicotannic acid, which have an astringent effect. In cases of tapeworm, the fresh bark can be taken in the form of a decoction, infusion or potion; since the drug only paralyses the parasite, an effective purgative must be taken an hour later to expel it.
Coralline	The true coralline (*Corallina officinalis*) is a light red seaweed, strongly impregnated with lime; it is usually fixed to its substrate by a disc, and has erect thalli 4 to 5 cm (1½ to 2 inches) long with irregular opposite primary and secondary branches. Until the late eighteenth century, coralline was known to pharmacists for its vermifugal action; it contains bromine, iodine, traces of arsenic and pentose. Several other red algae, mostly belonging to the genera *Fania*, *Gelidium* and *Grateloupia*, are used, particularly in Japan, for making agar; this is used for food and for making the jelly on which bacteria are grown in the laboratory.
Chenopodium	Anthelminthic ingredients are also present in *Chenopodium ambrosioides* var. *anthelminthicum* (known as American wormseed or Mexican tea), a herbaceous annual of waste places belonging to the family Chenopodiaceae. The plant is 30 to 50 cm (12 to 20 inches) high, with flowers clustered into spikelets that, in turn, form a panicle. The drug is made from the flowering and fruiting tops.

p. 56

Male fern	The male fern (*Dryopteris filix-mas*) belongs to the Aspidiaceae, a subfamily of the Polypodiaceae; it is found in shady, damp woods in submontane and mountainous regions. It is a perennial, with a rather short, thick rhizome, creeping or slightly erect,

covered with shiny brown or black leaflet bases and golden-brown scales and bearing numerous brown and black thread-like roots. The fronds are erect, petiolate, up to 50 cm (nearly 20 inches) long, doubly pinnatipartite, with small oval denticulate secondary lobes with a large tooth at the base. On the underside of the leaves, along the median vein, are two parallel rows of sori, covered by an indusium, containing small ovoid spores. The rhizome of the male fern is used; this contains filicic acid, also called filicine, flavaspidic acid, albaspidine, aspidinol and filmarone, as well as sugar, essential oil, fatty oil, waxes, green colouring matter, resins and so on. It has anthelminthic, especially taenifugal properties, if followed by an energetic purgative, but it should not be used without medical supervision.

Santolina *Santolina chamaecyparissus* is a Composite, found in dry, rocky regions in the Mediterranean area; it is sometimes grown in gardens under the name of lavender cotton. The plant is a small bush, reaching just over 50 cm (20 inches) in height, woody at the base, with numerous branches and an unpleasant odour. The fleshy leaves, 2 to 3 cm (about an inch) long, are composed of almost linear segments arranged in four rows. The yellow flowerheads consist entirely of tubular florets. The flowering heads are used in medicine; the seeds contain a bitter alkaloid, tannin, resins and an essential oil of complex composition. The drug acts as an anthelminthic, but its use has been discontinued.

Feverfew The feverfew (*Chrysanthemum parthenium*) is found particularly on walls and waste ground, sometimes as an escape from cultivation. It is a perennial Composite with erect stems up to 70 or 80 cm (around 2½ feet) high. It is very aromatic and has soft, petiolate leaves which are pinnatisect, with three to six pairs of segments. The flowerheads, up to 2 cm (0·8 inches) in diameter, are grouped in a terminal corymb. Feverfew is an emmenagogue and antispasmodic, recommended in cases of painful menstruation. A decoction of the flowers can be used as a poultice to treat bruises and skin ulcers.

p. 58 **Carob** The carob (*Ceratonia siliqua*) belongs to the family Leguminosae. It is a moderately tall tree with a globular head and a wrinkled and contorted trunk; it bears evergreen leaves, paripinnate with two to five pairs of leaflets, deep green in colour and fairly coriaceous. The flowers are also produced on the branches and even on the trunk. The fruits are large pods, indehiscent, brown in colour when ripe and containing numerous seeds embedded in juicy pulp containing sugar and gum; they are sometimes known as St John's bread. The carob originated in southeastern Europe and Asia Minor and is extensively cultivated in the Mediterranean area. In folk medicine, a decoction of the flowers, coarsely crumbled, is used as a laxative, while the meal made from the seeds is an excellent antidiarrhetic for young babies, and can be used to thicken liquid food or milk to prevent vomiting.

Black mulberry The black mulberry (*Morus nigra*) belongs to the family Moraceae. It is a tree of moderate height, formerly much cultivated for feeding silkworms; its appearance is often greatly modified by the practice of pollarding. Its leaves are rough; the fruits (mulberries) are multiple, each arising from a number of flowers. The leaves have hypoglycaemic and astringent properties; the fruits, in the form of a syrup, have been used in folk medicine as a laxative and intestinal regulator.

Manna ash Manna is provided largely by the manna ash or flowering ash (*Fraxinus ornus*), which belongs to the family Oleaceae. This is a tree of moderate height (up to 10 metres, or over 30 feet), with imparipinnate leaves having two to four pairs of leaflets, generally rather rounded. In spring the tree produces large inflorescences of fairly small white flowers. The fruit is a key (winged nut) about 2 cm (0·4 inches) long and 5 mm (0·1 inches) wide, which is scattered by the wind. The drug manna is derived from the sap which oozes from incisions purposely made in young plants; Sicily is the chief centre of collection. In this form, it is used as a mild purgative and intestinal regulator; the principal component, mannite, can be easily administered to children in sweetened milk.

p. 60 **Mullein** Of the various species of *Verbascum*, the one known in English as mullein or great mullein is the indigenous plant *Verbascum thapsus*; it belongs to the family Scrophulariaceae. It is a biennial herbaceous plant which can reach a height of 1·5 metres (5 feet) or

193

more when in flower; from a rosette of large, velvety whitish leaves arises a flowering stem which bears a large terminal spike. The flowers, of a pleasant golden yellow, are pentamerous, with rounded petals which are fused together and fall easily when the plant is shaken. The flowers and leaves of mullein are used. They should be gathered in summer and then dried rapidly, and can be used in various ways. An infusion of flowers, carefully filtered after an hour's maceration, or an infusion of leaves can be used to treat intestinal inflammation, and also as an emollient and pectoral remedy in cases of bronchial catarrh. The decoction can be used as an enema in the treatment of diarrhoea with griping. The fresh flowers can be used crushed as a poultice for insect bites, and an excellent ointment for easing the inflammation of haemorrhoids and chilblains can be obtained by macerating one part of flowers with two parts of olive oil for a week and then reducing the volume over very low heat.

Flax
The common flax or linseed (*Linum usitatissimum*) belongs to the family Linaceae. The seeds are readily available commercially. Because of their high mucilage content, they are used as general emollients, for either internal or external use. Macerated in water, they constitute an excellent bland intestinal regulator, indicated in troublesome forms of constipation; an infusion can also be employed. A decoction of the seeds, strained, can be used as an emollient and refreshing enema to relieve intestinal inflammation. For external use, a hot poultice, made by mixing equal parts of linseed meal and warm water and heating over a slow fire to obtain a satisfactory consistency, serves to resolve inflammations and to bring boils and abscesses to a head.

Tamarind
The tamarind (*Tamarindus indica*) is a tree of tropical origin, belonging to the Caesalpinioideae subfamily of the Leguminosae. The pulp of the fruit is available commercially in the form of a sugary mass containing fragments of the pod and seeds. A small dose has generally refreshing properties and can be used to make very pleasant drinks. The pulp is also a laxative.

p. 62   **Tormentil**
The tormentil (*Potentilla tormentilla* or *P. erecta*) is one of the many members of the family Rosaceae found in humid woods and fields in hills and mountains. It is a herbaceous perennial with a thick rhizome from which arise numerous slender stems, recumbent at the base and bearing many leaves. The whole plant is covered with appressed silky hairs. The radical leaves have long petioles and have already withered by the time of flowering; the upper leaves have little or no petiole and three (occasionally more) obovate-lanceolate, dentate leaflets. The flowers are borne on long peduncles and have golden yellow corollas, the petals being slightly longer than the sepals. The rhizome of the tormentil is used in pharmacology; its chief components are tormentillin, a crystalline glucoside with a high percentage of tannin, resin, chinonic acid, ellagic acid, calcium oxalate and starch. The presence of tannic substances gives tormentil antidiarrhetic and antidysenteric properties.

Cornelian cherry
The cornelian cherry or cornel (*Cornus mas*) is one of the few species belonging to the family Cornaceae and grows in wild and stony places. It is a bush or shrub, three to six metres (10 to 20 feet) high, rather slow-growing, with a greyish-brown, generally contorted trunk and greenish branches which may be reddish where they are exposed to the sun. The leaves are opposite, oval, slightly downy on the underside, and appear at the beginning of spring. The flowers, with yellow petals, appear before the leaves and are grouped in simple umbels. The fruits are red, the size of an olive, and ripen at the height of summer. The bark and the fruits have astringent properties, and also act as a tonic and febrifuge. Similar active principles are found in dogwood (*Cornus sanguinea*), a species which when not producing its white flowers is barely distinguishable from the cornelian cherry.

Sanicle
Sanicle (*Sanicula europaea*) is an Umbelliferous plant found in shady mountain situations, typically found in the undergrowth of beech woods. It is a herbaceous perennial with a short horizontal rhizome and a simple or slightly branched erect stem reaching a maximum height of 40 cm (nearly 16 inches). The leaves are shiny, those at the base being petiolate and divided into about five palmate segments or lobes, while the upper cauline leaves are reduced to the point of being almost sessile. The flowers, borne in umbels, vary in colour from white to pink. The drug is derived from the rhizome and leaves; it contains tannic and fatty substances, a saponin, a resin, a bitter principle and some essential oil, all of which confer astringent and vulnerary properties. An infusion of the drug is a mild astringent.

194

p. 64	**Arbutus**	The arbutus or strawberry tree (*Arbutus unedo*) belongs to the family Ericaceae. It is a large shrub with reddish bark, bearing elliptical to obovate leaves with a serrate margin and a glossy, dark green colour. It flowers in autumn, producing small whitish flowers with a characteristic pitcher-shaped corolla. The fruits are bright red berries with a granulated, tuberculated surface, and have a sweet, astringent flavour. The leaves act as an astringent, and also as a diuretic and urinary disinfectant. A decoction or a powder can be used in home medicine. A conserve of the fruit also has astringent properties.
	Oak galls	These galls are curious formations produced on oak trees (species of *Quercus*, especially *Q. infectoria*) by the puncture of a hymenopterous insect of the genus *Cynips*. They contain tannin and have astringent properties, but are used almost exclusively in industry as tanning material and for the manufacture of tannic acid.
	Salad burnet	Salad burnet (*Poterium sanguisorba* or *Sanguisorba minor*) belongs to the family Rosaceae. It is a perennial herbaceous plant with a short rhizome and pinnatisect leaves arranged in a rosette; the leaves have five to ten pairs of segments with toothed margins. The flowering stems are 20 to 50 cm (8 to 20 inches) high and are topped by small ovoidal heads. The drug is derived from the leaves or the entire plant. It is used in folk medicine as an astringent in the form of an infusion in hot water; after cold maceration; or as an alcoholic extract in an infusion of lemon-scented verbena. In the spring the young leaves, which have a pleasant taste, can be eaten in salads.
p. 66	**White dead-nettle**	The white dead-nettle (*Lamium album*) belongs to the family Labiatae. It is a herbaceous perennial, very common in Britain, found in humid grassy places. It produces annual erect, square stems 20 to 30 cm (8 to 12 inches) high, bearing decussate leaves with irregularly toothed margins resembling those of the stinging nettle (hence its common name). It flowers in the spring, producing terminal inflorescences known as verticillasters which are characteristic of the family; the flowers have white labiate corollas. White dead-nettle has astringent properties and can be used in cases of diarrhoea or other disturbances of the digestive system, and also as a diuretic, for gynaecological disorders, and externally as a vulnerary and resolvent in cases of burns, varicoses and ulcers. It can be used in the form of an infusion, a stronger one being prepared for external uses (compresses, poultices, vaginal douches).
	Purple loosestrife	The purple loosestrife or salicaria (*Lythrum salicaria*) belongs to the family Lythraceae, and is a herbaceous perennial typical of wet and marshy places. The annual aerial stems grow to a good two metres (over 6 feet) in height. It has sessile, lanceolate leaves, cordate at the base and slightly hairy. Each stem terminates in a large inflorescence formed of numerous dense whorls of five to eight red flowers. The flowering top has general astringent and haemostatic properties; it can be used as an infusion, a powder or a syrup. A poultice of ground-up leaves may be applied externally, to bruises, abrasions and so on.
p. 68	**Squirting cucumber**	The elaterium or squirting cucumber (*Ecballium elaterium*) is a Cucurbite typical of ruins and waste places in general in the Mediterranean region. It has a large fleshy root, creeping stems and large, petiolate greenish leaves. The flowers are yellowish and unisexual: the male flowers are borne in racemes, the female solitary and carried on a long peduncle. The fruit is an ovoid berry, deep green when immature and slightly yellowish when ripe; when fully ripe it virtually explodes, distributing the seeds for a long distance. The drug elaterium is extracted from the immature fruit, being the sediment from the juice; it was included in the British Pharmaceutical Codex down to 1963, supplies being imported from Malta. It contains elaterin, starch, phytosterol and fatty acids, and is a powerful purgative. Much research has been done in recent years on plants of the family Cucurbitaceae; they often contain some of the eleven known cucurbitacins, which have tumour-necrosing activity.
	Madder	Madder or dyer's madder (*Rubia tinctorum*) is a member of the family Rubiaceae found in western Asia and southern Europe. It is a perennial herbaceous plant with a creeping rhizome, numerous fruits, acute leaves arranged in whorls, and small yellow flowers. The

pharmacologically active parts are the rhizome and the roots, which contain a glycosidic principle; they have a basically purgative action, with secondary diuretic and astringent activity, and can be prepared, for instance, as a decoction.

Common buckthorn

The common buckthorn (*Rhamnus cathartica*) is a member of the family Rhamnaceae, found in woods and hedges. It is a spiny bush, rarely a shrub, growing to a height of one to five metres (3 to 16 feet). The leaves are dark green, nearly opposite, oval, slightly pointed near the top; they have a minutely toothed margin and five to seven well-marked veins. The plant flowers between April and June; the yellowish or greenish flowers are grouped in small bunches. The fruits are spherical drupes, at first greenish, turning violet-black when ripe. The berries are used in medicine, preferably when fresh, but also dried; they contain rhamnocathartin, rhamnotin, quercitin, sugars, acids, resins, pectins, etc. The drug has a strong purgative action; preparations of it can be used in cases of liver complaints, gout and skin conditions. The fresh berries should be used sparingly; overdoses produce diarrhoea with nausea and vomiting.

Alder buckthorn

The alder buckthorn or frangula (*Rhamnus frangula*) also belongs to the family Rhamnaceae. It is a bush or shrub, growing to a height of four to five metres (13 to 16 feet), and found in Britain in damp and wooded places. It has alternate, short-stalked leaves which may be elliptical, obtuse or pointed. It flowers in spring; the flowers, grouped in small axillary bunches, have five sepals and five whitish petals. The fruit is a small drupe, the size of a pea, which is reddish-purple at first, ripening to black, and contains three yellow seeds. The drug is derived from the bark of the branches and trunk. It contains the active principles frangulin, chrysophanic acid, glucofrangulin, pseudo-frangulin, and also rhamnotoxin, which tends to disappear with ageing or drying; for this reason, the bark is collected and then left to age for a year or else dried for a period dependent on the temperature used. In medicine, frangula is used in the form of a fluid or dry extract as a bland purge which does not give rise to tolerance; it is excellent in cases of chronic constipation, since it is capable of regulating intestinal peristalsis.

p.70

Convolvulus

Among the plants with purgative properties must be included the larger bindweed or convolvulus (*Convolvulus sepium*), a member of the family Convolvulaceae very common in hedgerows and thickets. It is a perennial plant with a long creeping rhizome and a twining stem that may be several metres in length. The petiolate leaves are usually cordate-lanceolate in shape, but can be sub-obtuse, acuminate or mucronate. The pink or white flowers are solitary, with funnel-shaped corollas. The active ingredients of the drug are fairly abundant throughout the plant, but most of it is extracted from the root; its medicinal properties are due to a resin with a purgative and anti-bilious action. It may be used as an infusion in boiling water.

Pokeweed

Pokeweed (*Phytolacca decandra*) is an American plant of the family Phytolaccaceae, now naturalized in many other parts of the world, including the Mediterranean region, where it often grows wild in pastures, along country lanes or on escarpments. It is a perennial herb with thick tap-roots; its annual stems, red in colour, are sometimes over two metres high (well over 6 feet). The alternate, lanceolate-oval leaves are smooth and rather soft. The flowers, blooming from July to October, are grouped in simple racemes and have whitish, five-lobed perianths. The fruit is a succulent purple berry surrounding shiny black kidney-shaped seeds. The root, gathered in winter, is the part most used for medicinal purposes. It contains saponins, starch, gum, and hemicellulose, and its ash is rich in potassium nitrate. Such active ingredients have an emetic and purgative, purifying and even slimming effect. The powdered root can be taken in water.

Castor oil plant

The castor oil plant (*Ricinus communis*) belongs to the family Euphorbiaceae. It originated in tropical Africa and is cultivated in Europe, sometimes growing wild in the southern part. An annual plant (perennial in warmer climates, where it forms a shrub or tree), it grows from its thick white roots to a height of two to three metres (6 to 10 feet); the fleshy leaves, on long petioles and often an attractive reddish-brown in colour, are alternate and palmatifid with dentate, palmately veined lobes. The flowers, growing in terminal or axillary clusters, are monoecious, the yellow male flowers being situated in the lower part of the inflorescence, the pink female flowers higher up. The fruit is a three-celled spiny capsule, containing the smooth, oval seeds with a protuberance at one end and divided into two lobes by a longitudinal ridge; they vary in colour, but are basically brown, black or red with paler stripes and spots. For medicinal use, the seeds must be gathered when very ripe, in September or soon after. They contain a fatty oil consisting largely of ricinolein, which is broken down in the duodenum, producing ricinoleic acid; also the albuminoid toxin ricin. By means of cold expression, the medicinal oil can be extracted without the ricin, which remains in the inner skin. Castor oil acts as an emollient, non-irritant purgative particularly suitable for treating constipation.

p. 72	**Aristolochia**	The genus *Aristolochia* of the family Aristolochiaceae comprises more than 300 species, distributed over the temperate and hot regions of both hemispheres. They are perennials with rhizomatous or tuberous roots. The leaves are simple and alternate, cordate at the base, occasionally tri- or bilobate; the flowers are rather large, irregular, solitary or in bunches, with an elongated corolla-like calyx and six short stamens. Some exotic species are cultivated for their beauty, others grow wild, including *Aristolochia clematitis* or birthwort, which grows in Britain, and *A. rotunda*; both of these possess similar pharmacological properties. An infusion or tincture can be prepared from the roots; such preparations have a drastic purgative action, and are also emmenagogic, to the extent of inducing abortion in certain circumstances. However, this type of purgative produces serious abdominal congestion and is seldom used today.
	Bryony	The bryony or white bryony (*Bryonia dioica*) belongs to the family Cucurbitaceae. It is a common plant in hedges in Britain. It has rather slender, branching stems, climbing by means of simple tendrils that grow near the small leaflets, though not in the axils, and frequently change the direction of their spirals. The alternate leaves are lobed, covered with hairs and rough to the touch. As its specific name suggests, the plant is dioecious; both male and female flowers are whitish, the male ones being grouped in racemes on peduncles about the same length as the leaves, the females, also grouped together, having much shorter peduncles and a large inferior ovary. The root of the bryony is thick and tuberous; it has a notoriously drastic purgative activity which is due to the presence of the particularly active principles bryonine and bryogenin. Bryony is also reputed to have diuretic and antihistamine properties. However, preparations of bryony should be administered only with caution because of their toxicity; their use is much less favoured nowadays than it used to be.
	Spindle tree	The bark and distinctive fruits of the spindle tree (*Euonymus europaeus*) have also been used as a purgative. This is a shrub belonging to the family Celastraceae, fairly common in hedges and woods. It has oblong or lanceolate, dentate leaves. The flowers are tetramerous, grouped in axillary cymes, and greenish-yellow in colour; the fruits are coriaceous, depressed in the centre, with four or five projecting lobes. The drastic purgative action is due, in particular, to the presence of 'euonymine', which is capable of increasing intestinal peristalsis and encouraging biliary secretion.

197

Cardiovascular system

p. 74 **Foxglove** The foxglove (*Digitalis purpurea*) belongs to the family Scrophulariaceae and grows in woods and on heaths in central and western Europe. It is a biennial (in warm climates a perennial) plant with a much-branched, reddish root; the stem, usually simple, is about half a metre (20 inches) high and greenish-grey in colour because of the soft, thick down covering the whole of the plant. The oval-lanceolate radical leaves, forming a rosette, taper abruptly towards the base, forming narrow wings along the sides of the stalk; the alternate, oval to oblong upper leaves become progressively smaller as they approach the top of the stem, taking the form of bracts near the flower. The flowers themselves, growing in a long raceme, have thimble-shaped, tubular corollas, reddish-purple outside with matching spots on the pink or white inner surface. From a pharmacological point of view, the foxglove possesses active principles with a cardiotonic and diuretic action. Its medicinal properties are due to glycosides contained in the leaves during the second year of growth; when broken down, they yield digitoxin and digitalin. Also present are a saponin, digitonin, and colouring matters and other substances. Digitalis regulates the activity of the heart, slowing down and steadying the rhythm, while arterial pressure rises and diuresis is incidentally increased. It can be taken in the form of powder, tincture, fluid extract or syrup, but it is difficult to eliminate from the system and, if taken for too long at a time, can accumulate and result in serious poisoning.

Yellow foxgloves Besides the purple foxglove, some related species grow wild (not in Britain) which have yellow corollas and are therefore known in general as yellow foxgloves. Among these are *Digitalis ambigua* (centre of illustration), with a unilateral inflorescence of large, downy flowers; *D. lutea* (right of illustration), with smaller, paler flowers marked with a couple of slightly darker spots inside the corolla; and *D. micrantha* (not illustrated), which, as its specific name suggests, has even smaller flowers than the preceding species. The leaves of these yellow foxgloves likewise contain active principles with cardiotonic and diuretic properties, possibly to a greater degree than the cultivated species.

p. 76 **Lily of the valley** The lily of the valley (*Convallaria majalis*) is a herbaceous perennial of the family Liliaceae, growing in woods and shady places, and often cultivated as a garden flower. It grows up to 10 to 20 cm (4 to 8 inches) high, and has a stoloniferous horizontal rhizome which produces every year a flowering scape enclosed at its base by two ovate-oblong petiolate leaves. The white, bell-shaped flowers have a strong, very pleasant perfume, and vary in number from six to twelve, collected in a raceme. The fruit is a globular red berry, a little larger than a pea, containing several blackish seeds. Either the entire plant, or preferably just the inflorescence, is used to produce the drug, which contains, among other substances, the glycosides convallatoxin, convallarin and convallamarin. It acts as a cardiotonic, cardiokinetic and diuretic. Preparations (such as infusions) for internal use should be taken only under medical supervision.

Oleander The oleander (*Nerium oleander*) is a member of the family Apocynaceae, growing wild in the Mediterranean region. It is an evergreen bush or shrub with coriaceous, glabrous lanceolate leaves in whorls of three. The flowers, blooming from May to September, are grouped in terminal corymbs; they have a delicate scent of bitter almonds and a rose-coloured, rarely white, corolla of five petals. Ornamental oleander varieties may have double the number of petals and a wider range of colours. The part used in pharmacology is the leaves, which should be gathered in June or July; they have cardiotonic and diuretic properties, containing a number of glycosides, including neriin and oleandrin, which have a similar action to digitalis. Because of the toxic nature of the plant, preparations for internal use should be taken only under strict medical supervision. A powder made from the leaves can be used externally against skin parasites.

Hawthorn The hawthorn (*Crataegus oxyacantha*), also known as may or whitethorn, belongs to the family Rosaceae and is a bush or shrub, commonly four to five metres (13 to 16 feet) high, found in western Europe in woods, thickets and hedges. It has scattered obovate leaves which may be dentately lobed or entire, but always incised. The flowers are white, occasionally deep pink, and scented; they have a five-petalled corolla, and stamens varying in number from five to 20. The drug is derived from the flowers and flowerheads; it contains quercetin and quercetrin, an essential oil and, when fresh, trimethylamine. It has antispasmodic, hypotensive, cardiotonic and nerve-sedative properties. Preparations (e.g. tinctures) of it are used therapeutically for normalizing blood pressure, and in arteriosclerosis, angina pectoris, cardiac neuroses caused by poor digestion, and insomnia.

p.78	**Squill**	The squill (*Scilla maritima* or *Urginea maritima*) belongs to the family Liliaceae, and grows widely in the Mediterranean region, especially the cooler areas. It is a herbaceous perennial with a large tunicate bulb, 10 to 12 cm (4 to 5 inches) in diameter, though occasionally up to 20 cm (8 inches); at the end of the summer, this produces a flowering scape a metre or more (over 3 feet) in height, terminating in a long cluster of white, pedunculate flowers formed from six oval petals, with six stamens and a three-carpelled ovary. The fruit is a trilobate membranous capsule, containing numerous seeds. The leaves have parallel veins and are soft and fleshy; they emerge after flowering and persist until the beginning of the following summer. The drug is derived from the bulb, and two types of squill are distinguished commercially: red squill, from larger, wine-red bulbs, and white squill, from smaller, whitish ones. These are used in folk medicine for their diuretic properties in the form of powder, tincture or medicated wine; other old preparations are squill vinegar, oxymel and squill honey.
	Summer adonis	Summer adonis (as opposed to the well-known perennial winter adonis *Adonis vernalis*) is the name given to the annual species of the genus *Adonis*, of the family Ranunculaceae, and in particular to the pheasant's eye illustrated (*A. annua* or *A. autumnalis*). This is a herbaceous plant of modest height, with leaves finely divided into numerous narrow linear segments. Despite its alternative specific name, it flowers in May and June; it is found in England in cornfields, and has flowers with bright scarlet petals with a dark spot at the base. It can be used as a substitute for *Adonis vernalis*.
p. 80	**Broom**	The common broom (*Cytisus scoparius* or *Sarothamnus scoparius*) belongs to the family Leguminosae, subfamily Papilionaceae. It is an evergreen shrub growing to a height of two metres or more (well over 6 feet); the branches are green, with five prominent ribs. The leaves, pubescent at first and glabrous later, are compound, with three ovate leaflets, or occasionally simple. The broom flowers in May and June; the abundant flowers, typical in shape of the Papilionaceae, are an attractive yellow in colour. The fruit is a legume, 3 to 4 cm (1 to 1·5 inches) long and 1 cm (0·4 inches) wide, hairy along the suture line and glabrous on the flat surfaces; when ripe, it bursts with an audible crack. The drug is derived from the flowers and young branches, gathered at or immediately after flowering; its principal activity is cardiotonic and diuretic. In home medicine, an infusion of the flowers (taking care that these have opened only recently and not begun to form the pods, which can cause gastric disturbances) or a decoction of young branches and flowers can be used as a diuretic. The decoction of young flowering branches can be applied externally as a poultice for the treatment of abscesses and swellings.
	Witch hazel	The witch hazel or hamamelis (*Hamamelis virginiana*) belongs to the family Hamamelidaceae; it originated in the Atlantic region of North America, and is occasionally cultivated in gardens in Europe. It is a bush or small tree with fairly sparse branches and leaves almost as large as those of the hazel tree. The plant starts flowering in the autumn and continues throughout the winter; the flowers are sessile, grouped in small axillary inflorescences of one to five flowers. The flowers and bark are used; various types of extract are prepared industrially, and there are numerous different formulas. None of them, however, is suitable for home medicine.

p. 82	**Motherwort**	The motherwort (*Leonurus cardiaca*) is a herbaceous perennial belonging to the family Labiatae. It has large, square annual stems, up to a metre ($3\frac{1}{4}$ feet) in height, with petiolate leaves which have a cordate base and a lamina divided into five to seven coarsely toothed lobes. The flowers are small and not very conspicuous, grouped in large whorls. The entire flowering plant is used as a sedative for cardiac and nervous patients. In folk medicine an infusion or a decoction is employed; for external use, a stronger decoction has a purifying and cicatrizing action.
	Aconites	The genus *Aconitum* contains herbaceous perennials belonging to the family Ranunculaceae; of the species illustrated, *A. variegatum* has flowers grouped in spikes, and is rather smaller than the better-known *A. napellus* (sometimes called monkshood or wolfsbane). The latter has a stem up to 60 cm high (nearly 2 feet) in wild plants, 1·5 metres (5 feet) in cultivated ones, petiolate, laciniate leaves, and flowers arranged in simple racemes. The flowers are zygomorphic, with five violet-blue petaloid sepals, the uppermost one being larger and resembling a helmet with a very short visor. The drug is derived from the roots or the leaves. The root of *Aconitum napellus* (v. illustration) is distinctive, being typically bifid. The aconites have a cardiac and nerve-sedative action, and there are many preparations known to folk medicine. However, the dangers arising from their poisonous properties make it inadvisable to recommend their use.
p. 84	**Mistletoe**	The mistletoe (*Viscum album*) belongs to the family Loranthaceae, and is found over the whole of temperate Europe, extending into northern Africa and Asia. It is a shrub living on the branches of trees (the pear, plum, almond, maple, fir and pine among others) into which it sinks its root-like haustoria or suckers; it is regarded as a semi-parasitic plant, since it draws from its host only in part the substances it is incapable of synthesizing. Mistletoe has cylindrical, much-branched stems and opposed, oblong-lanceolate leaves which are tough and fleshy and have three to six veins; the leaves persist throughout the winter. The flowers are insignificant, but the fruits are more noticeable, being spherical, translucent white berries with a gelatinous, viscous mesocarp. The parts of the plant that interest pharmacology are the young branches and, especially, the leaves, which are generally collected in the spring; they contain numerous active principles, including viscalbin, visciflavin, a saponin and choline. From ancient times to the nineteenth century, these substances have been considered to have antispasmodic activity; today, however, the active principles of the mistletoe are used exclusively for their vasodilatory, and thus hypotensive and diuretic, properties.
	Olive	The olive (*Olea europaea*) gives its name to the family Oleaceae. It is a shrub or tree, varying in height from a few metres to, in exceptional cases, 25 to 30 metres (80 to 100 feet). The trunk is particularly distinctive, being contorted, knobby and rough, often hollow. The branches are approximately four-sided, especially when young, and bear evergreen, short-stalked leaves, lanceolate or oval-lanceolate, thick and coriaceous with a slightly reflexed margin, clear green on the upper surface and silvery-white on the underside because of the presence of numerous stellate hairs. The flowers appear between April and June, growing in axillary inflorescences or terminal racemes; they have a four-toothed calyx and a white, tetramerous, gamopetalous corolla. The fruit is a fleshy drupe, with a pulp rich in oil surrounding a hard, oval stone. The drug is obtained from the leaves, which have no scent and are bitterish to taste. They contain several substances, such as oleuropine, which is a glucoside; elenolide, an unsaturated lactone; oleanolic acid; oleasterol; tartaric, lactic and glycolic acids; enzymes; tannin; glucose; and saccharose. Tinctures, potions and syrups can be prepared from the leaves; these are particularly effective in the treatment of hypertension, and also show some hypoglycaemic activity.

Respiratory system

p. 86   **Common mallow**

The common mallow (*Malva sylvestris*), belonging to the family Malvaceae, grows widely in woodland, on waste ground and by the side of roads and fields. It is a biennial or perennial herb with an erect, branching stem from a few centimetres to a metre ($3\frac{1}{4}$ feet) in height. The palmately lobed leaves grow on long, hairy petioles, the lobes of the upper leaves being shallow, those lower down more deeply incised. A rather bristly down covers the entire plant. The mauvish-pink flowers, veined with fine lines usually darker than their background but sometimes pink or white, grow in short cymes in the axils of the leaves. The leaves and the flowers are used in pharmacy. Both contain mucilage; the flowers also contain malvine anthocyanin, the leaves vitamins A, B, C and E and some acids. The emollient and relaxing properties of the common mallow are beneficial for coughs and in the treatment of inflammation of the respiratory, urinary and digestive tracts. A herbal tea may be prepared from an infusion of the flowers in boiling water.

Marsh mallow

The marsh mallow (*Althaea officinalis*) also belongs to the Malvaceae; it is a perennial herb, growing, as its common name suggests, in damp ground and marshes. The fleshy, fusiform roots are whitish outside and yellow internally; the stem is erect, only slightly branching, about a metre (over 3 feet) high. The alternate, petiolate leaves are large, with sharp, dentate lobes; the flowers, solitary or in small clusters, have a united calyx, and a corolla with five pink, white or mauve petals joined at the base to the bundle of filaments belonging to the numerous stamens. The whole plant, stem, leaves and inflorescence, is clothed with a soft velvety down. The root is the part used by herbalists; it has a 20–25% mucilage-content, the balance consisting of 11% sugar, 38% starch and 11% pectin, as well as asparagine, saccharose, galactose, fats, tannin, albumen and calcium oxalate. The active principles are soothing and tranquillizing, expectorant and mildly laxative. An infusion may be made from the grated root to relieve bronchial congestion. Marsh mallow can also be employed as an excipient in pills, or as a protective substance for irritant drugs.

Hollyhock

Another member of the family Malvaceae is the hollyhock (*Althaea rosea*), a garden plant, sometimes found growing wild as an escape in southern Europe. A herbaceous biennial or perennial, it has a simple flowering stem that can grow to a height of two or three metres (6 to 10 feet). The large radical leaves vary in shape from cordate-reniform to rounded, and are only shallowly lobed; the cauline leaves, on the other hand, are smaller and have deeper lobes. The large flowers grow from each leaf axil, in twos or threes or solitary; according to variety, the five-petalled corollas range in colour from white, through pale pink and bright red, to dark red. The drug is made from the flowers, which contain mucilage, tannin, pectin, anthocyanin and an essential oil. Infusions and decoctions of hollyhock are used to soothe and relieve coughing, as a refreshing drink in cases of gastritis, enteritis and cystitis, and as a gargle.

p. 88   **Cowslip**

The cowslip (*Primula veris* or *P. officinalis*) is a rhizomatose perennial herb of the family Primulaceae, growing in meadows. The radical rosette is composed of leaves on winged petioles, the laminae being nearly oval, with dentate margins; the flowering scape rises from the rosette slightly above the leaves, carrying at the top an umbel of flowers, each with a white, swollen calyx and a yellow corolla consisting of a narrow tube opening out into emarginate petals. The rhizome possesses expectorant and emollient properties, while the leaves and flowers, in the form of a decoction, act as a sedative and antispasmodic. The leaves also produce a decoction that can be used externally to stop bleeding and reduce bruises.

Violet

The sweet violet (*Viola odorata*) belongs to the family Violaceae. It is a little stemmed herb growing in woods and hedgerows, spreading by means of creeping runners or stolons. It has a rosette of oval to oblong, long-stalked leaves, cordate at the base; the flowers are irregular and pedunculate, with five violet or white petals. The flowers are most often used in pharmacy, the leaves and roots much more rarely. Soothing syrups

	and infusions, beneficial for coughs, can be prepared from the flowers, with or without pedicels, sweetened with sugar or honey.
Iceland moss	Iceland moss or cetraria (*Cetraria islandica*) is a lichen of the family Parmeliaceae, found on the ground or on rocks in the colder parts of Europe, Asia and North America. It consists of a low, bushy thallus with erect, almost leafy branches at the top of which appear scattered circular, dark brown apothecia, the fruit bodies. The whole lichen is used for medicinal purposes, but it must be picked before the apothecia appear. It is a useful emollient and pectoral remedy, besides having bitter-tonic and digestive properties. For bronchial catarrh, an infusion of the lichen can be used, or lozenges prepared by combining the lichen mucilage with gum arabic, sugar and flavouring. Lichen jelly is also beneficial in cases of respiratory troubles.
Lung lichen	Though it is less potent, the soothing effect of lung lichen (*Lobaria pulmonaria* or *Sticta pulmonaria*) of the family Stictaceae makes it a possible substitute for Iceland moss, whose bitter, mucilaginous characteristics it shares.

p. 90	**Lungwort**	Lungwort (*Pulmonaria officinalis*), a plant of the family Boraginaceae, is indigenous to parts of Europe and Asia; it is a garden plant in Britain, occasionally found growing wild. It is a perennial herb with a creeping rhizome and a hairy stem up to 40 cm (nearly 16 inches) in height. The leaves, also rough to the touch, are marked with yellowish spots; the radical leaves have long petioles and are oval to acute in shape, while the cauline leaves are sessile and slightly decurrent. The inflorescence grows in two scorpioid cymes, the few flowers that compose them being red when buds, and later violet-blue. The drug is made from the leaves, but the whole plant contains tannin, mucilage, saponins, vitamin C and carotene. Fresh lungwort has useful diaphoretic and emollient qualities, and can be used in a decoction or a herbal tea. The dried plant has an astringent action in cases of diarrhoea and dysentery.
	Soapwort	Soapwort (*Saponaria officinalis*) belongs to the family Caryophyllaceae and grows in damp, grassy places. It has an erect, stoloniferous stem about half a metre (20 inches) in height, with lanceolate to ovate-elliptical, opposite leaves which have three to five principal veins. The pink or white flowers, grouped in terminal heads, have obovate-spathulate petals. The drug is made from the root and the leaves, which contain a mixture of saponin glycosides. The leaves, macerated in water, have diaphoretic properties beneficial in cases of rheumatism and gout. The macerated roots produce a liquid to be taken only with extreme caution; it is claimed that this eases secretion from the inflamed mucous membranes of the respiratory, gastrointestinal, hepatic and genito-urinary tracts.
	Lime flowers	Pharmacologically speaking, this term refers not to a single species of lime or linden but to a number of related trees of the genus *Tilia* (family Tiliaceae). For convenience, these are usually divided into two groups: those with single flowers, which supply the drug *Tilia officinalis*, and those with double flowers, producing the so-called 'silver lime'. In general, it can be said that lime trees are often tall and have cordate, dentate pointed leaves, asymmetrical at the base and traversed by strongly marked veins. The sweet-scented flowers are clustered in small axillary cymes borne on long stalks attached to a wing-shaped bract. The drug is prepared from the flowers, either detached from or still in the cluster. They contain sugars and an essential oil with an action that is principally sudorific, but also soothing and antispasmodic. Lime-flower tea is a well-known health drink; it has cough-easing and diaphoretic properties and is reported to help in the treatment of arteriosclerosis by thinning the blood.

p. 92	**Elecampane**	Elecampane (*Inula helenium*) is a perennial herb of the family Compositae, growing wild in damp surroundings. It has a large, fleshy root and an erect stem, sometimes over a metre (more than 3 feet) high. Its ovate-lanceolate leaves, the radical ones noticeably larger than those above, all have downy undersides. The flowerheads are large and golden-yellow. The root contains essential oil and a mixture of sesquiterpene lactones, the chief being alantolactone. It has cough-easing, diuretic, diaphoretic and emmenagogic properties; its use as a vermifuge is comparatively recent, and attributed to the presence of helenine.

Corn poppy	The corn, field or scarlet poppy (*Papaver rhoeas*) is a member of the family Papaveraceae typical of both waste and arable land, and a familiar summer flower along field paths and roadsides. It is a herbaceous annual, seldom more than half a metre (20 inches) high, with pinnately or bipinnately divided leaves, the lobes being incised or dentate. The solitary flowers are composed of two hairy sepals, which fall early, and four large, rounded, bright scarlet petals, nearly always marked with a black patch near the base. The fruit is a smooth, top-shaped capsule holding numerous rough, grey reniform seeds. The drug comes from the petals, which contain alkaloids, including rhoeadin, and colouring matter; the seeds yield a fixed oil. The poppy's mildly sedative properties make it suitable for children; it is also used to ease coughs and treat bronchitis. A calming poppy tea is simple to prepare.
Wild pansy	*Viola tricolor*, the pretty wild pansy familiarly known as heartsease, is a member of the family Violaceae, growing abundantly in fields and on banks. It is an annual or biennial herb, with a stalk either branching or simple, reaching a maximum height of 30 to 40 cm (12 to 16 inches), usually much shorter. The lower leaves are sub-globular to oblong, the upper ones more elongated; all are dentate and have large, lyrate pinnatifid stipules. The flowers, variously coloured in combinations of white, yellow and violet, often with violet streaks or blotches, have five petals, the upper four being erect, the lowest one extended to form a hollow spur at the back of the flower. The fruit is a capsule, containing numerous round seeds. Used alone, the flower has an expectorant action that eases coughing; the plant as a whole possesses diuretic, depurative and laxative properties.

p. 94

Pines	The genus *Pinus* (family Pinaceae) is, from many points of view, the most important of the conifers. It comprises at least a hundred species, all but one found in the northern hemisphere; they grow in cold temperate regions, and at high altitudes in warmer regions. Pines are almost always found as trees, though there are also some shrubby forms, such as the Swiss mountain pine (*v.* below). They have persistent leaves, triangular in section, growing on short shoots in tufts of two to five leaves. Pines are monoecious and produce cones which ripen over a period of two to three years and contain winged seeds. Most pines contain oleo-resins which can be separated into resin and the essential oil turpentine. The following are some of the important ones. The Scots pine (*Pinus sylvestris*) is found in mountain forests in Europe and parts of Asia; it reaches a height of over 30 metres (100 feet). The bark of the branches is green at first, developing to a characteristic dark red. The leaves are needle-like, bound at their base into pairs; the cones are relatively small and pendulous. The Swiss mountain pine (*Pinus mugo*) has a rather more circumscribed distribution, including the central and eastern Alps and the Carpathians; it grows to no more than three to four metres (10 to 13 feet) in height and is often a procumbent shrub. The maritime pine (*Pinus pinaster*) is found in the Mediterranean region; it grows to 35 or 40 metres high (115 to 130 feet), with pairs of very long, needle-like leaves, green and more or less shiny, and the general outline of the tree is roughly oval. The Italian stone pine (*Pinus pinea*), on the other hand, which is found along the Mediterranean coastline, has a flat-topped, umbrella-like shape; it grows to 20 to 25 metres (65 to 80 feet), and has leaves grouped in pairs, or sometimes in threes, and cones that ripen over three years. Lastly, the Aleppo pine (*Pinus halepensis*), which rarely exceeds 20 metres (65 feet) in height, has elongated cones whose colour changes with the passage of time from green to violet-red to reddish-brown. The buds found at the tips of the shoots of the Scots pine, and also the leaves, are of pharmacological interest. The buds are gathered in March or the autumn; they contain an essential oil with balsamic, bechic, anti-catarrhal and diuretic properties. An infusion of the buds in boiling water, sweetened, can be taken in cases of bronchial and bladder infections; water distilled from the buds has similar properties. The leaves, gathered in summer, are known for their pectoral and anti-gout action; a decoction may be used in the treatment of rheumatism and gout. From the oleo-resin which drains from the bark is obtained turpentine, which is then distilled to produce oil of turpentine, which is used as an antiseptic and a nerve stimulant. The leaves of *Pinus pinaster*, *P. pinea* and *P. halepensis* have similar properties to those of *P. sylvestris* and are used and prepared in the same way. The Swiss mountain pine deserves especial mention, since it produces pine essence, an essential oil obtained by distillation of the young branches and the buds. This is used in the manufacture of bath salts and oils; in pharmacy, it is employed for its antiseptic and

203

decongestant effects on the respiratory system when taken internally (occasionally) or, better, by inhalation of the vapour.

p. 96	**Grindelia**	The grindelia illustrated (*Grindelia robusta*) belongs to the family Compositae, and comes originally from California; several other species of *Grindelia* such as *G. humilis*, *G. squarrosa* and *G. camporum*, commonly known as Californian gum plants, are also used. Grindelia is a herbaceous perennial, with stems 60 to 70 cm (2 to 2¼ feet) high. The leaves are rather fleshy; the inflorescence is in the form of small resinous heads with ligulate yellow flowers surrounded by several rows of bracts. The drug is derived either from the flowering heads alone or from the entire plant. It is used to treat bronchitis and certain forms of asthma. Various extracts are prepared industrially; it can be used in the form of a syrup, or as a tincture, combined with tinctures of stramonium and belladonna.
	Ephedra	The genus *Ephedra* is the only one in the family Ephedraceae, which belongs to the order Gnetales of the gymnosperms. The drug ephedrine comes from the branches of several species, some of which grow in the Mediterranean region in rocky places (*Ephedra nebrodensis*) or on sandy sea beaches (*E. distachya*). The branches of these plants are curiously jointed, green, with minute leaves; they somewhat resemble certain horsetails (*v.* p. 141). The drug is used for the relief of bronchial asthma and hay-fever. There are numerous industrial preparations, the simplest being a syrup.
	Lobelia	Lobelia or Indian tobacco (*Lobelia inflata*) belongs to the Lobelioideae, a subfamily of the Campanulaceae; its alternative name derives from its use by American Indians. It is a hairy, herbaceous annual, about 50 cm (20 inches) in height, with an angular, branched stem, and lower leaves on short petioles; the pale blue flowers form a spike. The entire plant, gathered in an advanced stage of flowering, is used; it has various activities, including action as a spasmolytic and anti-asthmatic. Various pharmaceutical products, such as extracts and syrups, are made; it may also be used in the form of cigarettes.
p. 98	**Coltsfoot**	The coltsfoot (*Tussilago farfara*) is a herbaceous perennial belonging to the family Compositae, and growing in wet and heavy soil. It has a robust white subterranean rhizome from which arise first the flowering stems, 10 to 20 cm high (4 to 8 inches), with small flowerheads of golden-yellow flowers, either during the winter or at the beginning of spring; these are followed by the leaves, which are palmate, and covered at first with white cottony hairs. Either the flowerheads, gathered at the point of opening, or the leaves are used; the latter should be picked when the cottony covering disappears from the under surface, and contain a bitter glucoside, resins, tannin, essential oil and organic acids. The leaves, flowerheads and rhizomes have emollient and pectoral properties. An infusion can be made from the flowerheads, strained and if need be sweetened with honey, and a decoction from the leaves and rhizome. The flowerheads can be mixed with mallow and mullein flowers and marsh mallow root, crumbled into boiling water and flavoured with aniseed.
	Wall mustard	Wall mustard or rocket (*Brassica tenuifolia* or *Diplotaxis tenuifolia*) is a fairly common herbaceous perennial belonging to the family Cruciferae, and found on waste ground and walls. The base of its stem is woody; it soon loses the basal rosette of leaves present in the young plant. The aerial parts, which also bear leaves, reach a good 50 cm (20 inches) in height. The yellow flowers are fairly conspicuous. The fresh sap can be used as an expectorant; an alcoholic preparation may also be employed, combined with alcoholic preparations of tansy or angelica, to disguise the unpleasant taste. Like other plants of the Cruciferae, it has stimulant, revulsant and antiscorbutic properties.
p. 100	**Ground ivy**	The ground ivy (*Nepeta hederacea* or *Glechoma hederacea*) is a perennial herb of the family Labiatae, found in fields and woods throughout Europe. The plant has an elongated

horizontal stolon, with fine roots, and erect flowering stems up to 30 cm (1 foot) high. The lower leaves are reniform, the upper ones orbicular to cordate, all petiolate and with crenate margins. The flowers grow in the leaf axils in groups of two to five, and have a bilabiate corolla, light violet to indigo in colour. The flowers and flowering tops provide the drug, which has expectorant and cough-sedative properties; an infusion of leaves or a tisane of tips may be efficacious for catarrh, cough and bronchitis.

Eucalyptus

The best-known eucalyptus is *Eucalyptus globulus*, or the blue gum tree, belonging to the family Myrtaceae. It originated in Australia, where it can reach exceptional heights, over 100 metres (325 feet); in the Mediterranean region, however, it seldom exceeds 20 metres (65 feet). The trunk has reddish-grey smooth bark which flakes off easily. The young branches are square in section, and the leaves change their shape and arrangement according to age: the young leaves are opposed, sessile and cordate, the older ones alternate, petiolate and scimitar-shaped. The flowers grow in the leaf axils; the teeth of the large calyx are fused to form a cap which eventually splits off to reveal the thick tuft of stamens. The leaves are used in pharmacy; they contain tannic acid, gallic acid, fats, resins and an essential oil, eucalyptus oil. This oil contains a high percentage of cineole (eucalyptol), terpenes and sesquiterpenes, and small amounts of aldehydes. Preparations can be made for use as infusions, fluid extracts, powders and tinctures, and decoctions for external use; they have balsamic, anticatarrhal, astringent, febrifugal and vermifugal properties.

Bignonia catalpa

The bignonia catalpa (*Catalpa bignonioides*) belongs to the family Bignoniaceae, and is often grown as an ornamental tree in parks and gardens in Europe. It grows up to 12 metres (nearly 40 feet) high, with numerous branches and large, entire ovate-cordate leaves on long petioles. The scented flowers are grouped in large terminal panicles, and have a bell-shaped white corolla with yellow and purple spots. The fruit is a siliquiform capsule, containing several compressed, hairy seeds. It is the principal source of the drug, preferably gathered when nearly ripe but still closed, so that the seeds are not scattered; the leaves, root and bark may also be used. A decoction of the fruit is a good remedy for whooping cough and asthma.

p. 102

Common milkwort

The common milkwort (*Polygala vulgaris*) belongs to the family Polygalaceae. and is a herbaceous perennial, commonly found in grassy places; older, vigorous plants may have 20 or 30 branches, with glabrous, obovate and elliptical leaves. The milkwort starts flowering between April and June, continuing through the entire summer and autumn up to the beginning of winter. The flowers are generally reddish-violet, but may be white, blue, greenish or yellowish. The fruits are paired, winged capsules. The roots, and occasionally the entire plant, are used, principally as an expectorant; the dried root contains senegin, saponins, and polygalic acid, which increases the flow of saliva. It may be used as a powder, or as a decoction, with the addition of aniseed for flavouring, and corn poppy syrup if desired. A syrup can also be made from the roots and aerial parts; these are macerated overnight and then strained, and an infusion made with the residue, cooled and strained, is added to the first batch of liquid, which is then sweetened.

Hart's tongue fern

The hart's tongue fern (*Scolopendrium vulgare*) belongs to the family Polypodiaceae. It grows in shady places, and has distinctive fronds up to 50 cm (20 inches) in length, petiolate, with an entire margin and long, narrow sori more or less perpendicular to the midrib. An infusion of the fronds can be taken as an expectorant in cases of bronchial catarrh, and also acts as a diuretic.

p. 104

Ivy

Ivy (*Hedera helix*) belongs to the family Araliaceae, and is a very common climbing plant. The leaves vary in shape from ovate to three- to five-lobed; the white, hairy flowers appear in October or November, followed by the black, round fruits. The leaves are used in medicine; a leaf tea may be taken to treat some forms of chronic catarrh, though the taste is extremely unpleasant. A poultice of fresh leaves may be used externally to help clear up ulcers and promote the healing of stubborn wounds.

205

Liquorice　Liquorice or licorice (*Glycyrrhiza glabra*) is a herbaceous perennial belonging to the subfamily Papilionaceae of the Leguminosae. It has large roots and long horizontal stolons; the aerial stems, up to a metre ($3\frac{1}{4}$ feet) in height, carry imparipinnate compound leaves with five to six pairs of leaflets, and inconspicuous flowers in erect racemes. The fruits are legumes, containing five or six seeds. The roots and stolons are chiefly used. The dry extract, easily available commercially in the form of pastilles (in England as 'Pontefract cakes') or small sticks, can be used in home medicine as an expectorant; two or three pastilles dissolved in warm milk are excellent for coughs or catarrh. The sticks may be chewed, or an infusion may be prepared; this is preferable to a decoction, which releases unwanted acrid and bitter substances into solution.

Wild thyme　The wild thyme illustrated, *Thymus serpyllum*, is closely related to garden thyme (*T. vulgaris*; *v.* p. 22), both being members of the family Labiatae. It is a small herbaceous perennial, woody at the base, found in dry and sunny places. It has long creeping stems, oval or elliptical leaves, and flowers grouped in more or less spherical small heads. The entire herb is used; it contains an essential oil rich in phenols such as thymol. The infusion can be used as an expectorant and antiseptic.

Nervous system

p. 106 **Passion flower**

Passiflora incarnata is a passion flower native to the southern United States and belonging to the family Passifloraceae. It is a perennial plant with long annual stems, alternate leaves with margins divided into three to five lobes, and tendrils which help it to climb. The flowers are distinctive, with five sepals fused into a cup, five white or mauvish-white petals, numerous filaments and, in the centre, a column called the androgynophore, composed of five stamens with hammer-like anthers and a tricarpellate ovary with three styles, each capped by a stigma. The green parts are used to make an infusion which acts as a sedative in cases of neuroses, anxiety states and gastric spasms of nervous origin.

White willow

The white willow (*Salix alba*) belongs to the family Salicaceae. It is a fairly common tree in damp places and alongside watercourses, and is easily recognizable by the silvery colour of the leaves. In cultivation, its natural shape is greatly altered by the practice of pollarding. The bark is used medicinally; it has sedative, anaphrodisiac and antirheumatic properties. As a sedative, a decoction of coarsely powdered bark may be taken, or the powder, or a medicated wine.

Hop

The hop (*Humulus lupulus*) is a herbaceous perennial belonging to the family Cannabinaceae, of the order Urticales. The annual aerial climbing stems arising from the perennial rhizome can reach several metres in length; the leaves are opposed, palmately lobed, and fairly rough to the touch. The hop is a dioecious plant: the male specimens produce panicles of flowers, while the females bear oval catkins which somewhat resemble pine cones, and are known botanically as strobiles. Industrially, hops are used to flavour beer. The drug consists of the strobiles, gathered in September when they are not completely ripe, or of the glands, known as lupulin, obtained by flailing and sifting the strobiles. Hops have a bitter-tonic action, as well as acting as a nerve sedative. They can be used in domestic medicine in a hot sedative infusion; hop pillows are also said to induce sleep.

p. 108 **Butterbur**

The butterbur (*Tussilago petasites* or *Petasites officinalis*) is a member of the family Compositae, found in damp places, particularly river banks. It has an erect, downy stem about half a metre (20 inches) high, and large leaves which are reniform-triangular to reniform-ovate in shape, with dentate margins and reticulated undersides. The mauve or flesh-pink flowers, which usually appear before the leaves, are grouped in a thyrsus. The medicinal properties of the butterbur are found in the large rhizomes, the roots and the leaves; the first two should be gathered in early spring, the last in May. In the past the plant was known for its diuretic, diaphoretic, anti-arthritic, stomachic and astringent properties; as a result of recent research on patients suffering from nervous tension, anxiety states, and over-excitability in infants, preparations based on butterbur are prescribed as sedatives and antispasmodics.

Lavenders

Lavenders are obtained from several species and hybrids of *Lavandula* (family Labiatae), several of which are used in pharmacy and perfumery; these include *Lavandula vera*, *L. spica* and the 'lavandins', which are hybrids of these two species. Lavenders are aromatic, evergreen shrubs with grey-green linear leaves narrowing towards their base. The small, strong-scented purple flowers form terminal spikes; they yield an essential oil with antispasmodic, bechic, carminative, diuretic and diaphoretic properties.

Valerian

The common valerian or all-heal (*Valeriana officinalis*) is a plant that has long interested herbalists and pharmacists. It is a perennial of the family Valerianaceae, growing in Europe and Asia in damp situations such as woods, ditches and marshes. It has a short, truncated rhizome with rather fleshy adventitious roots. The stems, up to a metre ($3\frac{1}{4}$ feet) in height, are straight, cylindrical, longitudinally grooved and hollow; they bear pinnatisect leaves with oval-lanceolate, dentate or entire leaflets, glabrous or rather hairy, the lower ones borne on short petioles, the upper ones sessile. The small white or pinkish flowers are clustered in branched corymbose cymes. The drug is obtained from the roots and the rhizome, often with a section of stem attached, and has the same characteristic pungent and unpleasant odour as the plant itself; the principal components are an essential oil from which valerianic acid is extracted, a glucoside, two alkaloids, tannin, starch and glucose. Valerian root and remedies prepared from it act as antispasmodics, sedatives and mild narcotics. A calming drink can also be made domestically, and white wine can be flavoured with tincture of valerian root.

p. 110	Red valerian	The red valerian (*Centranthus ruber*) is a herbaceous perennial belonging to the family Valerianaceae, a native of the Mediterranean area but long naturalized in England; it grows by preference on old walls, rocks and rocky slopes. The rhizome has similar properties to that of common valerian (*v.* above).
	Bastard balm	Bastard balm (*Melittis melissophyllum*) is a herbaceous perennial belonging to the family Labiatae; it grows in woods and shady places, but in England is confined to a few locations in the south and southwest. It has a short creeping rhizome which produces a few square aerial stems 10 to 40 cm (4 to 16 inches) high. The leaves are decussate, petiolate, with a coarsely toothed margin; the large flowers, pink or variegated with white and purple, are solitary or paired, with a pentamerous calyx and a typical Labiate corolla. The entire flowering plant is used; an infusion of it has antispasmodic and sedative, and also diuretic properties.
	Lemon verbena	The lemon verbena or lemon-scented verbena (*Lippia citriodora*) is a low bush, belonging to the family Verbenaceae, which originated in South America and is frequently cultivated in Europe as an ornamental plant. It has angular branches, leaves in whorls of three or four, and small pinkish flowers grouped in terminal spikes. The leaves, which are rough to the touch by reason of their characteristic hairs, and curl up into tubes when dry, can be used in an infusion as a nerve sedative and digestive, and also to disguise the unpleasant taste of other infusions.
p. 112	Cherry laurel	The cherry laurel (*Prunus laurocerasus*) belongs to the family Rosaceae; it originated in western Asia and is frequently cultivated in parks and gardens for the beauty of its foliage, particularly in hedges. It is a bush or shrub with large, glossy, leathery evergreen leaves, and flowers in spring, producing erect racemes of white flowers; the fruits are ovoid, shiny black drupes. The drug is derived from the leaves, which have protruding glands on the lower surface of the petiole near where it joins the lamina; crushed green leaves emit the odour of bitter almonds, though dry leaves are odourless. They have antispasmodic properties and are efficacious in the treatment of coughs of nervous origin, stomach and intestinal spasms, intractable vomiting and persistent insomnia. A distillate of the leaves is known as cherry-laurel water; this was formerly used in eye lotions. Because distillation of the leaves produces hydrocyanic (prussic) acid, it is advisable to obtain cherry-laurel water from a pharmacist. The fruits are also used to make a delicious digestive and antispasmodic liqueur.
	Bitter almond	The bitter almond (*Prunus amygdalus* var. *amara*), another member of the Rosaceae, originated in western Asia and is widely cultivated in the Mediterranean basin; the sweet almond is derived from the var. *dulcis*. It is a woody plant of modest height, very beautiful in early spring when it is covered with white or pink blossom. Almond oil, which is used like olive oil, is expressed from the seeds of both bitter and sweet almonds. The (quite different) essential oil of bitter almonds is obtained by distillation of the pulp remaining after expressing almond oil; it has similar properties to those of cherry-laurel distillate, but is much stronger. The active glycosides break down to yield prussic acid, benzaldehyde and sugars; the essential oil is often chemically treated to remove all the prussic acid, leaving the benzaldehyde, which gives the almond flavour, before being used for culinary purposes. Pharmacists usually stock this oil both with and without prussic acid.

208

Anemones

The genus *Anemone* of the family Ranunculaceae comprises many beautiful perennial flowering plants, some cultivated in gardens, others wild. They are all more or less poisonous and are now little used medicinally, except possibly for the pasque-flower (*Anemone pulsatilla*), the leaves and flowers of which are used in France; this plant is found widely in Europe, including several parts of England, and Asia, particularly on limestone pastures, and produces a purple flower in the spring.

The wood anemone (*Anemone nemorosa*) also has a wide distribution, including Britain, being very common in and near woods. It has a black, nearly horizontal rhizome; the two or three basal leaves develop on the rhizome after flowering time, and have long petioles with three ovate or lanceolate leaflets which are dentate or lobed. The flowers have long peduncles surrounded by an involucre of leaves which have shorter stalks and are smaller than those arising from the rhizome; the solitary flower has six to twelve completely glabrous sepals, and is white with a bluish or reddish tinge.

The yellow wood anemone (*Anemone ranunculoides*), which is found in Europe, the Caucasus and Siberia, grows by preference in meadows, cool woods and woodlands. It has a fleshy horizontal rhizome, and a stem at most 20 cm (8 inches) high. The radical leaves, one or two in number, develop on the rhizome near the flowering scape; they are pubescent, petiolate and have three or four ovate-cuneate segments. The leaves surrounding the flowers are three in number, similar to the radical leaves, on very short petioles. The flowers are generally solitary, carried on hairy peduncles, and have golden-yellow hairy sepals, varying in number from five to eight.

Anemone hepatica (or *Hepatica nobilis* as it is sometimes known) is found in Europe, Siberia, Japan and North America, though it does not grow wild in Britain; it is often found in woods, woodlands and hedgerows. It has a short rhizome, and petiolate radical leaves with a triangular lamina with three lobes, dark green and glabrous on the upper side, but with shaggy hairs and greenish-purple below. These leaves appear in spring, after flowering, and remain on the plant until the new leaves appear in the following spring; their colour and shape have given the names hepatica and, in the United States, liverleaf to this plant and its close relatives. The flowers are solitary, with six to ten petaloid sepals which are blue (more rarely white or pink) in colour.

The whole anemone plant has been used as a drug, with sedative, diuretic, expectorant and diaphoretic properties, also for painful spasms, neuralgia, migraine, dysmenorrhoea and dry, spasmodic coughs. The drug also has vesiculatory qualities. Infusions and tinctures can be prepared.

Cow parsnip

The cow parsnip or hogweed (*Heracleum sphondylium*) is a large herbaceous perennial, found in cool, damp pastures; it is one of the commonest British members of the family Umbelliferae. It varies in height, but can reach two metres (over 6 feet). It has large pinnatisect leaves with rough, stiff hairs, and erect, hollow, grooved angular flowering stems; the flowers are white, collected in large umbels with about ten rays. The green parts, the orbicular fruits or the roots may be used. In folk medicine cow parsnip is employed in the form of a powder or an alcoholic extract as a nerve sedative, anti-hysteric and analgesic. Some people are allergic to these plants, developing rashes, particularly after over-exposure to the sun.

Coca

The coca (*Erythroxylon* (or *Erythroxylum*) *coca*) belongs to the family Erythroxylaceae; it originated in South America and has probably died out in the wild, but is widely cultivated as a commercial crop, especially the var. *bolivianum*. It is a bush of modest size, with slender branches; the short-stalked, glabrous, slender leaves have an entire margin and two false lateral veins paralleling the median vein. The drug is derived from the leaves. This is not a plant for which there is any use in home medicine, though in its countries of origin the leaves are chewed for the sensation of resistance to fatigue and hunger they produce.

Cloves

Cloves are the immature flower buds of *Eugenia caryophyllus* or *caryophyllata*, which belongs to the family Myrtaceae; it is an attractive tree, cultivated in the Moluccas, Zanzibar and Madagascar, and can reach 20 metres (65 feet) in height. On examining a clove, one notices the 'stalk', which is the receptacle, while the globular 'head' is composed of the four-lobed calyx, petals and stamens. The essential oil of cloves is used in dentistry as an anaesthetic and antiseptic; its principal ingredient, eugenol, can be converted by chemical treatment into vanillin and used as a flavouring for chocolate and other preparations. Cloves are also used in liqueur manufacture and as a flavouring in cooking.

Chaste tree   The chaste tree (*Vitex agnus-castus*) is a shrub or small tree of the family Verbenaceae which grows wild in the Mediterranean region and is often cultivated as an ornamental. The opposite leaves are composed of five to seven lanceolate leaflets; the rather small violet flowers form slender, interrupted spikes. The medicinal substances, present in the leaves, inflorescence and fruit, consist mainly of castine, viticin, vitexine and vitexinine. At one time the plant was known only as an anaphrodisiac; today it is principally regarded as having digestive, emmenagogic, antispasmodic, aperient and soporific properties.

White waterlily   The white waterlily (*Nymphaea alba*), of the family Nymphaeaceae, is an aquatic plant, quite common on small lakes, pools and marshes, and often cultivated as an ornamental plant in park or garden ponds. It has a large rhizome, and cordate leaves that vary in shape and position according to age. The undersides of the floating leaves are reddened by anthocyanic colouring substances; the upper surfaces are green and covered with a more or less waterproof waxy layer. The large, white, solitary flower consists of a thick receptacle on which are arranged the numerous petals, stamens and carpels. The rhizome has been used for its supposed anaphrodisiac properties.

Rue   Rue or herb of grace (*Ruta graveolens*) is a member of the family Rutaceae native to southern Europe but growing readily in England. It is a low shrub, about 80 cm (over $2\frac{1}{2}$ feet) high, and the whole plant gives off a distinctive fragrance. It has bi- or tripinnatisect leaves divided into ovate-oblong, fleshy petiolate lacinia, with entire bracts. The yellow flowers form a corymb, the inner flowers having five petals, those on the outer rim only four. The pharmaceutically important part of the plant is the leaf, which should be picked a little before flowering and dried rapidly in the shade. It contains rutin and coumarins, but the main active ingredient is rue oil, a volatile essential oil of very complex structure. While it used to be considered only as an anaphrodisiac, rue is occasionally used as an emmenagogue, intestinal antispasmodic, uterine stimulant, haemostatic and vermifuge; infusions, fluid extracts and tinctures are prepared. However, any preparations of rue must be used with great caution and never in excessive doses; taken during pregnancy, it can cause abortion, and even in normal conditions an overdose can lead to serious, even fatal, forms of poisoning.

The three plant species described in this section are grouped together not only because they contain almost identical active principles with very similar medicinal properties, but also because they all belong to the same family, the Solanaceae.

Thornapple   The thornapple or stramonium (*Datura stramonium*), probably native to western Asia, but now diffused nearly all over the northern hemisphere, is a poisonous annual herb that grows on waste ground and roadsides; it is often a troublesome weed, and in the United States is known as Jimson or Jamestown weed. Its stalk, branching out near the base, grows to 1·5 metres (5 feet) in height. The bright green, long-stalked leaves are ovate or triangular-ovate, with sinuate-dentate margins; the flower, generally solitary, is white as a rule, but can be tinged with yellow or green, and has a trumpet-shaped corolla with shallow-lobed petals ending in a sharp point. The fruit is distinctive: a large capsule, up to 4 cm (1·6 inches) long, the exterior of which is covered with spines about 5 mm (0·2 inches) long. Leaves and seeds supply the drug.

Henbane   Henbane or hyoscyamus (*Hyoscyamus niger*) is a plant of Eurasia and North Africa, typical of waste and stony places. There are two varieties: an annual with an unbranched stem up to 50 cm (20 inches) high; and a biennial which produces a rosette of radical leaves in the first year and a branched stem up to 1·5 metres (5 feet) high in the second. The upper leaves are sessile, ovate-oblong to triangular-ovate, and have a deeply divided margin; the leaves on the annual variety are similar but smaller and less incised. All parts of the plant have abundant, rather sticky glandular hairs. The star-shaped flowers form a dense, short-stalked cluster; they are pale yellow with a network of red and purple veins which are more marked in the biennial variety. The leaves and seeds are used for their medicinal properties.

Deadly nightshade   Deadly nightshade or belladonna (*Atropa belladonna*) grows in cool woodland and on waste ground. It has a thick, fleshy root and a stout erect stem, simple at the base and branching above, 1 to 1·5 metres (3 to 5 feet) high. The bright green, short-stalked leaves are entire, oval, acuminate at the tip and ovate at the base; from the leaf axils grow the flowers, almost always solitary, deep purple in colour and shaped like a bell, divided at the end into five short petals. The fruit is a berry rather like a small cherry, green at first but darkest purple when ripe, and very poisonous. The drug comes from the root and the leaves.

As mentioned above, these three plants contain analogous active principles, the chief alkaloids being hyoscyamine and atropine, which is formed from hyoscyamine by racemization. These have antispasmodic, pain-killing, narcotic and mydriatic effects. Medicaments derived from the three plants are used in the treatment of chronic bronchitis, insomnia, neuralgia, asthma, spasmodic coughing, stomach pains, hepatic and nephritic colic, delirium tremens, and so on, and also in ophthalmology. The use of a variety of thornapple known as the Yang herb as an anaesthetic has been reported from China.

p. 122   **Spanish chestnut**

The Spanish or sweet chestnut (*Castanea sativa*) belongs to the family Fagaceae; it grows wild, particularly in the Mediterranean region, and is also widely cultivated for its edible fruit (chestnuts). It is a large tree with a straight trunk and furrowed bark; the leaves are oblong-lanceolate, strongly veined and serrate. The male flowers hang in long, loose, pale yellow catkins; the greenish female flowers grow in the axils. The chestnuts, one to three in number, are enclosed in a spiny involucre (the cupule or bur). The leaves are astringent (as is the bark) and also have sedative properties, particularly in cases of coughs. A hot infusion of crushed leaves may be taken, or the fluid extract used, in syrup or combined with other drugs.

Indian hemp

Indian hemp is derived from var. *indica* of the common hemp (*Cannabis sativa*), belonging to the family Cannabinaceae. It differs from common hemp, which is cultivated for textile and rope manufacture, by its smaller size and slenderer, more branching and compact habit. The lower leaves are digitate; the upper ones, found in the drug, consist of simple or lobed bracts. The drug is derived from the flowering and fruiting parts of the female plant; it has an analgesic and sedative action. Indian hemp is used by addicts in many parts of the world, being taken internally or smoked, and goes under a variety of names, including marihuana, hashish, bhang, kief and dagga.

Black nightshade

The black nightshade (*Solanum nigrum*) belongs to the family Solanaceae; it is found in England but is less widely distributed than the woody nightshade (*S. dulcamara*; *v.* p. 142). It is generally an annual plant of rather variable size, with branching green or violet stems. The leaves are petiolate and characteristically sticky; the pentamerous white flowers are borne in small corymbs of four to eight. The fruits are berries, usually black but sometimes yellow or carmine; those of the woody nightshade are always red. Black nightshade is fairly common as a weed in neglected kitchen gardens and on waste ground. It is a poisonous plant, although in some places the young plant has been eaten as a vegetable; indications for internal use have therefore been omitted. For external use, it can prove a good analgesic in cases of itching skin complaints, haemorrhoids and painful arthritic swelling; a compress soaked in a concentrated decoction can be used, or a poultice of freshly crushed leaves.

p. 124   **Corydalis**

Corydalis (*Corydalis cava*) is a member of the Papaveraceae belonging, with fumitory (*v.* p. 142), to a part of the family which is sometimes separated as the family Fumariaceae. It is a small herbaceous perennial about 10 cm (4 inches) in height, typically found in the undergrowth of woods or shady places; garden species of *Corydalis* are often grown in rock gardens. It has a yellow tuber which is hollow, giving the plant its specific name *cava*, and flowers in spring, producing characteristically spurred flowers which may be violet or white. The drug is derived from the tuber; it contains a potent alkaloid, corydaline, but its use in home medicine is definitely not recommended.

Opium poppy

The opium poppy (*Papaver somniferum*) belongs to the family Papaveraceae. It is a herbaceous annual, 50 to 150 cm (20 inches to 5 feet) high, with large, soft waxy leaves with dentate margins, sea-green in colour and amplexicaul. In addition to numerous garden hybrids, about four varieties of *Papaver somniferum* are recognized, differing in the colour of the petals, size and shape of the capsules, and colour of the seeds. These roughly correspond to geographical areas, e.g. var. *album* from India, var. *glabrum* from Turkey,

211

and varieties *nigrum* and *setigerum* from Europe. All contain latex from which opium is prepared. The non-poisonous seeds, particularly the slate-coloured 'maw seeds' produced in Europe, are used for decorating and flavouring bread and biscuits; on expression, the seeds also yield an oil which is used in cooking and by artists.

p. 126 **Coffee**

Coffee (*Coffea arabica*) is a member of the family Rubiaceae and grows in a belt between about 25° north and south of the equator, ranging from the sea coast up to about 1,500 metres (5,000 feet), as long as the climate guarantees an average temperature between 15°C (59°F) and 30°C (86°F) and at least 1,500 mm (about 60 inches) rainfall a year. When cultivated, coffee is pruned to keep the height to two to three metres (6½ to 10 feet). It has shiny, evergreen leathery leaves which are opposite, short-stalked and 10 to 12 cm (4 to 5 inches) in length, elliptical to lanceolate, with a very marked mid-vein. The flowers are white, highly scented, and grouped in clusters of three to seven at the axil of the leaves. Each flower produces a two-lobed fruit, the coffee berry or cherry, which is green at first, later reddish, then scarlet; each lobe of the fruit contains a seed, the coffee bean, with a convex dorsal face and a flat ventral face. The coffee beans are transported raw, in sacks, from the producer countries to the consumer countries, where they undergo a process of roasting which requires heat of up to 200°C (nearly 400°F); by the end of the process the beans have lost a fifth of their weight and a fifth of their caffeine content, increased in volume by a third and turned brown in colour, because of caramellization of the carbohydrates they contain. The constituents of coffee include several different sugars, fat, minerals and phenolic acids such as chlorogenic acid (caffeotannic acid), but the most important one is caffeine, which is responsible for coffee's stimulant properties.

Tea

Tea is derived from *Thea sinensis* (*Camellia sinensis* or *C. thea*), belonging to the camellia family, the Theaceae. It grows in tropical and monsoon regions with plentiful rainfall (about 3,000 mm or 120 inches annually), and is a small tree which can reach heights of up to ten metres (well over 30 feet) in the wild, but barely reaches two metres (6½ feet) when cultivated. The leaves are alternate, dark green in colour, elliptical-lanceolate, with a minutely serrate margin; the flowers are white and scented, and the fruits are trilobate capsules. The drug itself consists of the leaves; these are first harvested in the third year of the plant's life and are treated in various ways to provide the different qualities of tea used commercially: 'black tea' is made from the partly dried leaves which are piled up to ferment before being roasted, 'green tea' is unfermented, being fired as soon as it is harvested, and Oolong is semi-fermented. The dust left over from processing the leaves is used to prepare tea in the form of blocks, for the Russian market in particular, and for making caffeine. Tea contains theine (in fact identical with caffeine), tannin, xanthene and theophylline, and is stimulating, astringent, narcotic, analgesic, soothing, diaphoretic, digestive and indirectly nutritive. When prepared as an infusion it is an excellent nerve tonic which is free from the drawbacks of, for example, tobacco and alcohol; its effects are similar to those of coffee, and it also has certain diuretic properties. This is not to say that tea is completely innocuous; like coffee, it is not recommended for babies, for over-excitable people, or for neurasthenics.

Kola nuts

Kola or cola nuts are derived from *Cola nitida*, a plant belonging to the family Sterculiaceae and originating in the Gulf of Guinea; it is a tree which can grow to a height of 20 metres (65 feet), with petiolate leaves elliptical-oblong in shape, having a fairly large lamina and an acuminate apex. The flowers grow in small inflorescences; some are male, others female and others hermaphrodite. The fruits are follicles and contain between one and ten seeds, with two cotyledons each, white or russet in colour. Only the embryo of the seed, shelled of its husk, constitutes the kola nut. Kola nuts contain caffeine, a little theobromine, and also colanin, starch, glucose and rubber; they are less used in Europe than tea or coffee, but have similar properties. In their countries of origin they are valued as a nut to chew. They also have an important modern industrial use: together with the leaves of the coca (*Erythroxylon coca*; *v*. p. 116) freed of cocaine, they are used in the manufacture of gaseous soft drinks that have gone out from the United States to conquer every market in the Western world.

Genito-urinary system

p. 128 **Plantains**

The plantains illustrated are *Plantago media* (hoary plantain) and *P. lanceolata* (ribwort), perennial plants of the family Plantaginaceae, characteristic of grassy uncultivated places; another fairly widespread species is the greater plantain (*P. major*). They have large inflorescences in the form of a spike arising from the basal rosette of leaves. The drug is derived from the leaves, and has diuretic properties. An infusion can be made from the powdered leaves. Fresh leaves, washed and macerated in water, can also be used as a poultice for the treatment of ulcers, boils and wounds. The seeds of many species of *Plantago*, e.g. *P. psyllium*, are rich in mucilage and are used as demulcents and in the treatment of chronic constipation.

Rest-harrow

The rest-harrow *Ononis spinosa*, belonging to the subfamily Papilionaceae of the family Leguminosae, is often regarded as a form of *O. arvensis*. It is a perennial, much-branched, spiny undershrub about 30 cm (1 foot) high, with erect hairy stems and trifoliate, toothed leaves. The flowers are pink, appearing in the summer and autumn, and develop into a short pod containing two or three seeds. The root is said to have diuretic properties; it may be powdered and used in an infusion, either on its own, or combined with fennel fruits and sweetened with honey.

Woodruff

The woodruff (*Asperula odorata*) is a small herbaceous perennial of the family Rubiaceae, found in woods and shady places, and common in Britain. Slender, simple stems about 15 to 30 cm (6 to 12 inches) high arise from a creeping rhizome. The leaves, usually in whorls of eight, are oblong-lanceolate in shape: the white, stellate flowers are rather evanescent. The fruits are bifid, globular and very bristly because of the hooked hairs on their surface. The drug is derived from the entire flowering plant which, although odourless when fresh, assumes a distinctive pleasant odour of new-mown hay on drying; the chief odorous constituent is coumarin, but other glycosides are present. In the form of a decoction or infusion the plant has been recommended, particularly for children and old people, as a nervous sedative. It is also made into an aromatic wine (Vin de Mai) and employed in perfumery.

p. 130 **Butcher's broom**

Butcher's broom (*Ruscus aculeatus*) belongs to the family Liliaceae; three species of *Ruscus* occur in Europe, butcher's broom being found in southern England. It has a perennial rootstock and green branching stems 60 to 80 cm (about 2 to 2½ feet) high. A characteristic feature is the bright green cladodes (flattened stems that have assumed the shape and function of leaves), ovate-oblong in form, with a prolonged point at the apex; the true leaves are represented only by small scales, which bear the small, mostly unisexual flowers. The fruit is a highly ornamental red berry about the size of a cherry. The rootstock and roots of butcher's broom have diuretic properties and were formerly included in the French, Spanish and other pharmacopoeias. The plant is now known to contain steroidal saponins.

Asparagus

Asparagus or common asparagus (*Asparagus officinalis*) was, as its botanical name implies, formerly official in many pharmacopoeias. Like butcher's broom, it belongs to the Liliaceae and has diuretic properties. It occurs wild in Europe and Asia, but in England is confined to the shores of the west and southwest; it has long been cultivated for its young edible shoots, which arise in spring from the rhizome. If these shoots are allowed to grow, they develop into branched green stems with feathery cladodes which are often included in flower arrangements; the small, greenish-white flowers are succeeded by globular red berries. For use as a diuretic, the rhizome and roots, gathered in November, may be made into a decoction, but side-effects have reduced its popularity.

Pellitory

Pellitory or pellitory-of-the-wall (*Parietaria officinalis*) belongs to the stinging-nettle or Urticaceae family. It is a small perennial herb with a branched stem, often found on old walls in Europe, including Britain. The stem, rarely more than 20 cm (8 inches) long, is covered with downy hairs and bears stalked leaves which are ovate to lanceolate in shape and have entire margins. The leaves are generally used fresh, in the form of an infusion, for their diuretic effect, which is said to be due to the presence of potassium nitrate and flavonoids.

p. 132	**Borage**	Borage (*Borago officinalis*), of the family Boraginaceae, is a herb rather more than 60 cm (2 feet) high, almost completely covered with stiff, somewhat prickly hairs; it is found in waste places throughout Europe and is naturalized in England. The leaves are alternate and oval to lanceolate, the lower ones being long-stalked and large, the upper ones sessile to amplexicaul. The relatively large, bright blue flowers grow in loose forked cymes; they contain mineral matter, rich in potassium and mucilage. Both flowers and leaves are diuretic and emollient, and can be made into infusions, juice, or a refreshing summer drink.
	Chinese lantern	The bladder cherry or Chinese lantern (*Physalis alkekengii*) is a member of the family Solanaceae; it is often cultivated as a border plant and its dried fruits used for winter decoration. It is an annual or perennial herb, up to about 80 cm (over $2\frac{1}{2}$ feet) in height, though there are giant and dwarf varieties in cultivation. The angular aerial stems bear pairs of petiolate, oval or ovate leaves which have an entire or sinuate margin. The axillary, solitary flowers have a white corolla. The calyx, at first small and green, grows rapidly to enclose the fruit in a reticulately veined membrane which gradually becomes orange-red; an edible red berry develops within this 'lantern'. The berry forms the drug, and has a diuretic and mildly laxative action; it contains sugars, citric acid, vitamin C and carotenoids.
p. 134	**Couch grass**	Couch grass, quitch or twitch (*Agropyron (Agropyrum) repens* or *Triticum repens*), of the family Gramineae, is a common perennial weed in both Europe and America. It has a thin but deep-seated rhizome which is extremely difficult to eliminate from gardens and fields, for which reason it has various uncomplimentary names such as 'devil's guts'. The aerial parts are shown in the illustration. Up to the First World War, couch grass was included in both the British and the United States pharmacopoeias. Although the plant was only too common in England, supplies of the rhizome were often imported from the Continent; some of these were obtained from a different grass, dog's-tooth couch grass (*Cynodon dactylon*), a plant found not only in Europe but in many hot countries, where it has such names as Bermuda grass. Unlike that of true couch grass, its rhizome contains starch, which gives a blue colour with iodine; this simple test may be used to distinguish the two plants. Couch grass contains several carbohydrates, including both sugars and triticin, a vanilla-like glycoside and traces of essential oil. It has a diuretic action, and has recently been shown to have antimicrobial properties.
	Rusty-back fern	The rusty-back fern (*Ceterach officinarum*) is a small European and western Asiatic fern belonging to the Polypodiaceae, often found in Britain on rocks and old buildings or growing in cracks in walls. It is a perennial plant with a tufted rhizome from which arise several persistent, leathery, lanceolate fronds, pinnatipartite, with wide-based oblong or rounded lobes. They are bright green above, rusty red on the underside; brown scales cover the spore cases (sori) until these are old. About a century ago the fronds were official in some pharmacopoeias; the main constituents appear to be tannin, mucilage and a bitter substance. Infusions and decoctions have diuretic, expectorant and astringent properties.
	Elders	Three species of elder, of the family Caprifoliaceae, will be mentioned here, as they have similar characters and medicinal properties. The red-berried elder (*Sambucus racemosa*; *v.* illustration) occurs wild in Europe and is commonly cultivated in English shrubberies; the English common elder (*S. nigra*) and dwarf elder or danewort (*S. ebulus*) differ from it in having black berries. *Sambucus racemosa* is a shrub two to four metres ($6\frac{1}{2}$ to 13 feet) high, with compound leaves made up of lanceolate, acuminate, dentate leaflets. The faintly scented, greenish-yellow flowers form compact, oval panicles; the berries, when ripe in late summer or early autumn, are round and red. Bark, leaves, flowers and fruit all have uses in medicine: a decoction of the bark has diuretic properties; the flowers are made into a diaphoretic, diuretic and mildly laxative tea; a purgative and pain-killer can be prepared from a decoction of the leaves; and elderberry jam or decoction is a good laxative.
p. 136	**Bearberry**	The bearberry or common bearberry (*Arctostaphylos uva-ursi*), of the family Ericaceae, is found in Europe, including Britain. It is a small evergreen shrub with procumbent stems.

The leaves are obovate or oblong, entire, about 2 cm (nearly an inch) long and very leathery, dark green and shiny above, paler and duller below; the flowers are small, bell-shaped, white with pink tips. The fruit is a globular berry, red when ripe. The leaves are used to prepare infusions and decoctions with diuretic and antiseptic effects on the urinary tract.

Cowberry

The red whortleberry or cowberry (*Vaccinium vitis-idaea*), another member of the Ericaceae, grows widely, particularly on heaths, in the northern hemisphere. It is distinguished from the whortleberry or bilberry (*Vaccinium myrtillus*; *v.* p. 152 and below, p. 219) by its evergreen, obovate leaves with glandular dots on the underside and its berries, which are red when ripe.

Golden rod

Golden rod (*Solidago virgaurea*) is a large perennial plant of the family Compositae, very common in Europe and Asia. The stems, about 60 cm (2 feet) high, bear oblong or lanceolate, toothed leaves. The flowerheads are bright yellow, and are composed of ray florets surrounding tubular disc florets; they are diuretic and contain saponins and flavonoids. They are also used in homoeopathy.

Juniper

The common juniper (*Juniperus communis*) is a gymnosperm of the family Cupressaceae. It is widely distributed in the northern hemisphere, and may be a shrub or a small tree; in Britain it is usually a branched evergreen shrub up to three metres (10 feet) in height. It bears small, bright green, sharply pointed leaves in whorls of three. The very small catkins are followed by globular berries (galbuli); these have a deep purplish colour and a bluish-grey, waxy bloom, and are up to 1 cm (0·4 inches) in diameter. Juniper berries, the part used in medicine, contain an essential oil (oil of juniper), invert sugar and resin. The oil has diuretic and antiseptic properties. Large quantities of berries are used in the preparation of gin.

p. 138

Maize

Maize, Indian corn or sweet corn (*Zea mays*) belongs to the family Gramineae. Originating in America, it is widely grown for its grains, which are arranged in large cobs, and as a source of maize starch. The female flowers are enclosed in a large sheath of overlapping leafy bracts; from the top of this there emerges, at the time of pollination, a beard or silky tassel of thread-like styles. It is this hairy mass which is collected and used as a diuretic, generally in the form of an infusion.

Lycopodium

The lycopodium or club-moss (*Lycopodium clavatum*) is a pteridophyte belonging to the family Lycopodiaceae, and is a herbaceous perennial which is common in hilly pastures and heaths in northern Europe and Asia. It has long creeping stems with forked branches that are closely covered with extremely narrow leaves. The erect fruiting branches bear one or two (occasionally four) spikes of sporophylls carrying sporangia full of microscopic tetrahedral spores. The entire plant is used for its diuretic action, in the form of an infusion. The spores, collected in quantity in Poland and the USSR, form a light, mobile yellow powder which was at one time used for coating pills, as a dusting powder and in medicated snuffs; by virtue of its content of essential oil, it burns explosively and brightly, with some smoke, when blown into a flame, and is used to simulate explosions on the stage.

Herb mercury

The mercury or annual mercury (*Mercurialis annua*) belongs to the family Euphorbiaceae. It is a herbaceous annual, common on uncultivated land, in orchards and as a weed of cultivation, flowering the whole summer and autumn. It can vary in height from a few centimetres to a metre (3¼ feet); vigorous plants are well branched, the branches having rounded angles and swollen nodes. The leaves are opposite, petiolate, ovate or oblong, with a very thin lamina and a toothed margin. It is a dioecious plant; the flowers, especially the female ones, are inconspicuous. The drug is derived from the entire plant; it has diuretic and purgative properties, but the active constituents remain unknown.

p. 140

Everlastings

The everlastings or helichrysums are Compositous plants, members of a genus containing some 500 species of shrubs and perennial and annual herbs; the one illustrated, *Helichrysum italicum* (also known as *H. angustifolium* and curry plant), as its name implies, grows in Italy, where it is common on dry and stony soils, particularly in the centre and south of the country. It is a very aromatic perennial herb or small undershrub, about 50 cm (20 inches) high, much branched and bearing downy, contorted linear leaves. The inflorescence forms a dense but rather small, conical corymb with golden-yellow scale-like bracts that keep their colour even after the plant has dried up (hence the common name). The flowering season lasts from late spring to the end of September. Active principles are present in the entire flowering plant as well as the inflorescence itself; they consist of a very complex essential oil, caffeic acid and flavonoids. The plant is easily prepared as an infusion or decoction; it is used as a diuretic and in the treatment of diseases of the respiratory passages, liver and gall bladder, for rheumatism and in many cases of allergy.

Horsetails

The great horsetail (*Equisetum telmateia* or *E. maximum*) is a member of the family Equisetaceae, fairly common in cool, moist situations such as the vicinity of streams, pools and marshes. It is a perennial herb with simple, jointed fruiting stems about 40 cm (16 inches) high, almost covered from one joint to the next by sheaths marked with 25 to 30 longitudinal grooves and fringed with the same number of subulate teeth, which are in fact the leaves. It also has much taller, whitish, ungrooved sterile stems, appearing later and bearing whorls of 20 to 30 long, slender branches curving upwards and outwards; it is these sterile stems that supply the drug. The common horsetail (*Equisetum arvense*) is a similar plant, and its sterile shoots are also used medicinally. Equisetums contain a saponin, flavonoids and traces of alkaloids, and are very rich in mineral salts and silica. Their action is haemostatic, remineralizing and astringent; they are generally administered as a decoction.

Meadowsweet

Meadowsweet (*Filipendula ulmaria* or *Spiraea ulmaria*) belongs to the family Rosaceae and is fairly common in pastures and on river banks in Europe and western Asia, except for the extreme north and south. It is a perennial herb with a short rhizome and sparsely branched, angular annual stems up to a metre ($3\frac{1}{4}$ feet) high. The large leaves are pinnatisect, being composed of three to nine ovate to lanceolate segments which are whitish and downy on the underside. The yellowish-white flowers, in terminal cymes, are rather inconspicuous. The parts used in pharmacy are usually the flowers, but occasionally the leaves or even the whole flowering plant. The active principles are two glycosides, one of which breaks down, forming the volatile methyl salicylate. The plant's most important medicinal properties are antirheumatic and diuretic, but it is also astringent. Dropwort (*Spiraea filipendula*) has similar properties. Both species occur wild in Britain, and several other spiraeas are cultivated in gardens.

p. 142

Fumitory

Fumitory (*Fumaria officinalis*) is a herb belonging to the family Papaveraceae (sometimes classified as belonging to the separate family Fumariaceae), found in cultivated and waste places, on stony ground and ruined masonry in Europe, including England. It is a herbaceous annual, bright green to glaucous in colour, with branching stems and alternate leaves subdivided into segments which are generally three-lobed. The flowers form fairly loose racemes, and have whitish sepals and a tubular purplish-pink corolla. The inflorescence is used medicinally. Fumitory contains alkaloids and fumaric acid, and is rich in mineral matter, particularly potassium salts. It was known to Dioscorides and has long been used as a tonic, laxative and biliary stimulant.

Maidenhair fern

Maidenhair fern (*Adiantum capillus-veneris*) is a graceful little wild fern sometimes brought as an ornamental plant into the house, where it can survive often rather unfavourable conditions reasonably well; it belongs to the family Polypodiaceae. It has wiry, dark brown stems bearing fronds about 15 cm (6 inches) long, divided into bright green, stalked, obovate or fan-shaped segments. For medicinal use, the fronds should be collected in early summer. Although an old folk remedy, the maidenhair fern is still regarded as having pectoral and expectorant properties; it is easy to prepare as an infusion.

Woody nightshade

Woody nightshade or bittersweet (*Solanum dulcamara*), of the family Solanaceae, is an undershrub fairly common in hedges and on damp waste ground throughout Europe, including England. It has petiolate leaves, the lower ones ovate or ovate-lanceolate and cordate at the base, the upper ones tripartite and bearing additional small lobes or auricles. The flowers resemble those of the black nightshade (*v.* illustration p. 123), but differ in colour: each of the five petals surrounding the yellow stamens is violet and bears small spots of yellow or green at its base. The fruits are scarlet-red berries, which often attract children; luckily they are very much less toxic than the black berries of the deadly nightshade, but their consumption should be discouraged. The constituents of woody

216

nightshade are complex but include gluco-alkaloids and steroidal saponins. Although less used than formerly, the stems are employed in the form of a decoction or infusion as a diuretic and laxative or in the treatment of certain skin diseases.

p. 144 | **Shepherd's purse** | The shepherd's purse (*Capsella bursa-pastoris*) belongs to the family Cruciferae; it is a herbaceous annual, up to about 40 cm (16 inches) in height, widespread in gardens, fields and waste land, and flowering for most of the year. From a rosette of oblong radical leaves, which may be entire or pinnatifid, arises a simple or branched stem which bears small oblong or lanceolate leaves which clasp the stem, and inconspicuous white flowers in terminal racemes. The fruits are rather distinctive, being in the shape of a compressed triangle. The plant has haemostatic and astringent properties, and has been shown to contain tyramine and alkaloids. Its most common use in domestic medicine is as a uterine haemostatic in cases of excessive or painful menstrual flow.

Barberry The common barberry (*Berberis vulgaris*) belongs to the family Berberidaceae; with many other species of *Berberis*, it is widely cultivated. It is a perennial with a bushy habit, one to two metres (over 3 to over 6 feet) in height, with pale green, obovate, sharply toothed leaves some of which are modified to form sharp three-lobed thorns. The flowers are yellow, composed of six sepals, six to eight petals, and six stamens, and have a rather disagreeable odour; the fruit is a small red berry with an acidulous taste, containing two or three seeds. The bark of the roots and stem is employed in the form of a liquid extract or infusion; it contains a number of alkaloids, one of which is berberine. In folk medicine berberis is used as a bitter tonic, antihaemorrhagic and antipyretic. It is employed in homoeopathy.

p. 146 | **German chamomile** | The German chamomile (*Matricaria chamomilla*) is an erect, branched annual of the family Compositae, found in Europe and western Asia. The whole plant has a strong characteristic odour and a bitter taste. The leaves are sessile, divided pinnately into narrow linear segments. The flowerhead has an involucre of up to three rows of linear bracts. The receptacle is conical and hollow (unlike that of Roman chamomile; *v.* p. 156) and bears both ligulate and tubular florets; the outer ligulate florets are white, the central tubular ones yellow. The plant is widely cultivated and is used more on the Continent than in England, where the Roman chamomile is preferred. German chamomile contains essential oil, which is blue when freshly distilled because of the presence of chamazulene; other constituents are coumarins, a bitter principle and mucilage. The herb is used, generally in the form of an infusion (chamomile tea), as a bitter tonic, carminative and diuretic; and externally in hair lotions, shampoos and as an anti-inflammatory poultice.

Groundsel The groundsel (*Senecio vulgaris*), also belonging to the Compositae, is a small, very common weed in Europe and many other parts of the world. It has a glabrous stem, up to 40 cm (16 inches) high, bearing short-stalked lower leaves and sessile upper ones, the latter being oblong with a sinuate, dentately lobed margin. The small flowerheads have few or no ligulate florets, but numerous tubular disc florets. The entire aerial parts are used; the plant has been popular since Greek times, particularly for female complaints, but is now much less used. Like many other plants of the genus *Senecio*, it contains alkaloids.

Tansy The tansy (*Tanacetum vulgare*), another Composite, is common throughout Europe and western Asia. It is a perennial with an erect stem, up to 80 cm (over 2½ feet) high, with a powerful odour and bitter taste. The leaves are pinnate, oblong-linear and divided into pinnatifid or dentate segments; the flowerheads, arranged in terminal corymbs, are almost entirely composed of tubular, golden-yellow florets. The flowering tops are used as a domestic remedy for worms, but the essential oil of the plant, which is the active constituent, is toxic in excessive doses. The tansy is used in homoeopathy and in veterinary medicine.

217

p. 148	**Guelder rose**	The guelder rose (*Viburnum opulus*) belongs to the honeysuckle family, the Caprifoli-aceae. It is a well-branched shrub or small tree, common in hedges and woods throughout Europe, up to five metres (16 feet) in height. The petiolate leaves are divided into three or five lobes, coarsely toothed at the margin. The white flowers are gathered into drooping cymes; only the central flowers are fertile, those at the periphery being sterile. The fruit is a globular blackish-red drupe. The plant contains essential oil and catechols. The bark, used as an extract or infusion, has diuretic and antispasmodic properties.
	Ground pine	The ground pine (*Ajuga chamaepitys*), of the family Labiatae, is a small herbaceous plant, found by roadsides and in dry uncultivated places throughout Europe. It is hairy and sticky, and is usually a low, much-branched annual with crowded, deeply divided leaves. The flowers, in axillary pairs, are yellow. The flowering tops are occasionally used in popular medicine as an emmenagogue, but little is known about the constituents.
	Yew	The common yew (*Taxus baccata*) is a gymnosperm of the family Taxaceae. It is usually a small, dioecious evergreen tree; the linear leaves, up to 3 cm (1·2 inches) long, are in two ranks. The female plant produces isolated woody seeds, each enclosed in a fleshy cup, the aril, which becomes bright red when mature. All parts, except the aril, contain the very poisonous alkaloid taxine; if the trees are not well fenced, horses and cattle die through eating the leaves. The yew is no longer used in medicine.
p. 150	**Savin**	The savin (*Juniperus sabina*) is a gymnosperm of the family Cupressaceae. It is a shrub, sometimes lying close to the ground, but usually with erect branches, sometimes a small tree up to four metres (13 feet) high. The leaves are small, opposite and decussate, and overlapping; the flowers are always unisexual, on monoecious or dioecious plants. The fruit is a fleshy cone (galbulus), improperly called a berry, bluish-black when mature, carried on a recurved peduncle. The drug is derived from the young branches, but is dangerous and now rarely used. Savin contains an essential oil one of the constituents of which is a highly toxic alcohol, sabinol.
	Wallflower	The wallflower (*Cheiranthus cheiri*) belongs to the family Cruciferae. A native of southern Europe, it is now found wild in England, and is much cultivated in gardens; it is especially found in rocky places and (as its common name implies) old walls. The leaves are narrow, pointed, with an entire margin, and almost glabrous; the flowers are tetramerous, yellow, yellowish-brown to deep red in colour. The fruit is a tetragonal, elongated siliqua. In folk medicine wallflower has been used as a diuretic and in the treatment of dropsy. The seeds contain glycosides, one of which contains sulphur and another which has an action on the heart.
	Ergot of rye	Ergot of rye consists of the resting stage of a fungus, *Claviceps purpurea* (family Hypocreaceae), which sometimes grows on the ovary of the rye, *Secale cereale* (family Gramineae). Its use should be strictly confined to the medical profession. The same fungus infects other plants of the grass family, but there are many different races of the fungus which produce different constituents even when grown on the same host plant. The disease is spread by spores which are carried to the rye flowers either by the wind or by insects; these develop into the resting stage (sclerotium) shown in the illustration. The sclerotia eventually fall to the ground, where they produce stalk-like spore-bearing projections in the following spring. Rye flour contaminated with ergot, if eaten for any period, produces ergotism and may result in gangrene and death. The active constituents are alkaloids.

Endocrine system

p. 152

Onion

The onion (*Allium cepa*) belongs to the family Liliaceae; many other species of *Allium* are also cultivated, e.g. garlic, shallots and leeks. The onion is a biennial plant with a tunicated bulb, the size and colour of which varies in different cultivated varieties; the outer scales are tough and papery, the inner ones fleshy. From the bulb arises a rosette of large cylindrical leaves, enclosing the flowering scape which bears a globular umbel of flowers. The drug is derived from the bulbs. Onions are used for culinary purposes, and the fresh juice has diuretic and antibacterial properties. The bulb is rich in carbohydrates, including reducing sugars, and sulphur compounds; the coloured scales contain flavonoid pigments and phenolic substances.

Nettle

The common stinging nettle (*Urtica dioica*), of the family Urticaceae, is one of three species found in England. It is a herbaceous perennial with erect, square annual stems up to two metres (over 6 feet) in height, carrying large, dark green petiolate leaves; both leaves and stems are covered with stinging hairs. The flowers are usually dioecious, not very conspicuous, and arranged in spikes. In popular medicine, freshly expressed nettle juice or an infusion is used as a diuretic and hypoglycaemic; the leaves are sometimes used as a pot-herb for soups. The stinging properties, long thought to be due to formic acid, are now believed to be due to a histamine-like substance.

Bilberry

The bilberry, blaeberry or whortleberry (*Vaccinium myrtillus*) is a member of the family Ericaceae, widespread in Europe and Asia, particularly in mountain heaths and woods. It occurs in Britain; other British species of *Vaccinium* are *V. uliginosum* (bog whortleberry), *V. vitis-idaea* (red whortleberry or cowberry; *v.* p. 136) and *V. oxycoccus* (cranberry), all small shrubs with alternate leaves, and small flowers and berries. The bilberry attains a height of about 30 cm (1 foot) and has numerous erect or spreading branches, and ovate or obovate, very short-stalked deciduous leaves with a finely toothed margin. The flowers are pitcher-shaped, greenish-white with a tinge of red near the base; the fruit is a globular black berry with a waxy bloom, whereas the berries of the cowberry and cranberry are red. The leaves are hypoglycaemic and contain a variety of plant acids, flavonoids and tannins; they yield an ash which is rich in manganese. The fruits are valued for cooking and confectionery; they are astringent, and contain sugars, acids, tannin, pigments and vitamins A, C and P.

p. 154

Galega

Galega (*Galega officinalis*) belongs to the Papilionaceae, a subfamily of the Leguminosae. It is a large herbaceous perennial, with aerial stems up to a metre or more (over 3 feet) in height. The leaves are compound and imparipinnate, with eleven to seventeen lanceolate leaflets and sagittate stipules. In summer it produces dense axillary racemes of papilionaceous flowers with a pale blue-violet, or occasionally white, corolla; the fruits are legumes. The drug is derived from the entire flowering plant; galega has a hypoglycaemic and galactogenic action, and is used in the form of an infusion. It contains alkaloids which are derivatives of guanidine and quinazoline, and also a flavone glycoside.

Star anise

The star anise (*Illicium verum*) belongs to the family Magnoliaceae, and originated in southern China and Indochina, where it is still cultivated. It is an evergreen tree four to five metres (13 to 16 feet) high. The drug is derived from the fruits, which are composed of follicles fused in a radial pattern, each containing a single oval seed. The fruit is galactogenic, stimulant, digestive and carminative; it is widely used in liqueur manufacture. As already mentioned above (p. 189), this plant and European aniseed (*Pimpinella anisum*), though of different families, yield an almost identical oil; both oils are sold as aniseed oil.

Fennel

The fennel (*Foeniculum vulgare*) belongs to the family Umbelliferae. It is a herbaceous plant up to two metres (over 6 feet) high, perennial in the wild form and annual or biennial in the cultivated forms. The leaves have a sheathing base, and are finely divided into hair-like segments; the yellow flowers are borne in compound umbels without an involucre of bracts. The fruits are oblong and consist of a cremocarp of two joined mericarps, each with very distinct ridges. The fruits and roots are used, their action being galactogenic, carminative, stimulant and diuretic. The essential oil present in the plant consists mainly of anethole, but in the bitter variety of fennel a ketone, fenchone, is also present. In Italy the sweet variety of fennel has been used as a vegetable since Roman times; in England its main use is in a sauce, prepared from the leaves, to be served with salmon.

Skin

p. 156 **Walnut** The walnut tree (*Juglans regia*) belongs to the family Juglandaceae, and is now grown extensively in all of temperate Europe and in the Himalayas, China and Japan. It is an imposing tree, reaching some 20 metres (65 feet) in height. The bark is smooth at first, later becoming rough and whitish; the deciduous leaves are composed of up to nine elliptical, entire leaflets. It is a monoecious plant, the female flowers being solitary, the males clustered in a catkin. The fruit, a delicious nut, is made up of a rather fleshy outer case and a woody inner shell enclosing the seed or kernel, which consists of two large, wrinkled, oil-rich cotyledons. The leaves of the walnut tree contain tannin, essential oil and a purgative naphthaquinone known as juglone; they have astringent, antiscrofulous and antiperspirant properties. A decoction of leaves makes an effective mouthwash or douche and is good for eczema and skin eruptions.

Comfrey Common comfrey (*Symphytum officinale*), of the family Boraginaceae, is a rough, bristly plant covered with short stiff hairs, and often found in damp ground, beside watercourses and in shady hedgerows. It has a large rhizome and one or two fleshy, branched, leafy stems, sometimes over a metre (well over 3 feet) high, but usually much shorter. The basal leaves have long stalks and are larger than the upper ones, which are sessile and decurrent along the stem as far as the next leaf below; the white to dingy purple flowers grow in scorpioid cymes forming a multifloral pseudopanicle. The leaves can be used to make refreshing drinks, and are expectorant and diaphoretic, but their active principles are more abundant in the rhizome, from which astringent and healing poultices and powders can be prepared for external use; the rhizome contains allantoin, mucilage, tannin, resin and essential oil.

Roman chamomile The Roman chamomile (*Anthemis nobilis*), of the family Compositae, is more used in England than the German chamomile (*v.* p. 146). It is a creeping, branched perennial, and has been used to make chamomile lawns. The leaves are finely divided. The flowerheads have white ligulate ray florets and a few tubular disc florets; under cultivation the flowers have become 'double', that is, tubular florets have changed into ligulate ones. Chamomiles have a strong odour and a bitter taste and contain essential oil. The flowers are used in popular medicine and in shampoos.

Yellow chamomile The yellow chamomile (*Anthemis tinctoria*), as its specific name indicates, was formerly used by dyers. It occurs in Europe and occasionally, probably as an escape, in eastern England. It has pinnatifid leaves, and both the disc and the ray florets are bright yellow. Its constituents and uses resemble those of the Roman chamomile.

p. 158 **Betony** Betony (*Stachys officinalis*), of the family Labiatae, is a perennial herb widely distributed in Europe (including England) and Asia. Its stems, up to 60 cm (2 feet) in height, bear radical leaves which are oblong, cordate at the base, and have crenate margins; the upper leaves are narrower, non-cordate, with serrate margins. The flowers, in dense whorls, form terminal spikes; they have very pointed calyx teeth and bilabiate pink or mauve corollas. Betony is sometimes known as woundwort, and can be used for sores and ulcers in the form of a poultice made from the leaves. The plant contains tannin and bases such as betaine and stachydrine.

Myrtle The common myrtle (*Myrtus communis*) is a southern European shrub of the family Myrtaceae. It has opposite, ovate-lanceolate leaves which are minutely dotted with translucent oil glands; the lamina is bright green above but rather lighter on the underside. The solitary, long-stalked flower has a calyx of five sepals, a corolla of five petals which fall early, and numerous stamens. The fruit is a blue-black berry containing numerous seeds. The essential oil in the oil glands contains terpenes and the sesquiterpene alcohol myrtenol, and is used in perfumery; the leaves also contain tannin and resin. An infusion has astringent, antiseptic and haemostatic properties and is used for piles.

221

	Marigold	The marigold (*Calendula officinalis*), of the family Compositae, is a herbaceous annual found in the wild state in many parts of Europe and widely cultivated in gardens. It grows to a height of about 50 cm (20 inches). The leaves near the base are spathulate, those higher up smaller, lanceolate and amplexicaul. The flowerheads, up to 7 cm ($2\frac{3}{4}$ inches) in diameter, have an involucre of bracts, several rows of ligulate florets and a central mass of tubular florets; all the florets are orange-yellow. Marigolds contain a little essential oil, a bitter principle, and carotenoid and flavonoid colouring matters. Popular uses for the plant are as an infusion for use in anaemia and in an ointment for sores, cuts and bruises.

p. 160   **Burdock**

The burdock (*Arctium lappa*), of the family Compositae, is found throughout Europe and is common in Britain; it is a biennial herb with a stout stem up to 1·5 metres (5 feet) high. It has very large, long-stalked basal leaves which may be cordate at the base, with a denticulate margin; the upper leaves are smaller, broadly ovate, covered with cottony down on the underside. The flowering stems, which emerge in the second year, are longitudinally grooved and often reddish in colour. The flowers are purple and collected in globular heads surrounded by rows of scaly bracts with hooked points; the formation favours the dispersal of the seeds, since the ripe flowerheads catch on any animal or person that comes into contact with them. The part of the burdock used is the root, which should be collected in the autumn of the first year, and is generally broken into pieces of 2 to 3 cm (about an inch) and then dried at a fairly low temperature in a dry place. The roots contain about 50% of inulin, a bitter principle and an essential oil having a fungistatic and bacteriostatic action. Preparations of burdock root are used in the treatment of boils, eczema, acne and dandruff.

Birch

The common birch (*Betula alba*; sometimes divided into the species *B. pendula* or silver birch and *B. pubescens* or downy birch) is a tree of the family Betulaceae found in the hilly regions of Europe, Asia and North America; it can reach a height of 20 metres (65 feet), and is characterized by a silver-white bark which flakes off in parchment-like layers. The leaves are petiolate, usually ovate, taper to a point and have a doubly-dentate margin; the younger leaves are sticky, the older ones glabrous. The flowers are grouped in monoecious catkins, the male ones being sessile, the females pedunculate. The drug is derived from the bark and the leaves. The leaves contain tannin, essential oil and a saponin, and have diuretic properties. Dry distillation of the bark produces the so-called 'birch oil', which is efficacious in the case of certain skin complaints. Birch bark contains a glycoside which decomposes to give methyl salicylate. It is used as a remedy for rheumatism in Canada and the USA.

Toad-flax

Toad-flax (*Linaria vulgaris*) is a member of the foxglove family, the Scrophulariaceae; it occurs in hedges and on the borders of fields throughout Europe, and is common in England. It has a creeping rootstock and an erect stem up to a metre ($3\frac{1}{4}$ feet) high. The leaves are linear-lanceolate and the yellow flowers have a corolla-tube which projects as a conical spur. The constituents of the plant appear to require further investigation. An infusion is used in popular medicine for urinary troubles, and an ointment for the treatment of boils.

p. 162   **Mezereon**

The mezereon (*Daphne mezereum*) is a shrub, up to a metre ($3\frac{1}{4}$ feet) high, belonging to the family Thymelaeaceae, found, mainly in hilly districts, in both Europe and Asia, though occurring only in the south of England; it may be distinguished from the other British species, *D. laureola*, the spurge laurel, by the fact that its berries are red, those of the spurge laurel being black. Mezereon has glabrous, deciduous leaves about 7 cm (nearly 3 inches) long, which are oblong-lanceolate in shape; the purple, sweet-scented flowers appear in early spring, before the leaves. Mezereon is a very poisonous plant and the bark, although formerly official, is no longer used in medical practice; it contains an irritant resin and glycoside. In folk medicine the bark is sometimes used externally as a vesicant. Children should be warned not to eat the berries.

222

	Veratrums	Several species of *Veratrum*, of the family Liliaceae, have been used in medicine and, particularly in recent years, have been the objects of much research. The European white hellebore (*Veratrum album*) is very difficult to distinguish except when in flower from the American green hellebore (*V. viride*); another species or variety is *V. lobelianum*. White hellebore is a large perennial found in European mountain pastures up to a height of about 2,500 metres (8,000 feet). It has a short rhizome from which emerge aerial stems up to a metre ($3\frac{1}{4}$ feet) high. The leaves are large, alternate, oval and with well-marked veins which converge at the apex; the flowers are greenish-white. The rhizomes of these plants contain extremely toxic alkaloids, such as jervine and the protoveratrines, which have a hypotensive action. The plant has drastic purgative and emetic properties and is not suitable for home use. The veratrums should not be confused with the true hellebores (*v.* p. 52).
	Spotted hemlock	The spotted hemlock (*Conium maculatum*), of the family Umbelliferae, is one of the most poisonous wild plants found in Britain, and occurs in shady, moist places over most of Europe. It is a biennial with a branched, grooved stem up to two metres ($6\frac{1}{2}$ feet) high, often, but not invariably, marked with purple spots and giving off a disagreeable mouse-like odour when bruised. The large compound leaves are deeply segmented. The small white flowers are in terminal umbels with about ten to fifteen rays; the fruit is a small cremocarp. The plant is interesting historically, since it was used in classical Greece to make a draught by means of which criminals were put to death; further, its main constituent, the toxic liquid alkaloid coniine, was the first alkaloid to be synthesized, in 1886. Hemlock was used in Anglo-Saxon medicine, but now, even under medical supervision, it is rarely, if ever, used except by herbalists. A related plant, also very poisonous, is *Cicuta virosa*, the cowbane or water hemlock.
p. 164	**Periwinkles**	The larger periwinkle (*Vinca major*) and the lesser periwinkle (*V. minor*) are the only wild British representatives of the large, mainly tropical family Apocynaceae; these two species occur in many parts of Europe, and a third, *V. rosea* (*Catharanthus roseus*; *v.* p. 176), is cultivated. The larger periwinkle is a perennial with a creeping rootstock, often grown to provide ground cover in gardens; its trailing shoots bear shining, ovate leaves, and the erect flowering shoots bear large flowers of varying shades of blue and bluish-violet. The lesser periwinkle is similar, with smaller flowers and lanceolate leaves. The periwinkles are used in folk medicine in both the temperate and tropical zones and have been credited with various properties, including tonic, diuretic, purgative and vermifugal; they can be used as a mouthwash and in the form of a poultice for certain skin diseases. Research proceeds on the alkaloids they contain for the treatment of certain forms of cancer.
	Herb Robert	Herb Robert (*Geranium robertianum*), of the family Geraniaceae, is a small annual, up to 30 cm (1 foot) in height, usually found in shady locations near walls or hedges. All its parts are reddish and covered with soft hairs. It has an unpleasant odour when rubbed. The leaves are divided pinnately into three to five lobes; the rather small flowers have hairy, pointed sepals, and the petals are reddish-purple to rose in colour. The plant is rich in tannin, and the flowering tops are used as a mouthwash in the form of a decoction. It has an astringent action when used externally or internally. The genus *Geranium* should not be confused with the garden geraniums, which are species of the related genus *Pelargonium*.
p. 166	**Persicarias**	Several species of *Polygonum*, of the family Polygonaceae, are known in Italy as *persicaria*; the same plants occur in England under the names persicaria (*Polygonum persicaria*), pale persicaria (*P. lapathifolium*), which may be only a variety of persicaria, and water pepper (*P. hydropiper*). All are found in rocky but damp places, particularly ditches. Persicaria is an annual, up to 60 cm (2 feet) high, having lanceolate leaves which are petiolate on the lower part of the stem, but sessile on the upper; the flowering stem bears spikes of reddish flowers. The water pepper is a more slender plant than persicaria; its stem is often decumbent, its leaves and flowers are dotted with small glands, and it has a particularly

223

	Yarrow	acrid taste. The fruits of these plants are achenes, surrounded by the persistent perianth. The roots are used for their haemostatic, diuretic and hypotensive properties; they contain astringent substances such as tannins and flavonoids. The yarrow or milfoil (*Achillea millefolium*), of the family Compositae, is very abundant in Europe from the Mediterranean to the Arctic Circle. It is a perennial with a creeping rhizome and aerial stems up to a metre (3¼ feet) in height. The leaves are oblong or linear and deeply divided into pinnatifid segments. The flowerheads are in dense terminal corymbs; the ray florets are relatively few and, like the more numerous tubular florets, are white or pink in colour. In domestic medicine the flowering tops are infused as a tonic and febrifuge, and the fresh juice is applied to ulcers, haemorrhoids and boils. Yarrow contains an essential oil which, like chamomile oil, contains the blue compound azulene; also polyphenols and sesquiterpene lactones.
p. 168	**Solomon's seal**	The Solomon's seal illustrated (*Polygonatum officinale* or *P. vulgare*) belongs to the family Liliaceae and is common in Europe; a very similar plant, *P. multiflorum*, is found wild in Britain. Solomon's seal is a herbaceous perennial with a large nodular rhizome and an aerial stem up to 50 cm (20 inches) high. The leaves are sessile, ovate and parallel-veined; the flowers have six perianth segments and are solitary or paired. The fruit, a berry, is poisonous and said to cause vomiting. The drug is derived from the rhizome; it is used in popular medicine in the form of compresses made from a decoction or from the pounded rhizome to treat contusions, bruises or whitlows.
	Madonna lily	The madonna lily (*Lilium candidum*) also belongs to the Liliaceae, and is said to have been cultivated for over 3,000 years; it is a herbaceous perennial with an erect leafy stem and trumpet-shaped, six-petalled white flowers too well known to need further description. The drug is derived from the bulb, which has yellowish scales. In popular medicine the crushed fresh bulb or the petals are used to treat bruises, contusions or scalds. Oil of lily can be prepared by macerating the petals in olive oil. Little is known about the constituents.
	Arnica	The arnica (*Arnica montana*) belongs to the family Compositae, and is a herbaceous perennial with a subterranean horizontal rhizome. The plant has a basal rosette of pubescent, elliptical leaves, and a simple or slightly branched stem up to 40 cm (16 inches) high which bears smaller leaves in opposite pairs. The flowerhead is large, nearly always solitary, and surrounded by an involucre of lanceolate, hairy bracts; the tubular and the ligulate florets are both orange-yellow in colour. Leaves, flowers and rhizome are used. Arnica contains essential oil with terpene alcohols and acetylenic derivatives; the colouring matter consists of carotenoids and flavonoids. Arnica is seldom used internally, except in homoeopathy, but it is a popular external remedy for bruises, usually used in the form of a diluted tincture.
p. 170	**Agrimony**	Agrimony (*Agrimonia eupatoria*), of the family Rosaceae, is a herbaceous perennial with a short rhizome and usually a single aerial annual stem. The leaves are dense at the base, pinnatisect with two to five pairs of segments; the stem terminates in a long raceme of yellow flowers. All parts are hairy, and the calyx has hooked bristles. The leaves or the entire flowering plant can be used in the form of an infusion which contains tannin-like substances that make it suitable for a mouthwash. A decoction may be used as a lotion for boils and ulcerations.
	Columbine	The columbine (*Aquilegia vulgaris*) belongs to the family Ranunculaceae and is a perennial herb, common in woods and also cultivated in Europe and Asia. It produces a rosette of leaves and branched stems which may be up to a metre (3¼ feet) high. The flowers are blue, dull purple, rose or white, with petals terminating in a horn-shaped spur. The fruits are follicles containing numerous, very shiny seeds. The fresh juice is used to treat ulcers and boils, and an infusion of the leaves is used as a gargle or mouthwash.
	St John's wort	The common St John's wort (*Hypericum perforatum*) belongs to the family Hypericaceae and is found throughout Europe in woods and hedges. It is a herbaceous perennial with aerial annual stems up to 50 cm (20 inches) in height. The leaves are sessile, opposed and

elliptical-oval; when viewed against the light they show very numerous glands, appearing as small shining spots. St John's wort flowers at the beginning of summer; the flowers are pentamerous, of a pleasant golden yellow, grouped in a terminal corymb. The fruits are ovoid capsules, opening by three valves. The entire flowering plant is used; it contains an essential oil, polyphenols, tannin and a red pigment, hypericin. Used externally as an infusion, or decocted in a mixture of olive oil and wine, it acts as a vulnerary and astringent.

Terebinth

The terebinth (*Pistacia terebinthus*), of the family Anacardiaceae, is a bush or shrub found in the Mediterranean region. It has imparipinnate, deciduous leaves and inflorescences of inconspicuous flowers arising from the leaf axils. When the bark is incised, a greenish oleo-resin called 'Chian turpentine' exudes; this is used externally for the preparation of ointments and plasters. The presence of oleo-resin canals is a characteristic of the Anacardiaceae; the related species *Pistacia lentiscus* yields the solid oleo-resin known as mastic.

p. 172

Lesser celandine

The lesser celandine or pilewort (*Ranunculus ficaria* or *Ficaria ranunculoides*) belongs to the family Ranunculaceae; it should not be confused with the greater celandine (*Chelidonium majus*; *v.* p. 176), a member of the poppy family. The lesser celandine is a herbaceous perennial, fairly common in fields, small in size, with fibrous or occasionally tuberous roots; the stems are prostrate, bearing long-stalked fleshy leaves, bright green in colour and cordate at the base. The flowers have a long peduncle, three greenish sepals and eight to ten bright yellow petals; they begin to bloom in early spring. In popular medicine the crushed leaves are used for their revulsive and cicatrizing properties to treat cracks in the skin and stubborn boils. The fluid extract can be used as an antihaemorrhagic, and the soft extract used externally, mixed with poplar ointment (*v.* below).

Other ranunculi

Besides the lesser celandine, the genus *Ranunculus* contains some 400 species, of diverse form and habit; the Italian species illustrated is R. *velutinus*. Among the fifteen species which grow wild in Britain may be mentioned R. *aquatilis* (water crowfoot), R. *lingua* (great spearwort), R. *sceleratus* (celery-leaved crowfoot), R. *acris* (crowfoot or buttercup) and R. *repens* (creeping buttercup). The ranunculi generally favour damp situations and some are aquatic; many species, like the lesser celandine, develop tuberous roots. In the wild state the flowers are generally yellow or white and have five, or a few more, petals; under cultivation more petals may be developed, and there are double-flowered varieties such as bachelor's buttons. In spite of much chemical research, the constituents of many species remain unknown; among those reported are alkaloids, saponins, a cyanogenetic glycoside and tannin. Many species are more or less poisonous.

Poplar buds

The black poplar (*Populus nigra*) belongs to the family Salicaceae. It is a large tree, up to 20 metres (65 feet) in height; the Lombardy poplar (var. *italica* of this species) may reach 40 metres (130 feet). The leaves are deciduous, rhomboidal or triangular, and cuneate at the base. It is a dioecious plant, producing reddish pendulous catkins; the fruits are small capsules, containing seeds covered with cottony hairs which aid their dissemination by the wind. The drug is derived from the buds, which constitute the essential ingredient of an ointment used for the treatment of haemorrhoids, scalds, burns and boils. Poplar buds contain a glycoside called populoside; this resembles the glycoside salicin, found in many willows and poplars, which was much used in medicine until it was replaced by aspirin and similar synthetic drugs.

p. 174

White horehound

The white horehound (*Marrubium vulgare*) belongs to the family Labiatae and is found in Europe, western Asia and north Africa. It is a tomentose, whitish perennial, with a slight odour of musk. The square stems, up to 50 cm (20 inches) or a little more in height, bear opposed, orbicular leaves which are wrinkled or curled, and cordate to crenate at the base. The flowers are grouped in axillary whorls and have a whitish corolla protruding slightly from the calyx. The flowering tops are used, mainly as an expectorant but also as a bitter tonic and diuretic. The plant contains a bitter principle, marrubine, which is a diterpenic lactone; mineral matter rich in potassium and iron; and tannin, saponins and a little essential oil.

Horse chestnut	The horse chestnut (*Aesculus hippocastanum*), usually known on the Continent as the Indian chestnut, belongs to the small family Hippocastaneae, which is related to the Sapindaceae; it originated in the Near East but is now widely grown in Europe, and was introduced into England in the seventeenth century. It is not related to the sweet or Spanish chestnut (*Castanea sativa*; *v.* p. 122), a member of the Fagaceae. The horse chestnut grows to a height of about 25 metres (80 feet) and has a rather dark, cracked bark. The petiolate leaves are compound and have five to seven leaflets; these are oval-oblong, pinnately veined, with a dentate margin. The inflorescence is a group of cymes with small, scented, zygomorphic flowers which are white, tinged with red and yellow. The fruit is a large globular capsule with a rough spiny coat; this contains one to three seeds which resemble those of the sweet chestnut but have a bitter, unpleasant taste. Both the young bark and the seeds are used. The bark contains tannins and glycosides such as aesculin; the seeds contain much sugar and oil, triterpenic saponins, flavonoids and catechol tannins. A decoction of the bark is used in the treatment of haemorrhoids and varicose veins; preparations are also used in homoeopathy and in veterinary work. Besides its astringent action, the plant has vitamin P properties.
Cypress	The cypress (*Cupressus sempervirens*) is a gymnosperm which belongs to the same family as the junipers, the Cupressaceae. It is an evergreen shrub or tree, up to 20 metres (65 feet) high; it originated in the East but is widely cultivated in Mediterranean countries. It grows in a dense columnar or pyramidal shape. The leaves consist of closely pressed, fleshy scales covering the shoots; each leaf has a oleo-resin gland on its dorsal surface. The flowers are monoecious and grouped in catkins. The scale leaves surrounding the ovules are converted, after fertilization, into woody scales; the resultant berry-like fruit, known as a galbulus, is green at first, but becomes greyish-brown at maturity, when it is about 2 to 3 cm (roughly an inch) in diameter. For medicinal use, the fruits are collected whilst still green; they are used as an astringent and vasoconstrictor in the treatment of haemorrhoids and varicose veins. They contain essential oil in which are terpenes, sesquiterpenes and their derivatives; a catechol tannin is also present. The young branches of cypress also contain essential oil, which was formerly isolated by distillation and used as an inhalation for whooping-cough.
p. 176 **Meadow saffron**	The meadow saffron or colchicum (*Colchicum autumnale*) belongs to the family Liliaceae; although sometimes also called autumn crocus, it is not related to the true crocus, which belongs to the family Iridaceae. It is a herbaceous perennial, flowering in the autumn. The flowers have six rose- or lilac-coloured perianth segments and six stamens; the tubular perianth lies partly below ground and encloses the ovary at its base. The modified underground stem, the corm, is about 2 to 3 cm (roughly an inch) in diameter, white and starchy, and surrounded by membranous scales. The large, green, linear-lanceolate radical leaves appear only in the following spring. At the beginning of the summer the fruit, formed from the previous autumn's flowering, ripens. This is an ovoid, trilobate three-celled capsule; each of the chambers contains numerous small, globular, reddish-brown seeds. Both seeds and corm are used as a source of the toxic alkaloid colchicine; this should only be used, and then with extreme care, by qualified medical practitioners. Colchicine has profound effects on cell chromosomes and is used in biological experiments.
Celandine	The celandine or greater celandine (*Chelidonium majus*) belongs to the family Papaveraceae, and is a herbaceous perennial, up to 80 cm (over $2\frac{1}{2}$ feet) high, with swollen stems that are fragile at the nodes. The leaves are pinnatisect, with rounded, crenate and lobed segments. The flowers, grouped in simple umbels of two to seven, have two deciduous sepals, four yellow petals and numerous stamens; the fruits, formed from two carpels, are elongated capsules opening from the base upwards. The whole plant contains an orange-coloured latex the constituents of which include the alkaloid chelidonine and chelidonic acid. In domestic medicine the latex is used for caustic treatment of warts and to soften calluses and corns; it is also used in homoeopathy.
Rose periwinkle	The rose or Madagascar periwinkle (*Catharanthus roseus* or *Vinca rosea*) belongs to the family Apocynaceae; for the British periwinkles *v.* p. 164. The rose periwinkle is a native of tropical Africa but is now found in Asia, Australia and South America and is grown in British greenhouses; although it is naturally a perennial, it is often cultivated as an annual. It has glossy, oblong-ovate leaves and shiny stems. The rose-pink flowers, up to 4 cm (over half an inch) across, appear on English-grown plants from April to October.

Much research has been done on this plant in recent years, and some of the alkaloids it contains have anti-tumour activity. In Madagascar the plant has long been used for certain skin diseases and for its supposed anti-diabetic properties. It should be used only on medical advice and with medical supervision.

Pesticide

p. 178 **Pyrethrum**

The pyrethrum (*Chrysanthemum cinerariaefolium*), of the family Compositae, grows wild in Yugoslavia but is cultivated as an insecticide in many parts of the world, particularly Kenya. The plant grows to a height of about 80 cm (over 2½ feet) and is bushy and rather woody at the base. The lower leaves are alternate, petiolate and divided into lobed and dentate segments; on the flowering stems the leaves are smaller and have only two or three segments. The solitary flowerhead, carried on a striated stalk, has two or three rows of lanceolate hairy bracts forming the involucre; there is a single row of cream- or straw-coloured ligulate florets and a disc of numerous yellow tubular florets. The flowerheads are usually picked before they are fully open, and are then dried. Large quantities are used in the preparation of insecticidal sprays and as 'insect powder'. The active constituents, the so-called 'pyrethrins', are mixtures of complex esters. Pyrethrum has good insecticidal properties and has the great advantage of being non-toxic to man and domestic animals.

Thuja

The thuja (*Thuya occidentalis*) is a gymnosperm of the family Cupressaceae, and is a tree native to Canada and the USA, where it is known as white cedar, but also grown in Europe, often under the name of arbor-vitae. It has a brownish-red bark; the reddish twigs bear small, overlapping leaves and cones. The young twigs are used in domestic medicine and have astringent and anti-haemorrhoidal properties. The plant is poisonous in large doses; the chief constituents are essential oil, containing thujone and fenchone, and tannin and flavonoids.

Quassia

Two closely related trees, both of the family Simarubaceae, yield quassia wood. For historical reasons, the wood used in Britain is Jamaica quassia, derived from *Picrasma excelsa*, whilst most of that used in Continental Europe comes from *Quassia amara*, grown in Surinam, Guyana and French Guiana; the Jamaican plant is the larger and gives logs up to 30 cm (1 foot) in diameter, compared with about 10 cm (4 inches) from the South American plant. The trees have pinnate leaves with a winged petiole, and rose-coloured flowers. After removal of the bark, the white wood, which gradually turns yellowish on exposure to the air, is cut into small raspings (*v*. illustration). Quassia contains quassin, a lactone with an intensely bitter taste. Many years ago the scientific adviser for this book inspected some casks of West Indian honey which it was clear from the taste had been obtained largely from flowers of the quassia tree; it was quite unfit for consumption and had to be destroyed. Quassia was formerly regarded as having quinine-like properties but is now used in domestic medicine only as a bitter and a vermifuge. Sprayed on fruit trees, it may deter birds but only in the absence of rain.

Botanical Glossary

Achene Dry, indehiscent one-seeded fruit

Acuminate Tapering to a slender point

Acute Pointed, but not tapering

Adventitious Growing from some part of a plant other than the main root

Aerial Above ground level

Alternate Arranged successively on opposite sides of the stem (cf. **Opposite**)

Ament(um) *v.* **Catkin**

Amplexicaul With a base clasping the stem

Annual Completing its life cycle in the course of a year

Anther Pollen-bearing tip of a stamen

Apex Tip of a stem or other organ

Apothecium Spore-holding body of certain fungi and lichens

Appressed Lying flat against the surface

Aril Fleshy formation enclosing the seed of some gymnosperms

Auricle Small appendage at the base of a leaf

Axil Angle where a leaf or branch joins the stem

Basal *v.* **Radical**

Berry Indehiscent fruit, usually with the seed or seeds surrounded by a fleshy or pulpy pericarp

Bicarpellate Formed from two carpels

Biennial Completing its life cycle in the course of two years

Bifid Cleft into two, no deeper than half-way

Bilobate Two-lobed

Bipinnate Pinnately divided, with the leaflets themselves also pinnate

Bract Modified leaf growing just below the calyx

Bulb Modified subterranean bud with fleshy leaf-bases, acting as an organ of storage and vegetative reproduction

Calyx Outer covering of a flower, made up of sepals

Campanulate Bell-shaped

Capsule Dry, dehiscent fruit

Carpel Modified leaf forming the whole or part of the pistil

Catkin Dry, scaly spike of small, clustered flowers, usually unisexual. Also known as an ament or amentum

Cauline Growing from the stem

Cladode Flattened green stem fulfilling the function of a leaf

Composite Made up of numerous florets

Compound Composed of several smaller similar units, e.g. leaflets

Cone Pollen- or seed-bearing organ of most gymnosperms, usually composed of woody scales

Cordate Heart-shaped

Coriaceous Leathery

Corm Short, fleshy, bulb-like subterranean stem

Corolla Inner ring of a flower, composed of petals

Corymb Flat- or round-topped inflorescence of flowers on stalks of different lengths

Cotyledon Embryonic leaf present in the seed. Monocotyledonous plants have one, dicotyledonous plants two, gymnosperms several

Cremocarp Bicarpellate fruit splitting when ripe into two mericarps which remain hanging from the plant

Crenate With rounded teeth on the margin

Cryptogamous Flowerless

Cuneate Wedge-shaped

Cyme Inflorescence in which the stem terminates in a flower, the other flowers being at the end of lateral branches

Deciduous Falling off; shedding its leaves in autumn

Decurrent Extending down the stem from the junction

Decussate Arranged in pairs at right angles to each other

Dehiscent Splitting or opening when ripe to release the seeds

Dentate Toothed. A doubly dentate leaf has marginal teeth that are themselves dentate

Dioecious Having male flowers on one plant, female on another

Drupe Fruit with a hard kernel or stone and a fleshy pericarp

Elliptical Oval, acute at the ends

Emarginate With the margin slightly notched at the apex

Endocarp *v.* **Pericarp**

Entire With an even, unnotched margin

Epicarp *v.* **Pericarp**

Epiphyte Plant growing on another plant, but not deriving nourishment from it

Evanescent Soon withering

Filament Stalk of a stamen; microscopic thread forming vegetative part of a fungus

Filiform Thread-like

Floret Small flower, usually a component of a composite flowerhead

Flowerhead Dense group of flowers; composite inflorescence in which the tubular disc florets surrounded by the ligulate ray florets give the appearance of a single flower

Follicle Dry, monocarpellate many-seeded fruit, opening along one side when ripe

Frond Leaf-like part of a fern

Fruit Seed-bearing product of a plant. True fruits are produced by the transformation of the ovary; when any other part, e.g. receptacle, sepals, petals, bracts, is involved, the result is known botanically as a false fruit or pseudocarp

Fruit body Spore-producing part of, e.g. fungi

Galbulus Berry-like seed cone, composed of fleshy scales

Gamopetalous With petals fused to form a tube

Glabrous Smooth and hairless

Glandular Having an oil-containing gland, e.g. at the tip of a hair

Gymnosperm Plant, e.g. coniferous tree, of the class Gymnospermae, with ovules and seeds not enclosed in an ovary

Hastate Spearhead-shaped; triangular, with a triangular lobe on either side at the base

Haustoria Organs of a parasitic plant enabling it to attach itself to, and thus draw nourishment from, its host

Head *v.* **Flowerhead**

Herb Non-woody plant, usually with a stem dying down to the ground at the end of the season; plant used in cooking for its flavour, or in medicine

Hesperidium Berry of the citrus fruits and related plants, with pulpy pericarp and leathery rind

Hip False fruit of a rose, formed from the receptacle

Imparipinnate Pinnately divided, with a single terminal leaflet

Incised Cut

Indehiscent Not opening when ripe

Indusium Membrane covering the sori in some ferns

Inflorescence Cluster of flowers borne on one stalk

Integument Covering, usually of ovule or seed

Involucre Ring of bracts surrounding an inflorescence

Keel Two fused petals, enclosing the stamens and pistil

Key Dry, indehiscent winged fruit of certain trees

Labiate Having petals fused to form a tube with two lips

Laciniate Irregularly divided into long, narrow segments

Lamina Blade or expanded green portion of a leaf

Lanceolate Lancehead-shaped; narrow, tapering at the apex, more rounded at the base

Lateral At the side

Leaflet Division of a compound leaf

Legume Dry, monocarpellate

many-seeded fruit pod, splitting along both sides when ripe

Lichen Compound plant arising from the mutually beneficial association (symbiosis) of an alga and a fungus

Lignified Woody

Ligulate Strap-shaped; having the petals fused into a single petal-like corolla or ligule

Linear Narrow and pointed

Lobed Cleft, but not divided into leaflets

Margin Edge of the lamina of a leaf

Mericarp Half of a cremocarp, containing one seed

Mesocarp *v.* **Pericarp**

Monocarpellate Formed from one carpel

Monoecious Having both male and female flowers on the same plant

Mucronate With a short, straight point at the apex

Nectary Part of organ of a flower where nectar is secreted

Nut Hard, indehiscent fruit, usually single-seeded

Obovate Egg-shaped, with the narrow end at the base

Obtuse Blunt-ended

Opposite Arranged in pairs, one each side of the stem

Orbicular Nearly circular

Ovary The part of the pistil enclosing the ovules

Ovate Flat and egg-shaped

Ovoid Solid and egg-shaped

Ovule Outgrowth of the ovary, developing after fertilization into the seed

Palmate Radiating from a central point, e.g. veins from the base of a leaf; with lobes or leaflets so arranged. A palmately lobed leaf may be palmatifid, cleft to about half-way in from the margin; palmatipartite, more deeply cleft; or palmatisect, cleft almost to the midrib

Panicle Loose, pyramidal inflorescence, usually a compound raceme, i.e. one with branching pedicels

Papilionaceous With one erect petal, two side petals, and two petals below fused to form a keel

Paripinnate Pinnately divided, with an even number of leaflets

Pedicel Stalk of a single flower, especially in a branched inflorescence

Peduncle Stalk of an inflorescence or a solitary flower

Pentamerous Having five of each of its parts (sepals, petals, stamens, carpels)

Perennial Living for more than two years

Perianth The envelope of a flower, consisting of calyx and corolla

Pericarp Part of a fruit surrounding the seed, derived from the wall of the matured ovary. The outer layer is called the epicarp, the middle one the mesocarp and the inner one the endocarp

Persistent Withering, but staying on the plant through the winter

Petal Flower leaf, often colourful, forming part of the corolla

Petiole Stalk of a leaf

Pinnate Arranged on either side of a central vein or stalk; divided into leaflets so arranged. A pinnately lobed leaf may be pinnatifid, pinnatipartite or pinnatisect, according to the depth of incision (cf. **Palmate**)

Pistil Female organ of a flower, made up of one or more carpels and consisting of the ovary, style and stigma

Procumbent Trailing on the ground

Prostrate Lying closely on the ground

Pseudocarp *v.* **Fruit**

Pteridophyte Plant belonging or allied to the ferns

Pubescent Covered with downy hairs

Raceme Elongated inflorescence of flowers borne on short stalks

Rachis Central stalk of a compound leaf or inflorescence

Radical or **basal** Growing from the base of the stem, at ground level

Receptacle End, often enlarged, of a stalk bearing a flower or inflorescence

Recumbent Lying on the ground

Reniform Kidney-shaped

Reticulated Having a network of veins

Rhizome Root-like creeping subterranean stem, usually elongated horizontally. Also called a rootstock

Runcinate With pointed lobes curving backwards towards the base

Sagittate Arrowhead-shaped

Scale Modified leaf or leaf-base

Scape Leafless, flower-bearing stalk arising from the base of a plant

Sclerotium Compact mass of hardened filaments forming the resting stage of certain fungi

Scorpioid Curled up when immature, unrolling to bear flowers on one side only

Sepal Modified leaf forming part of the calyx

Septum Wall of tissue dividing an ovary, fruit etc. into cells

Serrate Sharply toothed

Sessile Without a stalk

Shrub Low, woody plant

Siliqua Elongated, many-seeded capsule

Simple Not compound; unbranched

Sinuate Deeply wavy

Sorus Cluster of spore cases

Spathe Bract sheathing an inflorescence

Spathulate Spoon-shaped; narrow, oval, tapering towards the base

Spike Raceme of sessile flowers

Sporangium Spore case

Spore Single-celled, asexual reproductive body of, e.g. fungi, ferns

Sporophyll Leaf or frond bearing spore cases

Stamen Male (pollen-bearing) part of a flower, consisting of the anther and filament

Stellate Star-shaped

Stigma Upper, pollen-receiving part of the pistil

Stipe Stalk of, e.g. a fern frond

Stipule Outgrowth from the base of a leaf stalk

Stolon Creeping subterranean stem, rooting at intervals

Striated Having narrow streaks or grooves

Style Part of the pistil joining the ovary to the stigma

Subulate Awl-shaped; with a long tapering point

Suture Line of junction between two parts; line along which a dehiscent fruit splits open

Tap-root Long, usually central root growing vertically downwards, bearing smaller lateral roots

Tendril Coiling, stem-like climbing organ

Terminal At the end

Tetramerous Having four of each of its parts (cf. **Pentamerous**)

Thallus Undifferentiated plant body of, e.g. fungi, algae

Thyrsus Panicle broadest in the middle, narrowing above and below

Tricarpellate Formed from three carpels

Trifid Cleft into three, no deeper than half-way

Trifoliate With three leaves or leaflets

Trilobate Three-lobed

Tuber Thickened part of a subterranean stem or root

Tubercle Small round swelling

Tunicate Enveloped in several concentric layers of scales

Umbel Flat-topped inflorescence with stalks arising from one point

Undulate Wavy

Unilateral Bearing flowers etc. on one side only

Verticillaster Inflorescence resembling a whorl, but composed of two cymes growing from the leaf axils on each side of the stem. Also called a false whorl

Whorl Ring of leaves or flowers around a stem at one level

Xerophyte Plant adapted to a limited water supply

Zygomorphic Symmetrical on either side of a single plane

Pharmacological Glossary

Abortifacient Inducing abortion

Active principle Constituent having a medicinal action

Alkaloid Basic, bitter-tasting organic compound containing nitrogen and forming water-soluble salts with acids

Alterative Correcting bodily functions

Anaesthetic Eliminating or reducing consciousness

Analeptic Restorative or fortifying

Analgesic Eliminating or reducing pain

Anaphrodisiac Reducing sexual stimulation and excitement

Anodyne Soothing or allaying pain

Anthelminthic Expelling worms

Antibilious Effective against biliousness

Antihaemorrhagic Arresting or reducing bleeding

Antiperspirant Reducing excessive sweating

Antiphlogistic Preventing or curing inflammation

Antirachitic Preventing or curing rickets

Antiscorbutic Preventing scurvy

Antiscrofulous Effective against tubercular swelling of the glands

Antiseptic Preventing infection; killing germs

Antispasmodic Calming nervous and muscular spasms

Antiuric Preventing or counteracting acid in the urine

Antiuricaemic Effective against excess uric acid in the blood

Antixerophthalmic Preventing the drying-up of the conjunctiva and cornea of the eye

Aperient Mildly purgative

Aperitive Stimulating the appetite

Aphrodisiac Increasing sexual stimulation and excitement

Astringent Diminishing secretion; contracting the tissues

Bacteriostatic Inhibiting the growth of bacteria

Balsamic Soothing mucous inflammation, especially of the respiratory and urinary tracts

Bechic Used to treat coughs and bronchial complaints

Bitter principle Substance the taste of which stimulates the secretion of saliva and gastric juices

Brachycardiac, bradycardiac Slowing down the heartbeat

Cardiokinetic Stimulating and regulating the heartbeat

Carminative Expelling gas from the stomach and intestines

Cathartic Purgative

Cholagogic, choleretic Promoting the flow of bile

Cicatrizing Encouraging the growth of new tissue over a wound

Cordial A stimulant

Corrective Additive, usually to improve the smell or flavour

Decoction Liquid prepared by boiling the drug up with water and straining the cooled solution

Decongestant Dispelling excess local blood supply

Demulcent Protecting and soothing the mucous membranes

Depurative Expelling impurities by way of perspiration and urine

Detergent Cleansing

Diaphoretic Increasing perspiration

Digestive Aiding digestion

Discutient Dispersing morbid matter

Diuretic Increasing the flow of urine

Drastic Violently purgative

Draught Dose to be drunk

Drug Part or parts of a plant in which the active principles are present

Elixir Alcoholic tincture with sugar

Emetic Causing vomiting

Emmenagogic Bringing on or regulating menstruation

Emollient Soothing; softening the skin

Essential oil Plant oil, usually scented, evaporating at a low temperature. Also known as volatile oil or ethereal oil

Eupeptic Promoting digestion

Excipient Substance into which a medicament is mixed, e.g. to make pills

Expectorant Helping to expel phlegm

Expression Squeezing out

Extract Dry, soft or liquid preparation of a drug. A fluid extract may be prepared with alcohol, distilled water (aqueous extract), alcohol and water (hydralcoholic) or ether (ethereal)

Febrifuge Substance lowering a high temperature or preventing fever

Fungistatic Inhibiting the growth of fungi

Galactogenic Promoting the flow of milk

Glucoside Glycoside containing glucose

Glycoside Compound combining sugar and non-sugar units

Haemagogic Promoting the flow of blood; emmenagogic

Haemostatic Arresting bleeding

Hepatic Beneficial to the liver

Homoeopathic dose Minute, very dilute dose

Hydragogue Expelling water, usually from the intestines

Hypnotic Inducing sleep

Infusion Liquid prepared by pouring boiling water on to the drug and later straining the cooled solution

Irritant Excessively stimulating; causing inflammation

Lactifuge Arresting or diminishing the secretion of milk

Laxative Mildly purgative

Local Confined to one spot or area

Macerated Soaked in liquid to soften and dissolve

Masticatory Substance chewed to stimulate the flow of saliva

Mucilage Gelatinous substance, swelling but not dissolving in water

Mydriatic Causing the pupil of the eye to dilate

Narcotic Inducing sleep or drowsiness

Nerve tonic, nervine Stimulating the nervous system

Oleo-resin Mixture of essential oil and resin

Oxymel Mixture of honey and dilute acetic acid

Pectoral Relieving coughing and promoting expectoration

Plaster Preparation spread on material and stuck on to the skin

Potion Liquid medicament taken by the spoonful

Poultice Soft paste, hot or cold, wrapped in cloth and applied externally

Powder Mass of minute particles obtained by milling or pounding

Reduce Diminish; concentrate by boiling down; remove oxygen from a compound

Refreshing Reducing overheating; in practical terms, mildly laxative

Refrigerant Cooling; reducing fever; allaying thirst

Resolvent Checking inflammation; dispersing swelling

Revulsive Counter-irritant; causing artificial local irritation to distract from pain elsewhere

Rubefacient Drawing blood into the capillaries of the skin

Saponin Glycoside that froths in water

Sedative Having a calming and soothing effect

Soporific Causing deep sleep

Sternutatory Causing sneezing by irritating the mucous membranes of the nose

Stimulant Exciting the functions of various organs

Stomachic Beneficial to the stomach; promoting digestion

Styptic Astringent; checking bleeding

Sudorific Stimulating perspiration

Syrup Liquid containing a drug mixed in a strong sugar solution

Taenifuge Substance expelling tapeworms

Tincture Extract of drug, usually dissolved in alcohol

Tisane Dilute plant infusion or tea

Tonic Stimulating the activity of an organ

Triturated Ground to a powder

Vasoconstrictive Contracting the blood-vessel walls, thus raising the blood pressure

Vasodilatory Expanding the blood vessels, thus reducing the blood pressure

Vermifuge Substance expelling worms

Vesicant Strong counter-irritant, possibly producing local blistering

Volatile oil *v.* **Essential oil**

Vulnerary Curing wounds and sores

Bibliography

F. Bianchini and F. Corbetta, *The Fruits of the Earth*, Cassell, London, 1975 (originally published in Italy under the title *I Frutti della Terra*, Mondadori, Milan, 1973)

Culpeper's Complete Herbal, pub. W. Foulsham & Co. Ltd., London

William Emboden, *Narcotic Plants*, Studio Vista, London, 1972

Gerard's Herball, ed. Marcus Woodward, Spring Books, London, 1964

Dorothy Jacob, *A Witche's Guide to Gardening*, Elek Books, London, 1964

W. Keble Martin, *The Concise British Flora in Colour*, Michael Joseph & the Ebury Press, London, 1965

Mrs C. F. Leyel, *Elixirs of Life*, Faber & Faber, London, 1948

Mrs C. F. Leyel, *Green Medicine*, Faber & Faber, London, 1952

Mrs C. F. Leyel, *Cinquefoil*, Faber & Faber, London, 1957

Florence Ranson, *British Herbs*, Penguin Books, Harmondsworth, Middlesex, 1954

A. W. Smith, *A Gardener's Dictionary of Plant Names*, Cassell, London, revised edition, 1972

G. E. Trease & W. C. Evans, *Pharmacognosy*, Baillière Tindall, London, 10th edition, 1972

Five Hundred Points of Good Husbandry by Thomas Tusser, ed. William Mavor, Ll.D., Lackington Allen & Co., London, 1812

Victorian Cups and Punches, ed. M. A. Dejey, Cassell, London, 1974

Index